Leo Strauss ON PLATO'S SYMPOSIUM

Leo Strauss

ON PLATO'S
SYMPOSIUM

Edited and with a Foreword by
SETH BENARDETE

THE UNIVERSITY OF CHICAGO PRESS
Chicago & London

Leo Strauss (1899–1973) was the Robert Maynard Hutchins Distinguished Service
Professor Emeritus of Political Science at the University of Chicago. His many contributions
to political philosophy include *The Political Philosophy of Hobbes, Persecution and the Art of
Writing,* and *On Tyranny,* all published by the University of Chicago Press.
Seth Benardete is professor of classics at New York University and the author, most recently,
of *Plato's "Laws": The Discovery of Being.*

The University of Chicago Press, Chicago 60637
The University of Chicago Press, Ltd., London
© 2001 by The University of Chicago
All rights reserved. Published 2001
Printed on the United States of America

10   09   08   07   06   05   04   03   02   5   4   3   2

ISBN (cloth): 0-226-77685-9

We would like to express our gratitude to the John M. Olin Center for Inquiry into the
Theory and Practice of Democracy, which, with the support of the John M. Olin Foundation
and the Lynde and Harry Bradley Foundation, provided invaluable assistance in preparing
the manuscript of this book for publication.

Library of Congress Cataloging-in-Publication Data

Strauss, Leo.
    Leo Strauss on Plato's Symposium / edited and with a foreword by Seth
Benardete.
        p.   cm.
    Includes index.
    ISBN 0-226-77685-9 (alk. paper)
        1. Plato. Symposium.   2. Political science—Philosophy—History.
I. Benardete, Seth.   II. Title.
B385 .S77   2001
184—dc21   00-012819

⊗ The paper used in this publication meets the minimum requirements of the American
National Standard for Information Sciences—Permanence of Paper for Printed Library
Materials, ANSI Z39.48-1992.

CONTENTS

FOREWORD

In the middle sixties of the last century Professor Hilail Gildin of Queens College suggested that the lectures Leo Strauss had given on the *Symposium* in 1959 be published in a readable form. Professor Strauss agreed to this proposal, with the proviso that the translation of the passages he had read in class be revised so as to conform more strictly with the original, and in the summer of 1966 I set to work making the changes he had requested. On first reading, Professor Strauss found the resulting manuscript unsatisfactory, but after a second reading he agreed to its publication. For several reasons this version never saw the light of day and was subsequently lost. In the summer of 1999 the project was resumed and done again from scratch. A very few changes were required to make the lectures flow smoothly on the printed page; heavier revisions are more frequent early in the series than at its end, since Professor Strauss often repeated points at the start of the early classes in order to confirm what he had established. On occasion these repetitions involved new formulations or insights, and these have been carefully preserved. The transcript from which this edition was made was not complete; the changing of the tape resulted in gaps of various length. When a gap could be filled in a fairly certain way, this has been done; where more has been lost than could safely be conjectured, an indication is given of the break in continuity, but it has not been possible to determine the length of the missing portions.

Professor Strauss gave this course on the *Symposium* partly in honor of his friend, Peter Heinrich von Blanckenhagen, who had accepted a position at the Institute of Fine Arts in New York and would leave Chicago by the fall of 1959. Judging from the transcript, they had often discussed the dialogue in the past, and they continued to talk about it during the course. It is, I believe, the furthest that Professor Strauss ever strayed in his courses on Plato from the strictly political dialogues: he taught the *Statesman* but neither the *Theaetetus* nor the *Sophist*. In his interpretation, however, this distinction proves to be somewhat illusory; without detracting from the nature and experience of Eros, Professor Strauss was able to show how political philosophy could still be a guide to its full understanding. The political in a narrow sense frames the dialogue, for Alcibiades is singled out at the beginning, along with Socrates and Agathon, as of interest to Apollodorus's acquaintance, and at the end it is he who disrupts the party, forces it to become a symposium, and completes the series of erotic speeches with a praise of Socrates. The year of the party also politicizes the unpolitical setting and theme, for it immediately precedes the Sicilian expedition that Alcibiades promoted. His subsequent withdrawal, which virtually guaranteed the failure of the venture, was due to the hysteria that swept Athens after the mutilation of the Hermae and the profanation of the mysteries, in which Alcibiades was thought to be involved. Strauss interprets the *Symposium* as Plato's version of that profanation: Socrates proves through his mouthpiece Diotima that Eros is not a god. The political and the theological thus come together and offer a way into Strauss's abiding concern.

Strauss's capacity to discern the ultimate import of seemingly minor things is nowhere more conspicuous than in his interpretation of the *Symposium*. He shows that Socrates' hubris, to which both Agathon and Alcibiades call attention, is equally involved in his teaching on Eros and his contest with Agathon, in which Alcibiades, in the guise of Dionysus, proves to be the judge. The contest with Agathon for supremacy in wisdom is in turn shown to be a contest between poetry and philosophy: Socrates had already observed to Aristodemus the hubris Homer committed against the good. The truly profound speech of Aristophanes and the seemingly silly speech of Agathon divide between them all that comedy and tragedy respectively can muster against philosophy. Only Aristophanes, Agathon, and Socrates, Strauss shows, give speeches that do not subordinate Eros to anything. Their speeches are the only inspired speeches, for Phaedrus looks at Eros through selfishness, Pausanias through morality, and Eryximachus through science. In each case Eros disappears into something else and does not emerge into its own until Aristophanes, recovered from the hiccups, speaks. His hiccups disturb the order of speeches and put the two poets on the same side as Socrates. Strauss's recognition of this division of the speeches into two triads does not affect his careful exposition of the first three speeches. Phaedrus's selfishness has a connection with Socrates' shifting of Eros from a concern with the beautiful—the ordinary understanding—to a concern with the good; Pausanias's unstable advocacy of freedom, philosophy, and morality at various stages of his argument encapsulates the political problem that the *Republic* sets out to solve; and Eryximachus's coordination of Eros with science already adumbrates the modern project that Plato uncannily foresaw and opposed.

In accordance with Socrates' own remarks on writing, Strauss sometimes compared the Platonic dialogues to animals in a zoo, in which the visitor is encouraged to classify the unique specimens on display into groups. Some of the more obvious taxonomic criteria were whether the dialogues were reported or not and, if reported, whether by Socrates or by others; whether their settings or times were given; and whether the characters were known. The *Symposium* is a reported dialogue at several removes from the occasion; it shares this peculiarity with the *Parmenides,* where Plato's relative reports on Socrates' second venture into philosophy. Phaedo reports Socrates' own account of his first venture in the *Phaedo,* and Apollodorus, who weeps continuously throughout the *Phaedo,* records Socrates' last in the *Symposium.* Strauss observed that Diotima's account of Eros as a *daimonion,* midway between gods and mortals, is plainly meant to overcome the difficulty Parmenides found in Socrates' ideas, which allowed there to be nothing except ideas and their participants. Strauss proposed that Eros, or the essence of soul, was meant to be an intermediary that could not be reduced to either a paradigmatic idea or its copies. Psychology therefore became paired with ontology or cosmology and offered a way to get around the Parmenidean paradox. Strauss went on to observe that the *Protagoras* included all the characters in the *Symposium,* with the exception of Aristophanes. He inferred that Aristophanes replaces Protagoras: the comic poet offers a myth about man's origin and nature that surpasses the sophist's, for it puts together man's impiety and man's civility, or the double nature of man, in a way that Protagoras utterly does not understand. The *Symposium*'s link with the *Protagoras* necessarily brings in its train the *Gorgias,* which handles the relation justice has with rhetoric, or the issue of rationality and punishment. Not only does the *Symposium* gain natural ties with the *Republic* through its association with these dialogues, but it also links up with the *Phaedrus,* whose theme is persuasion, dialectic, and writing in the element of Eros. Here is where Strauss's wholly unprejudiced viewpoint comes to the fore; it is not everyone who would see the kinship of the *Phaedrus* with the *Laws* or of the *Symposium* with the *Epinomis,* for writing connects the first pair and the notion of occasion the second. Strauss did not always develop these connections fully, but he suggested how one should proceed in trying to put together the necessarily imperfect cosmos of Platonic dialogues as an imitation of the true cosmos.

Seth Benardete

1 INTRODUCTORY REMARKS

This course will be on Plato's political philosophy and it will be conducted in the form of an explanation and an interpretation of the *Symposium*. By way of introduction I have to answer these two questions: (1) Why do we study Plato's political philosophy? and (2) Why did I select the *Symposium*? As for the first question, one could say that to give courses on Plato's political philosophy is the decent thing to do. It is admitted in the profession that political science students are supposed to have some knowledge of the history of political thought, the history of political philosophy. If this is so one surely must study it thoroughly, at least in graduate school, and the thorough treatment of the history of political philosophy requires specialized courses in the great political philosophers, hence also on Plato. This reasoning is rather poor for two reasons. In the first place, it would lead to the consequence that one should give such courses also, say, on Locke or Machiavelli, and I for one give such a course only on Plato. In the second place, though in all practical matters it is indispensable, either always or mostly, to follow custom, to do what is generally done, in theoretical matters it is simply untrue. In practical matters there is a right of the first occupant: what is established must be respected. In theoretical matters this cannot be. Differently stated: The rule of practice is "let sleeping dogs lie," do not disturb the established. In theoretical matters the rule is "do not let sleeping dogs lie." Therefore, we cannot defer to precedent and must raise the question, Why do we study Plato in particular?

When we look at the present situation in the world, this side of the Iron Curtain, we see that there are two powers determining present-day thought. I call them positivism and historicism. The defect of these powers today compels us to look out for an alternative. That alternative seems to be supplied by Plato rather than anyone else.

First positivism. Positivism makes the assertion that the only form of genuine knowledge is scientific knowledge. Physics is the model of all sciences and therefore of political science in particular. But this is more a promise than an achievement. This scientific political science does not exist.

In spite of this fact, we must take this position very seriously. Its motive can be crudely stated as follows: The same science—scientific method—which produced the H-bomb must also be able to prevent the use of the H-bomb. The science which produced the H-bomb, physics; the science dealing with the use of the H-bomb, political science. Now, you see immediately that this reasoning, that the same method which produced the II-bomb must also be able to prevent the use of the H-bomb, is very poor: the distinction between the use and misuse of anything—H-bomb included—means a distinction between good and bad, and this kind of distinction is now called a value judgment. According to the positivistic view value judgments are outside the scope of science. Therefore this positivistic political science promises something which it is, strictly speaking, unable and unwilling to supply. The characteristic thesis of positivism can be said to be that all values are equal. Positivistic science claims to be able to distinguish between attainable and unattainable ends. This is all. It cannot and does not claim more. It cannot even say that the quest for unattainable ends is foolish and therefore bad. This would be a value judgment. It can say only that they are unattainable. But it cannot say that the quest for unattainable ends is inferior to the quest for attainable ends. Positivists sometimes reject the imputation that according to their views all values are equal. But I can only say that this is merely an attempt to befog the issue. What they say in fact is that as far as human knowledge or reason is concerned, or as far as we know, all values are equal. This they certainly say, and there is no practical difference between the assertion 'as far as we know and shall ever be able to know' and the assertion that all values are equal.

The positivistic position can be characterized as follows: There is no position between the objectivity of science and the subjectivity of evaluations. The principles of thought, of thinking, of understanding, are objective. The principles of preference or action are necessarily subjective. I leave it at these brief remarks in order to characterize in a few words an alternative to positivism which I call historicism. There are all kinds of overlapping between these two areas of thinking, but it is unnecessary for us to go into them.

In the clear case, historicism admits that a value-free social science is impossible. But it asserts that both principles of thought and principles of action are essentially variable, or historical, and therefore in a radical sense subjective. In the vulgar form of this position we cannot arrive at any higher principles of understanding and of preferring than those of Western civilization. There are no principles of understanding and principles of preferring which belong to man as man, who can never go beyond a historically qualified humanity such as Western civilization. Historicism stems from Germany and is, therefore, far more developed there than, for example, in this country. But even in this country you find it in various forms. Carl Becker, I believe, was the most famous representative of historicism who denied the impossibility of any objective history. All historiography is based on the climate of the country and the age and can never transcend it. The difficulty with historicism, simply stated, is this: it cannot help transcending history by its very assertion. If we say every sort of man is radically historical, this assertion is no longer meant to be historical and therefore refutes the position. I cannot go into any further detail. I can only assert here that both positivism and historicism are not viable. But this is not the subject of this course. Assuming that they are viable, they are admittedly late positions. They are based on the experience of the failure of an earlier approach. This earlier approach is called in the loose language of this kind of literature the absolutist approach.

The absolutist approach asserts that there are invariable, unchangeable, universally valid principles of thought and action. This, it is said, has been destroyed by man's deeper reflection or by man's longer experience. From this it follows that if we as positivists or historicists want to understand ourselves we must understand our own ground, i.e., the absolutism of the past and the experience of the failure of that absolutism. Therefore a historicist or relativist, if he reflects on his position and wants to understand what he says, is compelled to understand the older position, the absolutist position, which he replaces. In other words, reflection, of which I have given here barely a specimen, on the defects of the views prevalent today, leads us to take a serious interest in the opposite view, in an evaluating social science that refers to invariable and universal principles. Such a social science was in existence at least until the end of the eighteenth century. The notion of a value-free social science emerged only in the last decade of the nineteenth century. The most talked about form of this older form of social science is the natural law teaching. This natural law teaching has its roots in the teaching of Plato and Aristotle, but it was not developed by them. It began to be developed by a certain Greek school, the so-called Stoics, which emerged after Aristotle, but we have barely sufficient evidence to speak about the Stoic natural law school. For all practical purposes, the classic of the natural law social science is Thomas Aquinas. As that part of the movement of thought which I have discussed up until now, Thomas Aquinas would be of the utmost interest to us.

But why concentrate on Plato as distinguished from Thomas Aquinas? In order to understand that, we have to consider a second meaning of relativism which has nothing to do with a value-free social science. If we look at what is going on in the sciences proper, in the natural sciences, and what is their peculiar character compared with earlier natural science, say up to the seventeenth and eighteenth centuries, we notice this: These sciences live in an open horizon. No results are regarded as definitive. All results, all theories, are regarded as open to future revision in the light of new evidence. This is a new phenomenon, that the highest authority for human society—and the highest authority for Western society is science—has this peculiarly open character. As someone who was very competent to speak about these matters, Nietzsche, put it, "We are the first men who do not possess the truth, but only seek it." Nietzsche had in mind all dogmas, all systems which predominated in the past and also sometime later. The novel thing was a society which apparently does not possess the truth. Now, there is an apparent modesty, an apparent commonsensical reasonableness in this open-mindedness, this refusal to say, "I possess the truth," which has surely some attraction for most of us. When we look back from this seeming peculiarity of the late nineteenth century and twentieth century to the past, we see that there is only one great philosopher who somehow seems to have stood for this principle, that the questions are clearer than the answers to the important questions. That was Plato.

Everyone knows, or has heard, that according to Plato man is incapable of acquiring full wisdom; that the very name of philosophy—a quest for wisdom, love of wisdom—indicates that wisdom proper is not accessible to men. Or to use the other formula, philosophy is knowledge of ignorance rather than the complete system. One can also indicate this historically as follows: Plato founded a school called the Academy. This school became, a few generations after Plato, the New Academy, a skeptical school. Whereas traditional Platonism was one of the most dogmatic schools, Plato gave rise to a most skeptical school as well, and this can be explained by the fact that while Plato himself was neither a dogmatist nor a skeptic, his successors were unable to remain on this level. There is a remarkable sentence of Pascal according to which we know too little to be dogmatists and too much to be skeptics, which expresses beautifully what Plato conveys through his dialogues. This peculiar openness of Plato seems to make him particularly attractive to our age, which has gone through so many moral and other disappointments. I will not now develop this notion of Plato as a thinker who cannot be properly characterized as either dogmatic or skeptic. I will leave it at the following remark. The very openness of Plato—the assertion that man does not possess wisdom, that he can only strive for wisdom—in a way also closes the issue. Human knowledge is imperfect. Human knowledge is at best progressive and never final. This is, of course, a final assertion. The great difference between Plato and his modern followers, or seeming followers, is that Plato knew that men cannot live and think without a finality of some sort. Plato contended that the finality of the insight that we are never fully knowing implies a final answer to the question of the good life, including the question of the best society. This is the problem we have to understand while trying to understand Plato's thought.

In what I said there is an implication which I would like to make explicit: Plato never wrote a system of philosophy. In a way, no one until the seventeenth century had a system, strictly speaking, but Plato did not even write treatises, as Aristotle did, for example. Plato wrote only dialogues. The dialogic character of the Platonic writings has something to do with this peculiar openness of Plato's inquiries. This, however, creates a difficulty which is very great. In his dialogues Plato never appears as a character. Plato never says a word. Socrates speaks, and other men speak, but with what right can we say that what Socrates says is Plato's view? If you say it is obvious, I can reply very simply that it is also obvious in the dialogues that Socrates is an ironical man. To have as one's spokesman a man most famous for his irony is almost the same as not having a spokesman at all. To say it differently: No one would dream of ascribing to Shakespeare every sentence expressed by any Shakespearean character, however attractive that character may be. It is wise to begin the study of Plato with this sober skepticism. Whether a certain sentiment or thought expressed by any character, however attractive, is Plato's view, we do not know. Plato expresses his views surely through his dialogues, but not simply through the explicit utterances of his speakers. From this follows a variety of rules of reading which we will take up on the proper occasions. But, to begin with, the rule can be stated in its universality as follows: Plato's dialogues demand to be read with exceeding care. There is nothing superfluous, nothing meaningless in a Platonic dialogue. Socrates in the *Phaedrus* compares the good writing, the perfect writing, to a living being in which each part, however small, has a necessary function for the life and activity of that living being. The Platonic dialogue has a function—the function is to make us understand. And the dialogue is comparable to an organism insofar as every part of it has a function in making us understand. Therefore we must consider everything in a dialogue. I leave it at these general remarks about why we turn to Plato and turn now to the question, Why do we choose the *Symposium?* What can we expect to learn from the *Symposium* that we are not likely to learn from any other dialogue?

I give two reasons provisionally: There are many competitors with philosophy or many alternatives to philosophy. But the most important of them, according to Plato, is poetry, not science. From Plato's point of view what we call science is simply and obviously subordinate to philosophy and therefore not a competitor. Nor can one say religion, because religion is not a Greek term. One would have to say piety. But piety is from Plato's point of view no competitor with philosophy because philosophy, rightly understood, is the true piety. The competitor is poetry, especially tragedy, which has the broadest and deepest appeal because it moves most men most deeply.

At the beginning of the tenth book of the *Republic,* Plato speaks of the feud between philosophy and poetry. In the *Apology of Socrates* the poet Meletus appears to be the chief accuser of Socrates. He acts against Socrates on behalf of the poets. The class interests of the poets have been endangered by Socrates. The foundation of the formal accusation against Socrates was led by an informal accusation that Aristophanes, the comic poet, did not indeed originate but expressed, in his *Clouds.*

Now what is the issue between philosophy and poetry? It is a contest for supremacy regarding wisdom. Let me illustrate this from Aristophanes' *Clouds:* Socrates is presented there as a student of nature, a student of the nature of all things, or of the whole, and also as a teacher of rhetoric. He is presented as corrupting the young by letting them see the victory of the argument for injustice over the argument in favor of justice. He transcends the ephemeral, ordinary life of man, the merely human, and realizes the conventional character of those things which are regarded as sacred by all men. Although he is a teacher of rhetoric, he is unable to win the argument in the end—he cannot persuade the many. His "think tank," his school, is burned down. Philosophy, Aristophanes suggests, in contradistinction to poetry, is unable to persuade or to charm the multitude. Philosophy transcends the ephemeral, the mundane, the political. However, it cannot find its way back to it. The philosopher as such is blind to the context within which philosophy exists, namely political life. He does not reflect on his own doing, he lacks self-knowledge—he lacks prudence in the wide Platonic sense of the word, because he does not understand political things. This is connected with the fact—again I follow Aristophanes' indication— that philosophy is unerotic and a-music, unpoetic. Philosophy is blind to the human things as experienced in life, in the acts of living. These acts of living are precisely the theme of poetry. Poetry integrates purely theoretical wisdom into a human context. It completes the completely theoretical wisdom by self-knowledge. Poetry is the capstone of wisdom. Poetry alone makes for the most comprehensive knowledge. By the way, you are all aware of this problem in present-day life. There is hardly anyone among you, I believe, who has not seen that a contemporary novelist with a reasonable degree of competence tells us much more about modern society than volumes of social science analysis. I don't question that social science analyses are very important, but still, if you want to get a broad view and a deep view you read a novel rather than social science.

Plato and Xenophon defend Socrates against this charge as follows: Socrates is so far from being blind to the political that he is truly the discoverer of the political in its own kind. Precisely Socrates understood the political as such, namely, the fact that the political is characterized by a certain recalcitrance to philosophy. In Plato's *Republic* we see that Socrates is a politically responsible man. It is Socrates' work that the argument in favor of justice wins out over the argument in favor of injustice. Socrates' philosophy is one act of obedience to the Delphic injunction "know thyself." His whole philosophy is self-knowledge or prudence. And Socrates, far from being an unerotic man, is the erotician. It is not true that poetry is the capstone of philosophy. On the contrary, philosophy is the capstone of poetry. This means not merely, as we shall see in the *Symposium,* that philosophy defeats poetry in the contest for supremacy regarding wisdom, it means also that the right kind of philosophy is more truly poetic than poetry in the common sense of the term. Poetry presents or interprets man's experience of human things according to their proper order, namely, the high is high and the low is low. But poetry must admit that the human things are not simply the highest things or the first things, that the true principles are no longer human. For example, in Homer the principle, the *arkhē,* is the Ocean—Okeanos. Yet Homer does not let us see, and cannot let us see, the principle becoming manifest in man above everything else, and become differently manifest in different men. When you see Hector or Achilles, you do not see Okeanos, the principle, in them. There is a crude juxtaposition, Plato implies, between the ultimate knowledge of the principle and poetry itself. Whereas Plato claims that by his understanding of the principle he is enabled to make the true principles transparent in human beings, in human action, in his characters. The reason he can raise that claim is his particular opinion, which we shall study later, of the human soul. For Plato, the human soul, and in a sense man, is, as it were, the concrescence, the growing together, of the highest principles. Therefore, if you have understood the soul in its essence, you can make these highest principles transparent in all human beings and all types of human beings. And this is precisely what Plato is trying to do in his dialogues. Platonic philosophy, by virtue of a deeper understanding of the principles, is able to see in men the manifestations of the principles.

The most extensive discussion of poetry in Plato occurs in the *Republic* and the *Laws*. But in those two dialogues we have no discussion with poets—no poets are present. The meeting of Socrates with poets, the contest of Socrates with poetry, is the *Symposium*. This is the first reason why the *Symposium* is of special importance. Lest you think that this is a question that involves a very special premise, namely, some sympathy for Plato, I assure you that the question is nothing less than the status of human reason. They all believe in human reason, but the poets imply somehow that something other than reason is superior to reason and must take its place.

The second reason why the *Symposium* is important is this: the theme common to poetry and philosophy is the human things. The human things, however, are primarily the political things, for mankind's greatest objectives, most impressive objectives, are political—freedom and empire. One might also say peace and war are clearly political phenomena. Don't forget that the title of what is somehow the greatest modern novel is *War and Peace*. Even today, Khrushchev and Eisenhower feed the headlines to a much higher degree than the White Sox or Ingrid Bergman's most recent matrimonial adventure. And the relation of Sputnik to the cold war is obvious to the meanest capacities. But what is the core of the political? Men killing men on the largest scale in broad daylight and with the greatest serenity. Today the most prominent fact is the cold war, communism versus liberal democracy, i.e., an antagonism of political orders, of regimes. Not Russia and the United States, not Russian culture and language versus English culture and language, they are only accidental.

The political in the political is the phenomenon which the Greeks called *politeia* (the title of Plato's *Republic* in the original). This word means, loosely explained, something like constitution. The politeia designates the character of the government, the powers of the government. Secondly, however, and this is the more important meaning, politeia designates a way of life. The way of life of a society is decisively determined by its hierarchy—its stratification, as it is now called. The most massive form of this stratification is expressed by this question: Which type of men predominate in broad daylight and with a view to compel power and obedience and respect? Which habits are fostered and admired by the society as a whole as it expresses itself in its actions as a society? Which moral taste is operating through the political order? We see immediately, on the basis of our present-day experiences, that there is a variety of such regimes. The conflict among them is only a conflict in the minds of men. Thus the question arises of what is the best regime. The first answer given by such men as Plato and Aristotle, and Socrates before them, is that in which the wise rule, absolutely and irresponsibly. Irresponsibly in the sense that they are not responsible to other human beings. That the wise should be responsible to the unwise seems to be against nature. But this regime is not possible, as both Plato and Aristotle knew. The few wise are too weak in body to force the many unwise, and they cannot persuade the many unwise sufficiently. Wisdom must be qualified by consent, it must be diluted by consent, i.e., by consent of the unwise. The political implies, in other words, something like a right of un-wisdom, a right of folly. This is the paradox of the political, that such a right of un-wisdom is admitted. The polis—the people—demand the highest respect without deserving the highest respect. This is the dilemma of the political. Not the pronouncements of wisdom, but laws rule. The rule of wisdom is possible only in this form: a wise legislator might devise a code which is then adopted through persuasion of the citizen body. It is clearly not enough that laws be adopted; there must also be those who are capable of applying and administering them equitably. The Greek word for equitable is the same as the word for gentleman. The right kind of rule is the rule of gentlemen. This does not mean exactly the same as it means in England; it means rather the urban patricians whose wealth is rural, not commercial. This is the famous economic condition of Greek thought, the famous prejudice, as some others say. I am now concerned with the crucial philosophic point, which is not affected fully by these things. The implication of the Platonic-Aristotelian philosophy is, then, that there cannot be a rational society, meaning a society consisting of fully rational human beings. The polis as polis is characterized by an essential, irremediable recalcitrance to reason. One could give many examples of that, which I will do on the proper occasion. There is something harsh in the political, something angry. Plato somewhere compares the laws with an angry and obstinate old man who always says the same thing without considering open-mindedly the circumstances (*Statesman* 294b8–c4). It is for this reason that Plato calls the political passion 'spiritedness' *(thumos)*, which also means something like anger. This harshness and severity is essential for constituting the polis and is, in a way, most characteristic of the polis.

In the *Republic* Plato teaches that this faculty which he calls spiritedness is higher than desire. You may recall that in the *Republic* we have three parts of the soul: let us call the first reason and then, the two nonrational ones, spiritedness and desire. Desire is also called 'eros', a key word for our present course. I would like to illustrate this by two more points. According to the teaching of the *Republic,* the tyrant, the most abominable ruler, justice and injustice incarnate, is eros incarnate. Another illustration: When Plato speaks in the second book of the *Republic* of the motives of men for establishing societies, he is completely silent about procreation. He speaks of hunger and thirst and need for shelter. The whole argument of the *Republic* is based on a deliberate, and deliberately exaggerated, demotion of eros, inasmuch as there is a tension between the political passion—spiritedness—and the erotic passion. The tension between spiritedness and eros corresponds somehow to the tension between the political and the nonpolitical. Now, whereas Plato's *Republic* can be said to be the political dialogue, we will tentatively say that the *Symposium* is the most emphatically nonpolitical dialogue of Plato, insofar as he deals with that element in man which is in essential tension with the political element.

Let me explain: As political scientists we are interested in political phenomena. But we must also be interested, simultaneously, in the political as political. What is it that gives elections, for example, their peculiarly political character? This more abstract question, What is the political, as distinguished from the study of particular political phenomena?, is for Plato a most important question. One cannot understand the political as such, without understanding somehow the nonpolitical. When you speak of the political, you imply that there is something outside the political and you must have some awareness of it. The nonpolitical may be entirely irrelevant for the political, e.g., digestion, or the backside of the moon, or it may be politically relevant. In the latter case, the nonpolitical is either subpolitical, say the economical, or suprapolitical—religion. The nonpolitical, as politically relevant, is the foundation of the political, either as condition or as the ultimate end. In both meanings, the nonpolitical was called traditionally the natural. There may be something natural which transcends the political in dignity and which gives politics its guidance. That is what was meant by those thinkers who spoke of the natural law and natural right. The word *natural* indicated the foundations of the political that are of themselves not simply political. The foundation of the political is, somehow, nature, and nature may be understood in different ways. One more thing: it is somehow the contention of Plato that the nature of man and, in a way, the nature of the whole, is eros.

To summarize: The *Symposium* is the dialogue of the conflict between philosophy and poetry where the poets are in a position to defend themselves. They cannot in the *Republic* and the *Laws*. Secondly, its subject is the foundation of the political—the natural. Somehow this is strongly identified with eros, poetry and eros. Somehow we feel that there is a certain connection between these two themes. Poets seem to be particularly expressive of eros, and eros seems to require poetic treatment. So much for the general introduction.

I begin in the beginning. In the beginning of any book is a title. The Platonic titles have this form: there is a general title, and then we have "or on wine." Then comes the description of the [category] to which the dialogue belongs: it might be called ethical, dialectical, or natural; it might also be called tentative or what have you. The general view today is that all this is surely not Platonic. I am inclined to believe that the latter part, "ethical" in the case of our dialogue, is really a scholastic addition that somehow does not fit the Platonic style. But the alternative title might possibly go back to Plato. I will say a few words about the alternative title of our dialogue. Our dialogue is called, in the subtitle, "on the good." Now this is seemingly strange because the theme of the *Symposium* is eros, not the good. Nevertheless, there is a good reason for taking the title "on the good" seriously: in the development of the theme of eros the good will appear to be the highest theme. In the *Republic* we have seen that the highest learning is called the good. But what was only alluded to in the *Republic* is developed at somewhat greater length in the *Symposium*. Therefore, the subtitle is of some meaning.

But let us turn to the title, and here again I must begin from the most external. As matters stand today, some of the dialogues which have come down to us as Platonic dialogues are regarded as spurious. I believe it is wise to suspend our judgment on this subject and simply to accept all dialogues which have come down to us as Platonic. The body of Platonic writings consists of nine groups of four (nine tetralogies). Thirty-five of these are dialogues and one consists of thirteen letters. Of the thirty-five dialogues, twenty-five have as their titles the names of participants in the conversation. Seven have as their titles a theme—that's the rare case: *Republic, Laws, Sophist, Statesman, Apology of Socrates, Minos, Hipparchus*. Six of these seven themes, as appears either immediately or else if you look at them, are political. In other words, when you look at a book called *Gorgias* you can't know what is in it, but when we hear *Statesman*, you have some notion of what will be in it. Therefore, the more revealing titles are those which indicate a

11

theme. As I said, six are political: *Republic; Laws; Sophist; Minos,* who was a legislator; *Hipparchus,* an Athenian tyrant; and the *Apology of Socrates,* which, as a forensic speech, is obviously also about political action. There are three remaining dialogues: the *Rivals (Erastae* or *Anterastae),* where the title indicates the participants. Here they have no names; the only way to indicate them was their common quality, rivals in love. *Epinomis* has its name from its position in the work, as a sequel to *Nomos,* i.e., to the *Laws.* The only remaining title is that of our work: the *Symposium.* This is a unique case. The *Symposium* is the only dialogue whose title indicates the occasion. Why not the name of a participant? The answer: there is not just one participant; there are six persons other than Socrates and, God knows, each may be as important as everyone else. It is also possible to make this tentative suggestion. The *Symposium* as you know or will find out soon, consists of six speeches on eros, and the last one is by Socrates. One is in-clined to assume that there is an ascent from the least interesting or least wise speech to Socrates' speech, which is the wisest. The speaker before Socrates is Agathon. Agathon is the most important individual after Socrates. But we don't know that. In Greek this name sounds almost like *agathon,* "the good." If the subtitle were really "on the good" this would not be a bad pun.

The *Symposium,* at any rate, is the only dialogue whose title designates an occasion. Why did Plato single out this occasion, a symposium? Plato's contemporary rival, ultimately friend, Xenophon, also wrote a *Symposium.* In the beginning this book says that it will treat the deeds of gentlemen per-formed in play, performed jocularly. In a way this is also true of Plato's *Sym-posium:* playful deeds of gentlemen. Symposia give rise to play and jokes, but at the same time they are susceptible of noble speeches. There are other human gatherings which are not so likely to give rise to delicate and noble speeches. You would have to reflect about the medium of symposia, which is wine, and the effects of wine. I mention only two of them, which have been articulated by Plato, so we are not substituting our own poor experi-ences for what Plato had in mind. But you will, I believe, recognize a phe-nomenon known to you from the daily papers. In the first place, wine gives rise to the ability or willingness to say everything—openness, frankness. Connected with this is what the Greeks called hubris, wantonness, doing things you would never do when sober, presumptuousness to take risks. In other words, this occasion is really a particularly important one. We are likely to hear interesting things which are not said on every occasion if we can listen to a symposium.

Another important distinction, apart from the character of the title of the dialogue, is this: a dialogue is either performed or narrated. A performed dialogue looks like a drama; we get a list of the characters in the beginning. In the narrated dialogue someone tells that he was present when people had this conversation—which is, of course, cumbersome, because he has to say all the time, "And then he said . . . ," but it has also certain great virtues because the narrator can say certain things. For example, if A and B were in a dialogue and at a certain point B made a particularly stupid expression, then interlocutor A cannot in propriety say, "Why do you look so stupid?" But the narrator can very well say, "Then he said, with a very stupid expression . . ." This has very broad implications.

Of the thirty-five Platonic dialogues, twenty-five are performed. We can say that is the normal case. There is one intermediate case in which we almost see a narrated dialogue transformed into a performed one, and that is the *Theaetetus.* Nine are simply narrated. Our dialogue belongs to the narrated dialogues. A narrated dialogue is either narrated by Socrates or by someone else. Six are narrated by Socrates. If Socrates is the narrator we find in the beginning of the dialogue either the name of Socrates without any addition or the name of Socrates and the man to whom he narrates: simply Socrates in the case of the *Republic, Charmides, Lysis,* and *Rivals,* Socrates to Crito in the *Euthydemus* or to a comrade in the *Protagoras.* Narrated by someone other than Socrates are three dialogues: *Parmenides, Phaedo,* and the *Symposium,* which is narrated by a man called Apollodorus to a comrade. I call him a comrade because in Greek he is not called a friend and he is also a bit closer than a mere acquaintance. The political implication that the word *comrade* has acquired in our age was present in the Greek, although from a different point of view. The oligarchic clubs were called comraderies. I only mention this point, which will later on take on some importance.

The *Symposium* and the *Protagoras* are both explicitly told to comrades.

[Tape change.] . . . a man of a very common sort, and this is a man called Aristodemus. He is a very important character, perhaps the most important character in the book, but he does not say a word. That happens sometimes in Platonic dialogues, that someone is silently there, and one misunderstands the whole situation if one does not look at that silent individual and what he shows by being present. Aristodemus, then, had told the story to both Phoenix and Apollodorus. Let me put it this way, crudely, but not unreasonably, I believe. Aristodemus was present at the symposium many years ago. He is older than the two men to whom he told it. He was associated with Socrates many years ago. Aristodemus is the leak to the younger friends of Socrates, and Apollodorus is the leak to the general public. We have to raise this question: Why was the story dormant for so long? And why is there only a one-way street to the truth? Namely, only through Apollodorus and Aristodemus. This must be connected to the character of Apollodorus and Aristodemus. Apollodorus is an enthusiast; he cannot help talking of Socrates, that marvelous man, all the time. But what is the place of Aristodemus? That is more difficult to say. Aristodemus knew it for many, many years, and only now does he talk about it. Was it not proper to tell the story earlier? Was Aristodemus the man most likely to do something perhaps slightly improper? I believe we can answer that question, but I postpone it because no answer is given here. We know the year the *Symposium* took place. It was the year Agathon won first prize. This is somehow known by tradition, and we arrive at the year 416. When was it told? I would like to give a tentative answer to this question, and develop it in greater detail later on.

Before I can give a tentative answer to this I must introduce another item. In the year 415 the Athenians began their expedition against Sicily, for which Alcibiades was chiefly responsible. This was a terrific gamble, but Alcibiades was such a genius that it might very well have been successful. The Athenians committed the folly, politically speaking, of calling back Alcibiades almost immediately after the expedition had sailed. Alcibiades didn't like it and fled to Sparta. He ruined Athens. He contributed more to the ruin of Athens than any other man. When the expedition was about to sail, the Athenians awoke one morning to find that most of the herms—pillars surmounted by a bust, usually of Hermes—had been defaced the night before. This was a great act of blasphemy, but it also had a certain political connotation. Somehow this Hermes statue was connected with the democracy, and the people had the feeling that some subversive activity had taken place. Then resident aliens (metics) revealed that other defacements of statues had happened earlier, but the big scandal was the profanation of the Eleusinian mysteries, the most sacred mysteries in Athens. The rumor was that the terrible fellow behind it all was Alcibiades. This was the background of the recall of Alcibiades and of Alcibiades' flight. He knew that condemnation of death was the only possibility those days for, as people now say, public hysteria.

Of the seven or eight characters in the *Symposium*, two others beside Alcibiades were implicated in this very dangerous undertaking: Phaedrus and Eryximachus. This has to be taken into consideration. A profanation of mystery occurs only when someone reveals it to another who is not already initiated. Later on in the *Symposium* we do find an explicit presentation of mystery, given by Socrates. I suggest tentatively that the dramatic play underlying the *Symposium* is that here you get the true report of what happened in 415 or 416. Not the vulgar, hysterical kind. This, after all, was very dignified, but we see how things become distorted.

Apollodorus is surprised that Glaucon thinks that the symposium took place only a short while ago. Glaucon knows only that there was in the house of Agathon a party at which Socrates and Alcibiades were present. Apollodorus says, this is absurd. Agathon left Athens many years ago—how could the party have taken place a short while ago? But why did he refer to Agathon? Socrates was always in Athens, his situation did not change. What about the other man, Alcibiades? If the thing had taken place in 415 it would be perfectly sufficient to say, "How can you say that that party took place now, since everyone knows Alcibiades left in 415 never to return?" Why refer to the obscure fact that Agathon won the prize? Answer: Because Alcibiades was in Athens. Alcibiades had returned to Athens in 407. He was such a genius that he compelled the city which he had betrayed to permit him to return, and to acquit him. That is also the reason why the story is told now. The open hysteria and terrible indignation have now been overcome. The most endangered Alcibiades is now restored. He is the leader of the procession to the shrine in Eleusis of Demeter and Kore, the object of this profanation of the mysteries.

Of course you can raise this question: Why does a serious man like Plato make such jokes? That will only gradually appear when we enter into the subject, but it is important to keep this in mind: the *Symposium* is a dialogue made unique by its title and by the fact that it is narrated by someone other than Socrates, secondhand, for the second time. It is a story that happened some years ago, but now we can finally hear it.

I mention another point which, I think, will be of some help. When you come to read the dialogue, you will see that the subject matter is eros. There is no question about that. But Phaedrus, a young man, proposes eros more specifically, and perhaps as a matter of course, as a god—the god Eros. Eros is not introduced as a power of the human soul, or what have you, but as the god Eros. Now, if we look around in the Platonic dialogues, we find the greatest variety of subject matter. We find many dialogues dealing with god or the gods, most specifically the *Laws*, the only dialogue which begins with the word *god*. We find something which is almost explicitly called the theology in the second book of the *Republic*. But no other di-

15

alogue is as a whole devoted to a god, goddess, or gods. The *Republic,* obviously, is devoted to justice, the *Laws* to law. The only dialogue devoted to a god—god with a small *g*—is the *Symposium.* From the point of view of the common notions prevailing at the time, a god is of course an infinitely higher subject than the just, or laws, or rhetoric, or any other subject. We must put these things together: the uniqueness of the character, the uniqueness of the circumstances of the narration, the uniqueness of the theme. Then we understand also this playful link-up with the profanation of the mysteries in 416 or 415. This is the gravest, the most dangerous thing, the profanation of the mysteries of the gods. This is, I think, the traditional description of what the *Symposium* is about.

Naturally we have to raise this question: If this is so, why is Eros and no other god singled out as the theme of a Platonic dialogue? And other questions follow from this: the ambiguity of eros as a god, the way the Greeks understood a god, and also what we mean by eros, a character of the human soul. This is essential for understanding the dialogue. I will leave it at that.

2 THE SETTING

I would like to say again a few words about the reasons which entitle one to speak of Plato's *Symposium* in a political science course. If scientific political science were the highest form of the understanding of political things then we should close Plato and return to Talcott Parsons or similar writers. But if scientific social science is not quite sufficient, then we need some supplement. This supplement is generally supplied by novels today. In other words, by utterances which are not scientific, not rational, which are subjective. This implies that there is a possible conflict between poetry, which includes novels, and philosophy. Perhaps philosophy can do the job that poetry claims to do and to some extent does.

A third consideration: the subject matter of the *Symposium* is eros. This does play a considerable role in scientific social science. Most of you will have heard the name of Harold Lasswell, who brought psychoanalysis into political science. This has had a very great success with the profession. To judge psychoanalysis and its contribution to political science one would have to have some awareness of alternative interpretations of eros. The alternative interpretation of eros is supplied in Plato's *Symposium*. One could give other reasons of a similar kind in case there is still someone among you who does not see the necessity for political scientists to study Plato's *Symposium*, and I am perfectly willing to open such a discussion.

To turn, then, to the *Symposium:* I said last time the theme is eros. The *Symposium* stands out among the Platonic titles in that its title is unique. The title indicates the occasion of the conversation. There is a connection between the unique character of the title and the unique character of the subject. The subject is not simply eros; it is the god Eros. The *Symposium* is the only Platonic dialogue explicitly devoted to a god. We have to consider also, and we began this last time, the peculiar position of the *Symposium* within the body of Platonic writings. There is no completely isolated Platonic dialogue. Every dialogue is connected with every other dialogue but sometimes in a very indirect way. One of the first steps one has to take in trying to understand a Platonic dialogue is to find out its nearest kin. I mentioned one point last time: the *Symposium* is one of the three dialogues which are not narrated by Socrates. The two others are the *Parmenides* and the *Phaedo*. They are the only Platonic dialogues dealing with the young Socrates explicitly. The young Socrates had been the subject of Aristophanes' comedy the *Clouds,* which, in terms of Socrates' biography, is still an earlier stage than the one presented in the *Parmenides* and the *Phaedo.*

The *Symposium* is the only dialogue in which Aristophanes, the author of the *Clouds,* appears. More obvious and clear is the relation to another dialogue: the *Phaedrus.* The subtitle of the *Phaedrus* is "on eros," whereas our dialogue is explicitly devoted to eros. The leading character in the *Phaedrus* is Phaedrus, who is responsible, as you will see, for the discussion in the *Symposium.* Obviously, then, these two dialogues are closely related.

I would like to make only one remark, which later on might prove to be helpful, about the relation of these two particularly beautiful dialogues— the *Symposium* and the *Phaedrus.* I think that the dramatic date—the inner date—of the *Symposium* is 416. I think the *Phaedrus* is later. Phaedrus, who is present in the discussion in the *Symposium,* as we shall see, turns up later, some years later, in a conversation which he has with Socrates in strict privacy, somewhere outside of Athens. I can only give one indication now. At the end of the *Phaedrus* a reference is made to a famous teacher of rhetoric, Isocrates, who was born in 436, and therefore was twenty years old at the time of the *Symposium.* But the reference at the end of the *Phaedrus* does not fit a very young man, a man of twenty. This is, I think, an indication that Isocrates was already at least twenty-five when the *Phaedrus* took place. This is for the time being a mere matter of information but will later on prove to be of some importance for the understanding of the speech of Phaedrus. His speech is the first one in the *Symposium.*

I will leave it at these general remarks and would like to turn now to the text.

> I seem to myself to be not unpracticed in what you ask about. I happened to be going up to town from Phaleron the day before yesterday. One of my acquaintance spotted me from behind and called from a distance, making a joke of his call: "Phalerian," he said. "You there, Apollodorus, aren't you going to wait up for me?" And I stopped and let him catch up. And he said, "Apollodorus, as a matter of fact I was just recently looking for you, as I wanted to learn about the get-together of Agathon, Socrates, and Alcibiades, as well as of all the rest who were present at the dinner party—about the erotic speeches, what they were. The reason is that someone else, who had heard it from Phoenix the son of Philippus, was narrating it to me, and he claimed that you too knew. He couldn't in fact say anything clearly. So you be the one to

narrate it to me, for it is most just that you report the speeches of your comrade." (172a1–b6)

Let us stop here for a moment. One thing we see immediately: there is a great kinship between this scene and the opening scene of another Platonic dialogue: the *Republic*. The name of the anonymous man has not yet been mentioned, but it is Glaucon. The *Republic* culminates in the assertion that the highest piece of learning is the good, and I mentioned last time that the subtitle of our dialogue is "on the good." But in the *Republic* the speakers stay outside the city, in the Piraeus, whereas the *Symposium* takes place in the city. There will be no newfangled things in the *Symposium*, no utopia as in the *Republic*.

I would like to say a word about the very beginning of the dialogue, which does not come out in the translation: it opens with a tone of extreme subjectivity. This will be of some meaning later on. Now we see Apollodorus is again away from home; two or three days before the same had happened. Probably he is on his way to Athens to seek Socrates. Glaucon, the anonymous man addressing him here, the day before had gone to Phaleron, also on the seaboard, in order to seek Apollodorus, the speaker. Glaucon wanted to know about the symposium, but he did not know anyone in Athens proper who could tell him about it. Therefore he had to go out to the suburbs to find out about it. The key names, as you see already here, are Socrates, Agathon, and Alcibiades. Socrates, everyone knows who that is; Alcibiades, the dangerous, glamorous politician, the most gifted man, politically, after Pericles; and Agathon, a tragic poet, of whom we shall hear later. Glaucon refers to a common meal which had taken place, not a common drinking. Not drinking together, but eating together. They really eat, and this is another nice difference from the *Republic*. In the *Republic* they are promised a meal but do not get it. The *Symposium* is much less ascetic than the *Republic*—they eat. And this is of very great importance. Therefore no utopia. They are satisfied, somehow.

Now, this Phoenix, the son of Philip, is a figure in Xenophon's *Symposium*. But this Philip is a clown, a maker of laughter. Philip, as we shall see later, belongs obviously to the older generation. Phoenix and Apollodorus are the younger generation. In Homer, Phoenix plays a certain role. He was the teacher of Achilles, cursed by his father. Perhaps the Phoenix here mentioned was also cursed by his father, Philip, for having turned to Socrates. Glaucon appeals to Apollodorus's special obligation to spread the knowledge of Socrates' speeches, and Apollodorus tacitly acknowledges this special obligation. We can leave it at these remarks for the time being.

> "But before anything else," he said, "tell me, were you yourself present at this get-together or not?" And I said, "It does seem that the narrator was giving you an absolutely unclear narration, if you believe that the get-together you're asking about occurred so recently that I too was present." "Yes," he said, "Indeed I did." "How could that be, Glaucon?" I said. "Don't you know that it's been many years now since Agathon has been in residence here, and since the time I pass the time with Socrates and have made it my concern to know on each and every day what he says and does has not yet been three years? Before that I used to run around haphazardly and believe I was doing something, and I was more wretched than anyone whatsoever, no less than you are now, you who believe you must do everything rather than philosophize." And he said, "Don't jeer, but tell me when that get-together occurred." (172b6–173a5)

Let us stop here. A get-together is a being together, and being together has also the meaning of sexually being together. This is not unimportant. Later on, very interestingly, this becomes the term for lectures. Of being together in all forms, even sexually, philosophy becomes the highest form of eroticism, and therefore also any common intellectual activity of some dignity.

Glaucon had heard of that symposium only recently, and he thought that it had taken place only very recently. But it could not have taken place recently for Agathon had emigrated many years ago. This is the refutation of the opinion Glaucon has. But why does Apollodorus use this argument? What about the two other men, Socrates and Alcibiades? Socrates is still in Athens. Therefore nothing has changed in his existence. But Alcibiades too must be present in Athens, otherwise the remark doesn't make sense. As I mentioned last time, Alcibiades had left Athens in 416. At the beginning of the Sicilian expedition (in 415), there was a big scandal, and he returned in 407 after the reconciliation with the Athenian city. So this, too, gives an idea of the date of the conversation. This is important, and I will mention it later, because of the change that took place in the situation between 416 and 407.

You see that Apollodorus is an enthusiast for philosophy. Only philosophizing is happiness, and everybody ought to philosophize. But Glaucon does not take this quite seriously. He takes the great rebuke rather as mocking. He is a businesslike fellow.

> And I said, "When we were still children, when Agathon won with his first tragedy, on the day after he and his chorus had offered the sacrifice for vic-

tory." "So it was after all," he said, "a very long time ago, it seems. But who narrated it to you? Or did Socrates himself?" "No, by Zeus," I said. (173a5–b1)

May I say only this: God forbid that Socrates would have told the story. The idea that Socrates could have told the story is impossible.

> "It was the same one who told Phoenix. It was a certain Aristodemus, from the deme Kydathenaion—small, always barefoot. He said he had been at the get-together, being more a lover of Socrates, it seems to me, than anyone else at that time. However, it is true that I also asked Socrates before now about some of the things I had heard from him [Aristodemus], and he agreed in just the way he narrated it." "Why, then, don't you narrate it to me?" he said. "The way to town in any case is as suitable for speaking as for hearing as we go along." (173b5–8)

Now we see that the date of the *Symposium* is here clearly given: after Agathon's first victory. It took place the day after the solemn celebration of that victory in the form of sacrifices. In the *Republic,* you will recall, the sacrifice takes place simultaneously with the discussion. Old Cephalus goes out while they make the discussion. Here there is no overlapping of sacrifice and conversation but a harmony between them because they are on different days. The naive Glaucon thinks that Socrates might have told of the symposium, but this is altogether unthinkable to Apollodorus. The source for the account is not Socrates but Aristodemus. Who is that Aristodemus? There is a reference to him in the fourth chapter of the first book of Xenophon's *Memorabilia,* where he is presented as a man who ridicules those who sacrifice to the gods and who use divination. In other words, he is a man of hubris, a word which is very hard to translate, the negative meaning of pride. This Aristodemus, who is a somewhat strange fellow, comes from the same deme—these were the administrative units of Athens—as Aristophanes.

Aristodemus is the only source of the exact report of that symposium. Phoenix is also mentioned but not precisely. Aristodemus is the source by way of which the older generation of Socratics informs the younger generation. Apollodorus is the only one who leaks that information to the outside public. This is somehow connected with the fact that Apollodorus is a very enthusiastic man and cannot keep back such an exciting story. Apollodorus checked with Socrates some of the points. Socrates said, "Yes, that's correct." Socrates takes an entirely passive role. When he is asked he says yes, but he would never tell the story on his own account.

21

The story is told on the way from Phaleron to Athens. Athens stands for something in Plato—for many things, but especially for freedom of speech, for the ability to say everything. And it is a way up, from the coast inland, in more than one respect. Let us continue:

> So as we were going on together we were talking about them, and hence, as I said at the start, I am not unpracticed. So if there's any need to narrate it to you all as well, then that's what I must do. For I too, whenever either I myself do some talking about philosophy or I hear it from others, quite apart from my belief that I am being benefited, you can't imagine how overwhelmingly I enjoy it; but whenever I hear some different sort of talk, especially your kind, the talk of the rich and moneymakers, I am as much distressed for myself as I pity those comrades of yours, because you believe you're doing something while doing nothing. And perhaps in turn you all suppose me to be a miserable wretch, and I believe your belief is true. I, however, don't believe it about you but know it well. (173b9–d3)

In spite of his missionary impulse, Apollodorus has learned this much from Socrates—that one must wait until the others feel a need, or a lack. In other words, one must not tell a story unasked. He tells the story on request. He is outstandingly glad when speaking or hearing speeches about philosophy. Up till now the interlocutors had only heard there were erotic speeches, but somehow that seems to be the same—unless we assume that speeches on eros are by their nature philosophic speeches. Apollodorus is also full of anger about the nonphilosophic speeches and full of compassion for those who turn their back on philosophy. Especially if they are wealthy, because they do not have the excuse of poverty. Now, in spite of his constantly hearing speeches about philosophy, Apollodorus is cursed, most unhappy. His turn to philosophy three years ago, when he met Socrates for the first time, has transformed his wretchedness, of which he did not know, into complete misery, of which he knows. In other words, he is not exactly a model of happiness. We also observe that this very humble man raises a high claim to superiority. The word *I* occurs all the time and also the word *narration*. This is of importance in another context which we may take up later.

> *Comrade:* You are always of a piece, Apollodorus. You are always speaking ill of yourself and everyone else, and you seem to me to suppose that simply everyone, starting with yourself, is wretched, except Socrates. And how you ever got the designation, to be called "soft," I do not know, for you are always of the same sort in your speeches, raging like a wild beast at yourself and everyone else, except for Socrates." (173d4–10)

The alternate reading, how he got the sobriquet "crazy," doesn't make sense because he is obviously crazy; but it is puzzling how such a passionate man should come to be called a softy. Now you see that this comrade is more friendly to Apollodorus than even Glaucon. Perhaps he knows him better. But why should this comrade ask Apollodorus after Glaucon had? Glaucon went to Phaleron in order to hear the speeches about that symposium. Perhaps Apollodorus had found, as an effect of his telling it to Glaucon, that he should tell it to others. Perhaps he induced that comrade and his companions to ask him, Apollodorus, for his report. This comrade finds Apollodorus to be without compassion, "raging like a wild beast" and savage in his condemnation of everyone except Socrates. Therefore, he rightly asks, "How come that they call you softy?" Why is he called a softy? To give in to emotion is soft. To be so full of enthusiasm for Socrates and so full of rage against the others is soft. This is a point of view which is not so visible today.

> *Apollodorus:* So it's perfectly clear, is it, my dearest one, that in thinking this about myself and about you all that I am crazy and out of my mind?
>
> *Comrade:* It's not worthwhile to quarrel about this now, Apollodorus; but just as we begged you, don't do otherwise but narrate what were the speeches.
>
> *Apollodorus:* Well, then, they were somewhat as follows—but rather, I shall try to narrate them to you from the beginning just as he [Aristodemus] narrated them. (173e1–174a2)

This is the end of the introductory conversation. Apollodorus admits that he is raging and out of tune. You notice perhaps the irony: the fact that I have a low opinion of myself and everyone else is a proof of my madness, he says. For it is sanity to think highly of oneself and everyone else, which is a good practical rule. His comrade does not deny that this subject is serious, but he thinks it is a subject not truthfully to be discussed with Apollodorus now. It is a rare case that a nameless comrade is somehow more sensible than a comrade of Socrates.

Let us stop here for a moment and enter into some broader considerations. The first point can only be a brief repetition of what I said last time at some length. The three participants, Phaedrus, Eriximachus, and Alcibiades, remind us of the great scandal of 415–416, the profanation of the mysteries. This was the great impious act underlying the accusation against Alcibiades in the following year, and all the great political tragedies which followed thereafter, because Alcibiades fled to the enemies of Athens. The *Symposium* tells us what really happened in that profanation of the mysteries. The true story is entirely different from what popular hysteria held. The mysteries divulged were not those of Eleusis but mysteries told by an entirely different priestess from Mantineia—we shall see that later—and the man who divulged them was Socrates himself. Alcibiades was completely innocent. He came in only after the whole thing was over. Therefore also the strange story about the dates; the story is told in 407, after Alcibiades had made his peace with Athens. The making of the peace culminated in the fact that the old procession to Eleusis, the seat of the mysteries, was carried on under the leadership and auspices of Alcibiades. The hysteria of 416 had completely disappeared; if we may use such a word, everything was fine. Now the story could with some safety be told. I do not agree with what some people have said about Senator McCarthy, but you know the popular language about it, and you know that there are quite a few things which could not be said in this country with grace some years ago that can now be said, after this hysteria has disappeared. This was a very small thing compared to what happened in Athens. No one was condemned to death because he had some dubious relations with communists, whereas in Athens they were killed by the dozens. It was certainly dangerous to tell something about it. This is the ironic background of the *Symposium*.

The allusion to an impious and criminal relation of mysteries ceases to be strange once one reflects on what philosophy or science is in Plato's view. Philosophy or science attempts to uncover all secrets and in this sense to profane all mysteries—to discover the truth and to proclaim it. But there is a difficulty here. Apollodorus proclaims the truth and this is connected with the fact that he does not quite know what he is doing. Apollodorus is not a theoretical man. Philosophy proper, while being concerned with uncovering the truth, does not reveal all mysteries to everyone, does not have missionary zeal. Socrates never told the story of the *Symposium*.

Another point: In the *Symposium* there are seven speakers. The first is Phaedrus, then Pausanias, then Eriximachus, then Aristophanes, then Agathon, and then Socrates. Later on, but not on eros, Alcibiades. The speakers on eros are the first six. All seven speakers have one very superficial characteristic in common: they are all Athenians. This is remarkable. If we think of the *Republic*, for example, one very important individual, Thrasymachus, is obviously not an Athenian, but even Cephalus and his whole family are, as we know from other sources, strangers. Or think of the *Phaedo*-Socrates' death. The key interlocutors are from Thebes—Simmias and Cebes. The *Symposium* is an Athenian affair. All speakers at the *Symposium,* with the exception of Aristophanes, appear in another Platonic dialogue: the *Protagoras.* These dialogues very much belong together. For the *Protagoras* is the only Platonic dialogue in which the cream of intellectuality is assembled, the three leading sophists: Protagoras, Hippias, and Prodicus. There are fantastic fireworks. The *Symposium* is related to that. These are all pupils of sophists. That is important as the background of the *Symposium.* The *Symposium* is an assembly of the cream of Athenian intellectuality. This we must never forget.

The relationship between the *Symposium* and the *Protagoras* is very important and very obvious, I think. I might mention some points. For example, in the beginning of the *Protagoras,* Socrates has a brief conversation with a young Athenian called Hippocrates. Hippocrates' full name is Hippocrates the son of Apollodorus. This is, of course, not our Apollodorus here, but a mere coincidence of the name. And then another scene which you will see immediately: When Socrates comes to the house in which all the sophists are assembled—the house of a culture vulture one could very well say, Callias—they are not admitted, the door is closed. In our case we shall see, the door is wide open. This very opposition indicates also a kinship. And, last but not least, when you look at the *Protagoras* you will see that Socrates comes in rather late. The illustrious society is almost completely assembled. But two people come in after Socrates: Critias and Alcibiades. Here, too, Alcibiades comes in at the end. There are many more such indications which we will take up when we come to it. I will leave it at these points for the time being.

One more little point: Four Athenians who are reputed sophists appear in this dialogue. This is reminiscent of another collective scene which I mention in passing for those who are interested in this sort of thing—they will not regret it. There is another dialogue with four Athenians, illustrious not as pupils of sophists but for the humbler quality of being fathers—four Athenian fathers. That is the dialogue *Laches,* which I recommend you read in connection with this. It is seemingly very remote, but in fact very close.

All speakers at the *Symposium* appear in the *Protagoras* with the exception of Aristophanes. Why did Aristophanes not appear in the *Protagoras?* Obvious: Aristophanes is a reactionary, an enemy of all newfangled things, of such things as the sophists and modern tragedy, of people such as Agathon, whom Aristophanes ridicules for his softness. But in the *Symposium* there is no enmity—rather, perfect harmony. The element in which the scene takes place—festivity, wine—is among well-bred human beings con-ducive to amity and harmony. Nevertheless there are important differences in the *Symposium,* as we shall see.

Aristophanes had attacked the new tragedy of Euripides and also Agathon, contrasting it with the old, ancient tragedy of Aeschylus. Aeschylus—Marathon fighter, American Legion. Euripides—what would be analogous to that in American life? I don't know. Now, the document of the attack on this new tragedy, in the name of the old tragedy, is Aristophanes' play the *Frogs.* In the *Frogs,* Dionysus, the god of wine and the theater, goes down to Hades where he becomes the witness to a venomous disputation between Aeschylus and Euripides for supremacy in tragedy. They behave completely like fishwives. Dionysus is made the judge between the two. He makes the decision eventually with a view not to the poetic quality but to the political judgment of the two tragedians. Euripides is opposed to Alcibiades; Aeschylus is willing to accept Alcibiades. Dionysus chooses Aeschylus, the man favorably disposed toward Alcibiades. In the *Frogs,* then, we have a contest between two tragic poets which is decided by Dionysus, the god of wine, with a view to Alcibiades. That is the model for the *Symposium.* In the *Symposium* the contest between the tragic poets is over: Agathon has won. We have a contest, as will appear, between a tragic poet, a comic poet, and Socrates. The scope is infinitely larger. Dionysus is explicitly said to be the judge, as we find near the beginning where Agathon says "Dionysus shall be the judge." But who judges? In a way Dionysus, but actually Alcibiades. The place of Dionysus is taken by Alcibiades who decides in favor of Socrates. So you see how elegantly Plato pays Aristophanes back. The man who is made the point of reference in a contest between tragic poets decides at the *Symposium* in favor of Socrates, whom you, Aristophanes, so unfairly ridiculed and attacked in your comedy. We can say that the *Symposium* is the reply of Plato to Aristophanes' *Frogs.* Aristophanes is the center figure among the seven speakers of the *Symposium,* and he appears nowhere else as a character in the Platonic dialogues. The *Symposium* is the Platonic reply to Aristophanes and to the poets altogether, because, as we shall see, Socrates wins also against the tragic poet.

The *Symposium* is the contest between Socrates and all other Athenian wisdom—sophistic or poetic—in which Socrates is given the crown by the most gifted Athenian statesman with a view to Socrates' whole life and not only to his tirades. But, we have to add, as we shall find later on, Alcibiades is drunk and he was not present at the contest proper, namely at the speeches, whereas Dionysus in the *Frogs* was present when Euripides and

Aeschylus fought it out. What is the conclusion? We cannot defer to Dionysus or Alcibiades; we must judge and see who is right. I think we shall leave
it at that and turn now to the beginning. Probably, the relations to the *Protagoras* and the *Frogs* are most revealing. We see an enormous feat: a comedy of Aristophanes, which is a very great piece of art, Plato claims to have
surpassed by this book—not only because it is more true theoretically, but
also as a work of poetry, and we must see that. In other words, Plato's *Symposium* must also contain the comical, amusing element in which the
Aristophanic comedies are so rich.

> He said that he met with Socrates fresh from the bath and wearing slip-
> pers—which he was seldom in the habit of doing—and he asked him
> where he was going, having become so beautiful. "To dinner at Aga-
> thon's," he said. "I avoided him yesterday at the victory celebration, in
> fear of the crowd, but I agreed I would come today. Accordingly, I beau-
> tified myself, in order that a beauty I may go to a beauty. But you," he said,
> "how do you feel about it: would you be willing to go uninvited to din-
> ner?" And I said, "In just the way you bid me." "Come along then," he
> said, "in order that we may corrupt the proverb by a change, 'Good on
> their own go to Agathon's feasts.' Though it's probable that Homer not
> only corrupted this proverb but also committed an outrage [hubris]
> against it: he made Agamemnon an exceptionally good man in martial af-
> fairs, and Menelaus a 'soft spearman,' but when Agamemnon arranged for
> a sacrifice and a feast he made Menelaus come to the banquet uninvited,
> an inferior to that of the better." (174b3–c4)

The joke consists partly in the fact that in all probability (it is an emenda-
tion, not in the manuscript) the good go on their own accord, i.e., without
invitation, to the meals of the good. "Of the good" *(agathōn),* in the
Greek, sounds exactly like Agathon. This would mean, then, that the good
go of their own accord to the meal of Agathon. So there is a Homeric basis
for this interlude. Now let us consider this: you see, Socrates is rarely beautiful. The word *beautiful* is, of course, in a way the key word of this book,
and it is translated differently by translators—understandably—because in
English it would have a more limited meaning than in Greek. In Greek, the
word *beautiful* means first of all what it does in English; it means also the
fair in the sense of fair action. In English I don't believe you can speak of a
beautiful action, but you can do it in German or French without difficulty.
In Greek the word beautiful means what is lovable, especially to the sense of
sight, but also what is lovable for the eye of the mind. It is the Greek word
for what we would call moral. This needs a minor qualification: there is a

Greek expression for what we call the moral, the noble and the just. The just things are things which you are obliged to do—pay debts, etc. But the noble is, in a way, that which is beyond the call of duty, that which you cannot expect everyone to do. The noble, then, has a higher status than the merely just. Both meanings are somehow always present in any Platonic reference, which can lead to all sorts of ironies, for example the man who is very beautiful to look at, but has a very lousy character. The contrast is more noticeable in Greek than if we would say "a handsome crook," and the other way around.

Socrates is rarely beautiful. He has made himself beautiful for the occasion. He goes as a beautiful man to the beautiful Agathon. Agathon, the host, is a beautiful man, notoriously beautiful. At Socrates' suggestion Aristodemus goes with him uninvited. The two of them go, as Socrates graciously suggests, of their own accord—for Socrates is, after all, invited; he includes himself in the same category as Aristodemus—to the meal of Agathon. Socrates is beautiful. He suggests that Aristodemus, too, is beautiful. But Aristodemus is obviously not dressed for the occasion. According to the proverb, "The good go of their own accord to the meal of the good." Socrates destroys the proverb by changing the good into the beautiful. The good is not identical with the beautiful, and that is the great theme of the *Symposium*, which is already announced in the beginning: whether eros is love of the beautiful or not rather love of the good. So far we know only that the two are beautiful; we don't know whether they are good. Socrates changes the good into the beautiful. What Socrates does is bad, but not as bad as what Homer did to the proverb. Homer presented a bad man going of his own accord to the meal of an outstandingly good man. Socrates changes the proverb, he makes a kind of pun, but it is not so bad. The substitution of beautiful for good is a corruption, a destruction, but the substitution of bad for good, as Homer did, is a corruption and, in addition, an insult. But Socrates is not beautiful. He has made himself as beautiful as he could, but there are limits to that, limits imposed by nature. Aristodemus, too, is not beautiful. How do we know that? He was small, and according to the Greek view small men cannot be beautiful, they can only be nice. Therefore we conclude with utmost precision that Aristodemus is not beautiful. Two nonbeautiful men go uninvited to the meal of a beautiful man. In other words, Socrates does the same as Homer, he commits a hubris as great as Homer's. This theme, Socrates' hubris, will be very important in the sequel. Let us go on from here.

Listener: Socrates changed to go to Agathon's, but Aristodemus did not; he is without shoes. Could you explain the substitution of the one for the other?

Mr. Strauss: Aristodemus is the most inconspicuous of all people there. He does not speak. He has a very distinguished seat somewhere, as we shall see later. He and his appearance are undistinguished. Aristodemus is in a way the true image of eros. Eros is not brilliant. Eros is a being in quest—needy. He is the opposite of luxurious, sleeping on hard floors, exposed to all sorts of difficulties. Socrates is a much greater man, better known, and therefore he is invited. Aristodemus is not invited. Aristodemus loves Socrates, just as the others do, just as Apollodorus does. We will come to this question later, but I wish to indicate the general character of this question.

There are six speeches on eros. In a way the first five are wrong. They are all refuted. But there cannot be absolute error; every theory contains an element of truth. You can easily see that if you take an atrocious untruth like "The sun is not shining now," which is obviously untrue, it nevertheless contains such important verities as "There is a sun" and "The sun is shining." At any rate, there is no untruth without primary truth. Therefore, none of these speeches is simply untrue. This is reflected in a complicated way in the characters. Each character is an erotic individual. So is Socrates. But whereas Socrates presents the erotic character on the highest level, the others represent the erotic character partially. Socrates is a completely erotic man, the others are incomplete. We must see therefore what kind of eroticism is characteristic of Aristodemus. One thing one can say to begin with: Aristodemus loves Socrates, Socrates does not love Aristodemus. Socrates is a lover, but a lover of something else.

There is a passage in the Second Letter of Plato, which is generally, perhaps universally, regarded as spurious, but this should not prevent one from reading it and enjoying it. It says that there are no writings of Plato's in existence. There are only speeches of Socrates having become young and beautiful (314c1–4). Socratic speeches are not simply the speeches of Socrates, realistically, but those of the Socrates who has been transformed, who has been beautified and rejuvenated.

> When he heard this, he [Aristodemus] said he said, "Perhaps, however, I too shall run the risk, not as you are saying, Socrates, but along the lines of Homer, of being no good and going uninvited to the banquet of a wise man. See what defense you will make for bringing me, since I shall not agree that I have come uninvited, but invited by you."
>
> "We shall plan what we shall say," he said, "as the pair of us go forward on the way together. But let's go." (174c5–d3)

[Tape change.]

. . . the beautiful go to the beautiful, but the Homeric version is that the bad, the low, the inferior go to the good. Aristodemus knows that Agathon is surely wise, being a tragic poet, and Aristodemus is not aware of possessing such gifts. But, in spite of knowing the facts, he is a reasonably proud man. He does not like to come in as a beggar.

> After some such conversation, he said they started off. Then Socrates, paying attention to himself for some reason or other, fell behind as he was going on the way, and when he waited for him to catch up [Socrates] urged him to go on ahead. (174d4–7)

Apparently they do not talk while walking. This is a famous theme which comes up frequently. The difficulty behind it is that intellectual activity and bodily activity do not go too well together. But this must be judiciously understood. In the *Laws*, for example, a large part of the conversation is explicitly made while they walk. Here, Socrates suddenly turns from paying attention to the goal, Agathon's house, to paying attention to himself. From Plato's point of view this means self-knowledge, as developed in another Platonic dialogue, the *Charmides;* it is not morbid brooding; self-knowledge is to recognize one's good or bad qualities. This presupposes standards. Therefore, self-knowledge is based and, in a way, consists in knowledge of the good. So, when Socrates turns to paying attention to himself, that means he is paying attention to the good. He turns to a silent meditation. Aristodemus again obeys Socrates without any fuss. Socrates stops because of his meditation and they come to the neighborhood of Agathon's house.

> When he got to Agathon's house he found the door open, and he said something funny happened to him there. Some boy, one of those within, met him at once and led him to where the rest were lying down, and he came upon them as they were about to dine. Agathon, in any case, when he saw him, said, "Oh Aristodemus, you've come at a fine time to dine with us. If you came for something else, put it off to another time, since even yesterday I was looking for you in order to invite you, but I was not able to see you. But how come you're not bringing Socrates to us?" (174d7–8)

You see the problem is very elegantly solved. Aristodemus does not have to give an excuse, he does not have to say anything, because Agathon, the gracious Athenian poet, has a beautiful, noble line.

Listener: This does not seem so nice on the part of Socrates. There he had promised to take him and now he lets him walk in by himself.

Mr. Strauss: But what if Socrates had anticipated that such a perfectly well-bred man would be gracious. This is not unreasonable to assume. I mentioned before that this scene reminds us of a similar scene in the *Protagoras* where they come to the house of Callias where all the intellectuals are assembled, and the door is locked. A eunuch watches the door. He does not want any other intellectuals to come in. Here the door is wide open, a much more liberal atmosphere prevails. There is an atmosphere of freedom, as distinguished from that of eastern despotism, as one could say on the basis of the reference to the eunuch. But we must also add that there is no meal in the *Protagoras*, whereas here the meal reinforces the atmosphere of freedom. Now, where is Socrates? It is well known that Aristodemus would not appear anywhere without the company of Socrates.

> And I, he said, turning around, see that Socrates is not following anywhere. So I said that I had in fact come with Socrates, invited by him to dinner there.
> "It was good of you to do so," he said. "But where is he?"
> "He was coming in just behind me, and I too am wondering where he could be."
> "Go look, boy," Agathon said, "and bring Socrates in. And you," he said, "lie down beside Eryximachus." (174e9–175a5)

There is nothing in particular to say here, but we must keep this in mind: gradually we will get a picture of the sitting arrangement which is not unimportant. Aristodemus will sit with Eryximachus, one of the six people, and a very important figure. We will see later on what this means. Let us go on.

> And he said the boy washed him off so he could lie down; and another of the boys came back to report, "Your Socrates has retreated into the doorway of the neighbors and stands there, and when I called him he refused to come in."
> "That is strange," he said. "Call him and don't let him go."
> And he said, "Don't do it, let him be. This is something of a habit with him; sometimes he withdraws wherever he is and stands. He will come immediately, I believe. So don't budge him, but leave him." (175a6–175b3)

Aristodemus knows the habits of Socrates and protects him. Agathon tries to disturb. By the way, servant is in Greek always boy, which is not entirely irrelevant, because the love of boys is in a way the great theme of the *Symposium*.

"Well," he said Agathon said, "that's what we must do, if you think so. But, my boys, feast all the rest of us. You serve whatever you want, in any case, whenever someone does not stand over you—something I have never yet done—so now, in the belief that I as well as all the rest here have been invited by you to dinner, treat us so we may praise you." (175b4–c1)

This is also meant to indicate the atmosphere: perfect absence of command, perfect anarchy in the literal sense of the term. The door is open and no one commands. Perfect liberty. Naturally Agathon pretends to be more anarchic than he actually is. Why does he have to give this command to the boys? There is, then, a certain element of pretense in this elegant man. Everyone is already there. Agathon is particularly gracious, and who would not be, after having won such prize? We can assume that he is not always in such a festive mood and then he may give commands to his servants for all we know. Socrates comes in last, in the midst of dinner.

After this he said they were dining, but Socrates did not come in. Agathon often bid them to send for Socrates, but he did not allow it. (175c3–4)

You see this conflict: Agathon the alleged perfect liberal, tried to interfere very much with Socrates' liberty, and Aristodemus protects him once again.

Then he did come, having passed the time as he usually did; and it was not very long, but they were about halfway through dinner. Then Agathon— he was lying alone in the last place—said, "Come here, Socrates, and lie down beside me, in order that I, in touching you, may enjoy the wise thing that occurred to you in the porch. It's clear you found it and have it; you would not have otherwise desisted." (175c6–d2)

This is the first indication we have of the seating arrangement. Agathon sits at the end. Since the order of speakers is that Socrates is last, the order of sitting is not identical with the order of speaking. Somewhere Eryximachus sits with Aristodemus. So far we don't know any more. Agathon begins with a joke: "Socrates you may have found some wise thought, and I am very anxious to hear that by just touching you."

Then Socrates sat down and said, "It would be a good thing," he said, "if wisdom were of the sort as to flow out from the fuller into the emptier of us if we touch one another, just as the water in wine cups flows through wool from the fuller cup into the emptier. For if wisdom too is of this sort, I put a high price on my lying beside you. My own [wisdom] would be a poor sort, or maybe disputable, being just like a dream, but your own is brilliant and admits of much progress, inasmuch as it flashed out so intensely from you while young and became conspicuous the day before yesterday before more than thirty thousand Greek witnesses." (175d3–e6)

Let us stop here. "Socrates you are a man of insolent pride" (175e7). Let us see if Agathon is not rude here or if he says something which is proper. What does Socrates say? He says it would be wonderful if mere bodily proximity and bodily touch—don't forget the dialogue deals with eros and therefore with bodily proximity—if mere bodily proximity would be the best purveyor of wisdom. Then it would flow from the full into the empty. "If wisdom were of such a nature, it would be a real boon to sit with you, Agathon." Think for a moment: is wisdom of such a nature? No. Hence it is not a boon and an honor to sit there. And what Agathon tells him later on is perfectly deserved. You see also here, "Since wisdom is not of this nature, I put not great store on sitting next to you." This is very nasty. And you see here also, though only provisionally, the contrast between poetic and philosophic wisdom regarding splendor. Poetic wisdom is not questionable. Poetic wisdom is, in the first place, splendid; philosophic wisdom is not. Secondly, philosophic wisdom is dubious, questionable, whereas poetic wisdom is not, which is ironical. Why is poetic wisdom not ambiguous? The tragic poet moves successfully many men. There must be something to it.

Agathon does not say here, as others sometimes do, you are ironical, but rather, you are insolent, proud, overbearing. In a way Socrates is that, and we will find quite a few examples of that later on. We see from this remark right in the beginning that Socrates is hubristic. But, as I said, the ordinary reaction to Socrates' remarks is that he is ironical, not that he is proud. What is the relation? What is irony? Starting from the outside the word means dissimulation, dissembling. But it takes on, in Plato and Xenophon, thanks to Socrates, the meaning of noble dissimulation. Now, what is noble dissimulation? The dissimulation on the part of a superior mind of his superiority. Something like politeness. A rich man who does not display his wealth but looks like an ordinary taxpayer. That is ironical, because it is a noble dissimulation. Socrates does this all the time, since he is manifestly wiser than almost anyone in the dialogues. He says he knows nothing, he always asks questions. "What do you think courage is?" This seems to imply that he doesn't know it, but the other fellow must. This is irony. Aristotle says somewhere in the *Ethics* that the magnanimous man is ironical toward the many, meaning he conceals his superiority in speaking to the many. But what has this to do with insolence? This is not a far-fetched question and I think you all know the answer from our present-day use of the word *ironical*. A man conceals his superiority out of politeness. His superiority is perceived but not heard. When the other man perceives it the irony ceases to be a consideration. Very frequently when we say a man is ironical we mean that he is a nasty fellow in the guise of politeness and self-effacement. Now, is it clear that if irony means the dissimulation of a man's superiority, when this dissimulation is noticed by the other it is insolent? There is something to that. We must not forget this side of Socrates.

In the vulgar sense of the word Socrates was, of course, not insolent. But we are concerned here with a somewhat more subtle thing. Irony is one of those things which fulfills its purpose only when unnoticed. Does this remind you of a problem which has been touched upon on other occasions? That there are things which are effective regardless of whether they are noticed or not and others which are effective only when noticed. In the so-called doctrine of the sophists the distinction was made between the virtues other than justice and justice. Take temperance. If the doctor prescribes for you not to drink cocktails because you will get into trouble, obedience to this prescription will have its effect regardless of whether anyone notices it or not. In other words, you may drink the cocktails in utmost secrecy but you will be punished for it. There are certain rules with which one must comply because of the consequences. Let us take the case of tax evasion. If someone evades taxes and he is an extremely clever tax lawyer and he is lucky, the tax evasion will pass unnoticed. Strictly speaking, crimes against justice are punished only, at least on earth, when one is caught, when they are noticed. Irony has something strangely in common with justice. Its effect depends entirely on not being noticed; whether it is noticed or not noticed is an essential element of its work. Therefore, the reference to insolence is a point in the right direction. Now let us go on.

> "Anyhow, we shall arrange for a trial, you and I, about wisdom a little later, using Dionysus as the judge; but now first turn to dinner." (175e7–10)

You see, Dionysus shall be our judge. That is, in a way, the formula for the whole thing. Dionysus shall judge which wisdom is the highest. Here understood by Agathon in a limited way. Agathon's wisdom or Socrates' wisdom. In the course of the evening it will be a contest between Socrates and everyone else regarding wisdom. But it also indicates that the contest between Socrates and Agathon is of special importance, and therefore Agathon's last speech is, in a way, the decisive speech, as we must see later.

After this, he said, when Socrates had lain down and dined along with the rest, they made libations, sang of the god, and did all the rest of the customary things, and then turned to drinking. He said then that Pausanias began a speech of this sort. "Well then, men, in what manner shall we drink most easily? Now I tell you for my part I am having a really hard time of it, on account of yesterday's drinking, and I need some respite—I suspect that many of you do too, for you were here yesterday—so consider in what manner we would drink as easily as possible." (176a1–b1)

Those of you who were ever drunk, which I trust is the minority, will know the relevance of that remark. This is, of course, a negative proposal which paves the way for the positive proposal, namely to make speeches instead of drinking.

Then Aristophanes said, "That is a good proposal, Pausanias, to arrange in any way possible for some ease of drinking, for I too am one of yesterday's soaks." He then said that Eryximachus, son of Acoumenus, when he heard them, said, "You are speaking beautifully. But I still need to hear from one of you, Agathon, whether he's feeling up to drinking."

"I myself am not," he said, "up to it either."

"It would, it seems, be a lucky find for us," he [Eryximachus] said, "for me, Aristodemus, Phaedrus, and those here, if you who are most capable of drinking have now given up, for we are always unable. I leave Socrates out of account, for he is capable either way, so it will suffice for him whichever we do. Since, then, it seems to me that no one of those present is eager to drink much wine, perhaps I would be less disagreeable if I should speak the truth about drunkenness, what sort of thing it is. On the basis of the art of medicine it has become, I believe, perfectly plain to me that drunkenness is a hard thing for human beings; I myself, as far as my will goes, would be unwilling to drink any further, and I would advise anyone else not to either, especially if he is still hung over from the day before." (176b2–d4)

We must watch the individuals. Pausanias and Aristophanes say they are still soaked from yesterday. But then Eryximachus takes over, who is, in a way, the most competent man, being a physician. "My science tells me that drunkenness is very bad." In addition, he is a very poor drinker. There is a perfect agreement between science and necessity. We learn certain things which are important for later developments about the characters of certain individuals. Phaedrus, for example, is also a poor drinker. Eryximachus and Aristodemus are both in a love relation. There is a similarity between them. Aristodemus, too, is not a good drinker, which shows a difference between him and Socrates. But the other fellows are very good drinkers. There is no moral principle involved, they just can't stand a second night. Socrates is an absolutely particular case, he is not anxious to drink, but if compelled he drinks more than anyone else without ill effect. There is a peculiarity which appears right in the beginning.

You see also something about the procedure which is not unimportant. Eryximachus had already found out before by a quiet opinion poll that Aristodemus, Phaedrus, and some others wouldn't drink any more. Pausanias and Aristophanes had already given their opinion. The only one who has not been asked is Socrates, but this is not rudeness because it is well known that Socrates can drink.

> Here Phaedrus of Myrrhinus intervened and said, "I, for my part, am accustomed to obey you, especially in whatever you say about medicine; and now, if they deliberate well, the rest will too." When they heard this, they all agreed not to make the present get-together through drunkenness, but to drink as it pleased them. (176d5–e3)

Do you notice anything about the character of this speech here, the language he uses? First they make the proposal not to drink. It is unanimously accepted. This is important—the unanimity of decision. The atmosphere of friendship, perfect harmony, in a way the atmosphere of eros. This is of some importance. Phaedrus is a younger man and he is, in a way, the leading individual as we shall see. He comes in after his older friend Eryximachus had taken over and become the chairman of the assembly. Of course the she-flute player is practically thrown out. She should play to the womenfolk; this is a strictly male affair. Only males are present.

Listener: In the only other dialogue where there is a woman, the *Phaedo*, she is also thrown out.

Mr. Strauss: That is not bad. But to be fair to the fair sex as well as to Plato we must make one remark right away: There is the highest speech at the peak, and it is presented to us is a woman, so they come back with a vengeance.

Listener: I get the impression that the strong drinkers can drink and are uncomfortable if they don't get a chance to, and the weak drinkers can't and are uncomfortable if they are made to. In both cases the capacity and the desire coincide. In Socrates' case the capacity is there but the desire is not such that he would be uncomfortable in either circumstance. Isn't there a case excluded of somebody with the desire but without the capacity? In other words he likes to drink but he is a bad drinker, he gets drunk.

Mr. Strauss: That's a good point. Of course it is clear that everyone may drink as much as he likes. There is no fixed rule. Now, the deliberation, the assembly, goes on. The main point, which is so emphatic here, is that all aspects of ordinary symposia—drinking plus flute playing, maybe other things—are excluded from the very beginning by unanimous decision. But it is important that some of these people who vote or steer the *Symposium* are induced to do so by a hangover from yesterday. In other words they are not always so severe. For Socrates it wouldn't have made any difference if it were yesterday. The poor drinkers would, of course, also have voted against heavy drinking, not because they are stronger than drinkers but because they are weaker.

3 PHAEDRUS

I repeat: the *Symposium* is the only Platonic dialogue explicitly devoted to a god, and it is, of course, a Socratic dialogue. Socrates is the chief speaker on the subject. Socrates denies the divinity of that being, eros, which is generally regarded as a god. He denies the divinity of the only being generally accepted as a god that is the theme of a Platonic dialogue. This forces us to remind ourselves of the accusation against Socrates. Socrates was accused of having denied that the gods worshiped by the city of Athens are. And this was preceded by Aristophanes' *Clouds*, in which Socrates was presented as saying, among other things, Zeus is not. In his *Apology*, written by Plato, we see that Anaxagoras said the sun is a stone, that is to say, not a god. In his *Apology* Socrates does not refute the charge that he does not believe in the existence of the gods worshiped by the city of Athens. He evades the charge in two ways: In the first place the accusation had committed the folly of saying that Socrates introduced new demonic things. Socrates asked, "What is a demon? A demon is an offspring of a god and a human being. Hence, by believing in demon, I believe of course in gods." The other point is the reference to the Delphic Apollo. Socrates had spent his whole life serving the Delphic Apollo, who had commanded him to devote his life to him. But, as a matter of fact, not Socrates had gone to Delphi but his younger friend Chaerophon, in order to ask whether there was anyone wiser than Socrates. When the oracle replied no, Socrates didn't believe him. He tried to refute the oracle. This was his service to the Delphic god. This is not a very convincing refutation of the charge.

There is one great Platonic dialogue which takes up this problem very obviously. That is the *Laws*. The *Laws* is the only Platonic dialogue beginning with the word *god*. In the tenth book of the *Laws* Plato presents what one might call his theology and also his political doctrine regarding gods. It consists in a substitution of the gods of the cosmos for the gods of the city. The impiety which is to be condemned is the impiety against the gods of the cosmos, but not the impiety against the gods of the city, which are merely a figment of the imagination. We can say Plato substitutes a natural theology for a civil theology.

In the *Symposium*, as distinguished from the *Apology of Socrates*, we find

Socrates' frank statement about a god. He is the only speaker who denies that eros is a god. The occasion is a symposium, where people drink wine, or are supposed to drink wine, and therefore a perfect time even for insolence or what is popularly thought to be impiety. Why did Plato choose the god Eros for this purpose? Eros was not an object of public worship in Athens, nor in most Greek cities. Therefore it was not protected by the law the way Zeus was. But, of course, there is another reason too. What was deified in the god Eros, namely, the phenomenon eros, is a natural phenomenon, for the knowledge of which we are not dependent on myths. It is a human phenomenon of the utmost importance, most powerful and most amiable, a kind of new god. I remind you that the charge against Socrates was that he had introduced new gods.

Eros is not simply above men, in the way Zeus is thought to be above men, but in men. One could, therefore, say, and this has been suggested by a very philosophic interpreter, Gerhard Krüger, in *Einsicht und Leidenschaft,* which appeared originally in 1939, that belief in the god Eros is the mythical expression of man's sovereignty. It is a question whether this is adequate. The basis of this view is that the Greek rationalism or Greek enlightenment, in contradistinction to the modern enlightenment, is able and compelled to give its views a mythical expression. Modern enlightenment is wholly unmythical. If it uses metaphoric expressions, like Prometheus etc., that is wholly unnecessary. According to this view, however, the Greek enlightenment was incapable of such unmythical expression.

Now, let us consider this for one moment, because it has very much to do with our theme. The speakers in the *Symposium* are enlightened people, pupils of sophists. They do not believe in the myths, but they express themselves in mythical language. I will not go now into the historical question of what this means; I will rather limit myself to the question of what is the characteristic thesis of the sophists according to the generally accepted view. Answer: the fundamental distinction between nature and convention. Nature and convention are distinguished and to some extent even opposed. And the gods exist merely by virtue of nomos. They owe their being to human enactments, tacit or explicit. This opposition between nature and convention implies the supremacy of nature. Man owes his best to nature, to gifts, as distinguished from his own achievements. Nature, therefore, can be called by these people divine. There is no sovereignty of man in Greek enlightenment, no conquest of nature. Law, convention, art, technology— all are subject to nature. The human things are a very small province within the whole. Inferior not only in size but also in dignity. The originating principles are not human. Therefore, all these men admit, in one way or another, standards of human conduct which are natural. They differ as to the content of these standards—they deny, for example, that the just is natural—but that there is something good by nature is not denied by anyone. From this it follows that all human activity, and especially the most highly renowned—political activity—is inferior to theoretical activity, to the understanding of the whole. This is an intellectual activity that transcends the political and can never be fully integrated into the political. There is a tension between intellectual perfection and political or social perfection. Therefore one can also say, though in the form of a footnote, that according to the classical enlightenment there is no harmony between intellectual progress and social progress. At any rate, from this older, this pre-Socratic rationalism which is ordinarily called sophistic, there follows of necessity that there cannot be a popular enlightenment. This is the reason why they are all compelled, more or less, to engage in a mythical presentation of their doctrines. In purely historical and external terms one can only state the massive fact, obscured by a certain eighteenth-century myth, that the Greek city was not liberal and therefore there were necessary limits to what a man could publicly teach. One way of evading this limitation was mythical speech. The most obvious example of that is the myth of Protagoras in Plato's dialogue *Protagoras*.

The *Symposium*, I said, presents Socrates' hubris. It presents his deviation from the accepted views with almost perfect frankness. What Plato further does in the *Symposium* is to link up this special case of Socrates with the biggest scandal related to impiety which ever happened in Athens, the profanation of the mysteries in 416 or 415. The worst offender, according to the rumor of the time, was Alcibiades, and the whole thing was followed by severe persecution. In 407, however, at the time the dialogue is told, a reconciliation has taken place. In 407 the true story can be told. It is told, because now it can be told. And what Aristodemus suggests is that the popular rumors about these terrible things were all wrong. Alcibiades was innocent. He came in after the whole thing was finished. The offender was Socrates. But he didn't offend the way popular rumor had it. There was nothing of black magic, as we would say, or of the mutilation of statues etc., nothing of vulgarity. What happened was very delicate and refined and took place at a symposium in the most refined society.

The original accuser of Socrates was Aristophanes, as Socrates himself suggests in his *Apology,* and the accusation was made in Aristophanes' comedy the *Clouds.* Here Plato shows us that Aristophanes was present, that he was an eyewitness of what happened. Plato replies on behalf of Socrates to Aristophanes' true accusation, which goes much beyond these vulgar things. The true accusation was that philosophy is inferior to poetry. Here, Socrates is contrasted with Aristophanes, indeed, with comedy and tragedy and all Athenian wisdom. This is modeled on an Aristophanic comedy, the *Frogs,* in which Aristophanes presents a contest between the tragic poets. Plato goes infinitely beyond that. There is no longer a contest between two tragic poets. That has already been finished, Agathon has won. Now we have a contest between all forms of Athenian wisdom, which Socrates wins with flying colors.

I have to say a word about the connection between the *Symposium* and another Platonic dialogue—the *Protagoras.* I mentioned last time that all speakers at the *Symposium* are Athenians, even the two reporters, Apollodorus and Aristodemus. This is very unusual in Platonic dialogues. I remind you only of the *Republic,* where the foreigner Thrasymachus plays such a large role. The *Symposium* is a distinctly Athenian affair. All speakers at the *Symposium,* with the exception of Aristophanes, appear in the *Protagoras,* i.e., in the company of the most illustrious sophists. When Socrates enters the house of Callias, where the most illustrious sophists stay, he finds Phaedrus and Eryximachus, speakers one and three at the *Symposium,* in the company of the sophist Hippias, and Pausanias and Agathon, speakers two and five, in the company of the sophist Prodicus. After Socrates enters, Alcibiades enters with someone else, just as Alcibiades enters at the end of the *Symposium.* What does this relationship of the *Protagoras* and the *Symposium* mean? In the *Protagoras,* Protagoras is presented as a teacher of good counsel and of virtue. There is a certain difficulty, which derives from the fact that there are many virtues, for example, courage and justice. This difficulty is to some extent overcome by the fact that one virtue is the highest, and that virtue is called knowledge or science. Yet knowledge or science does not guarantee goodness of action. We all know that we may know what is better and yet do what is worse. This difficulty is eventually overcome, at least apparently, by conceiving of knowledge as the calculation of pleasures. We all seek only pleasure, that is the assumption. We want a maximum of pleasure without any moral conversion, merely by greater shrewdness and calculation, i.e., by greater intelligence, by science, a calculus of pleasures. This is the theme of the *Protagoras.*

Socrates refutes Protagoras's claim. Protagoras is not a man of good counsel. Protagoras's actions in the dialogue always indicate the wrong choices. For example, he knows that his activity is very unpopular as a sophist. He thinks he can avoid all the difficulties by frankly professing to being a sophist, by revealing the mystery of his activity. But he fails in this. He is compelled to tell a myth. On the other hand, Socrates proves to be the man of good counsel. Socrates is presented, through some allusions, as Odysseus—the shrewd, wily man who can keep a secret. The relation of the *Protagoras* to the *Symposium* is this: In the *Symposium* Socrates is not presented as a wily man of good counsel. Odysseus is never mentioned. There is perfect frankness of speech, revelation of a mystery. This is an important part of the relation of the two dialogues.

We began to read the dialogue last time and we came to the passage where we found the silent meditation of Socrates. I would like to say a few words about that. As you recall, Socrates comes late because he had fallen into a silent meditation. Later on Alcibiades will speak of another occurrence of this kind. I would like, as I always do, to start from the most popular side of a man. The most obvious presentation of Socrates is given by Xenophon. In the first chapter of Xenophon's *Memorabilia,* vulgarly the memoirs of Socrates, Xenophon defends Socrates against the accusation of impiety as follows: Socrates had no secrets, he was always in the open, there was no monkey business of any kind. He was always talking. Of course this cannot be entirely maintained, because sometimes he had to stop, he had to sleep and go home. The opposite of that is, of course, silent meditation. There you do not know what a man thinks. This is an indication of the problem. We do not know whether what Socrates says later in the dialogue was the thought he discovered during that silent meditation.

After Socrates has begun his conversation with Agathon, he speaks of the lowness, the inconspicuousness of his wisdom. It cannot be moving, it cannot be charming in the way Agathon's, the tragic poet's, wisdom moves.

Two more points about what we discussed last time: The first concerns the order of sitting. I must indicate this now, because I cannot be certain that every one of you has reread the *Symposium.* The order of sitting is this: At the top is Phaedrus, who is called the father of the speeches. Then there are some missing, i.e., they are sitting but their names are not mentioned because they do not speak. Then we come to a man called Pausanias. Immediately following is Aristophanes, the comic poet; then the physician Eryximachus, and then come Agathon, the host, and then Socrates. This I learned only since the last meeting from Professor von Blanckenhagen, because I always thought that Agathon was sitting last. I am now satisfied that it's just the other way around. Socrates is sitting at the end. This is probably

due to the fact that the uninvited Aristodemus took Socrates' place. This is
the order of sitting, which is also the order of speaking, with one great exception: Eryximachus and Aristophanes change places because Aristophanes is temporarily disabled, as we shall see.

Someone made this point: When we get a description of the characters at
the beginning they are cataloged with a view to drinking. We find those who
are unable and unwilling to drink, people who are able but unwilling to
drink—they have a hangover—and one who is able to drink yet indifferent:
Socrates. Mr. Gildin made the point that this disjunction is not complete.
This is quite true. Which is omitted? Able and willing and unable and willing
are, of course, omitted because we want to have unanimity. No one must be
positively eager to drink. People who are unable to drink and yet indifferent
are omitted too, I suppose because they are not worth mentioning. But
there is another type which we could think of. We have people who are able
to drink and unwilling because of hangover. What about people who are
able to drink and unwilling on principle? I believe they too are out of place,
because they would hate the pleasure of drinking and, therefore, they would
be likely to be haters of eros as well. This is my tentative suggestion.

There has been a unanimous decision to devote the evening to speeches,
as distinguished from hard drinking. There is a proposal to devote this being together to speeches on eros. Socrates is silent in this first section, just as
he was absent for such a long time before. This is in accordance with the
general character of the *Symposium*. In all Socratic dialogues, that is in all dialogues in which Socrates occurs, he is the chief figure. But in the *Symposium* Socrates rules visibly in less than half of the book. First there was a
negative proposal about the procedure for this evening. It was started by
Pausanias, continued by Aristophanes, and concluded by Eryximachus, in
the order of sitting. Three speakers who are not young and who sit, somehow, farthest to the left. Phaedrus speaks after these three men, for the very
simple reason that he is young and modest. Socrates was not present yesterday for the drinking bout. The strongest drinkers are Aristophanes, Pausanias, and Agathon, to say nothing of Socrates. Phaedrus and Eryximachus
are not good at drinking; they are valitudinarians, which is of some importance for the later happenings. Eryximachus is that by profession, being a
physician. We have noted the unanimity of the decision and the parliamen-
tary procedure. Now let us read.

"Well, then," Eryximachus said, "since this has been resolved, to drink as
much as each one wants but there is to be no compulsion, I propose after
this that we dismiss the flute girl who has just now entered, and let her

flute for herself or, if she wants, for the women within. But we are to be to-gether with one another for today through speeches, and, if you want, I am willing to explain to you through what kind of speeches."

They all said they did want to and urged him to make the proposal. Then Eryximachus said, "The beginning of my speech is in line with the *Melanippe* of Euripides: 'The story is not mine.' What I am about to say belongs to Phaedrus here. Phaedrus on several occasions said to me in an-noyance, 'Isn't it terrible, Eryximachus,' he says, 'that hymns and paeans have been made by the poets for some of the other gods, but for Eros, who is so old and so great a god, not even one of the innumerable poets of the past has made even one encomium? And if you want in turn to con-sider the sophists, they compose in prose praises of Heracles and others, as, for example, the excellent Prodicus did—and this is less astonishing. But I have came across a certain book of a wise man in which salt had amazing praise for its usefulness, and you would see that many other things of the kind have received encomia. Isn't it terrible to be in great earnest about things of this sort, and for not one human being to have yet dared, up to this very day, to hymn Eros in a worthy manner, but so great a god has been so neglected?' Now Phaedrus, I think, speaks well. So I de-sire not only to offer him a voluntary contribution and gratify him, but it seems to me appropriate as well at the present time for us who are present to adorn the god. If you also think so, there would be an adequate pastime in speeches. It seems to me each of us ought to speak, starting on the left, a praise of Eros as beautiful as he can make it, and Phaedrus should be the first to speak, since he is lying in first place and is the father of the logos as well." (176e4–177d5)

Eros has never been praised, at least not properly, and therefore this sym-posium will be the first adequate praise of the god Eros. This proposal is again unanimously accepted—accepted, however, in a different way. The acceptance in the second place is strikingly different from the acceptance of the negative proposal. To mention this only briefly now, in the second case we have not a democratic decision but a dictatorial, authoritarian decision, made by Socrates. He decides it without having asked anyone. This is an-other sign of his strange hubris. Of course Socrates sensed the meaning of the assembly and therefore didn't have to take any votes. After this has been done, Phaedrus becomes the first speaker, first of all because it was his pro-posal and also because he sits at the front of the table. He is the first in the sitting order and therefore also the first in the speaking order.

Here, then, the theme is introduced—the god Eros. Why was Eros sin-gled out? He was not worshiped in Athens. It is easier, less dangerous. The theme is proposed by Phaedrus. Why does Plato make Phaedrus propose it, and why for the *Symposium* as a whole? In order to answer the question, we would have to know Phaedrus's point of view, which we do not know. We get a provisional answer in the immediate sequel where Socrates is said to have no other art except the erotic art. I said before, Eros is a god experienced by everyone. One could say this applies also to Helios, but there it is not evident; the sun might be a stone. Eros is the only god experienced by everyone of whom it is certain that he is a god, i.e., that he is living and superhuman, a living power stronger than us. This superhuman being which is experienced by everyone is lovable. At any rate, Eros is somehow the most important god, which does not necessarily mean the highest.

> "No one, Eryximachus," he said Socrates said, "will vote against you."
> (177d6–7)

You can compare this with the similar situation regarding the negative proposal. Eryximachus had the decency to look around and see what the others think. Here Socrates gives the answer without asking anyone, which is an insolent decision. You must keep in mind this theme of insolence, which is very important.

> "For just as I surely would not refuse, I who assert that I know nothing except the erotic things, so surely would neither Agathon and Pausanias— let alone Aristophanes, whose whole pastime is about Dionysus and Aphrodite—any more than anyone else of those I see here." (177d7–e3)

Aristophanes' whole activity is devoted to the praise of wine and to the praise of love. His subjects are two gods, Dionysus and Aphrodite. One of them has nothing to do with love as love—Dionysus—whereas Socrates is undividedly committed to eros.

> "Yet for us who are lying down last it is not equal, but if those before us speak adequately and beautifully it will be enough for us. Well, let Phaedrus start, and good luck to him. Let him praise Eros."
> Everyone else then assented and urged just what Socrates had. Now what each one said of all who spoke, Aristodemus could hardly remember, any more than I could recall all that he said, but I shall tell you the points in the logos of each of those I thought especially worth remembering. (177e3–178a5)

You see the theme is designated not only by the god Eros, but by the praise of the god Eros. If it is indeed the task of the poet to adore and magnify the god Eros, one can say all are partisans of the tragic and the comic poets for the evening. This is not a verbatim report because Aristodemus had forgotten some things, and Apollodorus had too. No one can use this for official purposes.

We begin, then, with the first speech, the speech of Phaedrus, and his speech will also give us an answer as to why Phaedrus suggested that subject.

Here there is a general reference to the missing speeches. At the end of Phaedrus's speech the missing speeches will be located; they are all here immediately after Phaedrus and before Pausanias. It must have something to do with Phaedrus's speech, at least indirectly.

Now we come to Phaedrus, the first speaker. He is responsible for the choice of the theme. The reason given was that Eros has never received his due praise, although he is so great a god. There were some difficulties someone suggested last time, and I myself had that question—what about the praise of eros in Sophocles' *Antigone*? Well, if you read it you see that eros is not praised as highly as it is here. Phaedrus appears in two dialogues in important roles: in the *Symposium* and in the dialogue called the *Phaedrus*. This of course does not prove that he is an important individual: the sophist Hippias was a very ridiculous figure, much less important than Prodicus, whom Socrates respected to some extent, yet Plato never wrote a Prodicus and he wrote two dialogues called Hippias. Why is Phaedrus selected? Well, he has two qualities: he is a modest man, a young man, and he is handsome; a most desirable combination as far as it goes. But he is also in both respects the opposite of Socrates. Socrates is ugly and he is not modest, as we have seen. There is another reason. He studies both physics and rhetoric. This combination reminds us of the young Socrates. In this dialogue he appears as connected with the physician Eryximachus. In the *Symposium* we see that Phaedrus is a very enlightened young man. He doesn't believe the old tales about the gods. In the *Phaedrus* he doesn't know by which god to swear. He says perhaps by the tree in front of him, it doesn't make any difference. Phaedrus was also accused of having profaned the mysteries in 416. So we see him as an avant-gardist, as we would say today. Now let us read.

> Now first, as I say, he said Phaedrus began to speak from somewhere like this, in saying that Eros was a great god, and wondrous among human beings and gods both in many other respects, but not least in point of birth. "For the god to be among the very oldest," he said, "is a point of honor, and there is proof of this. There are no parents of Eros, and they are not

spoken of by anyone, either by prose writer or poet, but Hesiod says
Chaos first came to be—
>'Then thereafter
>Broad-bosomed Earth, always a safe seat of all,
>And Eros.'
Hesiod says after Chaos these two have come into being, Earth and Eros.
And Parmenides says of genesis:
>'She devised first of all the gods Eros.'
Acousilaus agrees also with Hesiod." (178a6–c1)

There is a seeming tautology when Phaedrus renders Hesiod, but he does
not render him slavishly. First we have the verses, in which Hesiod says after
Chaos these two have come into being, Earth and Eros. Phaedrus then
changes something. He omits broad-bosomed Earth, always a safe seat of
all. Since the earth has come into being it cannot be always, and it is, of
course, not the seat for all things, as Hesiod erroneously said. It is not the
seat for the gods, for example, or for the stars. Eros is the oldest, for he has
no parents. All other gods have parents. He is not preceded by anyone, he
is the founder of the race. According to Hesiod he is the second of the two
first-born. So he is not so high according to Hesiod, but according to Parmenides, the philosopher, Eros is simply the first god invented by genesis,
by bringing into being.

There is a general rule, which I know only from practice and for which I
cannot quote chapter and verse, that the most important in Plato is always
in the center. The most important does not mean absolutely the most important. It means the most important in the context. Parmenides is the
most important in this context because he is the only one who simply says
Eros is the first god, whereas Hesiod makes him second to Earth. Parmenides' praise of Eros is the greatest, because he says Eros is the first and
the oldest one, and secondly Parmenides' account is more rational than
Hesiod's. He gives the cause of eros—genesis—a nondivine cause, of
course, because if Eros is the first god, genesis cannot be the first. Hesiod
doesn't give any cause, he simply says they jumped into being. Parmenides
is, as you know, the only great philosopher who was honored by Plato with
a book title. Plato indicates by this that he regarded Parmenides as the most
important of all the earlier philosophers. According to Parmenides' poem,
Eros and all other gods belong to the world of genesis, of coming into being and perishing. But, according to the first part of Parmenides' poem,
genesis—coming into being—cannot be, because coming into being

means a movement from nothing to being and nothing is not; hence, there cannot be genesis. This implies that the gods as having come into being cannot be. Only unchangeable being is. Parmenides replaces the gods by the unchangeable being.

Phaedrus's speech, being the first speech, is the most frenetic speech. But there is a close relation between the beginning and the end, between the seed and the fruit containing a new seed. There is a close kinship between Phaedrus's speech and its reference to Parmenides and Socrates' speech. Socrates no longer accepts the simple Parmenidean view, but it still reveals its origin from Parmenides.

The first praise of Eros is that he is the oldest one, and the oldest is the highest. This is an axiom for all earlier thinking. It has a deep root in human nature and, therefore, we still say "the good old times." There is a certain veneration for the old as old, which needs a long analysis and which is not sufficiently explained by our desire for stability. But in olden times "the good equal to the old" can be regarded as a primary axiom, which is then questioned. If the good is the old, the best must be the oldest. Eros being the oldest, must be the best god. In the sequel Phaedrus will draw this conclusion.

> "So it is agreed, on the basis of many sources, that Eros is the oldest. Being the oldest he is the cause of the greatest goods for us, for I cannot say what greater good there is for one, straight from youth on, than to have a good lover and for a lover a beloved." (178c1–5)

Since Eros is the oldest he is responsible for the greatest good. This is elementary, but Phaedrus is an enlightened young man and cannot leave it at that simple equation. He needs additional proof that the oldest is the best. He gives the proof in the following way: Goodness is virtue, but the cause of virtue is higher than virtue and, therefore, the best. Yet eros is the cause of virtue and that he will now prove.

> "For that which should guide human beings throughout their whole life, for those who are going to live nobly, neither kinship, honors, wealth, nor anything else can implant this as beautifully as eros. What do I say this is? It is shame for the shameful things and honorable ambition for the beautiful things, for it is impossible without them for either a city or private person to accomplish great and beautiful things. I say accordingly that a man, whoever is in love, if it should be evident that he is doing something shameful, or undergoing something shameful at someone else's hands, on account of unmanliness and without defending himself, neither were he seen by his father nor by his comrades nor by anyone else would he be dis-

tressed as painfully as were he seen by his beloved. And we see this same occurrence in the one who is loved, that he is exceptionally ashamed before his lovers, whenever he is seen to be engaged in something shameful. If, then, there should be some possibility for a city or army to come to be of lovers and beloveds, it is impossible that they would not manage their own city better than by abstaining from all shameful things and being ambitious for honors before one another; and besides, in fighting alongside one another, people of this sort would win, though they were few, over virtually all human beings. For a man in love would surely choose to be seen either leaving his post or throwing away his arms to a lesser degree by his beloved than by all others; before this he would prefer to die many times over. And as for deserting his beloved or not coming to his aid when he was in danger, no one is so bad [cowardly] that Eros himself would not make him inspired for virtue, so as to be like the best by nature; and simply, as Homer said, the strength the god breathed into some of the heroes—this, in coming from him, Eros supplies to lovers." (178c5–179b3)

What is Phaedrus's argument up to this point? Eros is the oldest, he is therefore the best. Now, he says, I will prove this independently of all mythical views. What is so productive of virtue as eros? Nothing else. No honor, no wealth, no kinship. Eros is the best because it is productive of virtue. This is true both in the lover and in the beloved. This is the thesis. Now, what does he understand by virtue? Virtue means here primarily courage, manliness, and eros produces manliness.

There are two sides to Eros. This motive for virtue is subdivided: One is sense of shame, and the other is love of honor. Which does Phaedrus emphasize? Shame. Eros, then, produces a sense of shame, bringing about virtue in general but manliness in particular. How does this show? In which case does he prove it? In the case of the lover, the beloved, or both? In the lover. Let us, then, make the thesis more precise: Eros produces a sense of shame in the lover which makes him courageous. This is the emphasis of the speech. How does this effect come about, how does it appear? When the lover is seen by the beloved. Therefore the question arises, will Eros have this effect when the lover is not seen by the beloved? This is not immediately clear, but Phaedrus goes on to say, "No one is so low that Eros would not inspire him to virtue, so as to be like the best by nature." The erotically inspired is not the best by nature. He is not even equal to him, he is similar. The best by nature will fight against the heaviest odds; so will the lover, but only when seen. The best by nature will do it simply. The praise of Eros, then, is amazingly qualified.

What he says is this: Eros acts as a tolerable substitute in the absence of virtue and produces something which looks like virtue. Whether Phaedrus is pretty clear about that is not our question. This is decisive for the rest of the speech.

> "Lovers alone, moreover, are willing to die on behalf [of their beloveds], and not only men but women too. Alcestis, the daughter of Pelias, offers adequate testimony for this to the Greeks on behalf of this logos: she alone was willing to die on behalf of her husband, though his father and mother were alive. She surpassed them to such a degree in friendship on account of her eros as to prove that they were alien to their own son and were related only in name, and in accomplishing this deed she seemed, not only to human beings but also to gods, to have accomplished so beautiful a deed that, though many accomplished many beautiful deeds, the gods gave this as a reward to some easily countable number, to send up the soul again from Hades; but in admiration of her deed they sent up hers. So the gods too honor especially the zeal and virtue in regard to eros." (179b4–d2)

Up to now we have spoken of eros and virtue as two different things. Eros as productive of virtue. Now he speaks of a virtue concerned with eros. For example, the virtue regarding eros is different from the virtue regarding the polis, of which he had spoken before. Here he turns to women as well, and to the love of a woman for a man. The previous examples were all implicitly of pederasty. I have to say a word about this somewhat unusual subject. The common view, of course, is that pederasty was the manner and custom of Greece, and Plato and Socrates suffered from this defect. It is usual therefore to give a kind of apology for this. I believe that this is really wrong.

[Tape change.]

Today a man of principle will not always underline that he is a man of principle. We must not be squeamish about these matters, but on the other hand we must be principled. I suggest already now that in a very playful and graceful way, the *Symposium* is among other things a criticism of pederasty and not a praise of it. Certain speakers praise pederasty as higher than heterosexual love. But the beauty is that they try to find a foundation for their habits and they fail in that. In the Socratic speech pederasty occurs only in a way which has nothing to do with certain criminal and indecent practices. And the drunken Alcibiades shamelessly tells a story that only redounds to the praise of Socrates' perfect propriety. It is an improper account of proper conduct. From Socrates' and Plato's point of view, pederasty, this deviation from the natural, points to something true and natural. I can only give one word, which is not an answer, and that word is philosophy.

You see here that Phaedrus himself turns to bisexual love, and apparently he admits it as equal in dignity to homosexual love. Which is a lot because the next speaker will assert that pederasty is much higher in dignity than heterosexual love.

Eros overcomes the fear of death. We have seen this before. Eros overcomes the greatest obstacle to manliness—fear of death. But this only means, according to what was said earlier, that eros is an inferior means for producing virtue and manliness, by making men ashamed to behave like cowards. In other words, eros would be inferior to nature, to the best nature. Now a turn takes place, a new logos begins. Alcestis had no concern with shame, meaning what others say, but she is possessed by the genuine thing, by friendship. She was truly a friend of her husband, whereas her husband's father and mother had only the name in common. This shows that eros, by nature, culminates in death for the beloved. Eros is not a means for virtue, but the object of virtue, the end of virtue. The virtue regarding eros, as distinguished from the virtue regarding the polis, for example. It is heroic virtue. Alcestis's husband was one of the Argonauts. Two other examples, Orpheus and Achilles, also have roles in this account. This heroic love is admired even by the gods, who, being immortal, do not possess it. But there is a difficulty. He refers here to the Greeks. Is this admiration of heroic love limited among men to the Greeks? And is this heroic eroticism not also in need of witnesses, if only of gods?

> "They sent Orpheus the son of Oeagrus out of Hades unfulfilled; they showed him a phantom of his wife for whom he had come but did not give her herself, because he was thought to be soft inasmuch as he was one who sang to the lyre and had not dared for the sake of eros to die, as Alcestis did, but contrived to enter Hades while alive. Accordingly, on account of this, they imposed a penalty on him, and made his death occur at the hands of women." (179d2–e1)

Orpheus, the husband of Eurydice, was punished by the gods because he did not dare to die for the sake of eros. We see here that there are demands of eros which are reinforced by the gods. There are external punishments, also rewards, for this virtue regarding eros, which consists in self-sacrifice.

In the second of the three examples eros does not make the lover courageous. Eros is not as such self-sufficient. But of course one could say this lover happened to be a singer, a poet. Perhaps we could say the poets have failed to praise Eros properly in their poems because they have failed to praise him properly in their actions in the first place. Orpheus was not punished simply for not having died for his beloved, but for having tried to evade death and yet enter Hades. What is the conclusion? He would not have been punished if he had died. But he also would not have been punished if he had limited himself to evading death and to merely lamenting the death of Eurydice, i.e., if he had practiced valetudinarianism. Let us not forget that the praiser of heroic dying is the valetudinarian Phaedrus. Now let us turn to the third example.

> "Not as they honored Achilles, the son of Thetis, and sent him away to the isles of the blessed, because, having learned from his mother that he would die if he killed Hector, but if he did not do it he would go home and die an old man, he dared to choose, in coming to the aid of his lover Patroclus and avenging him, not only to die on his behalf but also to die after him, when he was already dead. It was in great admiration for this fact that the gods honored him exceptionally, because he was holding his lover in such high esteem. Aeschylus talks nonsense in asserting that Achilles was in love with Patroclus, he who was more beautiful not only than Patroclus but than all the heroes together; and he was still beardless and, in the second place, far younger, as Homer says." (179e1–180a7)

Achilles is an entirely different case. Phaedrus has shown up to now the effect which eros has on the lover, not on the beloved. Here we find for the first time a case where the beloved becomes inspired by being beloved to die for his lover. Achilles is the beloved who dies for his lover Patroclus. This is a paradoxical assertion of Phaedrus. He defends it against Aeschylus who had said that Achilles was the lover, which would be the normal case. Achilles was the beloved for he was the most beautiful. How can we understand this absolutely paradoxical action of Achilles under the premise he had made?

> "As a matter of fact, though the gods really honor in the best possible case this virtue in regard to eros, they wonder at and admire and benefit more whenever the one who is loved cherishes the lover than whenever the lover does the beloved. The reason is that a lover is a more divine thing than a beloved, for he has the god in him. On account of this they honored Achilles more than they did Alcestis, by sending him away to the isles of the blessed." (180a7–b5)

Do you understand this reasoning? Why do the gods honor the beloved more than the lover? Let me try to explain this: The virtue regarding eros is more admired by the gods in the beloved than in the lover, for the god is in the lover, not in the beloved. You can interpret this in two ways: either the beloved who cherishes the lover is pious—he bows to the god—or it is much more difficult to have that virtue which consists in dying if one does not love than if one does. The gods themselves bear witness to the fact that virtue which is not god-inspired is higher than the virtue which is god-inspired. Lack of eros is superior to eros. In the *Phaedrus,* which in my opinion follows dramatically the *Symposium,* the whole thing begins with a speech elaborated by the orator Lysias, in which the nonlover is preferred to the lover. Let me take this example: If a girl today would raise the question With what kind of man would I like to have friendly relations, with a lover or with a nonlover? Lysias says with the nonlover; precisely because he has no passion, he will not do anything improper. This is what attracts Phaedrus, the preference for the nonlover. It is paradoxical that the non-passionate Phaedrus should wish Eros to be praised. We must try to understand that. The lover is older than the beloved, as appeared from the discussion of the Homeric example. The oldest god is in the older men, in the homosexual, not in the younger. But the younger, in whom the god is not, who is not inspired by the god, is superior in the eyes of the gods themselves, and, I might add, in the eyes of men. The lover recognizes by his pursuit a certain superiority of the pursued.

What is Phaedrus driving at? We know the contradiction between the two statements he made, the one at 179b and the other at 179e. He says only lovers are willing to die for the beloved. Later on he says Achilles the beloved was willing to die for his lover. Achilles received a unique honor from the gods. But what happens if we disregard this divine honor, or if we draw the proper lesson from Orpheus's half-hearted action. The beloved will not die for the lover, he will only be the beneficiary of other men's love. The beloved, especially if he is very beautiful, will be beloved by many people and will thus be the beneficiary precisely because the god is not in him. While the god is in the lover, the greatest benefit accrues to the beloved. It is really a triumph of valetudinarianism, or, to introduce a more precise term, what Phaedrus wittingly or unwittingly does is to subject eros to the criterion of gain, a selfish consideration. Therefore his speech is the lowest of all the speeches. I refer again to Phaedrus's admiration of Lysias's speech in the *Phaedrus,* where it is said that the young should prefer the nonlovers to the lovers—a calculating rule. I think that Lysias's speech in the *Phaedrus* is altogether a reflection on Phaedrus's speech here, modified by the other speeches we hear later on. In other words, Phaedrus, induced by the experience of our evening, has abandoned the admiration for eros completely. From the point of view of the calculating recipient the nonlover is preferable to the lover. Now, let us read the end of Phaedrus's speech.

> "It's in this way that I assert that of the gods Eros is the oldest, most honorable, and most authoritative for the acquisition of virtue and happiness for human beings when they are alive and dead." (180b6–8)

As we see, then, it is a limited praise even at the end. I shall suggest a provisional answer to the question of why Phaedrus thinks that Eros has not been sufficiently praised. He thinks that the benefits which lovers bestow on the beloved have never been sufficiently praised. Phaedrus speaks from the beloved's point of view, and this is very important because the next speaker will be a lover, with a completely different perspective.

Perhaps I should give now a presentation of the whole *Symposium* as it appears to me now. I am not only willing but eager to learn that I am wrong. It seems to me that we have six speeches on eros, because Alcibiades' speech at the end is a speech on Socrates, not on eros itself. The speeches fall naturally into two parts, the first three and the second three. Phaedrus, Pausanias, and Eryximachus—Aristophanes, Agathon, and Socrates. I believe that the first three speeches are deficient as praises of eros because they subject eros to something outside of eros: Phaedrus to gain, Pausanias to moral virtue, Eryximachus to techne, to science or art. The three others do not subject eros to something outside, they praise eros as such. Socrates, too, does not subject eros to something outside because that to which Socrates seemingly subjects eros is the natural end of eros. If the natural end of eros is wisdom in the highest case, then the love of wisdom doesn't subject eros to something alien to it. The distribution I think is this: Aristophanes' speech is characterized by ugliness, Agathon's is beauty incarnate; in Socrates eros is neither ugly nor beautiful. The last word, the key word, in Socrates' speech is neither ugliness nor beauty but the good. I believe there is a connection here with Phaedrus' speech. Love of gain was ordinarily regarded, and I believe in some quarters still is, as something mean, ugly. The connection between moral virtue and beauty is obvious, because in Greek it is the same word. Techne—science, art—corresponds on the lower level to what Socrates means by the good.

I would now like to summarize what I believe are the most important lessons of Phaedrus's speech. His speech is obviously of very great importance since he is the one who suggested the theme, on the grounds that eros had never been sufficiently praised. This evening is to be devoted to such praise. Phaedrus's speech is the beginning, just as Socrates' speech is the end. Phaedrus combines in his life physics and rhetoric, just as the young Socrates did. Then we have the key authority appealed to by Phaedrus, Parmenides. Parmenides is the only one with whom he fully agrees. With Homer he doesn't quite agree, and surely not with Aeschylus and the others. Parmenides means that the place ordinarily occupied by the gods is taken by purely intelligible principles. Phaedrus's speech is set off from all other speeches and in this respect it is akin to Socrates' speech, which by other devices is set off from all other speeches. There is, in spite of the lowness and poverty of Phaedrus's suggestion, a certain connection between Phaedrus and Socrates. Both say the beloved is higher than the lover; both say the oldest is the highest. But of course there is a difference. Plato understands by the oldest the most fundamental—soul. The soul is higher than the body. Last but not least, Phaedrus invokes Parmenides. And a modification of Parmenides' philosophy will be the background to what Socrates says in his speech, namely, the so-called Platonic background of ideas, the heterogeneous ideal cosmos, will replace the Parmenidean one—the homogeneous one—the pure intelligence. I will try to explain this when we get to it.

If we read the speech with some care and concentration, we see that Phaedrus gives a very strange praise of eros. In the first place he makes it clear that lovers, to say nothing of the beloved, are, as such, inferior to those who are by nature best, in regard to virtue. Furthermore, the motive of these lovers is a sense of shame rather than love of honor. They are concerned with acting nobly in the sight of the beloved. We hear nothing about their concerns when they are unobserved. Finally, the virtue which he praised is one virtue only, namely manliness or courage, which, from a certain point of view, is the lowest of the virtues. Phaedrus's speech is also made distinctive by an extraordinary emphasis on dying, on sacrifice. This will be important for the next two speeches, in which any allusion to these harsh things will be avoided. Phaedrus makes a distinction. He turns from virtue in general, i.e., the virtue primarily concerned with the polis, to the virtue concerned with eros—the virtue which does not only stem from love but is also concerned with love. But here we see also that this love does not necessarily culminate in what, from the point of view of courage, is the highest, namely the willingness to die. We have seen the example of Orpheus, who had this love to a high degree but could not bring himself to die for Eurydice. This erotic virtue is least effective in the case of the beloved. External rewards and punishments, rewards and punishments by the gods, are required for bringing this erotic virtue into its own. In his culminating thesis, the god is in the lover, not in the beloved, and yet the beloved proves to have a higher status than the lover. This is a very strange eros, that the

55

one who does not have eros in himself should be higher. I suggest this explanation: Phaedrus looks at the phenomenon of love from the point of view of the beloved, the beneficiary of other men's love. This man—or woman—does not need as such virtue. Their attractiveness, their beauty, is perfectly sufficient. Phaedrus's point of view, to state it succinctly, is that of profit, of calculation, of gain. Phaedrus also says Eros is the oldest god. The oldest means the most venerable. But why is Eros most venerable? Because he is most useful to the beloved, to such people as Phaedrus himself. It is not most useful to man as man, and here we shall see the great change occurring later in the fourth speech, Aristophanes' speech, where Eros is presented for the first time as the most philanthropic god, as the god who loves man as man.

Here, Apollodorus says, Phaedrus has made a speech of this kind, more or less exact, a remark which he makes in no other case. After this were some speeches which Aristodemus did not remember. There is a hiatus between Phaedrus's speech and all the other speeches. It is set off from all the others. It is the shortest of all speeches, but to its credit it indicates much. All the motives of Phaedrus's speech return in Socrates' speech in a modified way. Take only this crucial point, that the beloved is higher than the lover. What about Socrates? He says exactly the same thing, though he doesn't think of the beloved in terms of a human being. There is a one-way street of love from the lover to the beloved. Essentially love is only one-sided. We know this, in its highest theoretical development, in Aristotle's doctrine of the unmoved mover. The unmoved mover moves as beloved, not as lover. This is what Socrates indicates in his speech by making something which we may loosely call the ideas the highest object of love. The ideas do not love the men, the men love the ideas. Ultimately there must be principles which are self-sufficient, or not in any need, and therefore do not love or long for anything else. This applies to the metaphysics of both Plato and Aristotle. Today, people make the distinction between two understandings of love—eros and agape. Agape, the biblical understanding, means love out of abundance comes down.

4 PAUSANIAS (1)

There is one point which I would like to make right now: there is no Platonic dialogue which does not abstract from something important. Every dialogue is deliberately one-sided. In the *Phaedrus* just as in the *Republic*, you have a tripartition of the soul. There is a base eros, there is a noble eros, and above them is reason or intellect. What is called base love in the *Phaedrus* is called appetite or desire in the *Republic*; noble love is called spiritedness in the *Republic*. This tripartition does not occur in the *Symposium*. Instead you get another tripartition of eros in the simple sense, i.e., heterosexual love for the end of procreation; love of immortal fame, which has a certain kinship to spiritedness in the *Republic* but is not identical with it; and the third is love of wisdom. How these two tripartitions are related is a question. He who could give a true answer to that question could claim to have understood Plato's doctrine of man. The task of understanding this work completely is of enormous difficulty. Even if this schema which I present is true, it would only constitute a very small part since we would also have to understand the characters of the speakers. Why did Plato entrust the defense, say, of moral virtue to an elderly lover of a certain kind? Why did he entrust the defense of gain, the submission of eros to gain, to a young beloved, etc. These different attitudes toward love are connected with certain human characters, and one must also understand these characters, not only the attitudes in themselves.

[This incorporation of attitudes into characters] brings the nature of the thing into the open. That means, however, that it does not present the nature of the thing as that nature presents itself, but as hidden or half revealed or overlaid by opinion. Plato reproduces the natures of things as they first come to sight; he imitates them as they show themselves at first. This being the case, Plato always discusses, whatever he discusses, in a human context. Human beings talking about the phenomena at question. A human individual, a man with a proper name, a member of this or that society, is the one who talks about it. The reason is as follows: Philosophic inquiry, speculation, theoria, is in danger of forgetting itself, of losing itself in the contemplation of the subject. By this very fact speculation becomes very unphilosophic. Philosophy, or whatever you call this pursuit, must always know what it is doing—it must always be self-knowledge—and therefore it must always entail reflection on the philosophizer.

Philosophy cannot leave it at trying to find out what knowledge is—the problem of so-called epistemology; it must also raise the question Why knowledge? What is the meaning of knowledge in the human context? These problems are kept alive by the representation of philosophy which Plato gives. Here in the *Symposium* the human context is this: eros is to be praised and adorned as a god. This is imposed on eros. As critical men of science we naturally raise the question, "Is Eros a god?" Does he deserve praise? Perhaps love is a humdrum phenomenon as so many others. Therefore Plato is under obligation in some way to prove that eros deserves praise. To begin with the favor or prejudice we have regarding eros is only opinion. Yet it is not entirely groundless opinion, as simple reflection shows. Suffice it to compare the bodily pleasures somehow akin to eros, the desire for food and drink. Homer calls the pleasure of love the golden words and deeds of Aphrodite. It is obviously inappropriate to apply such a term to food and drink. But it is more than that. Food and drink are related to self-preservation, whereas eros has an essential relation to the preservation of the species. Eros, therefore, as such, raises men above the concern with self-preservation. Eros contains in itself the possibility of self-sacrifice, which we cannot say about the concern for food and drink. Therefore eros has a natural relation to heroism, as Phaedrus indicates in his speech. A man who dares everything in order to get food and drink can be somehow impressive, but no one would call him a heroic man.

In the *Symposium,* the analysis of eros is modified not only by the command to praise Eros. I refer to the allusions to the year 416, the gross impiety committed at that time and then somehow forgiven in 407. The background of that is the accusation against Socrates, and this means the question of the life of the philosopher in tension with the life of the polis. By the link-up of the years 416 and 407 Plato indicates that in studying eros we must not forget for one moment the highest activities of men—political and philosophic. This raises the question of the relationship of eros to political life on the one hand and to philosophy on the other. As to political life, we have seen in the *Republic* that in the purely political consideration on the highest level silence is preserved regarding procreation. In the second book, where he gives reasons for the desire of men to form society he mentions food, drink, and shelter but is completely silent about procreation. Later on, in the ninth book, the tyrant, the worst degradation of political life, is identified with eros. Furthermore, in the psychology of the

Republic, eros, which is the same as desire—in the Greek *epithumia*—as we shall see later in the *Symposium,* is presented as the lowest part of man, lower than spiritedness, to say nothing of reason. The polis, we can say, necessitates law, nomos, and eros is not essentially legal. I think that everyone must admit that—the final and essential concern of eros is not legality. Yet we could say, is not love of country a modification of eros? There is this difficulty: What is the opposite of love of country? Let us say treason. But what is the primary object of high treason? Is it selling out a given country, or is it not at least as much selling out the established order? Political crimes are never really crimes against the country; as political crimes they are directed against the constitution. The polity, however, never lets you meet the country naked. We always meet it clothed in a political form. And the loyalty which is demanded, as every loyalty discussion shows, refers not to the unclothed country but to the country defined in terms of its constitution. Love of country, then, is in a concrete form a love of country as modified and constituted by its polity, and the polity expresses itself in law. This means that the country is unthinkable without the element of compulsion—laws—and therefore of punishment. There is a certain harshness which essentially belongs to political life, which shows the tension between eros and political life.

To take a Platonic example, which is always best when discussing a Platonic problem, the best polity as presented in the *Republic* stands and falls by the noble lie. The indication is not that in imperfect polities we do not need a lie, but that they are based on base lies. There is an element of the artificial and untruth that is essential to political life. Philosophy, on the other hand, is love of truth. There is an old presentation of this difference: the naked soul confronted with the naked truth, in a *gymnasion,* the Greek word for gymnasium. In other contexts, this is also taken as a place for intellectual stripping. Eros is connected with stripping. Philosophy is a stripping on the highest level, the mind. The political life is never a life of stripping. I can also state this as follows: political life is, of course, public life. The erotic life is private life, and therefore there is a fundamental tension between the two. I can illustrate this as follows: There was a man who in a way demanded absolute politicization and that was Marx. Marx spoke of the collectivization of man to be brought about by the communist society. All privacy, all private property, as well as all misery, is connected with the division of labor, and therefore the perfect society would be one in which the division of labor is completely abolished. But the same Marx, at least in his early writings, mentions the fact that the root of the division of labor is man's bisexuality. He says in so many words that the fundamental act of the division of labor is the sexual act. The paradoxical conclusion would be that perfect communism would have to abolish sexual difference and produce men in test tubes. Whether Marx intended this is not for us to investigate here, but it only shows that if you think through the problem of public, publicity, collectivization, you see with the greatest clarity that there is something fundamentally and absolutely irreducible in man on the most massive level—the erotic life, which in this respect agrees with the life of the mind—which is not susceptible of being collectivized.

This difference between the political, which is akin to compulsion, and philosophy, which like eros is incompatible with compulsion, plays a certain role also for the externals of the Platonic dialogues. I have said on occasion that to begin one must look at the Platonic dialogues from the most obvious point of view, namely the titles, and also whether they are narrated or performed dialogues. A slightly more subtle distinction is that between the dialogues which are voluntary and the dialogues which are compulsory. This distinction reflects the distinction between the political and the philosophic. You can see this if you look at that dialogue which is the most compulsory. That is, of course the *Apology of Socrates,* which is called a dialogue with the Athenian demos in the *Apology* itself. The *Republic,* too, is a partly compulsory dialogue. At the beginning Polemarchus tries to keep them back by main force. The *Symposium* is an unusually voluntary dialogue, as you can see from the opening. Socrates dresses up and goes on his own.

In this connection I would like to mention in passing this characteristic feature of the *Symposium:* at the celebration of eros, the intellectual cream of Athens is assembled. Socrates is fifty-three years old, that is to say at the peak of his life, and the theme eros, which explains the atmosphere of the dialogue and which contrasts so sharply with a kindred dialogue, the *Phaedo*—Socrates' death, no celebration of anything. Yet they are closely akin because love and death are akin, as we shall hear later from Socrates' own mouth.

We have some prospect already, though very insufficient, to what is going to come. We see in the first place a specific point of view from which one can look at eros. This point of view is indeed the lowest, that of selfish gain. We must see what other points of view can arise. We must also consider how this is connected with the character of the speaker. There are two things about Phaedrus's character: he is young, he is at least potentially loved, and he is a valetudinarian. You remember he goes with the physician, he doesn't drink, and he is afraid of getting drunk. So, by merely finding out the connotations of these items—young and beloved and valetudinarian—we find four possibilities, the other three being old, beloved, and valetudinarian; young, lover, and valetudinarian; and old, lover, and valetudinarian. We must see if any of these occur. What is much more important, however, is to see what other forms of character traits could take the place of, say, the valetudinarian. In the end we must see whether the typology implied in that is complete. Whether Plato has succeeded in discussing all character traits relevant to eros and all possible approaches to eros. Then and only then can we say whether he has written through his dialogue the definitive treatise on eros.

[In answer to a question:] Many lovers, as we see in so many books, were very uncalculating precisely because they were young. I would say that a calculating young lover is the exception rather than the rule. There is a certain contradiction between calculation and eros. We know that people sometimes combine them but that is not the clearest phenomenon of eros. As if a man were to speak of this woman who is absolutely wonderful because she has millions. Calculation is one thing and love is another thing. If I now take in the scholastic term for eros, natural inclination, calculation is not natural inclination and vice versa. One can roughly divide all political doctrines into two kinds: whether they say political society rests on natural inclination or whether it rests on calculation. The Aristotelian doctrine is the most famous case of one where the polis is natural, which means there is a natural inclination in man for political society.

Listener: Is it necessary to view the notion of love as calculation in Phaedrus as a deliberate intention on his part? It seems to me that the whole example of Achilles suggests a notion of love that he is not fully aware of.

Mr. Strauss: I don't believe that Phaedrus understands the implication of what he says. To a great extent the irony is involuntary. But that it is not entirely involuntary can be proved as follows: We know from the *Phaedrus,* for example, that he was very skeptical, that he did not believe in the old tales. Now, whatever he says about Achilles, etc., is based on the old tales. In this case I believe he knew what he was doing. Also, we have the parallel of the *Protagoras* myth, where Protagoras consciously speaks ironically about these things, but there is a kind of irony beyond his irony of which he is not aware.

Pausanias begins with the very simple remark that it is preposterous to say, as Phaedrus seemed to have said in general, that eros is conducive to virtue, since we know of so many cases where eros has led to vice. He makes the distinction between a virtuous love and a vicious love. From this point of view Phaedrus's speech is obviously imperfect, and therefore we get Pausanias's speech. Let us remember what we know about Pausanias: Pausanias, in contradistinction with Phaedrus, is good at drinking, and he is a lover. He loves Agathon, the tragic poet, who is also good at drinking. Both, he and Agathon, are pupils of Prodicus, a sophist, whom Socrates regarded most highly. So there is an intellectual kinship. Pausanias's speech is the longest, apart from that of Socrates; Phaedrus's speech is the shortest, so they really are opposites.

The theses peculiar to Pausanias are at first glance two: First, there are two erotes, one for the noble and one for the base. Therefore, the noble eros will be committed to virtue and the base eros will be committed to vice. Secondly, the noble eros, the proper eros, is prescribed by the law of the land. Phaedrus has been completely silent about the law. Naturally, a man who is concerned predominantly with gain will think of law only when he has to. Now, the first thesis, the two forms of love, is directed against Phaedrus's speech, according to which nothing is as conducive to virtue, namely to courage, as eros. That thesis is open to the objection that eros may very well lead to vice. We do not have to go into any examples from the newspaper; we have the great example of Paris and Helen. If that was not love it is hard to see what is love. Yet Paris was not outstanding for courage. The solution to the problem is that there is a noble eros leading to virtue and a base eros leading to vice. But virtue means now the whole virtue, not merely courage, and that seems to be an improvement.

The second thesis, namely that the right form of eros is prescribed by the law, is directed against Phaedrus's thesis according to which the virtue concerned with eros, that one is willing to die for the other, is rewarded by the gods, and in its absence one is punished by the gods. That thesis is open to the objection that the goodness of this kind of virtue depends on the truth of these old tales, which Phaedrus himself does not believe. Therefore Pausanias, in a positive spirit, says, "No, this is caused by a human love, by a surely effective love, effective here and now."

Phaedrus says eros leads to courage by nature. Pausanias says the noble eros, in contradistinction to the base eros, leads to the whole virtue but is in need of support by the law. That means that both Phaedrus's and Pausanias's praise of eros are very weak, compared to the position that eros, without the need of man-made support, would lead to the highest virtue. This comes out, of course, in Socrates' speech. If you contrast the final remark of Phaedrus with the final remark of Pausanias you would see that Pausanias's praise of eros is actually weaker than Phaedrus's praise. But we must not forget that Phaedrus has some kind of irony which Pausanias lacks. Now let us read the sequel.

> He said that Phaedrus spoke a speech of this kind, and after Phaedrus there were some other speeches which he could hardly remember, and omitting them he proceeded to narrate the speech of Pausanias. He said that he said, "The logos, Phaedrus, seems to me to have been not beautifully proposed to us, the command to praise Eros so unqualifiedly." (180c1–5)

Pausanias takes issue not only with Phaedrus's thesis but with the theme proposed by Phaedrus.

> "If Eros were one, it would be fine; but, as it is, it is not, for he is not one; and if he is not one, it is more correct to have it stated beforehand which one is to be praised. So I will try to correct this, first to point out the Eros which one must praise, and then to make a praise worthy of the god. Everyone knows that there is no Aphrodite without Eros. Now if she were one, Eros would be one; but since in fact there are two, it is a necessity that there be two Erotes. How aren't there two goddesses? One is surely the older and the motherless daughter of Uranus. It is she whom we name Urania. The other is younger, daughter of Zeus and Dione. It is she whom we call Pandemus. So it's a necessity, in the case of Eros, that the one who is a coworker with the second [Aphrodite] be called correctly Pandemus, and the other Uranios." (180c6–e3)

Pausanias is very much concerned with correctness of speech, due to his connection with Prodicus, who was very much concerned with semantic problems. Now, which Eros is to be praised? There is more than one Eros and only one is to be praised. Pausanias does not refer to any myth in the beginning, as Phaedrus did. He refers to a common opinion implied in the official Athenian cult. Not an old story but a present opinion. Two Aphrodites were worshiped, the heavenly and the pandemian. *Pandemian* does not necessarily have a negative connotation because pandemian means common to all human beings. No Aphrodite without eros. But that has of course also another meaning. Eros is a condition of Aphrodite. Eros is, then, at least coeval with Aphrodite and not her son, as he was sometimes said to be. But there are two Aphrodites, hence there must be two erotes. That does not necessarily follow from the condition. Also, as I mentioned before, we must name things correctly, therefore we must give the two erotes different names. Dione is, of course, also a goddess. But the noble Aphrodite, and hence the noble eros, is older than the other. We see also that Eros is no longer simply the oldest god. This assertion of Phaedrus has gone. The best is no longer simply identical with the oldest. This is natural since he is going to defend the present Athenian law.

I think his argument is this, which is of course a political or popular argument: Every Athenian knows there are two Aphrodites; secondly, there is no Aphrodite without eros. Hence, since there are two Aphrodites there must be two erotes. He draws a new conclusion.

Listener: His insistence on two Aphrodites, of which one is best, would be much stronger if he had said there is no eros without Aphrodite, but this he could not say.

Mr. Strauss: If I understand you correctly, if there are erotes already at this time without Aphrodite, and Aphrodite is a kind of leftover from old mythology, why does he not drop her altogether? Then this thing would be much clearer. I have the impression that Simonides for example says that Aphrodite is the mother of Eros, but it is denied here that eros has a mother.

There is this difficulty in the beginning (180c). He says if there were one eros Phaedrus's proposition would be all right, but now as it is there is not only one eros. Since there is not only one it would be more correct to say which Eros should be praised. There is more than one eros, i.e., there may be many erotes. Then the question arises, with what right does he limit himself to two. Sometimes a logical lacuna occurs in one speech which is resolved later on. Socrates speaks of three erotes. In other words, this possibility remains sterile as far as Pausanias is concerned.

> "Now one must praise all gods, but regardless of that one must try to say what each of the two has obtained as his lot." (180e3–4)

This pious statement, that all gods must be praised, is contradicted by quite a few things, past and future.

> "Every action is of this kind. An action in being done alone by itself is neither beautiful nor ugly. To drink, for example, as we are now doing, or to sing, or to converse, not one of these things is in itself beautiful, but in whatever way it is done, it turns out to be of that sort in the doing. If it is beautifully and correctly done it proves to be beautiful; if incorrectly, ugly. So too loving and Eros is not in his entirety beautiful, any more than he is deserving of praise, but the [Eros] who [beautifully] induces one to love beautifully." (180e4–181a6)

This, of course, is a very important assertion, which has very grave consequences. Every action can be done nobly or basely. What about that proposition? Is every action susceptible of being done nobly or basely? No. Murder, for example, cannot be done nobly. There are, then, actions which in themselves are base. We must keep this in mind in order to understand Pausanias, because Pausanias is so much concerned with nobility, he only wants to praise the noble and he says all actions can be noble. In other words, he who is so concerned with the morality of eros is rather immoral.

> "Now the [Eros] of Aphrodite Pandemus is truly pandemus and does his work haphazardly; and this is he in respect to whom the base among human beings love. People of this sort love, in the first place, women no less than boys; second, of them, they love their bodies rather than their souls; third, [they love] those who are as mindless as possible, looking solely to the accomplishment and neglecting whether it is beautifully done or not. From this it follows that whatever they do they do haphazardly, the good as indifferently as its opposite. The reason is that he is from the goddess who is far younger than the other, and she partakes in her birth in female and male. The [Eros] of uranian [Aphrodite]—in the first place, she does not partake in female but only male—and this is the eros of boys; in the second place, she is older and has no share in hubris. It is on this basis that those who are inspired by this eros turn to the male, cherishing the stronger by nature and who have nous to a higher degree." (181a7–c6)

He gives first the description of the base eros. The base eros is directed toward the female sex too; secondly it is directed more toward the body than the soul and it prefers the most unintelligent beloved. Why? Because it is concerned only with what we may call sexual success. Therefore, and this is somewhat paradoxical, it is accidental whether the devotees of this vulgar eros act well or badly. Can you act well on that basis? We surely notice that mere concern with sexual success does not necessarily lead to virtue. While the base eros is concerned only with sexual success it may act well. I think this is connected with his general proposition that there is no action about which you can speak universally with respect. Though this is true, the base eros will lead to a good action only accidentally, and therefore it is base. This eros is base because it is not directed toward the good. What are the reasons for this? The younger Aphrodite has a mother, therefore she is bisexual as is also the Eros who accompanies her. Secondly, she is younger, and the younger are more unreasonable. Therefore she goes in for the love of the unreasonable, for very young boys.

A few more points: At 180c2, when he speaks of the other eros he does not mention the word *eros*, he only implies it. That, of course, does not come out in the translation. But the more important conclusion is this: no action is in itself noble or base. Every action is capable of being done nobly or badly. But how do we distinguish? Here we get a certain inkling of it. Here we have the noble eros put in terms of the male, which is by nature stronger and possesses intelligence to a higher degree. Love for those who are by nature stronger and more intelligent is nobler than love for the weaker and less intelligent. In the sequel the emphasis shifts immediately to intelligence alone. Homosexual love is nobler because it is concerned with the nobler sex. May I ask the ladies here to forgive me for introducing these statements, which are not my statements. Not even Plato makes them; they are statements of Pausanias. Let me make one general statement here: What Pausanias is after is a defense of pederasty.

[Tape change.]

It is directed toward the noble because it is directed toward intelligence, toward nous. Here we have already one difficulty, which is ultimately the downfall of Pausanias. Let us assume the noble love is love for intelligent human beings. What follows? The noblest love is love for the most intelligent. Who are, generally speaking, the most intelligent males? [Gap in the tape.] He tries to find a ground for pederasty and what he gets is the opposite. To make this a bit more clear, where do we find that noblest love presented in the *Symposium*? Aristodemus, the silent fellow, and in a cruder way Apollodorus.

> "And one would recognize also in pederasty itself those who have been purely prompted by this eros, for they do not love boys, except when they already begin to have nous, and this is close in time to the growth of the beard. I believe that those who begin to love from this time are fully prepared to be together their whole life and live together in common, and not, once they have taken him as young in his folly and deceived him, then disappear in scornful laughter and run off to another. There should also have been a law forbidding the love of boys, in order that much zeal would not have been expended for an unclear result. It is unclear where the end of boys ends up in regard to the virtue and vice of soul and body. Now the good voluntarily lay down this law for themselves, but there should have been a compulsion of this kind imposed on those pandemian lovers, just as we compel them, to the extent that we are able, not to love free women. It is these who have made it a reproach, so as for some to dare to say that it is shameful to gratify lovers; and they say this looking at them, seeing their untimeliness and injustice, since it is surely the case that there is no matter whatsoever, if it is done in an orderly and lawful way, that would justly incur blame." (181c7–182a6)

Pausanias, in contradistinction to Phaedrus, looks at the problem from the point of view of the lover, as distinguished from the beloved, that I think is clear. He is not primarily worried about the corruption of the boys by base lovers, but about the waste of time on the part of the lovers. He is concerned with the self-interest of the lovers. Phaedrus is concerned with the self-interest of the beloved. This is a great difference because there is no perfect parallelism between the lover and the beloved. Out of this self-interest of the lovers good men impose upon themselves a law. And you must not think here of Kant or Rousseau, that would be misleading, although the expression is the same. What he means is this: the good men are not merely by nature directed toward those above sixteen. If they were there would be no need for a law. Therefore they must impose on themselves a law. There is no natural difference between the devotees of the noble eros and the devotees of the base eros because there is no natural or intrinsic difference between good and bad actions. For example, the base eros directs itself equally toward free women and toward slave girls. But the nomos, the law, speaks. This is based on the fact that the law is the work of the free man, of the fathers, par excellence. These fathers protect not only their wives, they protect also the young boys naturally. The same fathers are concerned with the well-being of their young sons and thus make it disgraceful to be a corrupter of a boy. They go even beyond this and say all such love is disgraceful. The reasonable lovers anticipate this and impose the law on themselves not to run after young boys.

If there is no intrinsic or natural difference between the noble and the base eros but only a view to the consequences—you become disgraced in one case and not in the other—would one not have to show that love of women is inferior, and not only because it is more troublesome than love of boys? Why is love of adolescent males superior to love of girls as well as to love of women? Let us see how he goes on. If there were no defects in the so-called noble eros, if the noble eros were an entirely natural phenomenon, there would be no need for law. But somehow it is constituted by nomos. That nomos we find almost only in Athens. Of course it is not enough to defer to the positive law. What is the principle underlying the positive law? Is it nous, is it intelligence? But we see intelligence wouldn't work.

> "Further, the law about eros in all other cities is easy to understand, for it has been defined without qualification; but the law here and in Sparta is complicated. In Elis and among Boeotians, and wherever they are not

wise in speaking, it has been laid down by law that without qualification it is noble to gratify lovers, and no one, either young or old, would say that it is shameful, in order, I suspect, they might not have any trouble in try-ing to persuade the young by speech, because they are incapable of speak-ing; but in the case of Ionia and many other places, all who dwell under barbarians, it has been laid down by law as shameful. For in the eyes of bar-barians, on account of their tyrannies, this in fact, as well as philosophy and love of exercise, are shameful; for it is, I suspect, not advantageous to the rulers that there come to be great and proud thoughts among the ruled, any more than that there be strong friendships and partnerships. It is this that all the rest and especially eros are wont to instill. Even the tyrants here understood this in deed; the eros of Aristotogeiton and the friendship of Harmodius, in proving to be steadfast, destroyed their rule. So wherever it is laid down to be shameful to gratify lovers, it has been laid down by the vice of those who laid it down, by the overreaching of the rulers and the unmanliness of the ruled; but wherever it was held by law to be unqualifiedly noble, it was on account of the idleness of the soul of those who laid it down. But here it has been laid down by law in a far no-bler way than elsewhere, and, as I said, it's not easy to understand it." (182a7–d6)

Up to now we have only the assertion, and we see that it is a very character-istic one. There are two extremes and a mean. One extreme is never to grant favors, that's the barbaric one. The savage Greeks say grant favors as you please. The Athenians say grant favors with discretion. The Athenian and Spartan law regarding eros is praised. Elis and Boeotia have no restric-tion whatsoever—this is characteristic of the uncivilized Greeks—and ac-tual prohibition is characteristic of the Greeks living under barbarian rule, but it is a reflection of the barbarians themselves. The praise of the oldest is replaced by the praise of what is established, and as a political man he chooses the most renowned, Athens and Sparta.

There is a distinction between noble and base eros, therefore a distinc-tion between virtue and vice. Virtue itself is a mean between complete ab-stinence and complete self-indulgence. This is the theme of Pausanias's speech—moral virtue. Pausanias's speech is characterized by the attempt to look at eros from the point of view of moral virtue. But this is not the speech of an entirely disinterested man. It is the speech of a man who wants freedom for his practices, of which he says they are legal, but we shall see later on that they are not legal. He has to make them legal. His whole speech is, under the guise of a praise of the Athenian nomos, a suggestion of how to improve the Athenian nomos. Such speeches are called deliberative speeches, and I believe that Pausanias's speech is the only deliberative speech occurring in Plato. According to Aristotle there are three kinds of speeches: forensic, epideictic, and deliberative. Forensic concerns acquittal or condemnation under the law. Epideictic is a display of power which serves no practical purpose, for example, after-dinner speeches. Deliberative speeches are political speeches about peace and war, finance, and also law. That this is a political speech, i.e., a speech inspired by interest and possibly by self-interest of the speaker, may be shown by the fact that he is concerned with the law which permits the beloved to grant their favors. That's the tension. As for Sparta, which is omitted in some editions, that is awkward. He has this division: either they can't speak or they can and are, like the Spartans, sensitive about pederasty. The Greeks living under barbarian rule drop philosophy and love of exercise (182c1), but the Greek savages also have no philosophy. The reason he mentions Sparta is because Sparta adds luster to his law; the praise of the law is greater if it includes both Athens and Sparta. But then he must drop Sparta for a very good reason. Not because the practice of pederasty is necessarily different, though there are some indications, as we know from other Platonic dialogues, that there are differences. But the main point is that the connection between the noble eros and the cultivation of the mind is entirely different in Athens. The cultivation of the body is at least as good in Sparta. In his whole speech manliness or courage does not appear. There is a certain softness essential to Pausanias as well as to his beloved Agathon. He is not a valetudinarian.

In Elis and Boeotia the law was made by the lovers as such, therefore there is perfect freedom for the lovers. It was not made by the fathers as such, though the fathers may also be lovers. But in which capacity did they act when they made the law? The explanation suggested here is insufficient. Why is love of young men superior to that of boys and women? Let me state it as follows: In Elis there is no law forbidding this kind of thing; therefore the lovers are not interested in restraint. What is wrong with the law in Elis? That is not clear. Let us therefore look at the other example of the Greeks in Asia Minor living under barbarian rule. Freedom. Freedom requires erotic bonds among those who are best able to carry arms. Those who are best able to carry arms are, of course, neither women nor young boys. We get, then, an entirely different point of view. Hitherto we had nous—intelligence; this will never justify pederasty, as we have seen, because it will lead to love of the wiser, the older. But if it is a matter of political freedom, of those who can defend it best, then there is a link between men who are still able to carry on from the older generation—forty-five according to the Romans—and the younger generation, say of seventeen. We must see whether this is sufficient.

We see here by various examples, in 182c3–4, that eros produces lofty souls, but it is not the only thing that produces lofty souls. Here we have another consideration. Freedom is used as a support for pederasty. But why doesn't it work? Why is freedom insufficient? Anyone who has continued to read Pausanias's speech should know the answer. Why is the relation between eros and freedom not safe? The lover is supposed to serve as a slave. Nous—mind—fails. Freedom, too, is no good, since the relation is a slavish one.

There are some more points which we can briefly consider. One is of political interest in a narrower sense, when he speaks of the barbarians. "Wherever it is laid down to be shameful to gratify lovers, it has been laid down by the vice of those who laid it down." It was due to greed, to the desire to have more on the part of the rulers, and to unmanliness of the ruled. That is a very interesting remark. The ruled, even those ruled by a tyrant, are as much legislators as the ruler or the tyrant. This contains, of course, an element of truth which is so grossly overdone by certain trends in modern scientific political science. For example, in Bentley's theories of political government there doesn't exist simple tyranny. There is always some influence of the subjected population on the rulers. Therefore, in the spirit of this view, Pausanias says the legislators, even in a tyranny, are the ruled as well as the rulers. In the other case—where he speaks of the barbaric Greeks, where it was made a law to be simply noble, namely without any restraint—there it was done through the laziness of the soul of the legislators. Here you see he does not make any distinction between the rulers and ruled. Why? Obviously—they are republics; the distinction between rulers and ruled does not exist. They are truly free men. What do they say regarding pederasty? They say do as you wish. Therefore freedom does not require the noble eros. We have another proof that the second attempt of Pausanias to find a basis for pederasty—this time not in nous, in intelligence, but in freedom—breaks down. Where will he find the basis? Plato doesn't say, "That's my value judgment"; every idiot can say that. He asks, What's the reason for your value judgment? Why is pederasty good? Why should it be permitted by the law? You must give reasons. The fact that some people wish to engage in it or suffer from its prohibition is of course no reason for changing the law. There must be good reasons. Give me a good reason. Nous? No. Freedom? No. Because freedom would lead to an indiscriminate permission which no substantial part of the Athenian electorate would go for. So, he must find a third principle.

The third principle, to which he is going to appeal in the sequel, is moral virtue, not nous, not freedom. We have to see whether the moral education of a boy of seventeen is improved by doing all kinds of favors to a man of thirty or forty. That's a practical proposition; you have to think it out. The point toward which he is driving is this: You have a decent man, say of thirty, and you have a potentially decent boy of seventeen. They become friends so that the young boy might become decent. Wonderful. But why have this kind of bodily relation? Can anyone see any connection between the moral improvement of that boy and these bodily relations? So he doesn't find an answer. Nor will Eryximachus be able to find an answer. Only Aristophanes succeeds in giving an answer, but we must see about that. But, as far as I understand Pausanias's speech, I would say that Pausanias tries to establish the distinction between noble and base eros by giving three principles: nous, political freedom, and moral virtue. He does not succeed in any. This is by no means the full meaning of this speech because, moral freedom being his theme, he must give some analysis or at least some indication of an analysis of what moral virtue is. It will prove that nous and freedom are in a strange way the elements which compose moral virtue. So there is a real unity there. You see also the selfish motive of this political speech. This man as a lover has an entirely different interest, self-interest, from the beloved Phaedrus. He needs his reputation as a decent man for his erotic success. Therefore he must boost moral virtue.

Listener: Are there two problems in Pausanias's speech or merely one, namely homosexuality? Or does he really think that there are two different kinds of love intrinsically indistinguishable?

Mr. Strauss: The two things are united because he says the noble eros, in contradistinction to the base eros, is essentially homosexual. As I said in the beginning, Plato never presents an issue in a purely theoretical form. He presents here not a professor, discussing dispassionately this problem, but a man who has an interest in a certain solution. According to Plato there is only one self-interest which is legitimate; that is the self-interest of the virtuous man as virtuous man. The self-interest of the calculating beloved is of course entirely different from the self-interest of the elderly lover. Transform it into heterosexual relations: Think of an attractive secretary who is a gold digger, who would have an entirely different self-interest from an older man who falls in love with that girl. We must not snobbishly smile about these things, but we must take into consideration that these possibilities belong essentially to love, and although they are not very high they must be understood too. That is in a way more delicate but in a way more corrupt in the Greek examples, because it is not heterosexual but homosexual. Through this medium the true meaning of love gradually appears. To mention only one point, in Socrates' final speech bodily eros is legitimate only, according to nature, in heterosexual love for procreation, as all sensible people always said, though their saying it does not always have a universal effect on human practice. What Socrates and Plato added is that in the more dignified forms of homosexuality which they knew, some striving is recognizable which goes much higher than the concern with procreation. The first who brings up this distinction is Phaedrus. He says that people in love were so divine that it saved them. That is a more radical version of what Socrates says: eros is the human soul. Even in these problematic forms there is some striving of which ordinary practitioners are absolutely unaware but which has something to do with the right of the two sexes. Greek philosophy never deals with man without taking into consideration the difference between man and women. It does not deal with man as a purely spiritual thing, and this difference is for them of the greatest importance because it has something to do with philosophy. Plato's teaching in the *Republic,* as you recall, that the two sexes are equal, must be judiciously understood. Plato has no doubt that women could be political rulers, queens. But regarding philosophy there is a problem, and that has something to do with the single difference of the two sexes regarding procreation. The woman is much more involved in that. In fairness to Plato one must say, when one disregards all the bewildering facts and looks at the history of philosophy on the one hand and political history on the other, we see that the top men in the history of philosophy were all males. Among the top people in history were quite a few women. Somehow they are more earthy. This is not simply a Greek prejudice, and yet we must never forget: the teacher of the truth in the *Symposium* is a woman. Nevertheless the difference between the sexes is a great theme throughout Plato and particularly in the *Symposium.* These three speeches—Pausanias, Eryximachus, and Aristophanes— have the special theme of investigating the problem of pederasty in the literal and narrow sense, and these attempts fail. But Plato does more than this; to mention only one point, Pausanias looks at pederasty from the point of view of the moral, Eryximachus from the point of view of the medical art. These things, moral virtue and art, are subjected to analysis in this connection.

5 PAUSANIAS (2)

[The question of man] must be on our minds to the extent that we are social scientists. Social science tries to understand man and human affairs, but science itself is a human activity. Therefore, in a way, natural science presupposes man and the question is whether man as a presupposition of science must not be understood in a way which is not scientific. Man, as a starting point for the understanding of scientists, is perhaps not an object of science. The starting point for the understanding of science would be, in an expression which is today very frequently used, the situation of man. One can say that this is the initial theme of every Platonic dialogue. As experienced, the human situation is, of course, the experience of individuals in individual situations. In the case of Plato, it is almost always the situation of Socrates. The individual philosopher Socrates with these and these traits of body as well as of character, as Athenian citizen, etc., in his individual situation, transcends his individual situation insofar as he is a philosopher. There was an infinity of possible solutions which Plato could choose. For example, he could have chosen a situation between Socrates and Xanthippe. He did not do that, and we can perhaps discuss that for a moment. Even Xenophon never gave a conversation between Socrates and Xanthippe, but he did give a conversation between Socrates and his son about Xanthippe; a conversation with Xanthippe herself was out of the question. What both Plato and Xenophon did was to select situations fertile for the development of philosophic themes.

In our situation, the *Symposium,* we find the cream of Athenian wisdom. They are men who have transcended the traditional beliefs and therefore have an unusual freedom of speech—frankness—verging on hubris. Even Socrates himself is presented in the *Symposium* as hubristic. Socrates is not presented as a man of prudent counsel but rather as surrendering to the greatest power. This is brought out in contrast with alternatives, at least with the Athenian alternative. For some reason, Plato preferred to present Socrates in the *Symposium* only in contrast to other Athenians. These alternatives are presented, so it seems, in an ascending order. The first speaker was Phaedrus, who looks at the phenomenon of love, or rather of the god of love, from the point of view of the beloved, from the point of view of the beneficiary of love, of the man in whom the god Eros is not, the simply uninspired. All other speakers are inspired, either by eros—the lovers—or else as poets they are inspired by the muse. Phaedrus's thesis, you will recall, is that eros leads to virtue, here understood as courage, manliness. We know that this is not simply true, that eros may also lead to vice or cowardice. The simplest solution to this difficulty is to say there are two kinds of eros, a noble and a base eros. This is the thesis of the second speaker, Pausanias, and this thesis is accepted by the third speaker, Eryximachus. But since it is dropped, this solution to the problem of the distinction between a noble and a base eros is tacitly rejected by Plato. It is only a provisional solution. How this is compatible with the undeniable fact that eros leads sometimes to vice we must find out later, when we see what Socrates has to say on the subject.

Pausanias, the old lover, speaks from the point of view of the lover. His theses are two: first, there are two erotes, one noble and one base, and second, the noble eros is the concern of the law of the land, of the nomos. The first thesis is directed against Phaedrus's assertion that eros simply leads to virtue; the second thesis is directed against the assertion of Phaedrus that virtue regarding eros, virtue concerned with eros, not concerned with the polis, is supported by divine rewards and punishments. Of these rewards and punishments we know only by way of tales, as Phaedrus himself will admit, and therefore it is not a good point. The noble eros is supported by human law, by law effective here and now. Pausanias starts not as Phaedrus did from myth, but from facts of the Athenian cult. There are two Aphrodites and there is no Aphrodite without eros. Hence, there must be two erotes corresponding to the two Aphrodites. Pausanias does not say no eros without Aphrodite. It is important to observe that Pausanias leaves it open whether there may be an eros without Aphrodite—a male god of love without a female goddess of love. But Pausanias is not fully aware of this. Socrates will draw the conclusion. Why is Pausanias not aware of this? He is in need of support by accepted opinions, by the law, as his whole speech shows. The distinction between noble and base eros needs support by the law because it is not simply based on nature. Pausanias does not dare to say that those who are by nature best have the noble eros and those who are by nature inferior have the base eros. Phaedrus had spoken of those who are by nature best, and Aristophanes will reintroduce the natural hierarchy of men. But Pausanias as well as Eryximachus are silent about it. We must gradually see the reason for this. As far as Pausanias is concerned, I will say he is silent about the natural hierarchy because his point of view will prove to be that of moral virtue, and moral virtue as such is meant to be equally accessible to all men. The natural hierarchy is not of crucial importance as far as moral virtue is concerned. Pausanias speaks all the time of moderation and justice.

As we know from the *Republic* there are four virtues—wisdom, courage, moderation, and justice. Moderation and justice are the only virtues which are equally accessible to all. Courage is the preserve of the higher-ups, and wisdom is the preserve of the cream of the higher class, the philosophers.

One more word I must add about what is meant by nomos. Nomos has a much broader meaning than law has now. It includes also what we mean by custom and usage. Thus, when he speaks of the Athenian law regarding eros, we must not think that these were written laws enforced by legal officers of some kind, but it was the custom. In other words, that by virtue of which you earn disgrace. I prefer the simple word because it is important to realize that this sharp distinction between the written law properly enacted and radically distinguished from custom is not common to all of mankind and took a very long time until it became 100 percent clear as is believed today.

To come back to Pausanias's assertion: no Aphrodite without eros. This does not mean that Eros is the son of Aphrodite. Pausanias does not question Phaedrus's assertion that Eros has no parents. Eros is indeed connected with Aphrodite, who has parents. Nor does Eryximachus question that. The first to question this assertion that Eros has no parents or, more precisely, that Eros is the oldest of the gods, is Aristophanes; then Agathon and then Socrates. This is, incidentally, one of the differences between the first half of the *Symposium* and of the second half. The first is based on the premise that Eros is the oldest god and the second is based on the denial of that premise. Pausanias asserts that no action in itself is noble or base. Every action is capable of being done nobly or basely. However, we need a principle of distinction between the noble and the base. The general answer would be nature. With a view to what is according to nature we make the distinction between what is noble and what is base. Accordingly, Pausanias says that nous—intelligence, mind—is by nature higher than unreason or nonreason. From this it follows that love of the reasonable, of the more intelligent, is noble, and love of the less reasonable is base. But this wouldn't do as we have seen, because from this it follows that the true eros would be directed toward mature, wise men and never toward youths who, generally speaking, are presumed to be less wise. Or, as was suggested, there is certainly no necessary relation between love of nous and love of bodily beauty in bloom. From this it would follow that an ugly, intelligent youth is preferable as a beloved to a beautiful, stupid youth. Pausanias does not say that those who are by nature good are by nature directed toward male adolescents. He does say that certain men are directed toward what is by nature better, i.e., intelligence. But this does not justify his kind of pederasty. These men whom he praises avoid boys not so much because the boys are less intelligent than youths but out of fear of disgrace. The boys are protected by their fathers. Not nature but deliberation limits the desire of pederasts like Pausanias. These men impose upon themselves a law, a nomos. This law is in part a response to a preceding law laid down by the fathers, who protect their boys.

We have seen that such a law is by no means necessary or universal or according to nature. In Elis and Boeotia we see that no such law exists. The reason is this: the fathers who lay down the law are also potential lovers. In the latter capacity they may permit perfect license, which in their capacity as reasonable fathers they would, in all probability, restrict. Disgrace, then, is the reason which restrains these people from boys. Disgrace falls on the base eros, but this differs in different cities. We turn, therefore, to the laws of the intelligent and free cities, the two cities which have the qualities decisive for judgment of any city, that it is intelligent or highly civilized and, secondly, that it is free. These cities are Athens and Sparta. Pausanias refers to them in the beginning but he drops Sparta immediately; this is connected with the fact that in his whole speech there is no reference to manliness or courage. Pausanias is a softy; that is of some importance. He loves another softy, the poet Agathon, and this brings up a broad theme which we can here only mention, namely, to what extent poetry as such is, from Plato's point of view, a form of softness. For the time being I refer only to the poet Orpheus who, as we have seen, was not distinguished by courage.

To summarize: intelligence does not justify pederasty, political freedom might. We see it in Athens and among the free people of the west who practice unlimited pederasty, whereas the Greeks subject to barbarians do not. But here is the trouble: political liberty does not as such justify limitation to the noble love. Those people concerned only with freedom encourage pederasty without making any distinction. Also, there is a conflict between freedom and enslavement implied in pederasty, as Pausanias himself understands it. Eros is not even conducive to lofty thoughts and to freedom. Pausanias's beloved Agathon lived at the court of Archesilaos of Macedonia, whom some of you will remember from the *Gorgias,* where his evil deeds are described with great force.

What is the basis of the distinction between noble and base eros? Hitherto we have no answer to that question. Now let us turn to our text.

> "But here it has been laid down by law in a far nobler way than elsewhere, and, as I said, it is not easy to understand." (182d4–5)

He has before discussed the law, the law of the Greek savages of the west and the laws of the Greeks living under Persian domination in the east. Both are wrong, for different reasons. Now he turns to the Athenian law. Here at home in Athens everything is fine. The thesis which he will develop now in the first part of the sequel is that the Athenian law declares it is noble to love and it is noble to be gracious to the lover.

> "For if one considers that to love openly is spoken of as nobler than to love in secret, and especially to love the noblest-born and best, even if they are uglier than others, and in turn that the universal exhortation to the lover is amazing, not as if he were doing something shameful, and that if he seizes the beloved it is thought noble, and if he does not seize, disgraceful. And with regard to trying to seize, the law has granted to the lover the possibility of being praised in performing amazing deeds." (182d5–e3)

You see now he gives enumerations of what the Athenian law, i.e., custom, signifies. The style reminds one of Aristotle's *Rhetoric,* when Aristotle gives the enumeration of, for example, what is noble, or just, etc. Here is an enumeration of items from which one can see what people generally think. The Athenian law encourages the lover, that becomes perfectly clear by implication. It does not encourage the beloved. We shall see that later. There are five items here mentioned, the center one is the universal encouragement given to the lover.

> ". . . for which, if one should dare to do them in pursuing anything else whatsoever, in wanting to accomplish it, except this, one would reap the greatest reproaches hurled against philosophy. For if one should want to get money from someone or to occupy a magistracy or any other power and were willing to do the sorts of things lovers do in regard to their beloved—making supplications and entreaties in their requests, swearing oaths, sleeping in doorways, and willing to perform the sorts of slavery that not even one slave would—he would be hindered from doing an action of this kind both by friends and enemies, the latter reproaching him for his flattery and illiberality, the former admonishing him and being ashamed on his behalf. But there is a grace upon the lover if he does all these things, and it has been granted by the law for him to act without reproach, on the grounds that he is accomplishing some very noble thing." (182e3–183b5)

The Athenian law gives the lover amazing freedom regarding the actions leading to erotic success, but no such freedom in regard to the pursuit of anything else, for example, money or political power. The greatest servility, which is disgraceful in other pursuits, is praised in the case of love. If someone were to swear falsely in order to get money, for example, he would earn the greatest reproaches leveled against philosophy, namely—if you would look up Plato's *Apology* you would see that it is not to believe in gods. Perjury in the case of love is not regarded as impiety, whereas perjury for the sake of money would be a sure proof of not believing in the gods. You see here also why Pausanias wisely started from the principle that no action is simply base. Servile actions, begging, are noble in the case of love; even perjury is not base in the case of love.

> "And what is most terrible, as the many say at least, there is also forgiveness from the gods for him alone if he swears and then departs from his oaths—they deny that an oath holds in matters of sex. So both gods and human beings have made every possibility open to the lover, as the law here asserts. Now in this way one would believe it is lawfully maintained in this city that to love and be friends with the lovers is very noble." (183b5–c4)

You note that the Athenian law as stated hitherto encourages all love, not only the devotees of the noble love—no such limitation is mentioned. Phaedrus said that to die for one's beloved, and especially for one's lover, is highly rewarded by the gods and not to die is severely punished by the gods. Pausanias says to perjure oneself is forgiven by the gods to the lovers. The implication is clear. According to Pausanias lovers do not need a stimulus, they need only to be forgiven afterwards, especially since Pausanias is silent about the supreme sacrifice. He speaks of false oaths, but he does not speak of any obligation which is put on the lover to die.

> "But whenever fathers set up guardians over those who are loved and do not allow them to converse with their lovers, and these things have been prescribed to the guardian, and his contemporaries and comrades reproach him if they see anything of the sort happening, and the elders in turn do not reproach those who are finding fault, on the grounds that they are not speaking correctly, then if one looks at these things one would believe again that this sort of thing is lawfully maintained here to be most disgraceful." (183c4–d3)

Now we see the other side. Athenian law, which encourages the lovers, discourages the beloved from seeing the lover regardless of whether the lover is prompted by noble or base love. It forbids even conversation. This is not so difficult to understand for those of you who remember an older order of society antedating the psychoanalyzation of the Western world. At that time there was a thing called battle morality which gave great freedom to male lovers and very small freedom to the female beloved. Everything is fair in love and war, I believe people said. Obviously there is something like it in Athens. In a way the law is simply inconsistent, though in a way it is not because it simply says, as in business matters, the buyer should beware—in this case the girl should beware. Legislators in Athens are both fathers and lovers and in these two different capacities the same legislators have different interests, and they lay down the law according to this difference of interests. Pausanias is trying to overcome the contradiction by a distinction of his own which he imputes to the Athenian law. This he will do in the sequel.

> "But this is the way it is, I believe. It is not unqualified, but as it was said at the beginning, it is neither noble in itself nor shameful, but if it is nobly done it is noble, and if shamefully shameful. Now to gratify a base person and in a base way is shamefully done, but to gratify a good person and in a noble way is nobly done. That lover, the pandemian lover, is base; he loves the body rather than the soul. For he does not even last, because he is not in love with a lasting thing either. Along with the cessation of the bloom of the body, which was what he was in love with, 'he flies off and is gone,' and disgraces his many speeches and promises; but the lover of the good character lasts throughout life, because he is fused with that which is lasting." (183d3–e6)

The primary distinction made by Athenian law refers to what is proper for the beloved. The lover has perfect freedom. He produces now the crucial distinction. The noble lover loves a decent character. It is not his intelligence or his courage but his decent character. On this basis, Pausanius believes, he can make the distinction stick. What is noble for the beloved depends on the quality of the lover. Here Pausanias begins to answer the decisive question: What is the ground of the distinction between noble and base love? The signs of noble love were, you will recall, that it is *(a)* for males rather than females, *(b)* for souls rather than for bodies, and *(c)* for adolescents rather than for boys. The guiding point of view was mind or intelligence. But this doesn't work, as we have seen. Here things change. Here the point of view is abiding bloom or excellence. Since the bloom of the body does not abide the soul is preferred to the body. In other words, abidingness, lastingness, is a criterion for distinguishing between noble and base love, which makes some sense. But this does not lead to love of males in particular. Why could there not be abiding love of males for women? He sees the most lasting excellence as the excellence of souls who have the longest time to live. Who are those? They are the adolescents. Older men have less time to live than young ones. But again, this applies also to adolescent girls. Pausanias still cannot give an account for the superiority of love for adolescent males to love of adult males and to love of women. Still, he sees in this that the noble lover loves a decent character rather than the body. This, however, does not necessarily mean, and we must keep this in mind, that the lover possesses a decent character. The point of view is abidingness, and from abidingness he goes to that which is relatively most abiding in men, the character.

> "Our law wants to put them to the test in a good and noble way, and wants to have them gratify some and shun others. On account of this it encourages them to pursue and the others to flee, setting up a contest and testing to which group the lover belongs and to which the one who is loved." (183e6–184a5)

The Athenian law commands to the beloved, on the basis of the requests of those who love, a decent character. You may not accede to the request of the base lovers. You see also that Pausanias's concern is for what is proper for the beloved. Then he makes the transition from the distinction between noble and base lovers to the distinction between lovers and beloved. The Athenian law commands the lovers on the one hand and the beloved on the other in order to make manifest to either side the noble or base character of the partner. The Athenian law says you must wait some time before you see, and this offers the test of the character of the lover and to some extent of the beloved.

> "This is why, in the first place, to be caught quickly has been laid down by law as disgraceful, in order that time may pass—time is often thought to test beautifully—and in the second place, to be caught by money and by political powers is shameful, regardless of whether one cowers in being ill-treated and does not resist or, in being benefited in regard to money or political achievements, one does not despise them, for none of these things is thought to be either solid or lasting, even apart from the fact that there is not by nature a genuine friendship from these things." (184a5–b5)

Now for this reason, as he says, namely because noble love is love for the lasting, for decent character, our laws prescribe to the beloved to run away and not to get caught. Thus the lovers are tested. The lovers are only commanded to pursue and to catch. It is noble for them to catch quickly, as we have seen, but it is base for the beloved to be caught quickly. To be caught by money or political preferment is simply base, regardless of whether one is caught quickly or after a long time. For money and political power are not thought to be firm nor abiding. But what is then firm and abiding? Character. Hence, not only the beloved but also the lover must be of decent character. The noble erotic relation is, then, between a mature man of decent character and an adolescent of decent character. There is no tension between the noble lover and the noble beloved. One could still wonder whether the game of pursuit is so necessary if this is the essence of the erotic relation.

> "So one way is left for our law, if a beloved is going to gratify a lover in a noble manner." (184b5–6)

The problem is how can the beloved nobly grant favors to the lover according to the Athenian law? If both possess decent character and after a decent interval of waiting the beloved can be assured of the decent intentions of the lover, has the problem not yet been solved? Yet this long period tests the tenacity rather than the decency of the lover. So the problem is not solved. It is obvious that a base lover may be as tenacious as a decent lover.

> "Our law is that, just as it was agreed in the case of lovers that to be a slave voluntarily to a beloved in any sort of slavery whatsoever was not flattery or an object of reproach, so too there is only one voluntary slavery left that is not an object of reproach, and this is [slavery] in regard to virtue. It has been established by law for us, if one is willing to serve someone in the belief that one will be better on his account, either in terms of some wisdom or any other part of virtue, then this voluntary servitude is not shameful or flattery." (184b6–c7)

You remember he has spoken of two laws, encouraging the lover and discouraging the beloved. Nothing satisfactory came out of this solution because the testing of tenacity is not a test of decency. Now he brings in another Athenian law. To repeat: the first Athenian law entitles the lover to all kinds of things which are permitted in no other pursuit, to every kind of slavery, while discouraging the beloved. The new Athenian law, to which he turns now, encourages the beloved to thralldom toward the lover in order thus to acquire virtue. Think of a young Athenian looking up to Pericles as a man of outstanding virtue, and he may do for Pericles all kinds of things which in no other human relation would be regarded as proper. To take an example from Aristotle's *Politics*, he might even shine his shoes or shave

81

him, which would ordinarily be slavish, but in such relations it would do. Up to now we have seen that thralldom is encouraged in the case of the lover. Now we bring in another law, which has to do with virtue, not with eroticism, which encourages slavery in the case of the younger, the beloved. Let us see whether this leads to a satisfactory solution.

> "One must bring this pair of laws together, the law about pederasty and the law about philosophy and the rest of virtue, if the result, the gratification of the lover by the beloved, is going to turn out fine." (184c7–d3)

This is the proposition that he is trying to establish: it is noble for the beloved to grant favors to the lover. He is working toward it. He tried it with the Athenian law regarding love, and that was not good enough. Now he says we must combine these two laws—the law regarding eros and the law regarding the acquisition of virtue.

> "Whenever lover and beloved come together, each with a law, one that he would justly serve, in serving in anything whatsoever, a beloved who gratified him, and the other that he in turn would justly serve in anything whatsoever the one who is making him wise and good, and the one is able to contribute to intelligence and the rest of virtue, and the other needs to acquire education and the rest of wisdom, then, when these laws come together, only in this case does it turn out that for the beloved to gratify the lover is noble, but in no other case." (184d3–e4)

Now let us try to understand that. One thing is clear now: the Athenian law as it stands now is insufficient for Pausanias's purposes. In the guise of a praise of the established Athenian law Pausanias proposes a subtle change of the Athenian law. His speech is a deliberative speech, a speech about a change of law. As I mentioned at the end of the last meeting, it is the only deliberative speech occurring in Plato. Now, every deliberative speech, according to a vulgar interpretation, must raise the question, Who expects benefits from it? Here the answer is clear—the proposer. The lover demands that the prohibition addressed to the beloved be rescinded or that a new law be addressed to the beloved. The new law is the consistent formulation of two contradictory ones. Why does Pausanias want a change of the law? Because like every man of his character he needs legal support for his practice. He is decent—yes—but one could also say soft. There are two laws: one regarding pederasty, the other regarding philosophy. The former encourages the lovers and discourages the beloved; the latter encourages the beloved. But the law regarding pederasty is concerned with the protection of the boys' virtue. The law regarding philosophy is concerned with the boys' acquisition of virtue. The law entitles the boys to come together with respectable men of outstanding virtue. But it does not encourage them for that purpose, of course. What, then, is the solution? The adolescent seeks virtue, the lover possesses virtue. The adolescent is prompted by love of virtue; the lover, however, is prompted not by love of virtue but by love of youth in bloom. The motives of the two partners are heterogeneous. The allegedly perfectly virtuous relation is constituted by heterogeneous motives. One can, in a way, compare this to the relation between buyers and sellers, which brings about, in a way, a satisfactory relation. Still, the harmonious relation of buyer and seller remains a question even if they make a deal because of their opposing interests.

You will recall that in 183e Pausanias had ascribed to the adolescent a noble character, meaning possession of virtue.

> "Even to be deceived for this reason is in no way disgraceful; but it brings disgrace for all other reasons whether one is deceived or not. If someone should gratify a lover on the grounds that he is wealthy and then be deceived and not get any money when the lover shows up as poor, it is no less disgraceful; for he who is of this sort is thought to show his very self, that for the sake of money he would serve anyone at all in anything at all, and this is not noble. So on the basis of the same argument, should one gratify another on the grounds that he is good and that one would become good oneself on account of friendship with the lover, and were one then deceived when he showed up as bad and not possessing virtue, the deception all the same is noble, for he too is thought to have shown what he is, that just for the sake of virtue and of becoming better he would be wholly eager for anything, and this in turn is the noblest of all." (184e4–185b4)

The adolescent seeking virtue may fall into the hands of the mature man who merely pretends to be virtuous. It is not disgraceful for the adolescent if he grants favors to that pretender. The freedom given to the beloved is still more enlarged. He does not have to be certain that the lover is virtuous, it is sufficient if he believes him to be virtuous. The adolescent may grant any favor, in any manner, to anyone, provided that he believes that by so doing he acquires virtue. You must admit that Pausanias gets in this way absolutely everything. This is brought about by this wonderful combination of the Athenian law regarding pederasty and the Athenian law regarding the acquisition of virtue.

> "So it is totally noble in every way to gratify just for the sake of virtue only. This is the eros of the uranian goddess, and it is uranian, and worth much

for city and private persons, compelling the lover and the one who is loved to exert much care each for his own virtue. All the other lovers are of the other [Aphrodite], the Pandemus. These are the things, Phaedrus, that on the spur of the moment I contribute to you about Eros." (185b4–c3)

The noble eros is worth much for the acquisition of virtue on the part of the lover and the beloved. This seems to mean that both still have to acquire virtue, and we are not confronted with the situation of an established character who has already acquired virtue. Neither of them really possesses virtue; both acquire virtue in the process of their union. We see this also from the formulation that eros is neither indispensable nor sufficient for acquiring virtue. This, I think, becomes clear. Eros is altogether unrelated here to happiness or bliss. At the end Pausanius speaks of the vulgar Aphrodite but not of the vulgar eros per se. The last word, for which the best translation is "I contribute" *(sumballomai)*, is the same word he used before when he spoke of the bringing together *(sumbalein)* of the two laws. I think this is the final reference to this crucial bringing together, the novel bringing together of two hitherto disjointed Athenian laws.

Now, let us try to understand this as a whole. Whereas Phaedrus had completely disregarded the conflict between eros and morality or taken it in stride, Pausanias starts from that conflict between eros and the noble, and therefore he says there are two erotes. The noble eros consists in decent men loving decent youths with a view to the latter's decency, and decent youths will in their turn love the decent mature men in order thus to acquire decency. But why should the decent lovers love decent young men? Why not decent young girls? Why should the decent youths, possessing decency, grant all kinds of erotic favors to decent lovers in order thus to acquire decency? I don't want to develop this, but with a little imagination you must see the fantastic suggestion for a way to virtue. Why should decent lovers seek all kinds of erotic favors, especially from decent youths? You see, it really is a fantastic situation. Pausanias wants to make his kind of eroticism legal and proper. He is not impudent, he is rather a coward. Without knowing it, Pausanias refutes the sophisticated pederasty which he wants to establish. We will see there are two further defenses of pederasty coming in the next two speeches. But is this all that emerges from Pausanias's speech? What comes to sight through his speech?

Pausanias's position arises from the conflict between eros on the one hand and the noble and the law on the other. For this purpose he must represent the noble or the law, what we would call morality, in terms of the decent character. As you could see from the end of the first book of the *Laws*

(650a–d), characters are the theme of political science, and in Aristotle's *Ethics* we find that the chief work of the political art is to make the citizens good and doers of noble things. There is an essential connection between character and law. From the Greek point of view the function of the law is not merely to establish peace but to make men noble. The noble regarding eros is a mean between repression and complete license, as we have seen. This is, according to Aristotle, the character of moral virtue. We may expect to learn something from Pausanias's speech about moral virtue.

In order to establish the distinction between the two kinds of eros Pausanias refers successively to three different principles: intelligence (nous), freedom, moral virtue. Moral virtue does not legitimate his eroticism. Intelligence excludes love of boys and women and yet supports love of older men. Freedom leads to love of all those who can carry arms, the fighting men. Freedom would justify Pausanias's requirements but, as he points out, the principle of freedom alone leads to barbaric eroticism, not to the sophisticated eroticism with which he is concerned. It does not exclude boys, as the Greek example to which he refers shows. For his purpose, then, he needs a combination of these two principles, nous and freedom.

Pausanias demands a combination of two laws—the law regarding philosophy and the law regarding pederasty. The law regarding love of wisdom, i.e., the actualization of intelligence, and the law regarding the love of the bloom of the body. Is there a link between body and nous, its perfection, and freedom? Is there a connection between freedom, political freedom, and the body? This is the question we have to raise. Freedom is regarded as a desirable state for the polis. Why? Freedom needs consent, and consent is something fundamentally different from the principle of intelligence (I refer to *Laws* 684c). Consent means precisely that not-intelligence as such is the sole guiding principle. Because if intelligence were the sole guiding principle then we would have the dictatorship of the wise. Freedom means exactly the opposite. There is no dictatorship but consent, i.e., a decent contribution of nonwisdom to political life. Now the polis, which is essentially linked up with freedom, is primarily concerned with the well-being of the body, according to Plato. What do you say to this suggestion? Is it not obviously false to say that the polis as polis is primarily concerned with the well-being of the body? In the second book of the *Republic* Plato speaks of the city of pigs which has no other purpose than to satisfy the bodily needs of men. He calls this the true city and in some other place he calls it the city. The city as city is concerned with the body.

In order to reach its full stature the polis must combine freedom and wisdom. And the virtue directed toward the self-sufficient polis is moral virtue. The fully developed polis combines the satisfaction of the requirements of the mind and of the requirements of the body. But the same is intended by Pausanias's perfect erotic association. Pausanias's perfect erotic association, however, suffers from a fundamental defect: the motivations of the lover and the beloved do not agree. But the same is true of the polis and of moral virtue. The motivations of the body and those of the mind do not jibe. The needs of the body lead to society. Society as such requires political or vulgar virtue, which is merely a shadow of virtue, a daylight virtue. The needs of the mind, however, require genuine virtue (*Republic,* book 6). This is one of the great themes of the *Republic;* these four virtues, which are courage, wisdom, moderation, and justice, have the same name throughout. They mean something very different whether they occur on the level of the philosopher or on the lower level. The justice and moderation of the uneducated part of the population, we can say, is only a shadow, a very poor imitation, of the genuine virtues. Now, what is true of this most perfect city, the city of Plato's *Republic,* is still more true of ordinary cities. Phenomena of great variety which have a superficial resemblance and agree perhaps in their external action, are thought to be identical, and this is not the case. Moral virtue is a combination of these two heterogeneous moralities. If this is so, from Plato's point of view, there cannot be a natural desire for it. There is a natural desire for the protection of the body, there is a natural desire for the protection of the mind, but this necessary but not simply natural combination is not an object of a natural desire. There is no connection, certainly no identity between moral virtue and bliss or happiness. This is by no means completely changed in Aristotle or, for that matter, in Thomas Aquinas. I could refer you for example to Thomas Aquinas's *Summa contra gentiles,* book 3, chapter 34, where this is developed, and where the following remark is made: "The operations of justice are ordered for the purpose of preserving peace among men, through which each and every one possesses quietly what is his own." The ends are not these actions; the end is peace and quiet. Man cannot find his end in love or virtue as such. One can make this objection: Pausanias does not mention all moral virtues, in fact he puts a much stronger emphasis on the intellectual virtues—wisdom, nous, prudence. He barely alludes to justice and moderation, and he merely mentions unmanliness, not manliness itself. To this I would reply as follows: Pausanias presents morality or moralism as modified by a certain kind of eroticism—the love of a mature man for a youth who is afraid of impropriety. Pausanias's position is based on a clear idiosyncrasy. But what he says awakens us to the question as to the status of moral virtue in Socrates' speech. There we have to watch for the relation between eros and moral virtue. Secondly, Pausanias's position is a particular position, but so is that of every other speaker except Socrates. Socrates' speech supplies the synthesis of these particular positions, both regarding the teaching and regarding the life and character, or what is now called the attitude, of the speaker.

For the time being we know only Pausanias and Phaedrus. Let us look, in conclusion, at the relation of their eros to what they say about it. Phaedrus speaks from the point of view of the beloved. Every eros is welcome from the point of view of the prudent recipient of favors who is very beautiful. He apparently assigns to eros therefore the highest place. But in fact he assigns the highest place to those who are by nature the best, either by beauty or by insight. He is satisfied with the law, for the law encourages the lovers to woo and to serve and discourages the beloved to seek, which suits him well. Therefore his speech is the shortest speech. Pausanias, on the other hand, speaks from the point of view of the lover who competes with others because he does not outshine all others. He must promote his qualities and, in particular, his respectability. He needs external support against his more attractive competitors. Therefore he must have recourse to the law. But unfortunately the law is not quite sufficient for his purpose, and therefore he suggests an improvement of the law. Since the law is not entirely on his side and yet he needs the law, his speech is the longest, apart from Socrates'. This is very striking: the first speech is the shortest, the second the longest. We come now to the transition and Eryximachus's speech.

Listener: If all Pausanias wants is a justification for his particular kind of eroticism, why isn't he satisfied with allowing the greatest freedom to all?

Mr. Strauss: What you say, I think, is this: The striking thing here is the emphasis on thralldom in eros and not something grudgingly given. But does this not mean, since freedom is of the essence of moral virtue as he understands it, that eros is essentially in conflict with moral virtue? And therefore it brings out all the more the impossibility of what he is after. He never uses the word *freedom;* he only describes it indirectly. The reason is that if one were to think of freedom and give it its normally assigned place, one could not defend eros. The question would then be this: Is there not an element in this thralldom which in a true doctrine of eros must be preserved, and is it preserved in Socrates' speech? There are two possibilities: (1) it is not preserved, and then there is a fundamental defect in the Platonic doctrine of eros. [Gap in the tape.] I am not sure whether Plato did not mean to bring out very massively the contradictory character of the attempt to reconcile, to subject eros to moral virtue. Pausanias makes the remark "Every action can be noble or base." This is also a principal question of morality as morality. You have to take the two things together. He who presents the standpoint of moral virtue brings out two principles: *(a)* every action may be moral and *(b)* there is a thralldom superior in dignity to the freedom belonging to morality. We must keep this in mind. We must keep in mind how this element in the context of the Platonic analysis of eros comes out. . . .

In the next speech you will see an attempt to subject eros to art. In the last three speeches no attempt is made to subject eros to anything external. In Socrates' speech there is something higher than eros, but that is not external.

Listener: It seems to me that the stress you put on defining Pausanias's speech as essentially defending pederasty . . .

Mr. Strauss: There is no question about that, that he makes very clear. We must face that. I think this is part of the argument. Whereas there is still a certain ambiguity in Phaedrus's position, Pausanias, Eryximachus, and Aristophanes are defenders of pederasty. In the last two speeches this changes again. This implies that a careful study of these three speeches will reveal to us why Plato regarded pederasty as wrong. I think in the case of Pausanias it becomes fairly clear: the very comical presentation of uniting for the purpose of virtue and doing something which has no relation with it. . . . In a much more sophisticated way this comes out in the next speech.

If we stick to what Pausanias's speech does, its unique character among the six speeches—the emphasis on the Athenian law, and the fact that contrary to the original claim merely to reinterpret the Athenian law he suggests a change in it—I believe it is necessary to conclude that it is a deliberative speech. A deliberative speech is of course not a detached, rational analysis. That it is a seductive speech, like Agathon's for example, may very well be, but it is more than that. While it may be true that every speaker has in mind an individual, with the exception of Aristophanes—and I believe that Socrates had particularly Phaedrus in mind—it still means more than that. The engine used by individuals must be understood in its own terms, precisely if we want to understand the effect on certain individuals. I am sure there is a connection, but nevertheless we must also understand—in spite of the rhetorical elements which every speech contains—we must also consider it as it presents itself, a speech praising eros, presenting eros as the speaker sees it. In the case of seduction it is clear. Agathon later on presents eros as sheer beauty endowed with all virtues.

I will draw a picture here of the six speakers:

1 Phaedrus : gain :: 4 Aristophanes : ugliness
2 Pausanias : moral virtue :: 5 Agathon : beauty
3 Eryximachus : art :: 6 Socrates : philosophy

Listener: From Agathon's point of view, and I imagine from Pausanias's also, there is a certain conflict between Pausanias and Socrates. It seemed to me what Pausanias is saying is that there is a nobility in accepting a lover as virtuous even when he is not. That is, it is noble to be deceived in these terms. In a certain sense what he says is that it is a good thing to accept an imitation virtue. And I wonder whether this is not the reason why he places such emphasis on nomos. That is to say he tries to claim that he has the virtue which is by nomos, which is perhaps not the truest virtue, but which it is noble to accept.

Mr. Strauss: There are an infinite variety of levels. And that this could be higher than low suspiciousness is obvious. Though this does not guarantee that in itself it is very high. We are quite reasonably easily satisfied, and we admire many things which, on reflection, though they may have an element of nobility in them, looked at dispassionately are not very high. Pausanias is taken in completely by his desire and his understanding. Therefore we must distinguish between what Pausanias intends by his speech and what we are enabled, by Plato's superior art, to discern in his speech. Pausanias surely does not go beyond the description of what he regards as the perfect erotic association. I believe that Plato wants us to see something in that perfect erotic association, which in principle is not true of the perfect erotic association but is true of the polis. The polis is such a strange mixture of heterogeneous elements, unlike the perfect erotic association where both are animated by the same emotions. In Socrates' speech both love something; that is the truth. The eros for the truth, motivating both, makes possible the highest erotic association. I am sorry if I give the impression that I tried to denigrate the beauties of Pausanias's speech. But in the short time at our disposal I have to think of the *Symposium* as a whole and see what the whole work is after. Otherwise I could be blamed very severely for devoting so much time to a course such as this in the Department of Political Science.

Listener: I wonder whether Socrates has not already answered one of Pausanias's main points, and that is that moral virtue is transmitted by this erotic contact, in his general rebuff against Agathon in the beginning when Agathon says, "If you touch me I will get wisdom."

Mr. Strauss: Yes, this is of course of almost Aristophanean indecency. I didn't want to develop this because I know that you have read the literature on that one.

[In answer to a question:] The question is, What makes it possible that mind and body are united? If you answer moral virtue, that is not unreasonable. Therefore Plato makes the suggestion in the *Republic,* to which we might return, that what unites the highest and the lowest is philosophy. This, too, is enigmatic but indicates the problem. The *Symposium* is silent about that. But, as I said before, we find in Socrates' speech a doctrine of three erotes, none of which is base, only high and low. The low is not base. All are natural, and we must see whether we find there moral virtue as an object of a natural desire. In scholastic language we can say, although this will displease many who think of these matters in more poetic terms, the Platonic doctrine of eros is identical with his doctrine of the natural inclinations. I think Pausanias's speech brings this problem more into the open than any other speech. In a general way, all six speakers are decent men, that goes without saying.

[In answer to a question about the polis and calculation:] That is the way in which he presents it in the *Republic.* Eros is radically different from calculation. Eros is a kind of possession, therefore he uses the term madness in the *Phaedrus.* The *Republic,* however, is silent about eros in the second book when he speaks about the foundation; he presents the case as something which can be put together and should be put together entirely on the basis of calculation. The one who comes nearest to this in the *Symposium* is Phaedrus. The word which Socrates uses for virtue, which can be translated as prudence or practical wisdom, contains the element of calculation, and Socrates is by no means completely adverse to it. The true virtue is the one in which calculation and possession coincide. Throughout the Platonic dialogues we find that one and only one phenomenon will solve the problem he has stated in a particular dialogue, and that is philosophy. Whether he takes justice, and he shows us the just city—ultimately we do not find justice in any city, however virtuous; the only perfect form of justice is philosophy. Or, he takes freedom. The only one who is genuinely free is the philosopher. The same regarding eros. Only in philosophy does eros come fully into its own. That is not meant to be something superimposed, as Pausanias tries to superimpose. Contrary to all enthusiasts Socrates says love is not directed toward the beautiful. The element of splendor is absolutely unessential. To that extent Aristophanes is right when he presents an ugly creature. Agathon presents only the beautiful [Eros. For Socrates, eros] is neither ugly nor beautiful but good. And the good is the primary theme of human decency, as we would say. Then he tries to show that heterosexual desire for procreation does not get what it wants. The desire for a lasting good, transcending one's death, can come only in theoria.

6 ERYXIMACHUS

I suggested last time in my statements on Pausanias's speech . . . that it is inadequate for the work of Plato as a whole. On the basis of further readings there is always new light shed on things which one has read. Since I do not possess a complete interpretation of the whole Platonic body, I know that whatever I say is provisional. Some of you raised objections to my interpretation. These objections were based on powerful impressions. Such impressions are never, or hardly ever, groundless. They are in need of examination, but examination in the light of what? In the light of Plato's guiding intention. What is this guiding intention?

First, of the *Symposium* in general, the praise of the god Eros as a problem—that eros is a god and ought to be praised is imposed on them by Phaedrus and will be examined later. The second important consideration for establishing Plato's guiding intention is to consider Pausanias's speech in particular with regard to its guiding intention. Two considerations are decisive: First, the distinction between the noble and the base eros, a distinction not made by Phaedrus and not made by Aristophanes and the later speakers. This distinction is linked up with a praise of the Athenian law, a praise which conceals a suggested change of the Athenian law. These are the peculiar features of Pausanias's speech. Now there is a theme which I played down, if I may say so: Pausanias's emphasis on the element of slavery or thralldom in eros. Does Pausanias not bring out an essential element in eros, which must not be forgotten in the final reckoning? Is the emphasis on this slavery or thralldom not Pausanias's particular contribution? I believe that this element in eros is surrender without concern for one's dignity, without concern for the noble. What does this serving or slaving mean? The lover is the slave of the beloved so that the beloved grants favors to the lover. This is explicitly described in 183b5 as something terrible; but, as appears from the context, this is not the most awful. Worse than this is a kind of perjury. This kind of undignified begging is bad enough, but false oaths are even worse. This is the context.

What Pausanias wants to bring out is the immoral element in eros. Eros is immoral somehow and yet noble. Pausanias is concerned with legitimating eros in terms of the noble and the law. Therefore he must first state the difficulty, the opposition between eros and the noble, or you can say morality—I know this has a somewhat different connotation, but in the Greek it is expressed by their word for the noble. He must bring out the opposition between eros and morality by stating the principle that no action is in itself noble or base, whereas morality would always say there are certain actions which are in themselves either noble or base. The emphasis on this thralldom belongs to the context of the opposition, or tension, between eros and morality. This can be understood very simply as follows: Virtue, as Pausanias and other men of this kind understood it, means gentlemanship, and the gentleman is the opposite of the slave. Now if the erotic man behaves like a slave, he behaves contrary to the gentleman and there is surely a problem. But this does not do away with the fact that this slavery is of the essence of eros—surrender without concern for one's dignity. Yet, precisely, according to Pausanias, the noble eros is understood in contradistinction to the base eros. This must affect the meaning of slavery. Surrender for the sake of what? Surrender for the sake of bodily gratification of him who surrenders, surrender to the practice of pederasty for the sake of acquiring and disseminating moral virtue? That is an absurd suggestion. Nevertheless, something of this notion of surrender without concern for one's dignity and for the noble or beautiful remains on the highest level, namely, in the Socratic suggestion that the highest form of eros is philosophizing. Philosophizing is surrender to the truth without concern for one's dignity and without concern for even the noble, since the truth is not simply noble or beautiful but in a certain sense ugly.

The other element raised in the discussion concerns the element of deception in eros. Reference was made to the two remarks, one near the beginning and the other near the end of Pausanias's speech. First, perjury, which is, of course, a form of deception. Perjury by the lover is noble. Later on, being deceived on the part of the beloved is noble. In other words, love can be noble even if it exists in an element of deception. Whether this is the highest love is of course another question. I think what would help us to understand better what appears in Pausanias's speech is the polis. Think of the noble lie in the *Republic*. The rulers, the philosophers, deceive the demos, and it is noble for the demos to be deceived. It is also noble for the philosophers thus to deceive. More generally: the lover is the statesman, the beloved is the demos. That this is not an entirely fantastic suggestion can easily be seen, because in Plato's dialogue *Gorgias*, Callicles, in a way the political man, is described as the lover of the demos. Callicles is dominated by eros for the demos just as he is said to be dominated by love for an individual called Demos, a handsome young man. To come back to the main

93

point, the ordinary politician, which includes all those we call statesmen, has eros for the demos. This also throws light on the fact that the *Republic* is silent on eros, ultimately because the most interesting case of eros, namely eros of the ruler for the ruled, is not admitted on the highest level. The philosopher in the *Republic* rules not out of eros but out of compulsion, as is clearly stated in the sixth and seventh books.

To recapitulate in a few words the comparison between Pausanias's erotic association and the polis to which I referred: You will recall that Pausanias explicitly says the perfect erotic association is one in which mature, decent males educate potentially decent males. This, however, is exactly what the polis claims to do. Mature gentlemen educate potential gentlemen—the next generation. But, of course, we see the absurd combination of education for virtue and pederasty. Pausanias demands a nonexistent combination of the law on philosophy and the law on pederasty. These laws exist in Athens but they are not combined. In demanding the combination of these two distinct laws, he refers to two independent principles: intelligence—nous—and body. In his speech he refers to three principles altogether: intelligence, freedom, and moral virtue. He refers to them in order to justify pederasty. We have seen that intelligence, as he understands it, does not justify pederasty. It rather justifies love of old men like Socrates. As for political freedom, according to the argument it does justify pederasty but not the distinction between the noble and base eros. The third principle—moral virtue—is sufficient in Pausanias's own opinion. I think reflection shows that moral virtue itself is a union, a combination of these two different things—intelligence and freedom. Freedom is specifically political, what we ordinarily call consent. The political, in its turn, is primarily in the service of the body, in modern language of self-preservation. We have, then, two principles ultimately: intelligence and the body. Their union, which is complicated and difficult to understand, explains moral virtue. The basis is this: the requirements of intelligence and the requirements of the body, and therewith of society, meet. It is strange that they should meet because intelligence and the body are entirely different. Their meeting can be shown very simply: both in order to live with others and in order to think, you must have a certain amount of temperance. If you are constantly drunk you cannot be a citizen, nor can you be a thinker. Also courage: you cannot be a good soldier if you are absolutely cowardly, nor can you be a good thinker if you are absolutely cowardly. You would be constantly in fear and not have a free mind. One can say, then, strange as it sounds, that the requirements of the mind and the requirements of living together meet somehow; they are for practical purposes almost the same. But they are radically different in principle or in spirit. The purposes in each case are radically different. Moral virtue, which is for the sake of understanding, of theoria, and for the sake of society, presents itself as the end—the simple, clear, and homogeneous end of human life. We can call this position moralist. Although Aristotle presented this view to some extent, it was fully developed only by Kant. This will suffice as a summary of the points we discussed last time. Though this is an occasion for further discussion we must make some headway.

Let us turn to the beginning, 185c4. After Pausanias had paused which is, first of all, an allusion to the length of Pausanias's speech.

> When Pausanias had made a pausation—the wise teach me to speak in equal phrases in just this way—Aristodemus said that Aristophanes should have spoken . . . (185c4–6)

Who makes this pun—Pausanias and pause? Could it not have been made by Aristodemus in his report and stuck in Apollodorus's mind? They are very different men but they have something in common: they are young lovers of Socrates. I think this ambiguity, that we don't know who made this joke, is not unintended.

> . . . but hiccups had just come over him, either by satiety or by something else, and he was unable to speak. But he did say—the physician Eryximachus was lying in the couch below his—"Eryximachus, it is just that you either stop my hiccups or speak on my behalf, until I have stopped." And he said Eryximachus said, "Well, I'll do them both. I shall speak in your turn, and you, when you stop, will speak in mine, and while I am speaking, see whether the hiccup is willing to stop if you hold your breath for a long time; if not, gargle with water. But if it is very severe, pick up the sort of thing by which you might irritate your nose, and sneeze. And if you do this once or twice, even if it is very severe, it will stop." "You couldn't speak too soon," Aristophanes said, "and I shall do this." (185c6–e5)

This is a funny interlude which is probably not entirely meaningless. We see immediately that they speak in the order in which they sit. One change is made: Aristophanes and Eryximachus change the order of speaking. This is of some importance. The general meaning of such changes is that the speakers are interchangeable—they are in an important respect identical, though not simply identical. Plato had apparently some reasons for emphasizing such an identity in the case of Eryximachus and Aristophanes and only in that case. It leads also to the consequence that Eryximachus concludes the first half of the speeches and Socrates the second half. By virtue of this change we get Socrates and the poets in the second half. Incidentally, also only strong drinkers; the weak drinkers are in the first half. Still, could Plato not have arranged it in the first place so that we would have the order Phaedrus, Pausanias, Eryximachus in the first half, and in the second Aristophanes, Agathon, Socrates? We must see the dramatic meaning of this change. This sensible order is brought about by accident. Why is this better than if it had been planned? To put these three most outstanding men together would have been impolite. There is a disproportion between wisdom, which requires that they go together, and politeness, or the polis and society. This is a consideration in every Platonic dialogue. In this way Aristophanes' speech becomes the center of the whole. Aristophanes acquires this center position by a defect of his body. The body asserts itself after Pausanias's somewhat disingenuous attempt to put the body entirely in the second place: bodily gratifications are only in the service of moral education. You see also that Eryximachus shows that he is a physician, very clear and precise, but also very pedantic. As you can also see, he is eager to speak. There is a certain contrast between him and Socrates, as we shall see. Now let us turn to Eryximachus's speech.

> Then Eryximachus said, "Well, then, it seems to me to be necessary, since Pausanias started out toward the logos beautifully but did not complete it adequately, that I must try to put an end on the logos." (185e6–186a2)

This is important for the understanding of the whole. There was no such connection between Pausanias's and Phaedrus's speeches. Eryximachus's is a continuation or, as he claims, the consummation of Pausanias's speech. But he carefully says, "I must try," and we will see later on that he does not conclude it. The man who concludes the series which began with Pausanias is Aristophanes. These three speeches form an important subtheme.

> "His assertion that Eros is double seems to me to be a beautiful division; but I seem to have observed from the art of medicine, our art, that he is not only over the souls of human beings in regard to the beauties but also in regard to many other things and in everything else, the bodies of all animals, the things that grow in the earth, and virtually in all the beings, and how great and wonderful is the god, and how he pertains to everything throughout both human and divine matters. I shall begin speaking from the art of medicine, in order that we may also dignify the art." (186a2–b3)

A physician is speaking, a poor drinker, valetudinarian, and a pupil of the sophist Hippias, who in his way loves the young Phaedrus, also a poor drinker and a pupil of Hippias. He agrees with Pausanias that eros is twofold—noble or base. Pausanias and Eryximachus are the only ones who speak of these two erotes. They are the only moralists. But Pausanias had said that eros, both the noble and the base, exists only in the souls of human beings and is directed toward beautiful males, whereas medicine teaches that eros exists also in other things and is directed toward many things which are not noble. For example, there is an eros directed toward evacuation of the body. Eros is a cosmic principle, affecting all human beings at least. This is the new notion introduced by Eryximachus, foreshadowed (but only foreshadowed) by the fact that Pausanias spoke of the noble eros as the heavenly eros. This nonhuman, even subhuman, phenomenon to which Eryximachus refers is the one he calls the divine things, as distinguished from the human things. There is no reference to myth or to the Athenian cult, as in the case of Phaedrus and Pausanias. The authority of myth is abandoned. But it is not simply abandoned. It is replaced by another authority: art, medicine. The modern analogy to that is science.

Phaedrus looks at eros from the point of view of gain, Pausanias from the point of view of the noble or virtue; Eryximachus looks at it from the point of view of art. He embraces eros and his art in one breath as appears from the following sentence: "I shall begin speaking from the art of medicine, in order that we may also dignify the art." He gives the cosmic doctrine of the two erotes, but this cosmic doctrine is modified by a concern for the praise of his art. This implies, as we shall see later on, that the noble eros is not by nature. For Pausanias, too, it was not according to nature, but brought about by law. In this case it will be brought about not by law but by art, by his art-medicine.

Listener: Isn't it implied here already that eros is a god?

Mr. Strauss: I think this will become the theme in a methodical way only when we get to Agathon. Agathon is the only one who praises eros as a god. The others talk of eros as a god but mean by it a natural phenomenon.

Listener: But Eryximachus doesn't even seem to talk about him as a god.

Mr. Strauss: This is quite true, and to this extent he is an enlightened physician. But he pays for it dearly, because his speech ends with the praise of the art of divination. Just as Aristophanes, who is more impious than any of his predecessors, ends with a praise of piety. The obvious point is that he begins in a very positivistic spirit, no nonsense. We will see whether his pride will not be humbled. In 186b–e he speaks of eros in the nature of bodies as revealed by medicine. By bodies he means here human bodies, since medicine is human medicine. Eryximachus does not yet transcend the human things. He will do that later but he has this in mind.

> "The nature of bodies has this double Eros. The health and the sickness of the body are universally agreed to be different and dissimilar, and the dissimilar desires and loves dissimilars. Now the eros for the healthy is different, and the one for the sickly is different. As Pausanias was saying just now, it is noble to gratify the good of human beings and disgraceful to gratify the dissolute; so too in bodies themselves, it is noble to gratify (and one should) the good and healthy things of the body of each, and the name for this is the medical, but it is disgraceful [to gratify] the bad and diseased things and one should disoblige them if one is going to be skilled in the art." (186b4–c5)

Pausanias had said it is noble to grant favors to the good lovers, it is base to grant favors to the dissolute lovers. In medicine it is noble to satisfy love felt for what is healthy in the body, and it is base to satisfy the love felt for what is sick in the body. In other words, medicine identifies the good with the healthy and the dissolute with the sick. However, he brings in another consideration: the healthy body loves X, and the sick body loves Y. He says similar things love similar things. The word *similar* will be crucial in the sequel, therefore I mention it here. The physician does not feel love for that which he satisfies or for that which he does not satisfy. The loveless art regulates love. This is a certain difficulty which one must keep in mind. Just as virtue was not love in Pausanias and Phaedrus but either produced love or regulated it.

Up to this point Eryximachus has explained who or what is the lover. The lover is the body, but what does the body love? So far we don't know.

Listener: Isn't there nobility in the action of the physician in his permitting and helping to satisfy desire?

Mr. Strauss: This is an important question. The healthy body is good, and the sickly body as such is a bad body. What the physician does is either noble or base. This is very interesting because what is loving—the body—is called good or bad, whereas the loveless art is now called noble or base. Pausanias had distinguished between noble and base eros. Eryximachus here, at any rate, seems to distinguish between good and bad eros and a noble or base exercise of the art. How much this means we shall see.

Listener: He agrees with what Pausanias had said that it is right to gratify good men and base to gratify dissolute men. Pausanias ended with a contradiction. Wouldn't this show Eryximachus's ability to reason on matters of virtue?

Mr. Strauss: We can see all kinds of things even if we are much less intelligent than Eryximachus. But in hearing a speech once it is impossible to look up the beginning. You cannot study a speech while giving it. That requires an enormous intelligence, which Socrates apparently had, as indicated by his conversations. Eryximachus understands about as much as a summary of the speech would give him, perhaps a bit more since he is intelligent. The hopeless difficulties in which Pausanias got entangled are not apparent to him, one reason being that he also shares Pausanias's prejudices; he, too, is a pederast. In addition, he is a bit rigid because of his mastery of his art. Mr. Gildin's point is very important. It could perhaps mean this: it might be connected with his concern with his art.

> "Medicine is, to speak summarily, the science of the erotic things of the
> body in regard to repletion and evacuation, and he who discerns in them
> the noble and base eros, he is the most skilled in medicine; and he who
> makes them alter, so as to acquire the one eros instead of the other, and in
> which things eros is not but should come to be in them, if he knows how
> to implant it, and if it is there to remove it, he would be a good crafts-
> man." (186c5–d5)

The question here is: We know who or what is the lover—the body either healthy or sick—but who is the beloved? Repletion or evacuation. The body has love for either the right kind, and then it is noble, or for the wrong kind, and then it is base. The Greek verb from which repletion is derived is used as well for the pregnancy of females. So you see the connection with the erotic phenomenon. Medicine distinguishes between two kinds. It encourages and even allows or causes the right kind and takes away the wrong kind. We also see a distinction within medicine as knowledge. The one who recognizes, diagnoses, eros, and the other who is concerned with doing things—he is called a good craftsman. Thus the theoretical and practical aspects are distinguished and we shall see later that this is very important. In the case of bodies the beloved is repletion and evacuation. The question is, could this have any applicability to the soul? In other words, does the soul love repletion and evacuation? Perhaps we could connect repletion with knowledge, and evacuation might be the evacuation of ignorance or perhaps also the bad evacuation, namely forgetting of knowledge.

> "He must be able to make the most hateful things in the body friends and
> love one another. The most contrary things are the most hateful, cold to

hot, bitter to sweet, dry to liquid, everything of the kind. Our ancestor Asclepius knew how to instill eros and unanimity in these things, as the poets
here say and I am persuaded, and so he put together our art." (186d5–e3)

He drops the subject of repletion and evacuation, as we have seen, and, perhaps, replaces it by something more general—opposites. Clearly repletion
and evacuation are opposites, but he looks at it now from a different point
of view, opposites in the body, not opposites which the body seeks. The
body contains opposite elements. This is the basis for the very need for repletion and evacuation. Medicine must establish harmony between these
opposite elements, i.e., love of the most hostile. The lover is the beloved
and the beloved is the lover. The lover and beloved are no longer distinguished in the subject, eros, as they were in the speeches of Phaedrus and
Pausanias. Eryximachus drops now all one-sided love. A one-sided love
would be, for example, the love of the body for food. He is only concerned
with things capable of mutual love, namely, the elements of the body.

If one were to apply this simply to human beings, a rather fantastic result
would seem to come about—the best man must love the most dissolute
man, and the art regarding the soul would exist in establishing an equi-
librium of mediocrity between the best and the worst. Surely in Eryximachus's own case, because he and Phaedrus are similar people, there
would be base love, since true love seems to be only among opposites.
What strikes us immediately is the silence about male and female. In his
whole speech this is the most relevant opposite, if you talk about love.
There was this famous list of opposites drawn up by the Pythagoreans, and
male and female naturally figured in an important place. Eryximachus goes
so far as to be silent even about men—males. Our physician is silent about
the normal union of opposites in living beings. Why? Noble love is usually
love of opposites, and this is the work not of nature but of art. This, of
course, constitutes the highest praise of art. If the noble love is never
brought about by nature, but only by the medical art, he also implies something else. If by nature opposites hate each other, it means that similar
things by nature love each other. Simply and crudely expressed—pederasty.
Pederasty is natural, and this is, of course, what he is trying to prove. Eryximachus's cosmic doctrine of eros is nullified not only by his concern with
medicine but by his kind of eroticism as well. His cosmic doctrine of eros
proves to be an expression of these two concerns: art and pederasty. The
difficulty you see at this time is this: His art is opposed to his eroticism because his art is supposed to establish harmony between opposites. It is

therefore a great problem for him to praise eros and his art in the same breath.

> "The entirety of medicine, as I say, is governed through this god, and likewise gymnastics and farming as well." (186e4–187a1)

These three arts—medicine, gymnastics, and farming—are mentioned together also in the tenth book of the *Laws* (889b–e) in the context of a representation of the doctrine of the subversive people: Art is lower than nature, and the most respectable arts are, therefore, medicine, farming, gymnastics, because these are the arts which most cooperate with nature. In the political art there is nothing natural, it deals only with human artifacts, laws, etc. This is derivative from the view that to be means to be body. At this point Eryximachus has finished his discussion of medicine and we keep only one thing in mind: Medicine consists in bringing about love of opposites which are by nature hostile, which implies that by nature similars attract each other—love each other. Applied to human things this would mean that pederasty is natural and heterosexual love is to be brought about artificially by medicine, which is a very funny suggestion.

In the sequel he speaks of eros in music. Music, too, establishes harmony between opposites, i.e., the eros of opposites for one another.

> "It is plain to anyone who pays attention with even a little nous that music too is along the same lines as them, just as perhaps Heraclitus too wants to say, since if one just takes him literally he does not speak beautifully. He says of the one that in differing with itself it agrees with itself, 'just as is the harmony of bow and of lyre.' It is overwhelmingly irrational to assert that a harmony differs or is out of things that are still differing. But perhaps he wanted to say this, that of the prior differences of high and low a subsequent agreement has come about by the musical art. It is surely not the case that a harmony would be out of high and low while they were still differing. Harmony is consonance, and consonance a kind of agreement, but it is impossible that there be a harmony out of differing things as long as they are differing, just as rhythm too has come to be out of swift and slow, which have previously differed but subsequently came to an agreement." (187a1–c2)

As you see, this is a somewhat pedantic correction of the saying of Heraclitus. Heraclitus wrongly asserts the persistence of disharmony, of the opposites. Once you have harmony, Eryximachus says, the original disharmony has ceased to exist. Heraclitus, however, says the survival of the desire in the harmony is essential to make it a true harmony. One could say the Heraclitean rule is deeper than this somewhat schematic view of Eryximachus. The fact that he refers to Heraclitus is not accidental, because Heraclitus is the opposite number to Parmenides and Parmenides was the authority for Phaedrus and his speech. One can say that Phaedrus agrees with Plato, who, ultimately, prefers Parmenides to Heraclitus, as is indicated in various ways.

The characteristic point here is this: Parmenides has said that eros is the first and oldest of all gods. What did Heraclitus say about the same subject? War is the father of all things. In a way Eryximachus agrees with him when he says the fundamental fact is the war of the opposites. He says in effect that discord is by nature and harmony is by art, which is closer to Heraclitus than he seems to think.

> "In this case music instills harmony in all these things, just as in the other case medicine did, by the insertion of eros and unanimity among one another. Music too is in turn a science of erotic things, in regard to harmony and rhythm. And in the system itself of harmony and rhythm, it is not at all difficult to discern the erotic things, and the twofold eros is not yet there." (187c2–c8)

We find no instances of one-sided love, only noble love. We find a sphere in which there exists only noble love, in the case of music, whereas in the case of the body, and, anticipating later developments, in all spheres except one, there are both noble and base love. There is one sphere in which there is only noble love, and we have to consider that carefully. Music and medicine both produce love; that means mutual love of opposites. The difference between music and medicine is this: both consist of a theoretical part and a practical part. Theoretical music has to do with objects composed by art, and these objects do not know the twofold love. There is only the noble love among them. Eryximachus says that the distinction between noble and base is a universal distinction. There is only one little sphere in which it does not apply, regardless of whether Eryximachus sees it. That is the sphere of theoretical music, or, to identify it more simply, mathematics. From Plato's point of view, the root of all art, the art of arts, is mathematics, more specifically, arithmetic. This much is seen by Eryximachus. But, characteristically, he does not make any use of it. In other words, there is the first indication of what Socrates later on describes as the true object of eros—these pure beings, the ideas. If there is such a sphere, in which there is only noble eros, this would have to be the model for all eros. True eros would be the love of this sphere of pure harmony. But Eryximachus cannot accept that. For him love is mutuality. The sphere of pure numbers does not love the mathematician.

> "But whenever one has to employ rhythm and harmony in relation to human beings, either by making—it is what they call lyric poetry—or by using correctly the songs and meters that have been made—it is what has got the name education—then it is here that it is difficult and there is need of a good craftsman." (187c8–d4)

Eryximachus has spoken before of the craftsman, when speaking of the practical art of medicine in 186d3–5. While there is a radical difference between theoretical medicine and theoretical music—theoretical medicine has also to do with the base form of love, theoretical music does not know a base relation—there is a basic kinship between practical medicine and practical music. He refers to education. But education as he understands it excludes gymnastics. He is a mere physician. What is the true relation between medicine and gymnastics according to Plato? Gymnastics is the positive art, medicine is a corrective art, just as education is a positive art and punishment a negative art. Eryximachus deals only with sick bodies, and his emphasis on the dignity of art implies that by nature there are only sick bodies and that the art is required to cure the natural sickness.

> "The same argument has come back, that one must gratify the orderly among human beings and see how the not yet orderly might become more orderly, and one must guard the eros of these—and this is the beautiful eros, the uranian, the Eros of the uranian muse. But the eros of the pandemian Polyhymnia, that one must cautiously apply to whatever one applies it, in order that they may reap the pleasure of it, and not insert any licentiousness, just as in our art it is a great task to use the desires of the art of cookery beautifully, so as to reap the pleasure without disease. So in music, in medicine, and in all other things, both the human and the divine, one must guard each Eros, to the extent it is allowed, for the pair is in them." (187d4–188a1)

The art of cooking must be supervised by the medical art. The art of cooking is an art which supplies pleasure; the art of medicine does not, as we all know. He deals here with eroticism as a subdivision of music. He devotes only a small part to human love. A very small part of his speech is devoted to what was the sole subject of Pausanias and Phaedrus. The lesson derived from medicine and music is that noble love is love for harmony, which consists of opposites. Therefore, it is noble to grant favors to the well-behaved human beings and to the not yet well-behaved with a view to their becoming well-behaved and to preserve their love. It is base to grant favors to the dissolute. This base love should be extirpated, for it is sick love. But this is not what he says. Noble love—heavenly love—is love of the heavenly muse. Base love—vulgar love—is love of Polyhymnia, the love of vulgar music. The latter, however, is not to be extirpated but to be purged. Why is this base muse, corresponding to the base eros, not to be extirpated? Formerly, when he spoke of medicine, he said that the base love is to be extirpated. The noble muse does not give us pleasure, but the base muse gives us pleasure.

There is a certain connection with the principle of the *Philebus,* the dialogue preceding the *Symposium* in the traditional order. The theme of the *Philebus* is the whole human good, that it consists of two parts: knowledge and pleasure. Whatever this may mean in Plato, Eryximachus's thesis is in a certain way akin to it. But let us turn to our subject: noble love is related to base love as medicine is related to the art of cooking. This is more or less said in Plato's *Gorgias,* too. From here we understand the reference to the opposites of sweet and bitter. When he spoke of opposites he put this in the middle, already foreshadowing the crucial importance of this example. Now, the sweet is according to nature, the bitter is against nature. This is not a metaphysical but an empirical statement. What is sweet does not go against the grain, what is bitter goes against the grain of the palate. Just as nomos, the law, had to bring together in Pausanias's speech a few things, so the art regarding eros must bring together the two forms of eros and overcome their separation; but the opposites which it reconciles, which it induces to love one another, are the noble and the base eros, not the lover and the beloved. This problem does not exist because we have only mutual love. The eros which lacks pleasure and the eros which supplies pleasure, the eros which is directed toward good behavior and the eros which is directed toward bodily pleasure—this is the function of the art of eroticism.

Eryximachus is willing to praise eros most highly. Eros is the power which moves everything by nature, for every happening is due either to love of similars or love of opposites. You can put it in mechanical terms of attraction and repulsion, though you would miss something. It is, in human terms, either to homosexuality or to heterosexuality. But Eryximachus cannot leave it at this, since he must distinguish between noble and base eros; and when you speak of love of similars and love of opposites, are not both noble? The distinction is in this case supported by his preference for homosexuality. Noble eros is love of similars—pederasty. Yet, he also wishes to praise his art, the art of medicine. The noble eros does not rule by nature, because there is also a base eros. The supremacy of the noble eros is the product of art, it is not by nature. The unnatural character of pederasty permits Eryximachus to praise in one breath pederasty and art. Let me explain. At first glance you would say this: Those which are by nature opposites, the male and the female, tend by nature to love one another. This union is according to nature and is healthy. Those which are by nature similar—males—tend away from one another. Their union is against nature; it is sick. The art must bring about their separation if it should not act against nature. Medicine, in other words, would be for the cure of pederasty and not for heterosexual love which is natural. But this is, of course, unacceptable for Eryximachus. The principle of pederasty can be stated as follows: Things which are by nature similar tend by nature toward one another. Then, of course, it follows that those which are by nature opposite—males and females—tend away from one another and we need an art in order to make these opposites—males and females—love one another. Males and females must be brought together by art for the preservation of the human species. This would mean that the preservation of the human species depends entirely on the art of medicine, which is a gross exaggeration. But, on the other hand, this art has nothing to do with Eryximachus's kind of eroticism. He must praise both his art and his eroticism and must conceive of both as akin to each other. Otherwise he cannot be satisfied. If the principle stated—that things opposite tend away from one another and art is needed in order to make them love one another—if these principles are to be preserved and if his art is to be in harmony with his kind of eroticism, there must be some oppositeness which his art alone, or art alone, can overcome. This is the opposition not of male and female but of virtue and pleasure. He must seek for harmony between opposites, the artificial harmony between the opposites of males and females won't do. He finds what he seeks in the opposition of good behavior and pleasure. But then, of course, it is music rather than medicine which overcomes this opposition. If virtue and pleasure are opposites, then the noble and the pleasant are opposites, and the pleasant is the base. It is a tall order that the solution of the human problem should consist in establishing a working harmony between the noble and the base. This much, I think, appears up to this point.

Eryximachus told us of one sphere in which only one of the two forms of eros exists, what I call theoretical music and which reminds us somehow of mathematics. This is forgotten, or perhaps not forgotten. He implies that it does not belong to the human things, nor to the divine things. The divine things are practically identical for him with the natural things. There was a doctrine which held that mathematical things are not natural, and, of course, they are not human things, in the sense that in themselves they have anything to do with human well-being. I want to repeat one point. Originally he had said that the base eros must be taken away, meaning the love of the sick body for things which increase its sickness. Now he says the base eros must he preserved but subordinated to an integrated end, the noble eros, and that means pleasure. He wants to praise in one breath pederasty and his art. What would help? By nature man is heterosexual; his art brings about homosexuality. But for any sensible Greek to say something is against nature is a degradation. He cannot praise both. If he would say pederasty is according to nature, then his art, in bringing about the artificial union of male and female, has nothing in common with pederasty. Art and pederasty are mutually exclusive and this has something to do with the true nature of man as an animal and a thinking being. But these two different functions are more or less in a certain harmony which excludes this fanciful and adverse attempt of Eryximachus. In the rest of the speech he deals with the eros in divine things. Hitherto he had spoken of eros in human things and made a subdivision—eros in medicine, eros in music. The erotic doctrine proper was only a subdivision of the doctrine of eros in music. Now he turns to the eros in divine things. By the divine things he means the natural, the cosmic things, as we will see.

One could say Eryximachus has four subjects: medicine, which deals with the visible body; music, which deals with invisible sounds; astronomy, which deals with the visible bodies far away; and divination, which deals with the invisible gods. This is an ascent from the most obviously visible bodies nearby to the least accessible invisible gods. He implies that as a physician he deals with visible bodies nearby; his art is the most solid of all the arts mentioned. This was seen by Krüger in his book, to which I have referred on another occasion. But one must not overlook the other side, namely the following proportion: the nearby visible is to the nearby audible as the far away visible is to the far away audible. The connection between the first parts is clear. What about the audible? Where in the case of the gods does the element of audibility come in? The gods are known by sounds, by hearing, by tradition. Hearsay is a basis of knowledge of the gods. Yet we must also see the distinction between the human and the divine. Medicine and music deal with human things, astronomy and divination with divine things. The relationship between astronomy and divination will not prove to be like the relation between medicine and music. It is rather like the relation of theoretical medicine and music to practical medicine and music.

Now let us read the sequel.

"Since even the system of the seasons of the year is full of both of these, and whenever those things of which I was just speaking—the hot and cold things and the dry and liquid—obtain the orderly eros in relation to one another, and get a harmony and moderate blending, they bring in their coming a good season for human beings, all the other animals, and plants, and they commit no injustice; but whenever the Eros that goes along with hubris is more in power in regard to the seasons of the year, they do a great deal of damage and commit injustice. Plagues are wont to arise from things of this sort, and many other varieties of disease for beasts and plants. Frosts, for example, hailstorms, and rusts come about from the greediness and disorderliness of erotic things of this sort in relation to one another, the science of which, concerning the movements of the stars and seasons of the years, is called astronomy." (188a1–b6)

In other words, the first subdivision of human knowledge of divine things is astronomy, the science dealing with the heavenly bodies, which were regarded by the pagans as divine. He speaks here of the noble eros, which is not a work of art, and of the corresponding base eros, which is, of course, also not a work of art. The moderate eros of hot and cold, dry and wet, brings about the health of men, brutes, and plants. This noble eros does not does not do any injustice. The dissolute eros among these elements brings about plagues and commits injustice. If you contrast this with an earlier passage, 186d–e, you see this: mutual love of the most opposite—of hot and cold—for example, brings, as such, health. Now he says no, only a certain kind of such mutual love brings about health. Why this change? In the earlier passage he started from the primacy of opposites, i.e., the primacy of war. The love of opposites is, therefore, entirely the work of art. Now he makes a distinction. War of the opposites is itself a special kind of love or union. Which kind of union could be the war of opposites? The love of similars. The war of opposites, the mutual attraction of everything hot, is disunity of the hot from the cold. We come now to the root of the problem: eros rules universally, by nature. Art, in this particular case astronomy, cannot affect these two forms of eros, the eros of the similar for the similar and the opposite for the opposite. Art can only foresee them and, therefore, help man by warning him.

This doctrine of which he makes use, is the doctrine of a famous philosopher, Empedocles. You can read a brief sketch of his doctrine in the first book of Aristotle's *Metaphysics*, especially in 985a21–28. He was a philosopher somewhere in Sicily who wrote a poem of which large stretches have been preserved. There is a funny thing: Empedocles addressed that poem to a young man whose name was Pausanias, just as Eryximachus, in a way, addresses his speech to Pausanias. Let us see what these funny things mean: Empedocles said there are four elements and everything that happens is either union or disunion, either love or destruction. But this has a subtlety: war is only another form of love, namely the love of the similars. If the different elements come together, the cosmos disintegrates. The love of similars leads to chaos; the love of opposites leads to the cosmos. The joke consists in linking this up with the issue of pederasty and heterosexuality. From Empedocles' point of view, both forms of eros are effective in the whole and are, as such, divine. The fact that the one is harmful to men and beasts, leading to chaos, and the other helpful to men and beasts, the love of opposites, was of no ultimate concern to Empedocles as a theoretician. Both are equally necessary, equally divine; there must be disintegration and there must be integration. The spirit in which Empedocles said it is illustrated by the following remark of an earlier philosopher, Heraclitus: "For the god everything is noble, good, and just. But men have made the supposition that some things are unjust and others are just." From a divine point of view the destruction of the cosmos is as noble, just, and good as its contrary, but men from their narrow perspective say the one is noble and the other base.

In other words, this Empedoclean doctrine is a purely theoretical doctrine. It looks at the whole with perfect detachment from human needs; it is not sufficient for practical purposes. Eryximachus tries to link this up: he must call one of these noble love and the other base. Homosexuals or heterosexuals are consistent if they love the opposites, namely, when they say yes to the conditions of human life, the cosmos. They are inconsistent if they love similars, because in this way they contribute to the restoration of chaos, and therewith the destruction of reason and art itself. Reason and art can only be if the opposites are united. Eryximachus takes the well-known physiological, scientific doctrine and puts it to use in his understanding of eros. And don't believe that this Empedoclean doctrine, in making use of the four elements and discord and love, is scientifically inferior to more recent suggestions. We cannot accept it in these terms; it leaves many questions open. The correction which comes out in Eryximachus's doctrine is this: What is according to nature is love of the opposite, which alone makes possible the cosmos; love of pederasty means saying yes to the chaos, the destruction of nature. Eryximachus, however, is not aware of this. Now let us conclude his speech.

"All the sacrifices, moreover, and those things over which the art of divination presides—these are the community of gods and human beings with one another—are concerned with nothing else than the guarding and cure of Eros. For every impiety is wont to arise if someone does not gratify the orderly Eros and honor and dignify him in every deed, both in regard to parents living and dead and in regard to gods. In these matters it has been assigned to the art of divination to examine the loves and cure them, and divination is in turn the craftsman of friendship of gods and human beings, by its scientific knowledge of the erotic things of human beings, as many as pertain to sacred right and piety." (188b6–d3)

Astronomy, as we have seen, cannot affect these divine laws—namely, these opposite elements—cannot predict them, but divination can. Why? Because if you assume that behind the things going on in heaven there are gods, and the gods can be influenced not by astronomy but by divination in the widest sense, including sacrifices, etc., it becomes possible to establish love between gods and men. Astronomy culminates in divination, just as medicine culminated in music. The latter is easy to understand, for no matter what a physician may tell you, if your conduct is not temperate, the prescriptions of the physician are of no use. Similarly, astronomy is incomplete if it is not completed by divination, by the art which allows you to control these potentially hostile forces. Divination produces eros between men and gods. We can say divination is a kind of cosmic medicine, a human art establishing a cosmic order favorable to men and beasts by establishing friendship between gods and men.

It seems there is either war between gods and men or love. But this is not strictly true on the basis of the Empedoclean doctrine, where we have seen war as a form of love. Even if we take the final formulation of Eryximachus we have to say there is always love between gods and men, either orderly or disorderly. The art of divination brings about orderly love between gods and men. If either of the two partners loves the other dissolutely, impiety follows on the parts of gods or men. The two must learn to follow the noble eros, which is done by influencing the gods through sacrifices. You improve the gods by appeasing them.

One more word about the central thesis of Eryximachus: all love is mutual, therefore love between gods and men must be mutual. The only question is whether it is sober or dissolute. Think of the love stories about Zeus and humans. An art is necessary to sober up the gods; this is part of the art of divination. While Eryximachus surely means this with tongue in cheek, he does not quite see the irony beyond the irony, namely, why he is compelled to admit such a fantastic art as divination: it is a necessary consequence of his belief in techne. There must ultimately be an art to control chance. Every art has a limitation. A simple example: you build a house with the best architect, but you do not know whether you will live to inhabit it. You marry in the hope of being happy, but the art of marriage cannot guarantee happiness. You plant the best possible garden, but the fruit depends on chance. There is an element of chance which limits all arts. So if you are a radical believer in art you must look for an art which enables you to control chance. This art would be the highest and most simple solution—theoretically, at any rate—and since the gods control chance, men would need an art to control the gods—divination. We smile about this, though we also have an art which tries to control chance; today they are called the social sciences in their capacity as predicting sciences. This is something very close to that art of divination.

[The remainder of this lecture was not recorded.]

I shall give a summary of Eryximachus's speech. You may recall this point, which I would like to repeat: Eryximachus makes use of a certain cosmological doctrine according to which the fundamental facts—four elements and repulsion or attraction—are the clue to everything there is. We can very well call attraction and repulsion love and hate. That was the doctrine of Empedocles, to which I referred and which underlies Eryximachus's doctrine. But Empedocles was more profound: he discerned love in that hatred, what is called strife in the atomists—in fact, love of the similar. So if fire repels water, it means also that fire seeks its kindred, fire, and water seeks its kindred, water. So there are two phenomena of love: love of the similar and love of the opposites. This is a universal cosmic phenomenon which explains everything.

The joke which Eryximachus makes is this: He identifies the love of the similar with pederasty, and love of the opposite with heterosexual love. (Eryximachus is in a way akin to the mathematician Theodorus in Plato's *Theaetetus*. Some of you will remember this very nice and respectable man, a completely tactless individual, who says to Socrates, Theaetetus looks exactly like you, for he is as ugly as you. Here we have a pedantic physician, which is not quite the same, but neither laughs.) That leads to very funny conclusions, some of which we discussed last time. Love of the similar leads to the consequence that the similar always assembles in one place, and that means there is no cosmos. If all elements are separate no composites can exist. Love of the opposite therefore is identical with the formation of the cosmos, of beings which are composites. To simplify matters I will say love of similars leads to chaos, at least from our human point of view, and love of opposites leads to cosmos. Now you must admit that a pederast gets into difficulties. Because if he says that love of similars—homosexuality—is good, he says yes to chaos. Whereas he who says heterosexuality-love of opposites—is good, says yes to the cosmos. Which of course makes sense, because heterosexuality is a condition of human life.

Could one not, however, make this objection: Eryximachus should not have assumed either the superiority of homosexuality to heterosexuality or the opposite. Why not have a value-free discussion, as Mr. Kinsey and others have done, and say both are simply natural? We could say that this presupposition is his failure. What is the reasoning behind this seeming prejudice? What is the tacit premise of Kinsey and the others? One could say the separation of the sexual act from its function, its natural function, its telos, its end. If you take into account the end there can be only one type of natural sexuality. This point of view, then, decides against homosexuality. But why does Plato make him a spokesman for homosexuality? Is this a mere idiosyncrasy? What Plato implies is this: in this perversion something is divined, i.e., not understood. Namely, eros, which is primarily bodily desire of different sexes, is not exhausted in procreation. Man cannot find his satisfaction in procreation. Procreation is not man's complete telos, complete end. Pederasty may be understood as a divination of this fact, and from this point of view pederasty would be more true in what it divines than self-satisfied heterosexuality.

One can state this also as follows: The value-free consideration, which takes all forms of sex life as equally valid, is wrong because it is abstract, contrary to its claim to be concrete, to give every case and every possibility. The characteristic thesis of Eryximachus, then, is that love is a cosmic phenomenon; it is not merely directed toward beautiful human beings, beautiful males, it is also directed toward things other than beautiful. The second characteristic is the praise of his art. He completes the consideration of eros as subject to something extraneous to it. Is there a connection between these two most striking characteristics, eros as a cosmic force and concern with his art? To the universality of eros there corresponds a universality of techne, not merely of Eryximachus's art, but of art in general. This is connected in Eryximachus's thought in such a way that it means the supremacy of techne. Ultimately, not eros rules, but techne. This is the greatest difficulty in understanding Eryximachus's speech: why the universality of eros, as he understands it, leads to the assertion of the supremacy of techne. I use the Greek word techne because there is no strict equivalent in modern language. Art today excludes the shoemaker and the carpenter, whereas in Greek they would be examples of an art. Techne has much to do with what is called today science, namely, a subphilosophic pursuit of high exactness.

The connection between pederasty and the other matters is this: Pederasty is unnatural love. The expectation from art increases as the expectations from nature decrease and become insufficient. If you prefer the unnatural, consciously or unconsciously, you demand thereby an art that supports this unnatural thing.

Love is universal; it is mutual. Both partners are inspired by the same motive. This is different in Phaedrus and Pausanias, where the motive of the lover and the beloved were clearly distinct. Love is universal; everything that is loves. Attraction and repulsion are only different forms of love, love of the similar or love of the opposite as the case may be. Now, if you look at this scheme—love of the same, chaos, pederasty; love of the opposite, cosmos, heterosexuality—what is the function of art here? If love of the similar is against nature, as we here presuppose, then heterosexual love is according to nature. The medical art, then, has the function to cure pederasty. On the other hand, love of similars is according to nature. Nature abhors love of opposites. Then art alone can bring about procreation. If all men were by nature homosexual, there would still be a need for the procreation of the human race. Art alone can bring about procreation. Eryximachus's attempt to establish a harmony between his art and his eroticism failed. Therefore he turns to an alternative. He says the problem of art is to bring together opposites which by nature abhor one another. To reconcile this with pederasty is his problem. He does this in the following way: the opposites which have to be reconciled are not the two sexes but virtue and pleasure. The highest art, the musical art, brings about this harmony of virtue and pleasure and thus makes pederasty possible as a noble love. But in this understanding, virtue and pleasure are conceived as opposites. That means, of course, that pleasure is base, not just morally neutral. Not the extirpation of the base, of the ugly, which he originally demanded, but its reconciliation with the noble or beautiful is the task of the highest human art. Yet, as he indicated in his criticism of Heraclitus, does the base not cease to be base when the harmony between pleasure and virtue is achieved? What becomes, then, of the distinction between noble and base eros? Is the base eros more than an inchoate eros, i.e., not truly eros? Thus, he prepares the way for Aristophanes' tacit rejection of the distinction between a noble and a base eros strictly speaking.

Eryximachus's theme is mutual love, and this is connected with his silence on hierarchy. He does not have the possibility of distinguishing ranks of eros corresponding to ranks of human beings. You may remember that Phaedrus alluded to this hierarchy by speaking of those who are by nature best; but in his understanding these people had as such nothing to do with eros. Pausanias had dropped that. His distinction between noble and base eros had nothing to do with the natural distinction. The silence here on hierarchy and, therefore, the stress on simple mutuality lead to the conclusion that the love of similars is not superior to the love of opposites. There is no distinction; both are equal, which means, of course, that chaos and cosmos are equal. This we understand immediately today, because from our science we learn that the state in which it was six billion years ago is just a different state of the world; there is no objective superiority of one state to the other. We humans prefer the latter, but this is only a subjective and external distinction, not one inherent in the subject matter. We can put it this way perhaps: the highest praise of eros in the whole work occurs here. Eros rules everything. Everything loves. Therefore the distinction between lover and beloved ultimately makes no sense. All love is mutual. There is nothing which rules by nature. The complete silence in Eryximachus's speech about male and female—for Plato and Aristotle the most simple example for the natural difference between ruling and ruled—indicates this. No natural hierarchy. Therefore art rules, because we must make distinctions between the better and the worse. If it is not in nature it must be brought in by man, intelligently and reasonably—it must be done by art. Pan-eroticism implies the rule of art. This I wanted to say in conclusion to our discussion of Eryximachus's speech last time, and before we turn to the sequel I would like to see whether you have any difficulties which we may or may not be able to solve.

Listener: In 186b he says that the healthy state and the sick state of the body are dissimilar. Directly after that he says dissimilars love dissimilars. Would that imply that the healthy state loves the sick state and vice versa?

Mr. Strauss: I discussed this last time. This is an initial statement. which he retracts later on. I will try to retrace it. He starts from the distinction between two erotes—the noble and the base. As a physician he identifies the one with the healthy, and the base with the sick. Then he says the healthy body loves healthy things, the sick body loves sick things. Then, since there is this fundamental distinction, he says dissimilar things love dissimilar things. What does the body love? Repletion and evacuation. The healthy body loves the right kind of food and the sick body the wrong kind of food.

Then, for some reason, which is not given, he does not like that. The reason, I believe, is that the food does not love the body. If you think of a little lamb, potential food, it does not like to be eaten. In the case of repletion and evacuation, it is a nonmutual love and he is driving toward a conception of love which would be mutual. He is not satisfied and so he turns to the love of opposites, which has to be brought about by art. You see, not every statement is of equal weight and that applies to us too. In the beginning of an argument we might make a statement which we would not repeat a half hour later, because in the meantime it might have been proved insufficient. Still, it is important as a stage in the development of the argument.

[In answer to a question:] The fundamental difficulty was taken care of by Empedocles. He called it also a state of love, but the love of similars. He also called it strife. What is behind this notion: love of similars leading to the collection of similars and love of dissimilars which leads to the emergence of composite beings—plants, brutes, men? What is the difference between them? To which I think, Empedocles' answer is that from the point of view of god they are equally good; but we humans—and the same would apply to brutes and plants if they could speak—we say this is cosmos and that is chaos. Once you accept that, you have the justification for medicine, that which enables the body to grow and fulfill its function properly. This is of course the standard for medicine. It is the function of art to bring opposites together, and even on the highest level—even in astronomy, which deals with the visible bodies far away—there exists, Eryximachus says, a noble eros and a base eros. The noble eros leads to health, the seasons, etc.; the base eros leads to plagues and similar phenomena. In the case of the conflict between the two erotes in the visible bodies nearby, medicine can be effective; there medicine is ineffectual.

But we can't leave it at that: we have to find an art which controls the heavenly bodies, and that is the art of divination. His whole speech ends with his praise of the art of divination. Through the art of divination the noble eros of these things holds the balance. Why? Because the gods do that. But who moves the gods? The human artisan—the problem of the *Euthyphro*. What we find in the cosmos, according to Eryximachus, is the fight between the two erotes, the noble and the base, the cosmic and the chaotic. He asserts an ultimate rule of techne, not of medicine. The grand bodies with which astronomy deals are indirectly controlled, via the gods, by the mantic art. All arts are concerned with the human good, subordinately or architectonically. From the theoretical point of view, from the point of view of god, the human good is of no interest. But from man's point of view it is predominant. There is a necessary connection between pan-eroticism and the rule of techne. If pan-eroticism means that everything that is loves and there are no beings which are loved or beloved, then there is no hierarchy, and the distinction between good and bad must come from a subjective point of view. The classic statement, in the Fragments of Heraclitus, 102: "For god everything is just, noble, and good; but men have made the supposition that some things are just, others not." That is exactly what Socrates, Plato, and Aristotle deny. They assert that the distinction between good and bad, noble and base, just and unjust, are not merely human, although most of the use we make of these distinctions is merely human.

I have to add a few points regarding the Eryximachus speech which I either forgot or which were brought to my attention. First, Plato tries to show in Eryximachus the typical physician, just as in Theodorus in the *Theaetetus* he shows the typical mathematician. There is a certain pedanticism about Eryximachus but also a certain lewdness, if I may use this strong word. In a certain contemporary medical treatment of eros I always was reminded of a statement of Burke regarding certain doctrines of the eighteenth century: he uses the expression "an unfashioned, indelicate, sour, gloomy, ferocious medley of pedanticism and lewdness." I think this has some contemporary application.

The next point: I mentioned that the background of Eryximachus's speech is the philosophy of Empedocles, who addressed his philosophic poem to someone called Pausanias. Eryximachus addresses his speech to this Pausanias. Empedocles is the natural target here behind Eryximachus because Empedocles' philosophy is truly a pan-erotic philosophy. Love, either for the similar or for the opposite, rules everything. There is another strange thing about Empedocles. I read to you Fragment 111 in Kathleen Freeman's translation: "You shall learn all the drugs that exist as a defense against illness and old age. For you alone will I accomplish all this. You shall check the force of the unvarying winds which rush upon the earth with their blasts and lay waste the cultivated fields. And again, if you wish, you shall conduct the breezes back again. You shall create a seasonable dryness after the dark rain for mankind, and again you shall create after summer drought the water that nourishes the trees and which will flow in the sky. And you shall bring out of Hades a dead man restored to strength." In other words, Empedocles also teaches a universal power of techne, of art. As far as my recollection goes this is the only document in a philosophic text prior to Plato where the notion of science for the sake of power, the famous

Baconian formula, is somehow approached. Now, we have seen in Eryximachus's speech also this combination of pan-eroticism and a universality
of techne.

I would like to remind you of two things. The first is that there are three
speeches in which eros is viewed from a point of view outside of it—those
of Phaedrus, Pausanias, Eryximachus, who view eros with regard to gain,
moral virtue, art. Eros is regarded as sovereign in Aristophanes, Agathon,
and Socrates. This overlaps with another principle of the structure. Phaedrus speaks from the point of view of the beloved, Pausanias from the point
of view of the lover; for Eryximachus they are not mutual lovers but they
could be. Eryximachus and Aristophanes are both mature men and they do
not speak from the point of view of lover and beloved, but they take for
granted that love in its perfection is mutual. Agathon and Socrates could be
lover and beloved—the young Agathon and the older Socrates. The central
couple speaks of love in terms of mutuality and we must see later on what
that means. This is only a specification of the general problem of an apparent arbitrariness, characterizing the *Symposium* in particular and the Platonic dialogues in general. We find here individuals with individual characteristics—such as names, sex, noses, etc.—and they discuss eros. This
is an imitation of life. Whenever we see people discussing something, or doing anything, they are always specified individuals with individual characteristics. Life is in this sense random. The intention in trying to understand
life is to see the reason or causes of what happens, to discover the pattern,
but the order does not explain everything, for there are always loose ends
which cannot be understood in terms of any pattern. This is what the
Greeks meant by *tyche,* chance. This is the way it is in life, and Plato in his
dialogues imitates life. But this imitation is artistic because it is in a way a
falsification of life. A simple reproduction of life would not be artistic. The
principle of this artistic imitation is the denial of chance—everything is necessary. And we can say that the Platonic dialogue as a whole is based on this
noble delusion, noble lie, that in the dialogue everything is necessary.
Strictly speaking, this would apply even to the names, but naturally there
are limits to that.

The theme here is eros, a universal subject, discussed by individuals with
all kinds of accidental characters. There is a disproportion between the universal and the individual. There are infinite individual possibilities on eros
and only a few are selected. We must see through those individuals presented and see in them the typical. What Plato must presume to claim is
that he has selected the typical possibilities about eros. Said in another way,

you must see the connection between the doctrines and the human types of the speakers, not understood as mere individuals. This implies also that there must be a completeness in the selection of types presented. If the typology is not complete, which might be the case, then one cannot simply say Plato forgot about that; one must raise the question Why did Plato omit that type? Perhaps because he did not wish to present it, either because it is uninteresting, irrelevant, or for some other reason.

Let us consider the question of completeness. As I indicated by my schema we have here eros subject to something extraneous or sovereign eros. The first is subdivided into three—eros subject to gain, eros subject to moral virtue or law, and eros subject to art. We have to raise the question Is this a complete description? Is there an alternative to gain, virtue, techne, something to which eros could be thought to be subject, and for which we have to find a speech? I believe that on reflection we find that it is complete. Have we not at this point, at any rate, laid bare the principle governing the whole work? The class agreed with me by silence—there is no alternative. But, later on, a friend of mine who does not wish to be mentioned said, "Why not procreation?" In a way, this is indeed true. Procreation, we can say, comes in as the theme in the next three speeches in different ways. But I must add one point: gain, virtue, techne are strictly extraneous to eros; procreation is not. Therefore, your silence and my assertion were justified. This creates a prejudice in favor of the view that we will find at the end of the dialogue a complete discussion of eros. But once this is settled, and I do not claim that this remark of mine settles it, we have to raise this question: Is there a proper correlation between these types—gain, moral virtue, and art—and the human beings who present them? For instance, moral virtue: Could we not say that the best representative of the moral supervision of eros would have been a stern moralist, say, a puritan? In other words, by not taking a stern moralist, did not Plato forget something important? Should not the moralist be the speaker about the conflict between eros and morality? It is absolutely necessary to consider the alternatives for oneself in order to understand what Plato is doing. Plato made a decision—this book. The grounds of the decision he did not tell us, we have to find out ourselves. To understand a Platonic dialogue is not merely to take cognizance of the decision, but to understand the grounds of the decision. Why did Plato not present a severe puritan to present the moral point of view?

Listener: It is possible that the severe puritan escapes the realm of love.

Mr. Strauss: I am not speaking of Calvin of course, but there have been other puritans who have been bothered by eros. That is not an impossibility; Calvin may have been unaware of the problem, but not every puritan was. What is the true reason? He suppresses the problem. The supremacy of morality is so certain and evident that a conflict cannot really arise. The puritan would have been unable to praise eros, and that is an elementary condition for every speech here. Still, one could say it is a bit narrow of Plato not to give us this spectacle of puritan versus eros. To which the answer is extremely simple: he did that in the *Republic*. One could say he wrote a whole book to show us this conflict. The *Republic* begins with the story where a poet—and what a poet, Sophocles—complains in the strongest terms about eros as a terrible tyrant which he has fortunately escaped now, being an old man. If this is not a rejection of eros even by a poet, I don't know what it is. Plato did not forget that problem, but it was not proper in the *Symposium*. But why Pausanias? There are perhaps alternatives. It is not only necessary that the man know the problem from his own experience; he must also have a special concern. In other words, it is necessary to raise in each case this question: Does not the speaker have a selfish interest in his doctrine? Does he not speak pro domo? And I think we would have to make a distinction at the end between those speakers who do not simply speak pro domo and those who do. Pausanias surely does: an oldish lover who has not sufficient erotic recommendation and whose best recommendation is his respectability. He is naturally, in this context, the best speaker about this aspect of eros. I do not say that this suffices—very far from it. I only wanted to say that it is necessary, and a full understanding of any work of this kind would require a full demonstration.

To turn to Eryximachus. He represents the point of view of art in regard to eros. He is a physician. That is not difficult to understand. Who are the specialists regarding eros today? The psychoanalysts, they are physicians. Medicine is the art concerned with eros and its consequences—think of obstetrics and gynecology, which are surely medical disciplines. But, it is of course also true, medicine deals with sick bodies, not as gymnastics with healthy bodies. The whole problem of sickness and health is the theme of medicine; therefore the distinction between sick and healthy eros follows, from the medical point of view, the two erotes, just as it had for Pausanias, from his moral point of view.

7 ARISTOPHANES

Let us turn then to Aristophanes' speech and a few introductory remarks. Let us remember Phaedrus's and Pausanias's speeches: one must not look at eros from the point of view of the lover, especially the mere beneficiary of love, nor from the point of view of the self-interest of the lover who wants to use his doctrine of eros for succeeding with his beloved, nor from the point of view of the possessor of a techne who treats eros from above and controls it. The lover, the man who has felt the power of eros, must give adequate expression to his experiences.

Aristophanes is a man filled with eros, not for this or that individual, as Pausanias is for Agathon. To use a term which is later on used in Socrates' speech, there is no pettiness involved. From Socrates' point of view there is a pettiness, a limitation, involved in this essentially accidental individual, and love in the fuller sense has a wider scope. This revolts our feelings, but we must see whether this is justified.

All earlier speakers had some concern other than eros—gain, virtue, art. Aristophanes is exclusively concerned, as we have seen in the beginning, 177b, with Dionysus and Aphrodite, the god of wine and theater and the goddess of love. Or should Dionysus, the god of the theater, and in particular of comedy, exercise a deflecting influence on Aristophanes' presentation?

Further: Eryximachus was led to imply, as I tried to explain, that the pleasant is as such base. The true musical art reconciles virtue and pleasure, but it reconciles them as opposites; hence pleasure is base. This baseness or ugliness is the theme of comedy. In order to ridicule the base, the poet must present it. But how can we reconcile this art of presenting the base with the praise of eros? Aristophanes is confronted with the seemingly impossible task of praising eros in the element of ugliness or baseness. Furthermore, Eryximachus's art and his eros contradict one another. If pederasty is to be preserved, one must abandon art. Aristophanes can be said to draw that conclusion: he abandons art. The alternative would be another art such as midwifery and matchmaking, of which a certain individual—Socrates—boasts. But that comes later. Eryximachus, in contradistinction to Phaedrus and Pausanias, had known only mutual love, but he had divorced eros from the natural hierarchy to which Phaedrus had, indeed, referred. Aristophanes will link up the hierarchy of erotes, not a crude opposition of noble and base eros, but a hierarchy of erotes with a natural order of human beings.

As we have seen, he changes places with Eryximachus, and that means he is in a way exchangeable with him. Eryximachus is a physician and a physicist; Aristophanes will also prove to be a physiologist in the Greek sense of the word—a student of nature—but in such a way as to lead up to a natural hierarchy. In contradistinction to the two preceding speakers—Pausanias and Eryximachus—he will again put the emphasis on manliness, a virtue which was completely forgotten by the soft Pausanias and the valetudinarian Eryximachus. Now, let us turn to the transition to Aristophanes' speech. I will discuss these transitions later coherently. In the beginning the speeches follow without interruption, now we always have interludes. Why this is so we will discuss later. "Then [Aristodemus] said that Aristophanes took over" from Eryximachus. Aristophanes' speech is thus connected with Eryximachus's speech; and Eryximachus's speech, in its turn, was connected with Pausanias's speech. Apart from these two principles of construction, Pausanias, Eryximachus, and Aristophanes form a unit: they are explicit defenders of pederasty. Aristophanes will complete what Pausanias began. Why will Aristophanes be able to complete what Pausanias and Eryximachus were unable to complete? It has something to do with the fact that Aristophanes is a comic poet. Those of you who have ever looked at Aristophanes in the original, or even in a translation, will know that his plays are indescribably indecent. Perhaps the element of extreme indecency permits things which cannot be done in any other way.

> "It [the hiccup] did indeed stop; not, however, before the sneeze was applied to it, so I am wondering whether the orderliness of the body desires these kinds of noises and ticklings, such as the sneeze is, for it stopped at once when I applied the sneeze to it." (189a1–6)

The word *orderly* is a derivative from the word *cosmos*. What do we learn from it? The orderly, the decent, the well-behaved needs, apparently, the ugly—sneezing and such things—in the case of the body. Perhaps it is also true in the case of the soul. If this is true, then the praise of eros would require the praise of the base or ugly. We see also that Aristophanes' hiccup was quite severe.

> And Eryximachus said, "My good Aristophanes, see what you are doing. Being about to speak you make a joke, and you compel me to be a guardian of your own speech, if you say anything laughable, though it was possible for you to speak in peace." (189a7–b2)

Let us see whether we understand that. Eryximachus says, "Being about to speak you make a joke." He seems to imply that speaking and joking are incompatible. Does this make sense? Making funny noises is exactly what Aristophanes had been doing. Speech is serious. "By your remarks you compel me to watch your speech in case you say something ridiculous, and you compel me to watch your speech by tracing your ability to speak, as distinguished from your ability to make funny noises, to my art. But you do not have to worry—there will be no further need for funny noises, for sneezing or joking." I think that is what he means.

> And Aristophanes said with a laugh, "That's a good point, Eryximachus, and please let what I have said be unsaid. But don't keep watch over me, since I fear, in regard to what is going to be said, not that I not tell jokes [*geloia*]—this would indeed be a gain and native to our Muse—but that they be a joke [*katagelasta*]." (189b3–7)

Aristophanes laughs—that is very rare here. Let us see if we find another case. What does this mean, if someone laughs? For example, in the third book of the *Republic,* a man of laughter is one form of intemperance. Therefore, Socrates never laughs, except on the day of his death. The same intemperance which showed itself in the hiccup is shown in this laughing. Aristophanes retracts what he has said. Does he mean that orderly things require funny noises, or that they require ugly things? "Our muse"—Eryximachus had referred to "our art." The obvious difference between the muse and art is that the music man is inspired. Aristophanes' speech is the first inspired speech. We can say there are three uninspired speeches and three inspired speeches. We would have to make a minor subdivision—the simply uninspired speech is that of Phaedrus.

[Tape change.]

> "You think you can hit and run, Aristophanes," he said. "But pay attention and speak on the condition that you will give an account [logos]. Perhaps, however, if I decide to, I'll let you go." (189b8–c1)

Eryximachus says, you think you can get away with jokes; but be responsible to me, complete my logos, and do not make jokes. Not Dionysus will be the judge, but medicine. The radical difference between Eryximachus's and Aristophanes' speeches comes out in this short exchange, and yet they are exchangeable as I said. The comic poet, and only the comic poet, can bring out the full truth of this or any other physiology.

Listener: Is there any reference here to laughter as a funny noise itself?

Mr. Strauss: Is Aristophanes likely to laugh at his own jokes?

Listener: If other people laugh at what he says, and if it is a disease, then Eryximachus has a right to put a stop to it.

Mr. Strauss: I have to think that over. I can't answer that at the moment. I would also like to repeat again Mr. Gildin's remark regarding the interlude between Eryximachus and Aristophanes, where Eryximachus apparently makes a distinction between speaking and causing laughter. This seems to imply that speaking cannot create laughter. What creates laughter will be funny noises, and we have seen that there were some funny noises like hiccups and sneezes. Mr. Gildin rightly points out that laughing, in contradistinction to mere smiling, can of course also be called a funny noise. From this point of view Eryximachus's remark would mean, Just as I, as a physician, was under obligation to stop the funny noises of hiccups and sneezing, I am under obligation to stop the funny noise of laughing. This would again indicate his pedantic character.

> "And yet *[kai mēn]*, Eryximachus," Aristophanes said, "I intend to speak in a somewhat different way from how Pausanias and you spoke. Human beings seem to me not to have perceived at all the power of eros, since, were they aware of it, they would have built the greatest sanctuaries and altars to him, and would be making besides the greatest sacrifices, and not be doing as they are now when none of these things are being done about him, though they most certainly ought to be done. The reason is that he is the most philanthropic of gods . . ." (189c2–d1)

You see here that he refers only to Eryximachus and Pausanias. Only their speeches are relevant to his subject. What does he say? Men act as if they had never experienced the power of eros, for otherwise they would worship him more than any other god. They do not worship him properly now. What Aristophanes suggests is what we would call now a religious revolution, not merely the mild change of the law suggested by Pausanias. Aristophanes introduces in a way new divinities. In a way he commits the crime of which Socrates was accused. Eros deserves the greatest worship because he is the most philanthropic of all gods. Not because he is the oldest, the most powerful, or the most just god. Phaedrus had praised eros as most useful to the beloved—to him. Aristophanes says eros is most useful to mankind, a much broader consideration. We have, of course, to raise the question of what will be the rightful status of the worship of the other gods after Eros will have come into his own. Must there not be a certain denigration of the others?

"... being a helper to human beings and a physician of those things which, should they be cured, there would be the greatest happiness for the human race." (189d1–3)

Eros is the physician, not the medical art. Eros, including pederasty, as will appear from the sequel, is not a sickness but a cure. The cure brings about the greatest happiness. The sickness is unhappiness. In other words, eros cures not only this or that deficiency, it cures the essentials of human life, as will appear later. No such praise of eros has appeared hitherto.

"I shall try to explain to you his power, and you will be the teachers of everyone else." (189d3–4)

He will initiate those present into something hitherto unknown, a mystery. He will not be the one who is going to divulge it to the others. The others may divulge it.

"You must first understand human nature and its experiences." (189d5–6)

Aristophanes seems to oppose the cosmological doctrine of Eryximachus and limit himself to human things. But he says "first." He only starts from human things, or rather from human nature. He promises to discuss the nature of man, he does not promise to discuss the nature of eros. This will be the starting point for Agathon later. The nature of eros will remain obscure in spite of everything Aristophanes says.

"Our nature long ago was not that which it is now, but of a different sort. First, there were three genera of human beings, not just as now, male and female, but there was a third besides, common to both of them, the name for which remains but it itself has disappeared. There was one then that was androgynous, common in looks *(eidos)* and name from both, male and female, but now it is not, except for the name, which occurs as a reproach." (189d6–e5)

Aristophanes begins with the extinct sex of man. Naturally, because it is the most striking; also, now, the most in disrepute. That there were such men was taught by Empedocles, the originator of this scheme, who was Eryximachus's authority. Whereas today there is merely a shadow, a name, originally there was the thing itself and a respectable name. Now this has a general application. What if accepted opinion is not authoritative for Aristophanes, but the respected, the accepted, is an important form of the noble or fair. Aristophanes makes it clear from the beginning: precisely the disreputable will be brought out by him, the comic poet living in the element of the despicable and base.

> "Second, the looks of each human being was as a whole round, with back and sides in a circle, and he had four arms and hands, legs and feet equal to the arms and hands, and two faces on a circular neck, similar in all respects. There was single head for the two faces lying opposite, and four ears, two genitals, and everything else as one might conjecture from these." (189e5   190a4)

Every being was a whole. This means it was round. All parts of the body were doubled, except the head and the neck. A fantastic being, very ugly, but we must see what he does with it.

> "He used to walk upright, as he does now, in whichever direction he wanted; and whenever he started to run fast, just as acrobatic jumpers whirl around in a circle with their legs straight out, they, supporting themselves with the eight limbs they then had, used to rotate quickly." (190a4–8)

Now these round beings were also capable of fast circular motion. They could have rolled even without stretching their legs, as indicated here in 190a6. Why this is so we shall see in the sequel.

> "The reason why the genera were three and of this kind was this: the male was at the start the offspring of the sun, the female of the earth, and that which partakes of both of the moon, because the moon too partook of both. They were spherical, both they themselves and their movement, on account of their being similar to their parents." (190a8–b5)

Now we know why man was originally a circular thing, moving in circular motion. He gives the reason explicitly. We see, then, that Aristophanes transcends already here the merely human and enters into the sphere of cosmology. The very word *stroggulos,* which he uses in 189e6, occurs, for example, in Plato's *Phaedo* (97e1), where the question is discussed whether the earth is flat or round. Sun, moon, and earth are gods. To quote from an Aristophanean comedy, *Peace* 406–11, the sun and the moon are the gods to whom the barbarians sacrifice, whereas the Greeks sacrifice only to the Olympian gods. In Herodotus, book I.131, the Persians worship sun, moon, earth, fire, water, etc., and they do not believe like the Greeks that the gods have human shapes. Aristophanes here refers us to a barbaric notion. Originally men had the shape of the cosmic gods, because they were the descendants of the cosmic gods. In that shape, as will become clear in the sequel, they did not yet have eros, because the androgynous did not have eros. Each kind of man had the single shape of sun, moon, or earth. But where do the gods of human shape come in? They are decisive for the emergence of eros, as we can suspect. Original man had lofty thoughts, these round descendants of the cosmic gods. We can say the head of each was the head of two bodies. This could perhaps already explain it. But the phrase "lofty thoughts" reminds us of an earlier passage, in Pausanias's speech 182c2. The lofty thoughts are the thoughts of those not subject to tyrants. Being the descendants of the cosmic gods, they had lofty thoughts; they were not subject to tyrants, hence, they did not respect the Olympian gods, the gods of human shape. Nothing is said here whether original men were happy. What did they do?

> "They were awesome in their strength and vigor and had great and proud thoughts, and they made an attempt on the gods. And what Homer says about Ephialtes and Otus, that they tried to mount up to the sky, is said about them, with their intent to assault the gods. Then Zeus and the other gods were deliberating as to what they should do and were perplexed. They did not know how they could kill them and, as they had blasted the giants with lightning, wipe out the race—the honors and the sacrifices they had from human beings would be wiped out—any more than they could allow them to wax wanton." (190b5–c6)

Aristophanes replaces the speech, the logos, of the individual Homer by a general logos, a general story. Men, being the descendants of the cosmic gods, were from the beginning subject to the Olympian gods. They were from the beginning meant to be subject to the Olympian gods. But the Olympian gods were not the descendants of the cosmic gods, for otherwise they, too, would have globular shapes, and we know that the gods have human shape. These original men of cosmic origin refused to be subject to the Olympian gods. Their rebellion failed as a matter of course. Aristophanes doesn't even mention that. Every rebellion against the living gods fails naturally. It seems that originally men had honored the Olympian gods and brought sacrifices to them prior to the rebellion. The gods could not possibly tolerate man's licentious behavior, for, by so doing, they would have lost their power and everything else. Nor could they destroy men, for they needed the honors and sacrifices. The word means also sacrificial animals themselves, in a very material sense. This is, incidentally, a theme of the Aristophanean comedies, the gods being starved by the withholding of sacrifices. The gods, as you see here very clearly, were not prompted by philanthropy. Eros is the only philanthropic god. You understand, then, the predicament of Zeus. Every government could be in such a position. They can't destroy their subjects, and on the other hand they can't let them do what they want. You see Zeus thinking and finally he got a bright idea. Then he says, "I seem to myself." Does anything strike you? Well, that's the very beginning of the dialogue. The *Symposium* begins with the same two words. I regard it as possible that Plato directs our attention in advance to this speech of Zeus and that Aristophanes' speech is the central speech of the whole work. Zeus is introduced as a speaker by Protagoras in Plato's dialogue *Protagoras* and by Socrates in the *Gorgias*. In the dialogue *Critias*, where Critias is the chief speaker, the dialogue ends, "then Zeus said"—but the speech doesn't come. According to the accepted opinions the *Critias* has not been completed. I believe that Plato did not want Critias to make such a speech. Aristophanes at any rate gives here a speech by Zeus.

> "Then Zeus with difficulty conceived of a plan and says, 'I seem to myself,' he said, 'to have a device, how human beings may [still] be and by becoming weaker stop their licentiousness. I shall now cut each of them in two, and they will simultaneously be weaker and more useful to us on account of their having become more in number. And they will walk upright on two legs. And if they are still thought to wax wanton and are not willing to remain quiet, then I shall,' he said, 'cut them again in two, so they will go around hopping on one leg.'" (190c6–d6)

Zeus, who is presented by Homer as the perfect ruler, and therefore, of course, also as the most wily ruler, comes up with a solution: preserve men and weaken them. His scheme is an improvement in every respect: more men and weaker men. It increases man's usefulness to the gods, no question of philanthropy. Through Zeus's punitive action men became erect. Through Zeus's punitive action—this is a great paradox of this speech—men became men. For they also became tame, orderly. They ceased to be universally dissolute or unjust. So they lost their lofty thoughts, as we shall see. They became like the subjects of tyrants, i.e., they became civilized. Civilization is the acquisition of justice and orderliness, accompanied by the loss of lofty thoughts. This road has been repeated many times since. Civilization is domestication and does to men what it does to animals. Men became men, they ceased to be similar to the nonhuman earth and they took on the shape of the Olympian gods. This is very important.

But are the gods themselves really orderly and just? Not at all, as we have seen. They are prompted only by their self-interest. That which makes men just, the action of Zeus, is not itself just. But, we ask now, independent of the Platonic utterance, what is it that makes men just, simply, without any sophistication? Law makes men just. But is the law itself just? We have an interesting discussion of that, for example, in the first book of Plato's *Repub-*

lic. I am referring to Thrasymachus: the laws imposed by the stronger with a view to the stronger's self-interest. Zeus imposes something with a view to his self-interest. Let me make a big jump: The Olympian gods stand for the nomos, for the law. Men cannot become men without being subject to law, and to divine law. Man owes his humanity to divine law; hence the cause of law must be manlike, anthropomorphic, must have a human shape. This is therefore the problem of Aristophanes and Plato, and in the historical life of Socrates: the tension between original nature and law in the wide sense, what we call today civilization. The general thesis of Aristophanes' speech will be that eros is a barbarization of man's impaired nature against that imposition. Therefore the final problem is how to establish a working relation between this rebellion, the attempt to return to the original nature, and the Olympian gods, to whom men owe their life. Aristophanes' speech is the only speech which ends with a praise of piety. Eryximachus's speech, you may recall, ended with a praise of the mantic art, and that's not piety.

[In answer to a question:] The question is whether Zeus acted on this consideration: Original man, visibly akin to the cosmic gods; derivative man, visibly akin to humanly shaped gods, brought about by the gods not out of love for men but out of self-interest. If it had been done out of love the nomos would be sacred, but if it is done out of self-interest it is not. And the rebellion, which is the essence of eros, is made even clearer later on when eros becomes much more than the desire for self-gratification. Aristophanes indicates the problem of the being of these gods by being absolutely silent about their origin. It is clear by implication that they cannot be of cosmic origin. If they were of cosmic origin, they would be round. And who would have split them? The only beings capable of splitting them were the gods themselves. The question of the origin of the gods is taken up only in Agathon's speech and even there only in a very general way. The question for Aristophanes is what is the power of eros. And the crucial point he makes is this: You cannot understand eros if you do not see in it the element of rebellion. That is deeper than any desire for pleasure or for that matter for procreation. This is a thought that I would not dismiss as irrelevant. All asceticism, all religion, has some such notion. I will explain this next time.

[In answer to another question:] *Androgynous* we use as a term for a womanish man or a mannish woman. But to say there were such people literally is a fantastic thing. We must not forget that the dramatic poet is concerned with stage effects and that is much more striking. Later on, after they are split, there are only males and females.

127

A last point regarding the following question: What is the doctrine of an individual speaker, and what is the connection between the doctrine and this particular character? It must fit that character in such a way that this character, say a physician of this particular kind like Eryximachus or an oldish lover like Pausanias or a comic poet like Aristophanes, is the proper representative of the doctrine which he presents. It is, indeed, necessary to investigate this, and one cannot claim to have understood a Platonic dialogue if one has not answered this question. In the case of the Platonic dialogues, because of their great wealth, this is very difficult. I have tried to show the necessity of this procedure in an essay of mine called "On Tyranny" in a much simpler case, a dialogue of Xenophon. There only two characters occur, and other things, too, are very simple. There one can show that this selection of speakers, a tyrant and a lyric poet, is the necessary combination for having such a dialogue on tyranny. No other combination, say, for example, a tyrant and a philosopher, would be as good and as perfect a setting as this one. One must also consider the title. You remember I said in the beginning of the course that the *Symposium* has in a way a unique title. The ordinary Platonic title is the proper name of a participant or else a subject matter. For example, *Gorgias* would be an example of the first kind and *Laws* of the second. *Apology,* I would say, indicates the subject matter. The title *Symposium* doesn't indicate either. If we look over the whole body of Platonic titles we find only one dialogue which has a title akin to that of the *Symposium* and that is the *Epinomis.* It is a kind of appendix to Plato's *Laws.* I suggest that there is a connection of some importance between these two dialogues, and this remark will be more easily intelligible after we have begun to study Aristophanes' speech.

Aristophanes' speech, which is the center speech of the *Symposium,* permits us to answer this question. Aristophanes tacitly makes the distinction between the Olympian gods and the cosmic gods. Now the theme of the *Symposium* can be described as follows: the *Symposium* is the only dialogue devoted to a god—the god Eros. A Greek god allied to an Olympian goddess—Aphrodite. But a little god, not the object of public worship in Athens, for example. The *Symposium* as a whole, and especially Aristophanes, questions the Olympian gods, the gods worshiped by the city. But only Aristophanes speaks of the cosmic gods, though even he does not speak of them explicitly as gods. The question of the cosmic gods does not become the theme of the *Symposium.* It is, however, the theme of the *Epinomis,* the only Platonic dialogue devoted to the cosmic gods. This, I think, is the connection between these dialogues, and it shows the crucial importance of the theological problem for Plato.

> "With this remark he proceeded to cut human beings in two, just as those who cut sorb-apples when they are going to pickle them, or just as those who cut eggs with hairs." (190d7–e2)

This, of course, recalls Aristophanic examples in his comedies. You see also the contrast between the gods in their solemnity and these very humdrum things.

> "And whomever he cut, he told Apollo to turn the face and half of the neck around toward the cut, in order that the human being might, on seeing his slicing, become more orderly, and he ordered him to cure the rest. And he turned the face around, and drawing together the skin at what is now called the belly, by making a single mouth, just as in string bags, he bound it up at the middle of the belly. It is what we call the navel. And he smoothed out all the other many wrinkles and straightened out the chest, with the sort of tool shoemakers use in smoothing out the wrinkles around the last; but he left a few around the navel itself and the belly, to be a reminder of the ancient experience." (190e2–191a5)

Natural men are transformed by the art of the gods so as to become orderly. Apollo is a kind of physician but also a shoemaker. You see the example of domesticated apples, if we can use the expression, and domesticated eggs. They are no longer capable of bearing fruit. Man's civilization is a kind of castration. Apollo, as you may have observed, did not turn around the neck as Zeus had told him. Did Zeus, in Apollo's opinion, lack anatomical knowledge? There is a strange parallel to this story in Plato's dialogue *Protagoras*, which I would like to read to you:

> As often as men banded together they did wrong to one another, through the lack of civic art, and so they began to be scattered again and to perish. Zeus, then, fearing that our race was in danger of utter destruction sent Hermes to bring shame and right among men, to the end that there should be regulation of cities and friendly ties to draw them together. (322b6–c3)

The gods are responsible for man's civilization.

> Then Hermes asked Zeus in what manner was he to give men right and sense of shame. "Am I to deal them out as the arts have been dealt? The dealing was done in such wise that one man possessing the medical art is

able to treat many ordinary men, and so with the other crafts. Am I to place among men right and respect in this way also or deal them out to all?" "To all," replied Zeus. (322c3–d2)

Now the implication is that Hermes has to tell Zeus how the arts are divided. I raise this question, though I am by no means sure that I am right, but it's the best I can do. Zeus cut them to pieces; then Apollo sewed up the side on which they were cut. We see there was much skin. There were wrinkles and he had to use a shoemaker's instrument to smooth them out. Where did Apollo get the additional skin required so that there were even additional wrinkles which had to be smoothed out? He acts as if the skin of the whole man were now available for the half man, which of course was a mistake. Did he in each case discard one half; leaving it skinless and letting it perish? Did Apollo, in other words, behave like that Epimetheus of whom Protagoras speaks in the same story? I can read you that part: "Epimetheus being not so wise as he might be heedlessly squandered his stock of properties on the brutes. He still had left unequipped the race of man and was at a loss what to do with it" (321b6–c3). Man was left naked and only the theft of fire from Hephaestus on the part of Prometheus could save the human race. Are we not confronted here with a similar situation by the blundering activity of a god? In that situation a savior, Prometheus, was needed; there is no reference to such a savior here. Why? Because the place of Prometheus as a founder of civilization is in Aristophanes' speech taken by eros. Aristophanes gives no account of the origin of the arts in his speech. He disregards art altogether. However this may be, the sequel surely shows that the gods lacked foresight. This cutting and sewing together did not solve the problem at all. Apollo left man a sign to remember the original act, but this was also superfluous, as we shall see immediately.

> "When the nature was cut in two, each half in longing for his own came together, and throwing their arms around one another and intertwining, in their desire to grow together, were being killed off by hunger and the rest of their idleness on account of their unwillingness to do anything apart from one another. And whenever one of the halves died, and one was left, the one that was left went searching for another and intertwined itself with either half of a whole woman it encountered—it is what we call woman—or of a man, and so they kept on perishing." (191a5–b5)

You see the problem is not yet solved for the gods. The nature was cut in two, man's nature was impaired, namely, by nomos. It is for this reason that the universal expression "the nature," not merely human nature, is used. It is not uninteresting that "to cut" also means to castrate. Out of this situation eros arose. Eros is surely not the oldest god. You see Phaedrus's thesis, which was hitherto uncontested, is here implicitly contested. Agathon will question it explicitly. Eros is in no way connected with the Olympian gods and, therefore, in particular not with Aphrodite. Aristophanes makes true what Pausanias had only implied. As Professor von Blanckenhagen pointed out to us, eros is possible without Aphrodite. As desire for the restitution of the cosmic, globular shape, eros belongs to the cosmic gods. Eros, we can say already now, is a movement of nature, of impaired nature, against law. The direction of eros is inverse to the direction of the action of the Olympian gods. To overstate it in order to make it perfectly clear, eros is radically impious. I think this is not a wholly unintelligible thought, though it may not be theologically wholly correct. If you look at all innate actions of which man is capable, all his actions can in their performance be directed to the glory of god. The only action of which this is not possible in the performance is the sexual act. There was always a tension between the biblical religion and eros. Think only of the second chapter of Genesis, where the disobedience of Adam has some connection with the loss of sexual innocence.

You see at the end of the passage that we read, Aristophanes omits androgynes from the enumeration because there are no longer androgynes. Now there are only males and females. In the immediate sequel he says that Zeus became pitiful, merciful. On the basis of what we have heard before, this is a euphemism. Zeus's pity for man is prompted by his self-interest, as we have seen before.

> "In pity Zeus provides another device: he changes the place of their genitals to the front—for up to this time they also had them on the outside, and they used to generate and give birth not into one another but into the earth, just as cicadas do—so he changes them to the front and through this made generation in one another, through the male in the female, for these reasons: if a man should encounter a woman, they might generate in the embrace and the race continue, and if a male should encounter a male, repletion of intercourse [being together] at any rate might occur in the embrace, and they might stop and turn to deeds and take care of the rest of their life [livelihood]." (191b5–c8)

Now Zeus does the whole thing. He was dissatisfied with Apollo's blunder. Original man already possessed sexual organs and used them. In this respect, and in this respect only, they were originally similar to the Olympian gods as distinguished from the cosmic gods, sun, moon, and earth. What does this mean? This is, of course, a very malicious suggestion. According to Aristophanes, the specific difference of men is sexuality as distinguished from rationality. This needs a long comment because the brutes are also capable of sexuality. The point on which men agree in origin with the Olympian gods was not their erectness but sexuality. This connects man with the Olympian gods and separates him from the cosmic gods. Perhaps this fact was the reason why men were from the outset subject to the Olympian gods. Their dissoluteness in the use of their sexual organs called for subjection, if only to beings which were themselves not immune to dissoluteness. But this sexuality has as little to do with eros proper as any dissoluteness of the gods. That's the crucial thesis—sexuality is not eros. But how did original men use their sexual organs? They begot into the earth, namely the males, and they gave birth into the earth, namely the females. I can understand this only in this form: the males fertilized eggs left by the females in the earth. Originally all men came from the earth, like the old Athenians, and it was claimed for the Athenians alone. The change which Zeus effected was to change man into his own image as regards sexual relations too, but with this difference, what is mere pleasure in the case of the Olympian gods is for men a dire necessity. The survival of the human race and its satisfaction, so that men are free to work, depend on the change effected by Zeus. These two things, the survival of the human race and the satisfaction of the individual, ultimately serve one function: man can serve the Olympian gods. Therefore, Aristophanes' speech is bound to end with a praise of piety.

In the case of the meeting of male and female you see procreation, not satisfaction. In the case of the meeting of male and male—satisfaction, but not procreation. He is silent here about the meeting of female and female, a subject which he will take up later. You see the pederastic element in Aristophanes' speech, which will come out more fully, and which is a particularly malicious suggestion because pederasts are presented in the Aristophanean plays, at least in the first lines, as something ridiculous. Through the Olympian gods men acquired orderliness. Eryximachus had said that both orderliness and its opposites are of cosmic origin. Loves of similars—chaos; love of opposites—cosmos. Both are cosmic forces. For Aristophanes orderliness does not stem from the cosmic gods. This, we can say, is his cosmology. This is important in connection with Aristophanes' tacit denial of the significance of mind, or nous, and therefore his silence about the arts as well.

I have to proceed step by step, leaving loose ends while I go. At the end of the discussion I shall try to pull it together. Through the Olympian gods men acquired orderliness, erect stature, and the possibility of embrace. Originally, sexual relations were related to the earth. Erect stature and the possibility of embrace link men to the Olympian gods. In the case of the Olympian gods there is no connection between orderliness, on the one hand, and an erect stature and embrace, on the other. But in the case of man there is. Why? Men and the Olympian gods, we may say, and I use a crude expression which in the case of Aristophanes I don't think is completely improper, are the only sexy beings. Here we answer the question regarding the brutes. In the case of the brutes, the sex life is limited by nature to the seasons. This is surely not true of man and surely not of the Olympian gods. If we may call this for convenience's sake sexiness, then this is what leads men to the Olympian gods—they are not limited to mating seasons. But there is one obvious difference between men and the Olympian gods in this respect. There is a limitation without which man is not thinkable, and which is absent in the case of the Olympian gods: the prohibition against incest. In the case of men, incest, always a great theme in the Aristophanean comedies, comes in. Man has a natural latitude regarding sex. I remind you of the famous passage in the beginning of Aristotle's *Politics* 1253a39:

> By nature there is in all men the impulse toward political association, and he who first established it is responsible for the greatest good. For, just as man, when perfected, is the best of the animals, so he is when divorced from law and right the worst of all. For injustice is harshest if it has weapons. But man is born having the possession of weapons such as prudence and virtue which he can use to the highest degree for opposite ends. Therefore man is most impious and most savage without virtue, and worst with regard to sexual things and food.

Sexual things—incest; food—cannibalism. Because of this latitude man is by nature capable of living on members of his own species, which would not apply to lions and tigers. There is the same thought in Aristophanes, only from an entirely different point of view. Whereas Aristotle presents it from the point of view of civilization, Aristophanes presents it from the point of view of rebellion against civilization, as will become clear. Man has a natural latitude regarding sex, therefore the need for limitation, for nomos, law—for a divine law. Since it is of man's essence to be limited by divine law, eros cannot be understood except in relation to the gods, or law. A mere physiological understanding of eros is absolutely impossible.

> "It is, then, from ancient times that eros for one another is inborn in human beings, a bringer-together of the ancient nature in trying to make one out of two and cure human nature." (191c7–d3)

Sexual satisfaction should enable man to survive for the purpose of worshiping the gods. From the gods' point of view the end of sexual satisfaction is piety. From man's point of view the end is sexual gratification. These are two entirely different ends. We had a similar problem in Pausanias's speech, where the two partners, the lover and the beloved, are united in the perfect erotic association but inspired by different motives. Eros is the natural desire of human beings, not of brutes, for restoration of the ancient nature, the healer of human nature. To repeat: in Aristophanes' understanding eros is peculiar to man. Eros is a natural consequence of the artificial division of the ancient nature. Eros is not a gift of the Olympian gods.

Aristophanes' doctrine of eros is the counterpart of Plato's doctrine of recollection, a return to the ancient nature in the case of Aristophanes, a recollection of the originally perfect knowledge in the case of Plato. You see also the difference: For Plato the guiding consideration is the mind, the intellect, nous; for Aristophanes it is something else, and it can provisionally be described as the negative relation to nomos. This negative relation to nomos is more meaningful to Aristophanes than mere procreation and mere gratification.

Eros is striving for something unattainable, and this is also implied in procreation. This unity can never be achieved. It is essentially unsatisfactory. It is, therefore, man's present nature—man as we know him—to be unhappy, to be sick. It is not that some men are sick and others healthy, as Eryximachus had said, but that all men are sick. This misery of man is traced to hubris. It reminds strangely of biblical doctrines. Although Plato started from entirely different things he came up with notions similar to the biblical notions. Furthermore, what eros longs for is this union, this original unit, something which we would call, not being tutored by Aristophanes, something ugly. The beauty of the body is completely denied in favor of these strange round beings. All concern with the beautiful tends beyond the beautiful to something else. The striving force of the beautiful in erotic feelings leads eventually to the defeat of the beautiful. Eros is tragic, certainly in the sense in which we understand the word. It is interesting that this is imputed to the comic poet.

"Each of us is a token of a human being, because each has been sliced, just as flat fish, two out of one. So each is always seeking his own token." (191d3–5)

The seeking is always, there is no fulfillment. For each human being seeks not simply some other human being, but that individual human being which is by nature its other half. To show the impossibility of this situation we must remind ourselves of the possibility that through Apollo's blunder the other half might have been left skinless and might, therefore, have perished. Men will, therefore, never find the other half. All love is unhappy, visibly or invisibly—comically unhappy or tragically unhappy. This is a strange problem for a comic poet. But Aristophanes is not an ordinary comic poet.

"Now all men who are a slice of the common—it was then called androgynous—are lovers of women, and many of the adulterers have come to be from this genus, and all the women in turn who are lovers of men and adulteresses come to be from this genus. But all women who are a slice of woman, these hardly pay any attention to men, but rather they are turned toward women, and the lesbians come to be from this genus. But all who are a slice of male, they pursue the males, and as long as they are children, because they are cuts of the male, they love men and rejoice in lying down together with the men and embracing them, and these are the best of the children and youths, because they are most manly by nature." (191d6–192a2)

Here we find the question of the natural hierarchy brought up for the first time. The large majority of men are heterosexual, for they descend from original androgynes. This new doctrine of eros legitimates adultery as a matter of course, i.e., it legitimates what is forbidden, it legitimates the ignoble, the disgraceful, the base, and the ugly. Aristophanes is silent on justice, here as elsewhere. Eros, we could paradoxically say, justly overrides justice. In 192d8, as you will have seen, he does not say all adulterers, only most of them. Why not all? There are adulterers, as Aristotle in his wisdom tells us, who are prompted by love of gain, therefore they would not be prompted by eros. By the use of different tenses, he indicates that in former times adulterers were mostly prompted by love for the female sex. Not so now. Why are the women loving women in the center? There are only three cases. He started from the most common case, heterosexual love, and he wants to end with the highest case, the male homosexuals. The second case is not common but below the highest. That means that what is most disgraceful, the least high, is in the center. Why? Because the most disgraceful, the ugliest, is the theme of Aristophanes. In another speech the highest would be in the center.

Listener: How do these various divisions continue beyond the first generation?

Mr. Strauss: There is a limit to literalness in such an account.

> "Some say indeed that they are shameless. They lie. It is not by shamelessness that they do this but by confidence, manliness, and a manly look, embracing what is like themselves. The evidence is great: on becoming complete [perfect] only men of this sort go into politics." (192a2–7)

The best males, the homosexual males, turn to politics when they become old, and this proves not only that they are the best men but that they are free from shamelessness. Is it not a strange thing to say that politicians are characterized by absence of shamelessness? What does he mean? To prove that the homosexuals are not shameless he refers to the fact that they alone go into politics. Politics would seem to be the medium of bashful behavior. Let me return. I say first that Aristophanes succeeds where Pausanias and Eryximachus failed, namely in proving the supremacy of pederasty, because he links it up with the natural hierarchy. Pederasty is the preserve of those who are most male by nature. I do not deny that there is a certain joke in that—courageous, manly, and male. Manliness is the criterion. Why? The pure males, the males interested only in males, are descendants of the sun, as distinguished from the earth and the moon, from which the others are descendant. They are as little shameless as the sun, which sees everything, and no one would call the sun shameless.

Apparently he legitimates pederasty by reference to the polis, and then, of course, the argument would run as follows: The polis, according to a preposterous etymology, stems from war *(polemos)*. War is that in which at first glance the polis shows itself in all its splendor and force, and manliness is, of course, the virtue of war. In Pausanias's speech we have seen that political freedom justifies unlimited pederasty. In opposition to Pausanias, however, Aristophanes abolishes the distinction between noble and base pederasty. There is only a hierarchy of eros, none of which is base, for each is according to nature. Also here, in contradistinction to Pausanias, the boys are lovers of the adult men and vice versa. Mutual love is present here, just as it was in Eryximachus. Yet, to return to the main point: It seems that the polis is used for establishing the hierarchy of nature. What is most conducive to political life in its greatest splendor is the highest. But must not the hierarchy of eros be established on the basis of eros itself and not on the basis of something external to eros, such as the polis? What has the polis to do with the essence of eros, with man's desire to return to his original nature? Does not the polis belong together with nomos, and hence with the Olympian gods, or is there an eros for the polis? Let us see the sequel.

> "Whenever they become full-grown men, they are pederasts and naturally do not pay attention to marriages and acts of procreation, but they are compelled by the law; but it suffices for them to live with each other unmarried. Now he who is of this kind proves to be in any case a pederast and fond of lovers [philerastes], always embracing that which is akin." (192a7–192b5)

These he-men have no eros for the polis; they regard nomos merely as compulsion. They love only what is akin to them, and their fellow citizens are not akin to them. The political point of view has no legitimate place in Aristophanes' argument. For example, he does not refer to the obvious link between polis and eros which will come out in Agathon's speech, namely eros as love for honor, which turns naturally into the political. This is not even alluded to by Aristophanes. Precisely because he has experienced the power of eros or because he does not subordinate eros to any extraneous consideration, he cannot refer to the polis in order to legitimate eros. Does he basely bow to the taste of the public in the theater? No. Eros is a desire for the ancient nature, for the state in which man had the loftiest thoughts, in which he thought of conquering heaven, or rather Olympus. Eros is rebellion against nomos. Through eros men cease to be cowed and acquire again the loftiest thoughts. If this is the essence of eros, the community of those which are most manly by nature is most highly erotic to the deepest degree in regard to what eros is ultimately after—the state of completeness in which men could challenge the gods. Therefore Aristophanes succeeds where Pausanias and Eryximachus failed. Because he frees eros from subjection to anything not inherent in eros . . . [Tape change.] . . . therefore it can be understood only in terms of the extremes.

> "Now whenever the pederast and everyone else meets up with that very own half of his, then they are wondrously thunderstruck by friendship, kinship, and eros, unwilling to be separated from one another for virtually even a short time. And these are the ones who continue with one another throughout life, but who could not even say what they want for themselves from one another. No one would think that it was the intercourse [being together] of sex, that for its sake one, after all, would enjoy being with the other with such great seriousness; but it is evident that the soul of

each of the two wants something else, which it is not able to say, but it divines and hints at what it wants in riddles." (192b5–d2)

This is a typically Platonic expression: the soul divines something which it cannot express and this is truer than what the soul can say. In this section, we have seen, Aristophanes turns to all lovers and he speaks no longer of homosexuals in particular. Hitherto he had put the emphasis on desire, seeking, trying to be one. Now he stresses the achievement, the fact that man gets the half which he seeks and therefore friendship arises. But he adds eros. The eros survives in the embrace itself, for the danger of separation remains, nay, separation is inevitable. The ability to comply with the requirements of eros is not equal to the requirements of eros. The desire of the lovers is incompatible with the desire of the gods. If the lovers had their way the gods would never be honored, because the lovers would always stay together. The desire of the lovers is incompatible even with love itself. The lovers would simply perish if they could follow the requirements of eros, and love would perish if they could succeed. There is then in this way a harmony between the desire of the gods and the desire of love itself.

Not all men are genuinely erotic, either because of the effect of their nature or else because not all men find their natural alter ego. Many human beings cease to have desire for being together after the partner has lost his or her youthful bloom. The genuinely erotic human beings cannot say what they desire because the desire is in a way self-contradictory. But the self-contradiction points to a deeper truth which the soul divines without being able to state it clearly. There is a disproportion between the infinity of the love and the finiteness of the embrace. Men cannot say what they desire; a god must say it for them.

"And if while they were lying down in the same place, Hephaestus should stand over them with his tools and ask, 'What is it, human beings, that you want to get from one another?' And if he should again ask when they were at a loss for an answer, 'Do you actually desire this, to become, in the best possible case, in the same place with one another, so as not to be apart from one another day or night? If it is this that you desire, I am willing to melt you together and fuse you into the same, so as to become one, being two, and as long as you live, both, as if being one, to live in common, and when you die, there in turn in Hades, with the pair of you dead, instead of two, to be one in common. Well, see whether you love this and it is enough for you if you obtain this.' We know that not even one, if he heard this, would refuse, and it would be evident that he wants nothing else. He would simply believe he had heard that which for some time he had been, after all, desiring, to come together and melt together into the one being loved and become one out of two. The cause is this: that was our ancient nature, and we were wholes. So the name for the desire and pursuit of the whole is eros." (192d2–193a1)

The god who speaks to the lovers is Hephaestus, the blacksmith. Does this remind you of something you may know from other readings? Hephaestus comes up in a similar situation in the *Odyssey,* in the eighth book, where the story of Ares and Aphrodite is told. Aphrodite was the wife of Hephaestus and had an adulterous affair with Ares. Somehow Hephaestus catches them in the act. I read to you a few words from the prose translation. Hephaestus naturally makes a fuss and all the gods assemble. He complains bitterly to Zeus.

> His mouthing gathered the gods to the house of the brazen floor. Poseidon the Earth-girdler, beneficent Hermes, and royal Apollo the fardarting came: but the Lady Goddesses remained at home, all of them, quite out of countenance. In Hephaestus' forecourt collected the Givers of Weal and unquenchable was the laughter that arose from the blessed Gods as they studied the tricky device of Hephaestus. One would catch his neighbor's eye and gibe: "Bad deeds breed no merit. The slow outrun the speedy. See how poor crawling Hephaestus, despite that limp, has now overtaken Ares (much the most swift of all divine dwellers upon Olympus) and cleverly caught him. Ares will owe him the adulterer's fine." Words like this one whispered to the other: but of Hermes did Zeus' royal son Apollo loudly ask, "Hermes, son of Zeus, messenger and giver of good things: would you not choose even the bondage of these tough chains, if so you might sleep in the one bed by golden Aphrodite?" And to him the Gods' messenger, Argus-bane replied: "If only this might be, kingly, fardarting Apollo! If there were chains without end, thrice as many as are here, and all you Gods with all the Goddesses to look on, yet would I be happy beside the Golden One." (*Odyssey* 8.321–43)

This story is now transferred from the immortals to the mortals. The unquenchable laughter about the two immortals caught in the act of adultery and the frank expression by Hermes about his desire to lie publicly with Aphrodite, while fettered to her literally, is the comedy in eros. He contradicts propriety. What he says is improper but it is natural. When these two things clash laughter arises. Not in every case, naturally, but in the case of certain clashes we laugh. For example, at the story of a murder we don't laugh, but at a confidence man we do. Not all successful crimes are laughable.

Aristophanes' Hephaestus doesn't address gods but mortals. There is therefore love only until death, or rather, beyond death, and tragedy is necessary in human love. The Olympian gods love eros because they are deathless. Hephaestus is not angry here but friendly; he is philanthropic. He was connected with Prometheus because Prometheus stole Hephaestus's art—fire. Here there is complete silence about Aphrodite because Aristophanes knows only eros without Aphrodite. But, however philanthropic Hephaestus may be, and that is a crucial implication of this speech, he cannot bring about what men so deeply desire. The unity can never be restored. Eros is infinitely more than the desire of lust, it is the desire for oneness, wholeness, and integrity in the literal sense, everlasting integrity, a desire which cannot be fulfilled.

What is the consequence of the fact that eros cannot be satisfied? Ever-new embraces—that's Tantalus. The consequence of Aristophanes seems to suggest piety. The gods could make possible what is by nature impossible. Yet the gods would thus expose themselves to the original danger by restoring the original units. Furthermore, piety could fulfill what eros promises if the objects of piety, namely the gods, were themselves wholes. But the Olympian gods, being the models of human beings, are not wholes in this sense. The true wholes are sun, moon, and earth. Piety would then consist, in the highest possible case, not in restoring the original unity but in looking at the cosmic gods, sun, moon, and earth. The fulfillment of eros would be contemplation. In that case eros would tend by its own nature toward contemplation. The looking at available in amorous embrace would be only a foretaste of the true looking at. Yet, if the end is union, it cannot be theoria, contemplation. The unity would destroy the possibility of contemplation, in modern language, the vis-à-vis of subject and object. Only a part which remains apart can have contemplation.

We can also say that eros, as understood by Aristophanes, is, in modern language, extinction of the self. Aristophanes is unable to recognize eros in philosophy—that should be clear—because the end of man as he understands it is a being incapable of philosophy. Therefore, he tacitly accuses Socrates in his comedies of being unerotic. He cannot conceive of eros except horizontally, on the same level, not vertically, as Socrates understands it. He can conceive of eros only in terms of mutuality. He does not understand the mind—nous—and its one-sided direction. Pausanias, we may recall, brought in the mind in connection with pederasty. You may remember, his first attempt to justify pederasty was by arguing that the males are superior in intellect to the females. Eryximachus was silent about the mind, but he brought in art, and especially theoretical music, which reminds of the problem of the mind. Aristophanes drops the mind altogether. There is accordingly is a strange connection between that and his successful defense of pederasty.

In what sense can piety solve the problem which eros cannot solve? The ultimate answer in Aristophanes' speech will be that piety does not solve the problem. Piety is merely compatible with eros; it is even required for eros, but it does not solve the problem. The end of Aristophanes' teaching regarding eros is that eros cannot be fulfilled; it is striving for the impossible. It is very hard to say what is tragic and what is comic and, naturally, we think of it in modern terms. The question of what is tragic in the Platonic sense we have to take up when we come to the tragic poet Agathon. I may be permitted to use the term tragic now in the modern sense, the common sense. Aristophanes, the comic poet, is the only one who teaches that eros is essentially tragic. Behind the play and fun and absurdity of the Aristophanean comedies there is a very serious and profound teaching.

> "Formerly, as I say, we were one, but now, on account of our injustice, we have been settled apart by the god, just as the Arcadians were by the Spartans. So there is a fear, if we are not orderly in regard to the gods, that we shall be split again and go around in the state of those who have been sculpted in relief on stelae, sawed apart along our noses, and become like die cut in two." (193a1–7)

The motive of piety, it appears here, is fear, fear of superior power like the power of the Spartans. This fear demands not orderliness regarding eros, but orderliness regarding the gods. The example he gives here is recorded by Xenophon in his *Greek History,* book 5, chapter 2. I will tell you the gist of the story: There were people living in the Peloponnesus who had been the allies of the Spartans and then came over to the Athenian side, i.e., they became democratic. The Spartans vanquished them and established an aristocracy and destroyed the democracy. They restored the original way of life of the Mantineans, which was to live in villages. Xenophon uses the phrase "as they lived in the olden times." This is difficult to understand. From a Platonic point of view the Spartans deserve respect and not merely fear because they established aristocracy, which from Plato's point of view is superior to democracy, or because they restored the ancient. The gods can demand only fear because they do not establish the ancient, they prevent the establishment of the ancient. Yet, on the other hand, the Spartans, by compelling the Arcadians to live in villages and not in the city, may be said to have decivilized the Mantineans, and the gods are somehow the cause of civilization. Even according to Aristophanes' doctrine, or precisely because of Aristophanes' doctrine, it would seem that the gods deserve respect and not merely fear. What I am driving at is this: the story told by Xenophon is absolutely ambiguous in connection with this passage. It can be understood to mean that the gods deserve only fear, or they may also deserve respect.

> "But for these reasons everyone must exhort every man to be pious about gods, in order that we may escape one [fate] and obtain the other, as Eros is our guide and general." (193a7–b2)

Aristophanes says here that one must admonish every man, male man. He is not concerned with the piety of women. Piety is required so that the other gods do not prevent us from getting what the god Eros leads us to. The service of the other gods has merely a negative function, like evil ghosts as it were. The positive good comes from the god Eros alone. Yet Eros is the leader of an army and, as you know, an army consists of males. Eros is the leader of an army of males which strives for original unity, for the recovery of lofty thoughts, which implies the thought of rebellion against the gods. The fundamental antagonism between the Olympian gods and eros remains preserved. Piety in this sense is merely a dire necessity and concession. We will complete our discussion of Aristophanes' speech next time.

8 AGATHON

Today I plan to finish my discussion of Aristophanes' speech and begin the discussion of Agathon's speech. I have no quarrel with those among you who say that we proceed too fast. My defense is that one must also have a view of the whole and this requires necessarily some neglect of details if one has only sixteen meetings. It would do us no harm to reflect on the fact that the understanding of the whole must cooperate with the understanding of the parts and vice versa; and on how the understanding of the whole is and is not identical with the understanding of the parts. Especially we must consider that this applies not only to Plato's *Symposium* or any other Platonic dialogue but to all human understanding. One is always troubled about where to begin, with the whole or the parts. Unfortunately we cannot do this here. Others among you might say that we proceed too slowly, but I can only repeat, if political theory is a legitimate subject one must also study the classics of political theory and if they are to be studied, they must be studied carefully. There may be other complaints, other objections, other questions, and I am perfectly willing to discuss them but not at this moment. I think we should first finish our discussion of Aristophanes' speech.

Aristophanes is, as I said, the first inspired speaker. The first who speaks of eros as something not subservient to something extraneous to eros. Also, Aristophanes completes something which Pausanias had begun and Eryximachus had continued, namely, to show the superiority of pederasty. Pausanias had started from the distinction between the noble and the base eros. Yet, as became clear, according to him this distinction is not by nature but by law. He tried to find a natural principle of that distinction by having recourse to nous, to the mind. The male sex, as the more intellectual sex, should be preferred. But he failed. Therefore Eryximachus and Aristophanes abandon this attempt. Eryximachus refers indeed to art, to techne, which is an intellectual thing, but this techne is unerotic. Aristophanes is silent about nous altogether. In abandoning the orientation by the mind, Eryximachus and Aristophanes are compelled to conceive of eros as mutual.

The two preceding speakers, you will recall—Phaedrus and Pausanias— spoke of eros from the point of view of either the lover or the beloved. Why is this so? Mutuality, horizontality, as distinguished from verticality, eros directed toward the higher—this is connected with the problem of the mind as follows: The object of the mind is higher than the mind itself, since the mind follows its object and not the other way around. Eryximachus had also made the distinction between noble and base eros. The distinction, as he presented it, is not a natural distinction but is established by art with a view to what is useful to man. Remember particularly what he said about the seasons. The healthy seasons and the unhealthy seasons are equally natural. The prevalence of one or the other is achieved by art. Therefore he ends with the assertion of the supremacy of art. If the distinction between noble and base eros, then, is not by nature, it ought to be dropped. And this is exactly what Aristophanes does. Aristophanes does have recourse to a natural hierarchy among men. Yet that hierarchy is determined not by nous but only by manliness. Eros, according to him, is rebellion and military action; eros is the leader of an army.

A few words about Aristophanes' story. Man, the descendant of the cosmic gods, therefore round, was to be subject to the Olympian gods. But since he had lofty thoughts he refused to submit. Why was man subject from the beginning to the Olympian gods? Man, in contradistinction to his progenitors, the cosmic gods, is in need of procreation. And, in contradistinction to the brutes, he is not limited to mating seasons. In the latter respect, and only in that respect, he is like the Olympian gods. The relationship between man and the Olympian gods is based on the sexual latitude of both. The specific difference of man among the animals is this sexual latitude.

Through the punitive action of the Olympian gods men become well behaved, *kosmios* in Greek, which recalls "cosmos." This orderliness does not come from the cosmic gods but from the Olympian gods. Men acquired erect stature, the shape of the Olympian gods. The Olympian gods molded men in their image, you could say, to use the biblical parallel. Men became human through the action of Zeus, for man becomes human through law, nomos. And the cause of the nomos, which makes man human, must be manlike. The Olympian gods are manlike. On the basis of the comedies of Aristophanes one could say, since man's sex life is not limited by nature to seasons it must be limited by law. The most massive limitation of man's sex life by law is the prohibition against incest. The Olympian gods are not limited by seasons or by prohibitions against incest. Man is not limited by seasons but is limited by the prohibition against incest; not by nature but by convention. The brutes are limited by nature and not by convention. They have mating seasons but no prohibition against incest, a theme which occurs repeatedly in Aristophanes, for instance in the *Birds*.

Man acquired his humanity by Zeus's punitive action. That action limited man's sexuality by imposing the prohibition against incest, but he acquired erect stature. Thus men were enabled to see one another in amorous embrace. Men do not possess erect stature, as in the Platonic view, for looking up to heaven and to the cosmic gods. They do not have erect stature in order to be astronomers in the highest sense, but so that they can lie together. Bliss consists in amorous embrace.

Man seeks his alter ego, the other part of himself. What does this mean? He seeks his nearest relative, his own flesh and blood. Eros is essentially incestuous. I exaggerate, but this exaggeration is justified by a crucial part of the Aristophanean comedies. However this may be, it is man's essence to be constituted by both—limitless sexual desire and law. Law is as essential to man as is sexual desire: eros must be understood in the light of this duality. You cannot disregard nomos and regard it as entirely extraneous. This means, however, that eros must be understood in the light of the antagonism between nature and convention. Eros is at the same time desire for amorous embrace and rebellion of nature against convention, nay, eros is that rebellion rather than sexual desire, as Aristophanes makes clear when he says, "They could not even say what they want for themselves from one another" (192c3–4. That they want embrace they know, but the deeper meaning they do not know, the desire for the original oneness. It is the desire for the ancient nature not impaired by convention, for original wholeness or integrity. But if this is eros, its goal is not attainable. Zeus has taken care of that. It is at this point that the need for piety seems to arise. Eros can never be fulfillment and a supplement is needed.

> "Let no one act contrary to him—and he acts contrary whoever incurs the enmity of the gods—for if we become friends and reconciled to the god we shall find and meet up with our very own beloved, which few nowadays do." (193b2–6)

One must follow Eros, who is a leader of an army, therefore a male. This includes avoiding becoming hateful to the gods. As for Eros, one must become a friend of Eros and become reconciled to him. Aristophanes does not speak of friendship between men and the Olympian gods, whereas Eryximachus had ended his speech with the demand for friendship. There is need for reconciliation with Eros. Why? So that we can discover and encounter our young beloved, which Aristophanes ordinarily refers to as a male beloved by males. At present this happens only to a few. Why? At present there is no proper worship of Eros, i.e., there is too great a worship of the other gods. Eros is angry with us for this neglect. If he were properly worshiped he would help us find our natural alter ego. Surely the Olympian gods are of no positive help as regards the erotic pursuit.

> "And please let not Eryximachus suppose, in making my logos into a comedy, that I mean Pausanias and Agathon—for perhaps they in fact do obtain this, and both are males, in their nature manly." (193b6–c2)

Aristophanes does not for one moment regard Eryximachus and Phaedrus as lovers. Of those present, he refers only to Pausanias and Agathon as lovers. But he ironically imputes to Eryximachus the desire to misrepresent comically his speech, namely, to suppose that Aristophanes had been admonishing Pausanias and Agathon in particular to be pious. Perhaps, Aristophanes says in his own name, Pausanias and Agathon belong to the few who are erotically successful but are endangered by their lack of piety. And, perhaps, they are by nature males—which implies that by convention they appear to be females. This is natural, for they were notorious for their softness, their womanish behavior. And there is another little joke—the name Pausanias ends in *as,* and according to Aristophanes' *Clouds* names ending in *as* bespeak a female nature. To come back to the main point: only those who are by nature males can be full devotees of eros, the fulfillment of eros, the regained unity; this goes together with lofty thoughts, which as such are directed toward dethroning the gods, and this is particularly a male affair. From this it would seem that the restoration of our ancient nature is possible.

> "But, regardless of this, I am speaking of all men and women, in saying that in this way our race would be happy, if we should complete our eros and each one, in obtaining his own beloved, should go back to his ancient nature. And if this is the best, it is necessary that in the present that which is nearest to it is the best; and this is to obtain a beloved who is naturally to one's mind." (193c2–8)

He speaks here explicitly of men and women but by the use of this word *beloveds (paidika),* which means predominantly male favorites, a preponderance of the pederastic thought remains. The return to the original nature proves now to be a utopia. It is the best in itself but at present is not available. Only the closest approximation to it is the best possible as matters stand. And what is that best possible? To find not one's natural male alter ego, if you are a natural male, but a youth whose nature is in accordance with your mind—your taste, one could almost say.

> "If we should hymn the god who is the cause of this, we would justly be hymning Eros, who in the present benefits us the most, by leading us into our own, and holds out for the future the greatest hopes: if we show piety toward the gods, he will by his restoration of our ancient nature and healing of us make us blessed and happy." (193c8–d5)

This phrase "into our own" will prove to be in Socrates' speech the key problem. Aristophanes will prove to have said ultimately that love is essentially love of one's own, but there is an entirely different understanding of love, according to which love is the love of the beautiful, and this will come out in Agathon's speech. Socrates is going to side with Agathon, but, in contradistinction to Agathon, Socrates knows that the other love, love of one's own, also exists and is important. In other words, the issue of incest is only a comic exaggeration of the love of one's own. The practically important form of the love of one's own is patriotism, the love of your fellow citizens and, therefore, of your polis. Love of one's own is in necessary tension with love of the beautiful, which does not recognize boundaries. What the conclusion amounts to is that there is hope that eros may perpetuate this second best—you are united with someone who is to your mind by nature, but he is not your own by nature. Eros may perpetuate this second best after death, or perhaps make us find our natural alter ego after death. These hopes for the future, as distinguished from what is possible now, depend on piety. Erotic fulfillment as sexual gratification does not depend on the gods, but in itself, as original unity, it will be prevented by the gods. The conclusion would be that bliss and happiness could be supplied by eros alone if we could deceive the gods so that they would not prevent the restoration of the original unity.

I would like to make a few general remarks about Aristophanes' speech: In reading Aristophanes' speech one gets the impression that there remains nothing for man but, at best, homosexual gratification and a vain longing beyond it, accompanied by the fear of the Olympian gods, whom Aristophanes despises. This heterogeneous mixture takes the place of the original oneness, of the lofty thoughts that go with the original oneness. Man's origin from the sun remains ineffective and forgotten because there is no theoria, no contemplation. Piety is needed because of the unsatisfactory character of eros and because of the tacit exclusion of contemplation. In other words, eros as a reaction to nomos can never be truly free from nomos.

Eros, as Aristophanes understands it, is longing for a fantastic oneness, for an unnatural oneness. But, as such, it is the most important case of unnatural oneness: it is the nomos. Namely, the law presents itself, if not rightly understood, as something ultimate, which applies equally to all and is just because of this equal validity. But since men are different and human situations are different, the law is inferior in this respect to the wise decisions of wise men on the spot. This is a great theme throughout Plato, but also in that little dialogue, *Minos,* which is an introduction to Plato's *Laws,* where the problem of the spurious oneness of the law is contrasted with genuine oneness.

Aristophanes' notion of original unity is a fantastic and grotesque expression of his concern with nomos, with the polis, which comes out in spite of his concern with nature as the opposite of nomos. What is suggested here can be expressed as follows: eros is concerned with the natural one, but that is the human species, because eros serves procreation. But the preservation of the human species is effected only by heterosexual love. Pederastic, unnatural love reflects satisfaction with the unnatural unity of the nomos. Aristophanes' daring attack on nomos and the gods is harmless because it is based on an insufficient understanding of what the issues are— it is a harmless untruth, a harmless evil. But what do we call harmless evil? Ridiculous. Aristophanes' doctrine is, contrary to what he intends, not only amusing but ridiculous.

A word about the connection between the speeches of Eryximachus and Aristophanes, the two central speakers. First the difference: Eryximachus says that eros rules everything, but he is led to say that techne rules everything. Aristophanes is wiser than Eryximachus; he says, as it were, that nomos is the ruler of everything. Now, Eryximachus and Aristophanes are exchangeable, they are identical in the decisive respect. Both say that all love, if not imperfect, is mutual, i.e., the motivations of the partners are identical. There are no different motivations on the part of the lover and the beloved. And another important similarity: Eryximachus ends with a praise of the art of soothsaying; Aristophanes ends with a praise of piety. This implies that according to Eryximachus there can be friendship between gods and men, for there is an art, soothsaying, which brings about that friendship. Aristophanes implies that there cannot be friendship between gods and men, for art and law are weaker than nature. Eryximachus asserts the ultimate supremacy of art, but art, whatever form it takes, is limited by chance. Therefore, what we would wish to have is an art of all arts, an art which controls chance. That is the art of soothsaying, the art which controls the gods. There is some strange corollary in Aristophanes. Eros is desire for union with the alter ego, the other part of yourself. What does this mean? It means that the importance of chance in eros is denied. You know from literature and your own experience that when two people are truly in love they believe it could not have been another person—we were destined for one another. Aristophanes, and this is part of the charm of his speech, makes himself the spokesman of the delusion of eros. What we ultimately seek is something wherein chance does not enter. His inspiration seems also to be under the spell of the delusion; but Aristophanes knows that it is not true: we cannot find the other partner if Apollo was a blunderer, as I expect him to be, namely, if he left the other half skinless and it perished. We have, then, no techne, no art for finding the truly other half, and the only way out is piety. In other words, what Plato suggests is, "However ironical you, Aristophanes, might have been regarding piety, if you had been consistent you would have been seriously pious."

To summarize: Plato comedizes, if I may say so; he makes Aristophanes the subject of a comedy, just as Aristophanes made Socrates an object of comedy. Plato's tacit claim is that his comedy is much more spiritual and much more refined than the rather crude, if still subtle, comedy of Aristophanes. Plato apparently makes a mere caricature of Aristophanes, just as the *Clouds* at first glance is a mere caricature of Socrates. This becomes especially clear if you compare Aristophanes' speech in Plato with Aristophanes' comedies: there is almost a complete absence of Aristophanes' political concepts from the speech which Plato put into his mouth. In Aristophanes there is a constant political preoccupation, and the standard by which Aristophanes judges the mischief done in Athens in his time is that of the old Athens—the good old times, Marathon fighters, American Legion. Those who were responsible for the greatest glory of Athens are naturally the representatives. The ancestral is the standard for ridiculing the contemporary extreme democracy. The old polity is somehow much more rural than present-day Athens. The old is the more rural, and that means, however, that the pleasures of country life and of peace are identical with the ancient polis, the ancient, stern polity of the Marathon fighters, people living on their farms, large or small, enjoying the pleasures of farm life, wine, and women. Ultimately, then, the standard is private pleasure rather than the glory of the city. There proves to be a tension even between that private pleasure and the glory of the city, a tension which is ultimately the same as that between nature and convention. In other words, Plato's silence on the political orientation of Aristophanes is based on the profound understanding of what is really going on in the Aristophanean comedies. The other striking feature about Aristophanes is the massive indecency and obscenity with which his comedies abound. That again is beautifully represented by Plato in the pansexualist Weltanschauung which Plato imputes to Aristophanes in his speech. The link between men and gods is sexual latitude. The purpose of the erect stature of man is to see the partner in amorous embrace and not be reduced to the situation of the brutes. Furthermore, Aristophanes attacked Socrates in the *Clouds* in the name of piety. Aristophanes' speech in Plato culminates in what looks like a praise of piety, but, if carefully considered, not Socrates but Aristophanes is the impious man. Aristophanes' impiety is linked up with his sexualism, if I may say so, by the fact that his impiety is the core of eros as he understands it, since eros is essentially rebellion against the gods.

Aristophanes' attack on Socrates is an attack on philosophy, on the supremacy of the mind. Aristophanes therefore presents eros as incompatible with the mind. Eros is the desire for becoming merely cosmic again. Aristophanes says in his speech that the Olympian gods are the origin of civility and are despicable, given the contrast between claim and fulfillment. They are not even, let alone that they should be, venerable. The cosmic gods, on the other hand, are, as understood by Aristophanes, akin to what we would call chaos. His position can be stated as follows: The Olympian gods are despicable; they are not the cosmic gods but are akin to nous and are the origin of civility. Now this much about Aristophanes.

Listener: Does Aristophanes ever mention pleasure in his speech?

Mr. Strauss: That is a very good question. I am sorry to say I can't answer that. I haven't watched for it.

[In answer to a question:] There are two different elements here in what you say. What I said was that Plato speaks of recollection, i.e., man had an original state of perfect vision of the ideas, which he has lost. But he lives on that recollection. Similarly, Aristophanes speaks of an original state of perfection which man has lost. The difference is this: for Plato, recollection is of an original vision; for Aristophanes, the desire for reunion is for a condition in which a vision would be impossible. There is a parallel, but it only points out the radical antagonism. The fact that Plato can also speak of the highest love as love of one's own is true. But love of one's own is not meant as love of *x* or *y* but of that in you which is no longer the individual individuality. Plato can very well say that this is the true self, but that true self is, to use later language, not the empirical self. In the simpler term love of one's own means the love of the whole being in his individuality and his relatives in the widest sense. This means a scission not of the individual, but of mankind into different groups, each with an interest of its own. The love of one's own in this sense is radically different from the love of the beautiful which transcends this scission and boundaries. You see, involuntarily one discovers the inner layer of meaning just in trying to speak about it, without any malice aforethought. The scission in Aristophanes can remind us of the true scission of the human race into independent states, societies, cultures. It is perfectly possible that this was implied in Aristophanes' speech.

The greatest individual in this dialogue, apart from Socrates himself, and disregarding for a moment Alcibiades, is Aristophanes. His speech has more power and more imagination. On the other hand, while Aristophanes is the greatest individual, his speech is not the highest of the pre-Socratic speeches. Agathon, who is womanish, soft, and what have you, is higher, not as an individual but in what he says. Therefore, in the end, when they are all knocked out, the one who survives, apart from Socrates, is Agathon, not Aristophanes. Aristophanes holds out longer than anyone else but not as long as Agathon. Aristophanes has seen a great truth, which no one has brought out as clearly and as forcefully as he does, and that is love of one's own—but that appears only later, when Socrates comes up. This is deliberately suppressed in the *Symposium*. For a full understanding of the phenomenon of love, the way Plato understood it, both would have to be recognized, but I still believe, with this important proviso: that the love of one's own is lower than the love of the beautiful. When Socrates occasionally says he likes to talk to fellow citizens and strangers but has somehow greater interest in his fellow citizens, that's it. Man is a composite of heterogeneous elements even though he is a unity. This is particularly clearly visible in the polis. In the polis it is writ large, as he says in the *Republic*. But what is true of the polis is also true of man as an individual—he is a composite of heterogeneous things limited to a very special place, like a brute in a way but open to all, which no brute is. Man consists of both elements in such a way that most of the time, against nature, the lower takes precedence. You can state it without paradox by using Aristotle's sober formulation: our nature is slavish in many ways. Figure out how much time you use every day for the lower needs compared to what you use for the higher needs. The terrible thing is the inversion of the order: the lower is more urgent than the higher, that is the human situation. If we disregard any of this we get a distorted picture of man.

[In answer to a question:] We must not forget this, Plato tried to treat love in a dialogue and that means essentially and deliberately an incomplete one-sided treatment, not only in individual speeches but in the dialogue as a whole. A full understanding of the dialogue would imply an understanding of what is deliberately omitted. Plato was not a blunderer. But it is important not only that Plato was not a blunderer but that we not be blunderers. For practical purposes no one would agree more than Plato that eros must be controlled by law, but the question is whether there is not something lost in that. Everyone who does not say that moral virtue is the highest consideration admits by implication that there must be something in eros as the essence of man which cannot be satisfied that way. What Plato means is that the natural inclination does not go toward moral virtue as moral virtue. But in a crude, practical way, for the legislator this is a sound position to take. The problem of the legislator is to control eros and regulate it, not to understand its full message.

Let us go on then to the transition to Agathon's speech. But first the end of Aristophanes' speech.

> "Here," he said, "Eryximachus, you have my logos about Eros, different from yours. So, just as I asked you, don't make a comedy of it, in order that we may hear the rest, what each will say, but rather what each of the two [will say], for Agathon and Socrates are left." (193d6–e2)

You see Aristophanes' self-confidence. You, Eryximachus, and I have nothing in common. His ironical request that Eryximachus not ridicule his speech is, of course, particularly funny for the reader, since Plato had comedized Aristophanes. Aristophanes' view is that Agathon and Socrates belong together. This is quite natural since Agathon was allied to Euripides, and Euripides and Socrates were allied, and this triumvirate is an object of Aristophanes' mockery in his comedies. Aristophanes ignores poor Aristodemus, who came prior to Agathon in the order of sitting. Perhaps it is Aristophanes' fault that Aristodemus does not speak.

> "Well, I shall obey you," he said Eryximachus said, "for your speech was for me a pleasure. And if I did not know that Socrates and Agathon were skilled in the erotic things, I would be very much afraid that they would be at a loss on account of the variety of the many things that have been said, but as it is I am confident all the same." (193e3–7)

Eryximachus is the judge. You remember he made it clear, prior to Aristophanes' speech, that Aristophanes had to be responsible to him, Eryximachus. Now, in a way, Aristophanes has acted responsibly to Eryximachus. He expresses again what he believes to be a unanimous view. You remember in the beginning when they deliberated about what to do with the evening, there was also a unanimous view expressed by Eryximachus. But this time Eryximachus does not wait for the others to express their approval. Why? How does he know that the others liked the speech? How could they have expressed their approval of Aristophanes' speech? By laughter. Should Socrates have joined in the laughter? Eryximachus is the first speaker in this interlude. We are reminded of the preponderant role he played in the beginning. We note that his speech was the center speech in the speeches prior to Socrates, and this is not insignificant. I remind you only that behind Eryximachus there is a great philosophical doctrine, the doctrine of Empedocles, and this doctrine—which says that eros rules the whole—is ultimately the target of Plato's doctrine of eros. According to Plato this is not true and we shall find the reasons later on. You see that Eryximachus changes the order: he puts Socrates in the first place. Socrates and Agathon are somehow exchangeable.

> Then Socrates said, "The reason is, Eryximachus, that you yourself have competed beautifully; but if you should be where I am now or rather, perhaps, where I shall be when Agathon too speaks well, then you would be very afraid and at total risk, as I am now." (194a1–4)

Socrates praises here Eryximachus's speech; he does not praise Aristophanes' speech. This shows again the special significance of Eryximachus's speech. The remark here recalls a parallel in the dialogue *Critias* (108c5–6), in which there is a similar scene where Critias says, "You are posted on the last rung of the speakers and therefore courageous." Here, Socrates is posted on the last rung.

[Tape change.]

Did not Plato deliberately arrange the dialogue in such a way so as to prevent legitimate criticism of Socrates' speech? We must see whether this is true.

> "You want to bewitch me, Socrates," Agathon said, "in order that I be thrown into confusion on account of my belief that the audience *[theatron]* has great expectations that I will speak well." (194a5–7)

In other words, he suspects Socrates of a slightly unfair trick. He links up this exchange of speeches with his contest regarding tragedy. Unwittingly he tells us that hearers of the speeches must also be lookers-on [*theatron* means the place of seeing], lookers at the speakers.

> "In that case, Agathon, I would be forgetful," Socrates said, "if—though I saw your manliness and greatness of pride when you went up on the plat-

form with the actors, and with a glance straight out at so large an audience
when you were about to make an exhibition of your own speeches, and
you were not at all baffled—I should believe that now you will be in confusion on account of a few human beings like us.'" (194a8–b5)

In other words, You, Agathon, who had the courage to appear on the stage
in your own play, will not be afraid to address us few fellows.

"What, Socrates?" Agathon said. "You surely don't believe I am so full of
the audience that I am not aware that for a man of intelligence a few who
are sensible are more to be feared that the many who are senseless."

"Well, in that case, Agathon, should I imagine there was anything un-
refined about you, it wouldn't be a fine thing for me to do; I know well
that should you meet up with some who you believe are wise, you would
have greater regard for them than for the many. But I am afraid we are not
they—we too were present there and were of the many—though if you
should meet up with others who are wise, perhaps you would be ashamed
before them, should you perhaps believe that you were doing something
shameful."

"You speak the truth," he said.

"But would you not be ashamed before the many should you believe
you were doing something shameful?"

And he said that Phaedrus interrupted and said, "My dear Agathon, if
you answer Socrates, it will no longer make any difference to him how any
of the things here turn out, only provided he has anyone to converse with,
especially if he is beautiful. I myself would listen with pleasure to Socrates'
conversation, but it is necessary for me to take care of the encomium to
Eros and to receive from each one of you the logos; so let each of you render his due to the god and then on this condition go on conversing."

"Well, Phaedrus, you speak well," Agathon said. "There's nothing to
prevent me from speaking, for it will be possible at many other times to
converse with Socrates." (194b6–e3)

Phaedrus thinks that Socrates and Agathon will have their dialogue immediately after their speeches, and Agathon thinks that he and Socrates will
have their dialogue frequently hereafter. Who is the better diviner of the
two? The main point, however, is the fourfold reference to conversation.
Now, what is the meaning of this interlude? As you know, it is not the first
interlude. The first interlude came prior to Eryximachus's speech and was
due to Aristophanes' incapacitation. In the course of the evening, with the
progressive exhaustion of the subject, the general incapacitation increases,
not only the particular one of Aristophanes. There is a general incapacity

for long speeches. When people are too tired to make long speeches, they are not too tired to make conversation, engage in dialogue. The dialogues come in as a mere substitute for long speeches. This, however, is changed with Socrates' speech, which is, as it were, nothing but a dialogue, although it claims to be a speech. The first interludes were the dialogues between Eryximachus and Aristophanes. They dealt with Aristophanes' ridiculous bodily handicap, of which Aristophanes himself was in no way ashamed. The present interlude is chiefly a dialogue between Socrates and Agathon—Aristophanes is completely silent—and it deals with fear of disgrace, as distinguished from hiccups. Agathon and Socrates claim to have fear of disgrace, and this is a natural introduction to the subject of the beauty of eros. But Socrates and Agathon only claim to have such fear; in fact they don't fear it. Yet only Agathon is found out, as you have seen. Agathon walks into the trap which Socrates had set. There was no reason for Agathon to speak at this point in the presence of Socrates. Agathon becomes ridiculous; his beauty, his grace, his charm, is somewhat spurious. He is a beautiful young man, as we have seen, and, as we will see later, with a not so beautiful inside, contrasted with the ugly, oldish Socrates with a beautiful inside. Perhaps this applies to their speeches too. We must also consider this, and this is a good introduction to Agathon's speech: nowhere in the dialogue do we find perfect beauty. It is always tainted, if only by a snub nose. Now we turn to Agathon's speech.

> "I want first to speak of how I must speak, and then speak. All those who have spoken before seem to me not to be praising the god but blessing human beings for the goods for which the god is responsible; but as to what sort he himself is in bestowing these gifts, no one has spoken. There is one correct manner of every praise for everything, to go through in speech, whomever the speech is about, and say in being of what sort he is in fact the cause of what sort of things. So too in the case of Eros, it is just for us to praise him first as to what sort he is, and then his gifts." (194e4–195a5)

As it appears in the Greek, Agathon is the only one who begins with an emphatic I—*ego*. Naturally, he is beautiful and successful and he knows it. He makes the distinction between how one ought to speak and when one speaks. To speak of how one ought to speak is not truly to speak. Is this intelligible? For example, if you have a methodology of the social sciences, do you say anything about social phenomena? In a way you are silent. There is a formality about it which is empty. It would be different in one case: if the art of how to speak were the other side of psychology, knowledge of the soul; then the science of how to speak would be full of content. This is, of course, Plato's notion of rhetoric: it is only the doctrine of the soul viewed from the point of view of how to influence or persuade other people.

Aristophanes had blamed all earlier human beings for not having worshiped Eros; Agathon blames only all earlier speakers tonight. From this point of view he is much more modest. He certainly is no revolutionary, as Aristophanes was, an iconoclast. Iconoclasm is incompatible with beauty. I cannot always repeat that the latitude of the Greek word *kalon*—which is beautiful, fair, respectable—includes everything resplendent for the eyes or the mind. In Agathon's speech for the first time the god himself becomes the theme, not as something existing merely in the soul of man, but as self-subsistent, and the question is raised, Of what quality is the god? Aristophanes almost touched on that. He spoke of the power of eros and the nature of man. He did not speak of the nature of eros; he did not even speak of that quality of eros which Agathon refers to. We have to raise this question: Will Agathon discuss the nature of eros or only his quality? You see also in the way Agathon speaks that it is a very orderly speech, with an orderly beginning. A universal statement on every kind of praise, regarding every possible thing. Then the application: this and this is the right way to praise anything. But now we are supposed to praise eros, and this is the right way for praising eros in particular. The gifts of eros—that means that of which eros is the cause—is a metaphoric expression.

> "I assert that though all the gods are happy, Eros, if sacred right permits it and it is not offensive to say so, is the happiest of them, being the most beautiful and the best." (195a5–7)

This gives the plan of his speech. First, Eros's qualities: *(a)* the most beautiful; *(b)* the best. Second, Eros as cause of things outside of himself. The whole speech of Agathon is characterized by an unusually clear order. This has very much to do with beauty, because clear order is an element of beauty. But he does not raise the primary question, namely, What is eros? What is its essence, its nature? This will be done only in Socrates' speech. His praise of Eros is necessarily a critique of the other gods. His very excuse, "if . . . it is not offensive to say so," indicates that there is some prima facie reason for offense; otherwise he would never say that. The other gods are all less than perfect regarding both beauty and goodness; otherwise Eros could not be the most beautiful and the best.

> "Being most beautiful he is of the following sort. First, he is the youngest of gods, Phaedrus. He himself offers great evidence to the logos, avoiding

by flight old age, though it is plainly swift, for it approaches us at any rate faster than it should. It is that which Eros has a nature to hate and not to come even within hailing distance of." (195a7–b4)

We all believe, we older people, that we get old too fast.

"He is always with the young and is himself young, for the old logos holds good: like always draws near to like." (195b4–5)

The first subdivision regarding Eros's beauty is his youthfulness, proven by the fact that Eros is always with the young and runs away from the old. This of course does not yet prove that he is the youngest of the gods. What Agathon implies is that Eros is wholly young, young in every respect. Therefore, he is the youngest. His youthfulness would be defective if he were not the youngest. This is a very Platonic way of looking at it. The idea of beauty is the most beautiful thing there is. You can bring out the paradox by saying, in un-Platonic terms: the concept of beauty is the most beautiful thing in the world; the concept of justice is the most just thing in the world. Plato surely says that beauty itself, as distinguished from any particular manifestation of beauty, is the most beautiful. (This means, of course, that Plato's ideas are not concepts.) All other gods are older than Eros, but if oldness is deficient beauty, that means that all other gods are more or less ugly, or at least not perfectly beautiful. Only love of similar for the similar— the theme of pederasty as we have seen. But this is not used by Agathon for this purpose; he does not make a defense of pederasty.

"Though I agree with Phaedrus on many points I don't agree with him on this, that Eros is older than Cronus and Iapetus; but I assert that he is the youngest of gods and ever young, and the ancient business about gods, which Hesiod and Parmenides speak of, happened, if they were telling the truth, by Necessity and not by Eros. Otherwise, there would not have been castrations, any more than bindings of one another and many other violent things, if Eros were among them, but there would have been friendship and peace, just as there now is, since the time that Eros has been king of the gods." (195b6–c6)

He refers to Phaedrus and says that he agrees with him in many things. What things, he doesn't tell us. Does he grant, for example, that eros is not in the beloved? We must see. Agathon disagrees with Hesiod and Parmenides, not with Homer, though Homer, too, speaks of terrible fights among the gods. He does not wish to blame Homer. There is a strange difficulty here since Homer is the oldest poet. Is there not a contrast between the blame of old age and the praise of Homer? Originally, he says, Necessity ruled over the gods, now Eros rules over the gods. This means that Zeus is not the king of the gods, but Eros. If the stories told by Hesiod and Parmenides are true, Eros vanquished Necessity. Yet Eros is the youngest god; he cannot always have ruled. Hence, Necessity must have ruled prior to Eros. Hence, the stories told by Hesiod and Parmenides are true. The gods, other than Eros, lack virtue. Agathon tacitly opposes Aristophanes, who implied that Necessity is stronger than Eros. The implication is familiar: savage beginnings, progress; first Necessity, then progress to civility and peace. The good is not identical with the old, as Phaedrus implied and no one, not even Aristophanes, contested. On the contrary, Aristophanes said the oldest is the best. Agathon, in contesting this, brings himself closer to Socrates. It is a Platonic doctrine that the beginnings were savage: if anyone doubts it he need only read the third book of Plato's *Laws*. But Aristophanes contested already the assertion that Eros is the oldest. Implicitly this means that there is a progress of enlightenment, a progress of progress in the speech. First, Eros is the oldest god; then, according to Aristophanes, Eros is younger than the Olympian gods; then, according to Agathon, Eros is explicitly said to be the youngest god; finally, according to Socrates, eros is not a god at all. There is a constant demotion, parallel with an increase of praise.

If Eros is the oldest god, Eros affects all things—all things love. Eros is not specifically human, as Eryximachus had said. If, however, Eros is not the oldest god then it is not necessary that all things love. Agathon will get to that later. In the sequel Agathon pursues the theme of Eros's beauty by speaking of his tenderness or delicacy. It is obvious that if you want to praise the beauty of someone it is not sufficient to say "young." We have seen young people who were not beautiful.

> "Now he is young, and in addition to young, tender; and he needs a poet such as Homer was to show the tenderness of a god. Homer says that Ate is a goddess and tender—her feet at any rate are tender—saying,
> 'Her feet, however, are tender, for she does not draw near
> To the ground, but lo! she walks on the heads of men.'
> He seems to me to show her tenderness by a fine proof, in saying that she walks not on the rough, but on the soft. So we shall use the same piece of evidence about Eros, that he is tender. He does not go on the earth, or even on skulls, which are hardly soft; he goes and dwells in the softest of the things that are. He has settled his abode in the characters and souls of gods and human beings, and not in all souls in succession; but whatever

soul he encounters with a rough character, he goes away from it, and
whatever soul he encounters with a soft character, he takes up residence
there. So if he is always touching with his feet and everywhere the softest
of the softest, it is a necessity that he be most tender. So he is youngest and
tenderest and, besides this, fluid in respect to his shape *[eidos]*." (195c6–
196a2)

You see the praise of Homer. Yet Homer did not praise Eros, he praised
Ate, the goddess of mischief, an avenging god. The old gods, as seen by the
old poets, are basically avenging gods. Homer did not praise a male god in
this way but a female god, and he didn't praise in this way love but mischief.
Homer conceived of eros as something much sterner than the soft, modern
Agathon does. With due euphemism, the elegant Agathon suggests that
the oldest of all poets could not have done justice to the youngest of all
gods. Only the youngest poet, who is in his way eternally young, can do
this, probably by means of cosmetics. In the thought of the ancients, Ate,
the daughter of Zeus, occupies the place which in the thought of the mod-
erns is occupied by Eros. You know this phenomenon: the softening of
manners. Agathon transforms Ate into Eros, something not beautiful into
something beautiful. There is a parallel to that in Aristophanes' speech. For
Aristophanes, the god who solves the riddle of the human soul is Hephaestus, the limping god who, in addition, was deceived by his wife.

In Agathon the world of beauty rules unimpaired. Homer places the
softness of Ate only in her feet, not in her whole being. Here, too, Agathon
improves. Homer, in the nineteenth book of the *Iliad,* continues, when
speaking of Ate, "she who damages or hurts human beings." This is completely suppressed by our refined poet. Eros walks only on delicate, soft
things—on souls—and only on some; he walks on the softest of the soft, on
the souls of the soft. Souls are the softest of beings; souls as souls are soft.
Characters which are somehow made out of souls may be hard or soft, but
the souls as souls are soft. Eros does not dwell in the souls of all, he does not
dwell in the souls of harsh gods. Which god is harsher and harder than Ares,
the god of war? And Eros dwells in the soul of Ares. Perhaps Agathon
would say Eros makes Ares soft, but that remains to be seen.

"Otherwise he would not be able to fold himself about everywhere, any
more than he could, if he were rough, be unobserved in entering every
soul and exiting it. His gracefulness is a great piece of evidence for his
commensurate and fluid form *[idea]*, and this is agreed upon by all to be
something that Eros has to an exceptional degree, for there is always a mutual war between gracelessness and Eros. The god's way of life among

flowers signifies the beauty of his complexion, for Eros does not settle in a flowerless body and soul, or in anything else whatsoever that has faded and lost its bloom; but wherever there is a place of flowers and sweet odors, there he settles and remains. Now about the beauty of the god these things suffice, but still much is omitted." (196a2–b5)

He makes here a clear division, and in the next section he will speak of the virtue of the god. Now let us see what he has said in this section. The beauty of tenderness and the beauty of something which we can translate as pliancy—the word means literally wet, fluid, and therefore also pliant, of languishing shape. *Eidos,* shape, which is the word for the Platonic idea, occurs here only in the sense of visible shape. The *eidos,* the essence, of Eros himself does not become the theme of Agathon. Because he is so pliant he can pass through every soul, for every soul as soul is soft. This constitutes the symmetry of Eros. He makes himself symmetrical. His symmetry is his whole pliancy. By being pliable he is also pliable to the measureless, to the dissolute. Surely Agathon does not make any distinction between noble and base eros. Next is Eros's beauty of color or complexion. Since he dwells among souls of beautiful color he must possess beautiful color. Incidentally, *Flower* was the title of a tragedy by Agathon. Aristotle speaks of it in his *Poetics* (1451b21).

Now let us summarize what Agathon says about the beauty of Eros: Beauty here is the beauty of the body of Eros. He is young, delicate, of a pliant shape, and of beautiful color. If we look at Greek concepts of beauty in Aristotle's *Rhetoric,* we find that there are also two other elements of bodily beauty which Agathon omits: strength and size. Eros is neither strong nor large. Furthermore, even if we add to Agathon's four qualities the two qualities of strength and size, these qualities would not be sufficient for making a human being beautiful. A strong man of proper size who is young, delicate, of a pliant shape, and of beautiful color is not yet for these reasons beautiful as a human being; the proportions are missing. We note to our surprise that there is not a word said about a human shape of Eros in a passage dealing with Eros's bodily beauty. One could say that Eros, as described by Agathon, has the beauty of a serpent or a butterfly rather than the beauty of a human shape. Of course, as he said at the end of the speech, the enumeration of the beautiful qualities of Eros is not complete and perhaps he would have mentioned also the human beauty of Eros. However, it is strange that in what he did say nothing suggests the human shape.

There is a transition now from Eros's beauty to Eros's goodness or virtue. This means one thing: virtue is not beautiful, for beauty means beauty of the body. There is a peculiar parallelism between the praise of Eros's beauty and the praise of Eros's goodness. We have four qualities of beauty and four virtues: in beauty we have youth, delicacy, pliancy, and beautiful color; in goodness we have justice, moderation, courage, and wisdom. The question would be whether there is any meaning to that parallelism, or are they perhaps opposites? I would suggest that you look at a parallel in another Platonic dialogue, the first book of Plato's *Laws* (631b ff.), where you find a similar parallelism of the virtues of the body and the virtues of the soul. There we have a strict correspondence of the two.

> "After this one must speak about the virtue of Eros. The greatest is that Eros neither commits injustice against a god or human being nor suffers injustice at the hands of a god or human being." (196b5–7)

Agathon is very far from denying what Aristophanes had said, that he was the most philanthropic god. Not justice is the greatest but the combination of justice and immunity from injustice. If you do not do injustice to others and at the same time you cannot be hurt by others, this is the most desirable condition.

> "Neither does he suffer anything by violence, if he suffers anything—for violence does not touch Eros—nor does he in acting act [by violence]— for everyone serves Eros in everything voluntarily, and whatever one agrees to voluntarily with someone who is willing, the laws of the city say is just." (196b7–c3)

As we have seen, Eros rules over the gods, and the laws are the king of the city. Is there a connection between these two ruler-ruled relationships? There is a difficulty, for Eros's rule is gentle, the rule of law not necessarily gentle.

> "In addition to justice, he partakes in the greatest portion of moderation. To hold the upper hand *[kratein]* over pleasures and desires is agreed to be moderation, but [it is agreed] no pleasure is stronger *[kreitton]* than Eros; and if they are weaker, they would be mastered *[kratoito]* by Eros, and he would have the upper hand *[kratoi]*, and in mastering *[kraton]* pleasures and desires Eros would be exceptionally moderate." (196c3–8)

I trust you see the difficulty of this argument: uncontrollable desire is moderation and temperance.

> "And further, in point of manliness, 'not even Ares resists' Eros. For Ares does not have Eros, but Eros has Ares—[eros] of Aphrodite—as is the

story, and he who has is stronger *[kreitton]* than him who is had, and in prevailing *[kraton]* over him who is more manly than anyone else, he would be the most manly of all. Now about the justice, moderation, and manliness of the god it has been stated, but it is left [to speak about] wisdom.'" (196c8–d5)

You see the emphasis on the orderly path all the time. What about this argument about Eros's courage of manliness? This is as weak, I take it, as the preceding argument: a very great coward of the greatest pliancy could control the bravest very well without being the bravest. With a view to the later developments of the speech, it is important to observe that when he speaks of the love of Ares he says, "Eros . . . has Ares," to which he adds, "the eros of Aphrodite, as is the story." Eros is a self-subsisting being; but then the eros of Aphrodite is not a self-subsisting being but something in Ares. In the first case eros is something outside of Ares and keeps him; in the other case eros is something in Ares. This will be very important later on. The word in Greek is *sophia,* and Agathon adds, "So, as far as possible, I must try to omit nothing." The account of Eros's wisdom will be as complete as Agathon can make it. The previous accounts were not so complete.

"So, as far as possible, I must try to omit nothing. And first, in order that I too, in turn, may honor our art, as Eryximachus did his own, the god is so wise a poet as to make another a poet as well; everyone at any rate becomes a poet, 'even if he is un-music before,' whomever Eros touches. It is fitting that we use this as a witness to the effect that Eros is a good poet in general in all poetry that involves music, for whatever one does not have or does not know, he would neither give to another nor teach another." (196d6–e6)

Agathon praises his art, techne, as Eryximachus did his. He does not praise his muse, as Aristophanes did, which was connected with the fact that in Aristophanes' speech the intellectual part of man is played down. Therefore he spoke of the Muse (189b7), something inspiring and not rational as an art is. Eros is wise in the first place because he is a poet and one who makes others poetic. You will see that Agathon does not say that eros is indispensable for poetry. He does not say that all poets become poets through eros. On the contrary: all men, including all nonpoetic men, become poets under the influence of eros, not the other way around. This reminds us of Phaedrus's speech in the beginning, where Phaedrus made a distinction between those who are by nature best and who are imitated in a lesser way by those who are inspired by eros. Those who are by nature best are brave.

When the greatest cowards while in love behave in the presence of their beloved like the brave, they are not truly brave. To repeat this point: Agathon does not say that eros is indispensable for poetry, but eros may incite people to become poetic.

> "And furthermore, who will object, in the case of the making *[poiesis]* of all animals, and deny that this is the wisdom of Eros by which all animals come to be and are born?'" (196e6–197a3)

Again he uses the word *poiesis,* which underlies the word *poetry* and which, literally, means making, producing. The first form of producing was poetry in the ordinary sense; the second is the making of all living beings, all animals. In the wide sense this includes man. Eros is effective in generation. Agathon tacitly excludes pederasty. There is no coming into being, no emergence of any living beings prior to eros. You remember, he had said before there was a rule of compulsion. There could not have been generation then. In particular, the gods could not have come into being by generation through parents because eros is the youngest of the gods. What about the gods then? Were they always, or if not, how did they come into being? Agathon does not answer this question, for it is only with one god, with Eros, that he is concerned. Eros was not always, for he is the youngest god. He was surely not generated by parents. This is not surprising because Phaedrus had said in the beginning that nothing is known of Eros's parents, and no one had contested that. You will remember that Agathon said he agrees with many things that Phaedrus had said but did not say with which. One of them is that eros has no parents.

Every generation by parents presupposes eros, but where does Eros himself come from? That's the question. And this becomes the question for the first time here again. It was for a moment the question in Phaedrus's speech, when he quoted the verse from Hesiod saying that eros emerged first together with the earth, and that was superseded by the words of Parmenides, in which genesis, coming into being, produced eros first. Coming into being was given as the cause of eros. The question comes up again now of the cause of eros. Let us continue now with the third and final sign of Eros's wisdom.

> "And in the case of the craftsmanship of the arts, don't we know that of whomever this god is the teacher, he turns out noteworthy and brilliant, but whomever Eros does not touch, obscure? Apollo, moreover, discovered archery, medicine, and divination when desire and eros led the way, so that he too would be a pupil of Eros. And the Muses of music, He-

phaestus of forging, Athena of weaving, and Zeus 'to pilot gods and human beings.'" (197a3–b3)

Eros is wise, thirdly, in being the inspirer of (literally by putting his hand on) the arts. Fame in any art is due to one's being touched by eros. For example, fame in poetry as distinguished from poetry itself. You see that poetry is mentioned twice in two different contexts. The emphasis now is on fame. Agathon mentions only gods who became famous in the arts, not men. These gods became famous in the arts because they were led by desire and eros; desire and eros are used synonymously. Eros is desire, but no one ever said desire is a god or goddess. He mentions five gods and seven arts; the central art is the musical art. This is intelligible, so that we may better see the contrast between what he says here about music arts, poetry in particular, and what he said before regarding poetry. Poetry, as distinguished from fame for poetry, does not require eros. The central god of the five gods is Hephaestus. Love for whom makes Hephaestus famous in his art? Love for his wife, Aphrodite? Hephaestus is also famous for his wife Aphrodite's love for Ares. Did Aphrodite and Ares become famous as inventors by virtue of their love? Did they become famous as inventors at all? There is something new coming up here which has never occurred before and that is a new kind of eros. Eros not as erotic desire strictly understood but as love of fame, which will come out in the immediate sequel. You see also in passing that, contrary to Aristophanes, Agathon conceives of eros as a civilizing force; it was eros which inspired the invention of the arts. Eros is not directed toward that ancient nature, toward that aboriginal state antedating all arts. Eros is in harmony with civility or civilization.

The last god mentioned was Zeus. Through eros Zeus learned to rule gods and men. Zeus rules men too. But the cities are ruled by laws. What is the relation between the rule of Zeus, which in itself goes back to the rule of eros, on the one hand, and the rule of laws, on the other? Zeus rules gods and men, but eros rules Zeus. But if Zeus ruled the gods, he rules also Eros. Did Eros teach Zeus how to rule him, Eros, or is Eros not a god at all? This would be another way to solve the difficulty.

> "It's from him also that the affairs of the gods were arranged when Eros came to be among them—clearly the eros of beauty, for there is no eros for ugliness. Previously, as I said at the beginning, many dreadful things occurred among the gods, as it is said, on account of the kingship of Necessity; but once this god was born, from the loving of the beautiful things all goods have come to be for gods and men.'" (197b3–9)

Since eros taught Zeus to rule gods and men, there arose friendship and peace among the gods. Must the gods rule men so that there can be peace among the gods. Are men absorbed into the gods or vice versa? The most important point here: eros is no longer an absolute, an absolute in the very simple sense, like a tree. Eros is eros of—of beauty. You see also that Agathon now explicitly grants the truth of the stories told by Hesiod and Parmenides. But the most important point: peace and friendship arose among the gods not since eros ruled as a king, as was said before, but since eros came into being or sprang forth; his kingly rule is coeval with his being. Eros came into being or sprang forth—from what or through what? Out of nothing and through nothing? Then he is nothing. And, in a way, this is true: he is nothing as a self-subsisting being. We have seen some changes: from Eros as a self-subsisting being, i.e., a god, to eros as an activity of the soul, or as something directed toward—toward the beautiful. As a god Eros is nothing. But he is most powerfully in the soul, hence he has no human shape, for instance. As a self-subsisting being Eros is nothing. Yet we speak of him as a self-subsisting being. In a way he is a self-subsisting being. In which way? He becomes a self-subsisting being through poetry, through tragic poetry. For poetry as poetry precedes eros and eros rules Zeus. More simply: the other gods presuppose eros, for they have parents. Their self-subsistence breaks down with Eros's self-subsistence.

Eros is eros of beauty. More precisely—the verbal expression in 197b8, "from the loving of the beautiful things"—it is not a being, it is an action. The loving of the beautiful—that is eros. Now we have seen that Agathon uses beautiful, noble—*kalon*—originally only in the sense of bodily beauty, and he never applies this word to the virtues. From this it seems that the love of bodily beauty is the ground for everything good for gods and men. But this expression, "the loving of the beautiful things," has a broader meaning. It may also mean the love of honors. There is a particularly clear passage regarding this usage in the beginning of the third book of Xenophon's *Memorabilia,* where Xenophon says, "In this book I want to discuss how Socrates treated those who were longing for the beautiful things." But this means primarily the people who were ambitious, desirous of honors. Love of honor—ambition—is not merely a by-product of eros, as Phaedrus had said, but a kind of eros, the love of fame. The gods who became famous as artisan artists were indeed inspired by eros, not by eros for bodily beauty but by eros for fame; and that is the difference between Hephaestus, on the one hand, and Ares and Aphrodite, on the other. The latter loved only bodily beauty, so that they did not become famous as inventors, whereas Hephaestus did.

The gods were the originators of civilization. Not, indeed, out of love of mankind, *philanthropia,* but because they loved glory and fame. Agathon is the first speaker to transcend the level of bodily love. Surely, Eryximachus had spoken of art, but this was always as something extraneous to bodily love. Agathon is the first to discern in eros itself a tendency toward something higher than bodily love. Since eros is, on the highest level, love of fame, eros is in harmony with civilization. Through loving beautiful things, he says, which means now no longer bodily beauty but fame above all, all good things have arisen for both gods and men. Namely, via the gods' love of fame. Or was human love perhaps sufficient for the origination of civilization? This we must see in the sequel. Up to this point Agathon had spoken of eros himself, and now he will turn to the gifts of eros, of what eros is the cause.

> "So Eros seems to me, Phaedrus, in being himself the first who is most beautiful and best, to be after this the cause for everyone else of other things of the kind. It occurs to me to say something also in meter, that he is the one who makes
>> 'Peace among human beings, and windless calm for the sea,
>> Repose of the winds and sleep in the midst of care.'"
> (197c1–6)

Eros "being himself the first who is most beautiful and best," there was no goodness and beauty before Eros. He is thereafter responsible for others possessing other suchlike things. Prior to Eros there were no beautiful and good things; the gods themselves were not beautiful and good. Then he gives a poetic expression. It is the one poetic expression on eros occurring in this book. Two verses made by Agathon in honor of eros. They attract our attention for this very reason. Eros causes peace among men. Note that: he doesn't say anything about peace among the gods; he drops that subject. Eros, as human love of fame, would be a sufficient motivation for establishing peace among men. But this limitation to human things is strangely contradicted by the next two items. How can eros as human love be responsible for quieting winds and waves? There are limits to poetic license. There is only one way, and it is fit for a poet to reflect on that: metaphorically. If we compare the human passions, as the poets have always done, to strong winds and waves, then eros as human love can appease them. And then the fourth item is obviously human again. Eros supplies sleep. One could, of course, say that this is not exactly a characteristic effect of eros. You have heard of people who have been kept awake by love of fame and I suppose also by other eros. What is the connection? The lie implied in the metaphoric description of the true effects of eros, namely, that it appeases passions of hatred and this kind of thing, leads to a lie regarding the effects of eros. So that it is a kind of parody of what poetry does with eros, i.e., it goes over from the truth regarding eros—if a limited truth, because one could also question whether eros is simply a peace maker, though it is this to some extent of course. This is, I think, the meaning of these two verses. Whether or not they are good as verses is here not my concern, but they are meaningful in this speech by the poet.

> "It is he who empties us of estrangement, fills us with attachment, arranging for us to come together with one another in all sorts of gatherings of this kind, becoming the leader in festivals, in choruses, in sacrifices; providing gentleness, banishing wildness; the loving giver of amity, no giver of enmity; gracious, good; to the wise spectacular, to the gods wonderful [note the contradistinction of gods and the wise]; to be emulated by the have-nots, to be possessed by the haves; the father of daintiness, delicacy, luxury, grace, desire, longing; caring of the good, careless of the bad; in toil, in fear, in longing, in speech, captain, mariner, excellent fellow warrior, and savior; ornament *[kosmos]* of all gods and human beings together [this implies eros is neither god nor man], most beautiful and best leader [not leader of an army; for Aristophanes, the all-male eros was leader of an army], whom every man must follow, hymning him beautifully, partaking of the song which he sings, enchanting the mind of gods and human beings." (197d1–e5)

The thesis developed here is that eros is simply the good. Not only desire for the good, it is the good. But if this is so, eros—desire—is no desire. This is another expression of the absurdity in deifying eros. If eros is deified he becomes the good and he is no longer desire. And now the concluding remarks:

> "Here you have it, Phaedrus," he said, "the speech from me: let it be dedicated to the god, partly partaking of playfulness, partly of a measured seriousness, to the extent that I am able." (197e6–8)

An amusing play with a proper seriousness. He addresses Phaedrus at the end, and he had done this before. This is meaningful because Phaedrus started the whole thing with the remark voiced through Eryximachus, that the god had never been praised properly by the poets, and what Agathon now says is, I, Agathon, am the poet who has done what according to you no poet has ever done, namely to praise eros properly. I have done my utmost, he says. Pausanias, for example, had only said, I did what I could improvise; and the remarks of Eryximachus and even of Aristophanes are all much more restrained than this remark of Agathon's.

I would now like to give a summary of Agathon's speech and then we may discuss it: The starting point for understanding Agathon's speech is the fact that he is a tragic poet. Somehow he represents tragic poetry, just as Aristophanes represents comic poetry. But he is not as a tragic poet what Aristophanes is as a comic poet. His vanity, his insincerity, his softness and the too obvious and too external beauty of his speech indicate the lower level. The delicacy, not only of eros as he describes him, but also of his own speech on eros has nothing harsh. The souls are the softest of things. Eros harmonizes everything. His speech is, as he says at the end, half playful, free from all passion, because eros, as he presents it, does not constrain any suffering, in contrast to eros as Aristophanes presented it, where there is passion because there is suffering in eros.

Agathon's art is loveless; it is not inspired by eros and yet is enchanting. The sound and the rhythm are beautiful. Shall we then say that he is a degenerate tragic poet, an epigonic tragic poet? Perhaps. This would even be historically correct. One has only to read Aristotle's *Poetics* to get this impression. But Agathon is closer to Socrates than any other speaker. He sits closest to him and he alone is awake at the end together with Socrates, when everyone else is drunk. This applies not only to the fact that he can drink so well but also to his doctrine. It is Agathon who teaches that eros is eros of beauty or the beautiful things. He does not say, as some of the earlier speakers had said, that eros is love of beautiful human beings, or love of opposites, or love of the ancient nature. He is in agreement with Socrates in saying that eros is love of the beautiful and he does not recognize anything superior to eros which is alien to eros.

Secondly, in this brief sentence, when he speaks of eros's wisdom, he says eros is universal among the animals. How sober! He doesn't go as far as Eryximachus, who had said that eros rules everything—even the general phenomena of attraction and repulsion are erotic phenomena—nor does he limit eros, as Aristophanes had done, to human beings alone. You will remember, eros as understood by Aristophanes is a merely human phenomenon.

Thirdly, and this is perhaps the most important point, Agathon is the only one who raises the question regarding eros himself and not only his effects. He does not say, What is eros?, but he comes very close to raising this question. As an epigonic tragic poet he has undergone the influence of philosophy. He cannot take tragedy as seriously as the original tragic poets. But even in his degeneracy tragedy seems to be superior to comedy. How is this intelligible? Agathon praises the arts; he is not a rebel against the law, the nomos, the intellect. Comedy, Aristophanean comedy, is such a rebellion. Agathon is in harmony with civility and civilization, with cosmos. For eros is also, and above all, love of fame. Therefore, the positive presentation of the Olympian gods. The Olympian gods, as the originators of civilization, are praised, contrary to Aristophanes, where they also come up as originators of civilization, but eros is directed against them. Yet Agathon does not believe in the Olympian gods. He is the only one who makes the being of the god his theme. He faces this problem, whereas the others dismiss it. Surely the others don't believe in the Olympian gods, but they don't face the problem. His thesis is that Eros is the youngest god and yet has no parents. He makes the question of his origins more clearly felt.

Eros, as presented by him, has no human shape, though he speaks of his bodily beauty more than anyone else. Eros is nothing self-subsisting: Eros is *eran;* Love is loving. He is the youngest god. The Olympian gods cannot have been generated because they antedate eros. The Olympian gods came into being out of nothing and through nothing, if they are taken as they present themselves. But they were made, they do have an origin. By whom? Answer: by the makers, the poets, the tragic poets. They are the makers of the gods of human shape. They deify what in itself is not divine. They create the gods. Why? Because they are inspired by love of beauty. They idealize man, as we say. They do this out of love of beauty—the human beauty which they see does not satisfy them—and in doing so they raise the stature of man. They visualize something which looks like man but which is deathless and free from any other defect. They create the gods because they are inspired by love of beauty. They are the true founders of civility insofar as they are solemn. The solemnity of tragedy is higher than comedy, which is a rebellion against the gods, an attempt to undo what the tragic poets did.

Tragedy is higher than comedy provided the tragic poet knows what he is doing, provided he himself is free from the spell which he creates, and Agathon is obviously free from that spell. The tragic poet establishes the beautiful delusion, the salutary delusion, which the comic poet destroys. But this superiority of tragedy is not simply true. At the end we shall find a remark to this effect. Both tragedy and comedy are equally necessary. If tragic poetry enchants, comic poetry disenchants. We don't have to go back to Aristophanes; think only of Don Quixote, the whole splendor of knight-errantry. Cervantes raises the low, practical, commonsensical question: did the knights not have clean shirts with them on their trips? This is never mentioned in the books on knight-errantry. Disenchanting, but true. This question must be raised.

Comedy is essentially commonsensical and prosaic, in spite of the verses. There is a fragment of Heraclitus of which one cannot help thinking in this connection. There is one thing and only one thing which is wise, which wishes and does not wish to be called Zeus, i.e., to be seen in human shape. It wishes to be seen, to be called Zeus—tragedy; it does not wish to be called Zeus—comedy, which destroys that. Tragedy, then, is not simply superior to comedy. This superiority in the *Symposium* is due to the particular situation in the *Symposium*.

I will mention one or two points: The *Symposium* is, among other things, Plato's reply to Aristophanes, as I have said before. Aristophanes had attacked Socrates and Euripides in the same breath, and Euripides in his turn was connected with Agathon. But why was there a sympathy between Socrates and Euripides, i.e., tragedy, in the first place? In other words, what is the principle behind the antagonism, the obvious and manifest antagonism between Socrates and Aristophanes which led Aristophanes to attack Socrates? The philosopher is not a tragic figure from the classical point of view, but a comical figure necessarily, because he must appear comical to the nonphilosophers. From the very beginning, in the story of Thales, the first philosopher, he fell into a pit because he looked at the stars; this is surely comical. Concerned with the highest he is foolish as no ordinary human being would be. The philosopher is a comic and not a tragic figure, and therefore he can be presented only in comedy. In the comedy he is necessarily presented from the point of view of the common opinions, i.e., as ridiculous. Comedy is able and compelled, if it takes a sufficiently large view of its field, to attack philosophy. Comedy must present itself as antiphilosophic if it makes full use of its possibilities. Tragedy can never do that. Comedy has to do with the ridiculous in opposition to the serious or the solemn. In fact, tragedy and comedy present both, the ridiculous and the solemn, but in different ways. Comedy presents the serious beneath the ridiculous. What meets the eye is the ridiculous. Tragedy, on the other hand, presents the ridiculous beneath the serious. The first impression is the solemn and serious, the dignified. Philosophy, however, must present itself, because it is the most serious, as dignified, if it is to fulfill its function and not destroy itself. This much for the speech of Agathon and the most obvious suggestions which it leads to.

Before we get to Socrates' speech, are there any questions?

Listener: I am not sure what Agathon says. At one point he seems to say eros is the good, at another point he says it is love of fame.

Mr. Strauss: One must always start from the most massive and obvious. First he says eros is the youngest. But even before that he says how eros himself is, as distinguished from its effects. Therefore, whereas in the former speeches it could legitimately be doubted whether eros is a self-subsisting being or something which is only in other things, in Agathon's speech this can no longer be doubted. It must become the theme. He describes first, at great length, eros as a self-subsisting being. Then, precisely for this reason, the reduction of eros as love to the acts of loving shows the difficulty. The fact that he is the first to speak of eros himself means that he is the first to raise the question almost explicitly whether eros is a self-subsisting being. This is, I think, the crucial point, and one must connect this with the fact that he is a tragic poet. Aristophanes doesn't even suggest that eros is a self-subsisting being. He conceived of eros as rebellion against the Olympian gods. In Agathon there is a perfect harmony between eros and the Olympian gods. The Olympian gods, inspired by eros, by love of fame, are the originators of civilization. How can this be understood? If tragedy, by creating the gods of human shape, lays the foundation for civilization and therefore also limits human life, comedy is the rebellion against this and, therefore, restores the original freedom. In the center of the *Republic,* more or less, there occurs the simile of the cave, in which human life is compared to living in a cave, seeing only shadows of things. Of what do men see shadows in the cave? In the first place, one can show that the cave is also the polis, and this is especially important in our connection. They see the shadows of artifacts, imitating living beings which are carried around the cave. These are the visible gods, created by artisans. This limits the polis, therefore it also makes possible the polis and yet, at the same time, keeps the polis from seeing the truth. Therefore, the men who leave the cave, the philosophers, never see these shadows. This is perhaps the most striking parallel to what I suggested here, to which Agathon comes very close in his own speech.

To repeat: Tragedy and comedy are from Plato's point of view equally necessary and equally problematic. He has indicated in the clearest possible way how problematic they are in the *Republic,* in the famous criticism of poetry in the second and third book and, to some extent, also in the tenth book. But this is really only the crudest political expression of what Plato thinks about poetry. His serious views are, of course, much more favorable to poetry and, therefore, also more particularly to tragedy and comedy.

One could show this, perhaps, in the *Laws,* a political work, very clearly, that, while it is true that poetry is in need of political supervision, censorship—Plato was not a liberal—he knew very well that from another point of view the poet is the teacher of the legislators. The legislator has to learn to understand men by studying the poet. Otherwise he will be a very poor legislator. In spite of that, the legislator must judge on the basis of his own responsibility which poetry may or may not be publicly used. There is no contradiction there. There is a tension between the two things, but Plato admits this tension in this or that form throughout his work.

Listener: Why is it so easy to recognize what is comical in Aristophanes' speech and so difficult to recognize what is tragic in Agathon's speech?

Mr. Strauss: There is nothing tragic about it, I believe. On the contrary, I would say that Aristophanes' speech shows both the comic and tragic elements in eros. That is the greatness of Aristophanes. The comic element is obvious. If you take part of his argument literally and think it through, you arrive at the conclusion that all love is unhappy. This is, obviously, something that is both comic and tragic.

Listener: Why didn't he have a tragic poet trying to show both? Would the picture have been the same even if he had been great enough to show both?

Mr. Strauss: A great tragic poet might not have been willing to bring in this great element of playfulness of which Agathon boasts. If Plato found the most fertile setting was a *Symposium* after Agathon's winning the contest, he could not very well bring in Euripides, for example, instead of Agathon. These defective things, imposed on a man by chance, present also very great opportunities. The overly sweet in Agathon's speech is very helpful in Socrates' speech later on.

[Tape change.] . . . and then the polis arises as somehow above these things. That's not the doing of the philosopher, that is human nature. The philosopher tries only to understand that, perhaps to improve it to the extent to which it can be improved. That there be tragedy and comedy is a demand of the nature of man. If this were simply a Greek phenomenon, Plato would simply show that the Greeks were in this respect a particularly lucky people. But you know that this is not simply true.

The fact that Aristophanes is a much more powerful individual and his speech much deeper and richer than anyone else's speech, I take for granted. On the other hand, from Socrates' point of view it is the most wrong, because it goes in the false direction most passionately. I use this hesitant language partly because I do not want to anticipate a very big surprise which comes later. Agathon is not as right as he would seem to be up to this point, and Aristophanes got a very important point to which Agathon is blind, and which Socrates knows but will refrain from pointing out in this dialogue. Therefore, when Socrates is through, Aristophanes wants to speak and is prevented by the most unfair means, by the chairman, so to speak.

Love of the beautiful is Agathon's principle. There is an entirely different kind of love from that which Aristophanes had in mind, and that is the love of one's own. The love of the beautiful, which is so imperfectly expressed by Agathon, though externally wonderful, is truly expressed by Socrates. But Socrates does not bring out in this dialogue the true element in Aristophanes' speech, and the justification is that the love of the beautiful is higher from Socrates' point of view than the love of one's own. Both together are the complete phenomenon of eros and, in a sense, the complete phenomenon of man. But if you have to abstract, you should abstract from the lower rather than the higher.

9 SOCRATES (1)

When Agathon had spoken, Aristodemus said everyone present applauded loudly, on the grounds that the young man had spoken in a way as fitting for himself as for the god. Then Socrates said, with a glance at Eryximachus, "Do I really seem to you, son of Akoumenos, to have feared for some time now a fear not to be feared? Did I not mantically say what I was just now saying, that Agathon would speak in an amazing way, and I would be at a loss?" (198a1–7)

Agathon's speech is the only one treated with universal enthusiasm. This is, of course, partly due to the youth and special position of Agathon. But, also, tragedy, for which he stands, is the most pleasing, most pleasing for the demos, for the multitude. So Socrates says, I am defeated in advance as a speaker on eros, but my honor as a diviner, a soothsayer, has been saved. I predicted the outcome. Socrates here treats eros and soothsaying as two entirely different things. The secret of Socrates is that, rightly understood, they are identical, and the word for that is the *daimonion,* which Socrates claims to posses and which is both Socrates' eroticism and his divining power. In a crude way, you all know that love makes one keen-sighted. What does Eryximachus reply?

"In the one case," Eryximachus said, "you seem to me have spoken mantically, in saying, 'Agathon will speak well'; but in the other, that you would be at a loss, I don't believe it." (198a8–10)

Eryximachus says, You did not prophesy that Agathon would speak marvelously; you said that he would speak well, and this was not difficult to prophesy. As for your prophecy regarding yourself, I think you are mistaken. In other words, Socrates, you are no good as a soothsayer. Socrates' attempt to save his honor as a soothsayer, if not as a speaker, has failed. Now let us see how he goes on.

"But just how, you blessed innocent," Socrates said, "am I not to be at a loss, both myself and anyone else whatsoever, if he is going to speak after the speaking of so beautiful and varied a speech? Now all the rest was not equally marvelous, but the things at the end—who would not be thunderstruck on hearing the beauty of the words and phrases? As for myself, on reflecting that I won't myself be able to speak anything that is even close to it, I almost ran off and disappeared out of shame if I knew of any place to go. The speech even reminded me of Gorgias, so that I simply experienced the remark of Homer. I was afraid that Agathon would finally in his speech send in the head of Gorgias—an uncanny speaker—against my speech, and make me myself a stone in voicelessness." (198b1–c5)

Let us see. Socrates says, I am truly embarrassed; no one can possibly compete with Agathon. All of you, including Eryximachus, have been surpassed. Except, of course, Gorgias himself, the teacher of Agathon. If you would look up Homer you would see not the head of Gorgias, of course, but the head of the Gorgon. Who is in that position in the *Odyssey?* Odysseus. Socrates tacitly compares himself here to Odysseus in Hades. This, incidentally, shows also the connection between the *Symposium* and the *Protagoras.* In the *Protagoras* Socrates presents himself as another Odysseus; he has gone down to Hades, only now the illustrious shades are the living sophists. Socrates compares himself to an Odysseus trapped in Hades by a promise. This will come out in the immediate sequel. An Odyssean problem—trapped by an oath. How can he get out?

"And then I realized that I was, after all, ridiculous when I came to an agreement with you that I would praise Eros along with you in my turn and said that I was skilled [uncanny] in erotic things, knowing nothing of the matter, as it turned out, how one should praise anything whatsoever. For I, in my silliness, believed that one had to tell the truth about each thing that was being praised, and this was the starting point, and on this very basis we should select the most beautiful things and arrange them as fittingly as possible. And I was very greatly proud, on the assumption that I would speak well, since I knew the truth about praising anything." (198c5–d7)

What is Socrates' embarrassment? He is committed to making a speech and now he can't do it. In the former interlude it was because he is such a poor speaker compared to the others. Now he has a slightly different version. He made his promise honestly. But since he was silly, he did not understand the terms of the promise. All the others understood the terms of the promise and kept the promise. In the context this means that he criticizes no longer merely Agathon but all previous speakers. Socrates thought that praise must be true, whereas the others believed that praise may be entirely untrue and they acted on that belief. All the others were liars and he is the only honest man.

Socrates believed that a praise must be true. What does this mean here? He gives his own interpretation. Praise must consist in selecting the most beautiful things out of the true qualities of the thing to be praised. In other words, he admits that a praise cannot possibly be true, that it demands silence about the seamy side of the thing to be praised. If you make a eulogy you must say this man is a model of virtue, though in reality he is a miser: He got up at four o'clock in the morning, he exposed himself to the most terrible disgraces and bore them like a man, he lived on bread and water, he was the most patient man—but you never say a word of why he did that. Then you have said the truth. But you have selected only the most beautiful things. What Socrates says is really most ironical, of course, but we draw one conclusion: Socrates' praise of eros will be selectively true; he will speak only of the most beautiful side of eros and not of its seamy side. This fits very well with something I mentioned before: every Platonic dialogue abstracts from something, and the *Symposium* will abstract from important and essential elements of eros. For example, he may abstract from certain features of eros which have been mentioned by earlier speakers. We have to be watchful. Crude insolence in Plato's Socrates is impossible. In Aristophanes' Socrates it is a bit different. Here he is always well behaved. As I mentioned before when we discussed irony: irony noticed by the one who is being ironized is insolence. Try this experiment and you will see that this is true. Irony is a very interesting phenomenon because its primary inspiration is humanity, of course. Not to hurt other people by showing one's own superiority—this is the primary meaning of irony in the higher sense of the word. But if this is noticed, if the superior man is indelicate, stupid in his irony, then he hurts someone. We, who have so much time to read this at leisure, can of course find out what the people present at the moment could not. They couldn't rehear it, they couldn't say, as a student I knew said, repeat that sentence you just said and repeat it again. Ordinarily in conversation one cannot do this. Xenophon always tries to suppress the unpleasant things. When he comes to a deserted town with his expedition he never says the town was deserted; he will say it was a big town and will not add that it was inhabited. He will not say that someone is a coward, he will speak of his moderation and his skill and omit the rest.

Socrates says, I know the truth regarding the praise of things, and that truth is knowledge of the truth regarding the thing concerned; secondly, selection of the most beautiful parts of it; and thirdly, presenting them in the most becoming manner. This is a good rudimentary statement of what a perfect speaker is. Socrates claims here, in his perfect modesty, that he believes himself a perfect orator.

"But this, after all, it seems, was not the way of praising anything beautifully, but rather is was to attach to the matter the greatest and most beautiful things possible, regardless of whether it was the case or not; and if it was not, it was, after all, no big deal. It had been prescribed, that each one of us will be thought to praise Eros, but not how one will praise him. It's for this reason I suspect that you leave no logos unturned and assign them all to Eros; you assert he is of this sort and responsible for so many things, in order that he may appear as beautiful and good as possible—clearly to those who do not know, surely not to the knowers—and the praise is beautiful and august." (198d7–199a3)

You others held a radically different view of rhetoric. Concern with truth did not enter your rhetoric at all. Which, of course, could not be literally true. If you would say of a man who was a notorious coward that he was a notoriously brave man, this would be the height of ineptitude. This goes without saying. You have to know the truth, if you want to be an orator, from every point of view. You spoke according to the principles of sham rhetoric, which, as such, is useful only when addressing ignoramuses. Each of you regards everyone else among you as an ignoramus. He goes on and on, heaping insult on injury. Socrates has really hubris here in this dialogue.

"But, as a matter of fact, I did not after all know the manner of the praise, and in not knowing I came to an agreement with you that I too would praise in turn. So 'the tongue promised, but the mind not'; so let it go." (199a3–6)

This is a quotation from a tragedy by Euripides, which Aristophanes liked to quote but which, in the original, refers to an oath. The tongue has sworn, not the mind, which is the easiest way to get out of any oath. Socrates goes very far here. Odysseus-Socrates gets out of his oath by declaring that he had not understood the meaning of the oath.

"I no longer praise in this manner—" (199a6–7)

Socrates uses the present tense; perhaps Socrates had in the past. We will hear of this later: when he was young he adhered to that false rhetoric which he now rejects.

"for I would not be able—though I am willing, however, to tell the truth, if you want, in my own way, not in comparison with your speeches, in order that I may not incur ridicule." (199a7–b2)

I will not speak in your manner, he says, lest I deserve laughter. You see this is much stronger. Not because I cannot do what you do, but because this is in itself ridiculous.

> "See to it, then, Phaedrus, whether you at all need a speech of this kind, to hear the truth being said about Eros, with the nomenclature and arrangement of phrases to be of whatever sort it happens to be as it occurs." He said Phaedrus and all the rest urged him to speak in whatever way he himself believed he should speak. "Well, then, Phaedrus," he said, "allow me still to ask Agathon some small things, in order that with the gain of an agreement from him I may then speak on this condition."
>
> "Well, I allow it," Phaedrus said. "Go ahead and ask." So after this, he said, Socrates began from some point like this. (199b2–c2)

Socrates will not begin with a speech, he will begin with a dialogue, with asking others. He picks Agathon because he is closest to him, both in space and in kind. This Socratic rhetoric is essentially dialogic. This is only meant to prepare the speech, the speech will come later.

The difference between Socrates and all the other speakers is made clear by this interlude. It is greater than the difference among any others of them. There is a radical difference regarding the meaning of rhetoric. Socrates is, as you must have seen, a master of the mise-en-scène, of a certain theatrical art of presenting himself. You only have to contrast these remarks of his, these extremely modest remarks of his, with the comparatively weak and conventional protestations in the beginning of even Aristophanes' speech, where he says, "I will speak in a different way." How weak this is compared to this challenge here. Socrates shows by deed that he is different from all other speakers. We must also see how Aristophanes, his great antagonist, introduced himself. He introduced himself by his hiccuping. That was Aristophanes' aporia, his lack of a way out. Socrates' embarrassment, on the other hand, was moral. He had committed himself to something which he couldn't achieve. But he doesn't need a physician; he is his own physician, being, in a way, Odysseus himself.

At this point the dialogue with Agathon starts. As a preparation for our discussion of Socrates' speech I would like to read to you a passage which is absolutely crucial for the understanding of Socratic rhetoric or dialectic, but which is neglected today because of the contempt for Xenophon which has been so powerful since the last century. Xenophon came to be regarded as a retired colonel, who was chiefly interested in dogs and horses and could not possibly have had any understanding of Socrates. In the *Memorabilia,* book 4, chapter 6, paragraphs 13–15, we get the following account:

If someone contradicted Socrates on any point without being able to make himself clear, but asserted without proof that so and so was wiser or an abler statesman, or braver or what not than someone else, Socrates would lead the whole discussion back to the definition required in about this way: "You say that your fellow is a better citizen than mine." "I do." "Then, why don't we first consider the function of the good citizen." Then they establish it. By this process of leading back to the premise, even his opponent came to see the truth clearly. That was one way. But when he himself argued something, then he marched through the most generally agreed upon things, believing that in this consisted the safety of speech. Accordingly, whenever he argued, he gained a measure of assent from his hearers greater than any man I have known. He said that Homer gave Odysseus the credit of being a safe speaker because he had a way of leading the discussion through those things which appear to be true to human beings.

A word of interpretation. There were two kinds of rhetoric: when Socrates talked to contradictors he chose a way which led to the truth; but when he did not talk to contradictors, when he had entirely the initiative, he argued only on the basis of accepted premises, in the first place accepted by the men to whom he talked, and secondly generally accepted premises. This second kind of rhetoric is the Odyssean rhetoric, the rhetoric which Homer allegedly ascribed to Odysseus. This is a simple statement, simplified beyond what Xenophon himself needed for his purposes, but it indicates the problem. What Socrates does very manifestly in the discussion with Agathon is to argue on the basis of what Agathon agrees upon. There will be constant reference to the fact of agreement between them. Men may agree, and that doesn't have to be true: universal agreement could claim the truth. We will have to take up this question next time. The main point you must keep in mind is that we have been given advance warning that Socrates' speech on eros will not be the simple truth but a selective truth. Socrates will select the most beautiful things about eros, and if eros should have a seamy side, Socrates would not mention it. We cannot take for granted that our view of eros and its seamy side is Socrates' view. We have to watch the speech very carefully and see whether there is not some indication in his discussion of something which is omitted.

> "And yet *(kai mēn)*, my dear Agathon, I thought you led the way into your speech beautifully, in saying that you first had to show what sort Eros is, and later his deeds. I altogether admire this beginning." (199c3–6)

The first two words of Socrates are the same as those with which Aristophanes' speech begins. These are the only speeches beginning in this way, and this is only a confirmation of what we all felt, that Aristophanes' speech is particularly important. It is the opposite of Socrates' speech as far as its thesis is concerned, but almost on the same level. You see also how this beginning—"I altogether admire"—is also a cautious statement. He does not say that he admired the whole speech.

> "So please, since you went through everything else beautifully and magnificently about what sort Eros is, tell me also this: Is Eros of the sort as to be eros of something or of nothing? I am not asking whether he is of some mother or father—the question whether Eros is eros of a mother or a father would be ridiculous—but just as would be the case were I asking about this very thing 'father': 'Is a father a father of someone or not?' You would surely have told me, if you wanted to answer beautifully, 'Yes, the father is father of a son or daughter.' Or is he not?"
> "Yes, of course," Agathon said. (199c6–d8)

The question here is a fairly simple one: is eros not something like father or mother, i.e., something which is essentially of something. Is eros not essentially relative, in this sense of the word *relative*. For example, "tree." Tree is not essentially of. It is accidental that it is the tree of Mr. Smith. The tree as tree is a tree. But father is essentially related to a son or a daughter. Is eros not something of this kind?

In passing, as a joke, he says, I don't mean that eros is eros of a father or a mother, or the eros of a father for his daughter, or a mother for her son. This is not quite uninteresting because it has something to do with the problem of incest. What Socrates implies here is that incestuous eros does not exist. This is a great theme in Aristophanes, where the problem of incest is brought up, also in connection with Socrates' teaching, in the *Clouds,* where Socrates is accused of teaching his pupils to beat their fathers. This is a simple proposition, which follows in strict logic from the principle that the only title to rule is wisdom. Then, of course, the wise son is by nature the ruler of his unwise father. But ruling may include compulsion and this may include beating. Thus, it follows that the son may beat his father. This seems to be a perfectly innocent thesis, but when the pupil goes on to say he may also beat his mother; then the pupil's father is shocked. The indication in the context, which I cannot now develop, is the whole problem of incest. Here, Socrates seems to say that incestuous eros simply does not exist. In the immediate sequel he gives another example.

> "Isn't that also the case for the mother?" This too was agreed. "Well, then," Socrates said, "answer a little bit more, in order that you may un-

derstand better what I want. Should I ask, What about this point? A brother, that very thing which is just what it is—is he a brother of someone or not?" He said he was. "Isn't he of a brother or a sister?" He agreed. (199d9–e5)

A brother is also a relative in the sense in which father and mother are relative. Here he no longer asks whether there can be eros of a brother for his sister, for example. This has been disposed of by the remark about incestuous relations between parents and children. But this is not quite solved. If you would turn to the *Republic* (461d–e) you would see the famous laws regarding sexual relations in the best polity. Incestuous relations between brothers and sisters are not excluded. What are excluded are incestuous relations between parents and children, between the older and the younger generation. Within each generation no one knows who his brother or sister is because of the communism. Whether this is Plato's last word on the subject is another matter. The parallel in Xenophon's *Memorabilia,* book 4, chapter 4, sections 20–23, concerns the same thing. The fact that intercourse between parents and children is reasonably forbidden would not prove, of course, that there is no such eros. So the problem of incest remains. The sequel has to be read with great care.

"So try," he said, "to speak of eros too. Is Eros eros of nothing or of something?"

"He certainly is."

"Well, then," Socrates said, "guard this with yourself and remember of what he is; but tell me so much, Of that of which there is eros, does Eros desire it or not?" (200a1–3)

This is important. Agathon is asked to remember what the object of eros is but to give only the answer to the following question. What is that which Agathon is asked to keep for himself? What is Agathon's thesis regarding eros? Of what is eros eros, what is the object of eros? The beautiful. That is one view, but there is also another possibility regarding what eros is of, and that is the one indicated by Aristophanes, namely, love of one's other half, love of one's own flesh and blood. Therefore, ironically overstated, incestuous love, more simply stated, love of one's own. This question is here left open.

[Gap in tape concerning 200a4–201b8.]

"Do you still agree that Eros is beautiful if these things are so?"

And Agathon said, "It's probable, Socrates, that I knew nothing of what I said then."

"And yet for all of that, Agathon," he said, "you spoke beautifully. But speak still of a small point. Don't you think that the good things are also beautiful?"

"Yes, I do." (201b9–c3)

In the context good and noble are interchangeable. But they are not interchangeable, as the very context shows.

"If then Eros is in need of the beautiful things, and the good things are beautiful, he would also be in need of the good things."

"Socrates," he said, "I could not contradict you, but let it be as you say."

"No," he said, "It is the truth, rather, my dear Agathon, that you are unable to contradict, since it is not at all difficult to contradict merely Socrates." (201c4–9)

This is the height of irony, naturally, for it is impossible for Agathon to contradict Socrates. He can easily contradict the unarmed truth. Truth wouldn't shout when violated by Agathon's statement, but he can never contradict Socrates. That this is in an ultimate sense true I do not deny. In the dramatic context it is ironical.

Since eros can't be beautiful, he can't be good. But for the same reason, since the gods, according to Agathon, are prompted by love of the beautiful and therefore lack beauty, they also lack goodness. Love of the beautiful equals lack of beauty; beautiful equals good; therefore that which loves beauty is characterized by absence of beauty, which equals absence of good. The gods are also prompted by love of beauty. This is the end of the first part of Socrates' speech, the dialogue between Socrates and Agathon. I would like to summarize.

The argument starts from the premise that love cannot be love for the available, and that can also mean, properly enlarged, love for one's own. First, there cannot be eros for one's parents, bothers, and sisters; incestuous eros is impossible. Second, there cannot be eros for one's wife, nor third, for one's polis; fourth, not for sexual gratification. The copresence of desire and satisfaction is impossible. Fifth, only human beings who are not beautiful can have eros, if it is true that only the nonbeautiful can love the beautiful. Sixth, the gods are neither beautiful nor good. Seven, one cannot distinguish between beautiful and ugly, noble and base eros. The latter follows from the fact that there cannot be eros for sexual gratification, which, after all, was the phenomenon which made it necessary to distinguish between noble and base eros. All these points, with the exception of the statement regarding the gods, offer a perfect justification for Socrates' eros. Socrates is not interested in incestuous eros, not in eros for his wife, not for his polis, not for sexual gratification; that only human beings who are not beautiful can have eros suits him excellently, and that one cannot distinguish between noble and base eros. So much for the dialogue with Agathon.

At this point begins the high point of the *Symposium,* the conversation between Socrates and Diotima. For the better understanding, I would like to make a prefatory remark which I hope I can prove when we go on. The whole speech of Socrates, which is, after all, that toward which we have been building, consists of the following parts: (1) the introduction, the discussion of Socrates' rhetoric; (2) Socrates and Agathon, the dialogue which we have seen and which culminates in the assertion that eros is neither beautiful nor good, which includes, in this context, that the gods are neither beautiful nor good. Then we get (3) the dialogue with Diotima. This dialogue is subdivided into three parts [later referred to as IIIA, IIIB, and IIIC]. The first part stops at 204c7; the second part stops at 207a4; and the third part at the end of it. The third part is again subdivided into three parts [IIIC1 etc.]. The interesting point is this: if you count the parts which are no longer divisible you get seven parts, i.e., as many parts as the whole dialogue possesses. The real question would be whether there is some real correspondence between the seven parts of Socrates' speech and the seven speeches. The first part of Socrates' speech deals with rhetoric; the first speaker is Phaedrus, the interlocutor in the dialogue on rhetoric.

In my opinion Socrates clearly abstracted from love of one's own. This would make sense under one condition: A true speech of praise must concentrate on the most noble and beautiful and disregard the less noble. Now, if love of one's own is less noble than love of the beautiful, he would at least have the merit of consistency. The question is, is this a sensible proposition, that love of one's own is lower than love of the beautiful? Is it an intelligible thesis? Love of one's own we see constantly around us. A mother loving her child, etc. Is it possible to see this love as inferior to love of the beautiful? I do not mean cutting oneself off from the love of one's own, but simply to state that it is subordinate to something higher which does not have that relation to one's own. There is one thing one can say: if there is such a thing as philosophy, or love of truth, it is more akin to the love of the beautiful than to the love of one's own. In the realm of speech on general matters, the love of one's own leads to ideology; the love of the beautiful leads to the truth. If the fundamental fact is love of one's own, one absolutizes one's own and one seeks reasons for it. This is ideology, if one can use this abominable word, whereas love of truth is not primarily concerned with one's own. So it does make some sense. Surely this has nothing to do with the argument here, the argument is adapted entirely to what Agathon can digest or not digest at the moment. Surely the analysis is in no way complete, because Plato or Socrates has a certain object in mind which will gradually become clear.

[In answer to a question:] Can there be love for the ugly? If love is only love of the beautiful, there cannot be love for the ugly, but there can very well be love for the ugly which is one's own. Love of one's own is compatible with love of the ugly.

Listener: Love of one's own is somehow identical with love of the beautiful from the point of view of the subject, because it is my eros and I want to make this object mine.

Mr. Strauss: Let me state it a little more precisely: I love the beautiful, I want to own the beautiful. Still, it is important that it is the beautiful you want to own. There are three elements involved, as will appear later: *(a)* I, as the lover, *(b)* the beautiful beloved, and *(c)* its perpetual possession, which will be the theme of the central part. Let us then turn to the Diotima section.

> "And I shall let you go for now; but the logos about Eros, which I once heard from Diotima, a Mantinean woman . . . " (201d1–2)

Here the dialogue ends and Socrates's speech, the logos, begins. What was said before? He would give a speech after the dialogue. But we are in for a great disappointment. Socrates' speech does not begin, it is the speech of someone else. This is strange. Socrates really breaks his promises, we must say. As the name Diotima indicates—from *Dio-,* genitive of Zeus *(Dios),* and *tima,* honoring, and Mantinea, the name of a town, reminding of *mantis,* soothsayer—she is a prophetess. We have seen in our simple schema of the six speeches, Agathon and Socrates are inspired speakers. But no, Diotima is the inspired speaker, Socrates merely transmits what he has heard from an inspired speaker. In addition, this inspired speaker has the strange quality of being a woman. This contrasts with the all-male society. You remember in the beginning there was a woman, the flute player, and she was thrown out—and now she comes back. In addition, she is a foreign woman, which makes it worse. This contrasts with the fact the we have here an all-Athenian society. There is a parallel to that in Plato elsewhere, in the small dialogue called *Menexenus.* There, Socrates reports a conversation he has had with a foreign woman. But this was not a prophetess from Manti-

nea but the famous Aspasia, the quasi mistress of Pericles. The context is
particularly comical, because the question is a funeral speech which is to be
given, and Socrates gives the sketch of a funeral speech for the Athenian
fallen which had been sketched by the foreign woman Aspasia, with the implication that this funeral speech by a foreign woman was superior even to
the famous funeral speech of Pericles himself. Now, she comes from Mantinea, which is from the region of Arcadia. The Arcadians were punished by
the Spartans, you may remember, and were reduced to village life, to a
primitive form of life. What does he say? Diotima was wise in these things
and in many others.

> ". . . who was wise in these things and many others, and once when the
> Athenians consulted her on sacrificing, ten years before the plague, she
> made a delay of the disease." (201d2–5)

There is a parallel to that: there was a similar story about another prophetic
human being, Epimenides of Crete, told in the first book of Plato's *Laws*.
Epimenides of Crete was also a foreign soothsayer who had helped Athens
in a critical situation prior to the Persian war. The Cretans were famous, as
Plato indicates in the *Laws*, for pederasty, and Arcadia was a neighbor of
Elis, the country mentioned by Pausanias as particularly dissolute in this respect. Diotima was Socrates' teacher in erotic things. In other words, Socrates was young when he had this conversation. If the plague referred to is
that of 430, of which Pericles was the most famous victim, the dialogue
must have taken place in 440, if not earlier, when Socrates was relatively
young, thirty or younger.

> "It was she who taught also me the erotic things. So I will try to recount
> to you the speech she spoke, as far as I am able, on the basis of what has
> been agreed upon by Agathon and me. So, Agathon, one must account
> for Eros himself in just the manner you explained, first, who is he and of
> what sort, and then his deeds." (201d5–e2)

It is not a question of essence, but what kind of a guy he is. One dialogue—
if I remember well, the *Euthydemus*—begins with Crito asking Socrates a
question, "Who was it?"; that is the difference between the curious man
and the philosophic man. The question as stated here is not the philosophic
question What is eros? but Who is eros?

> "It seems to be easiest, in fact, to give an account in just the way the
> stranger [female] once went through it in quizzing me. I too was saying to
> her pretty nearly the sorts of things that Agathon just now was telling me,

in saying that Eros is a great god, and he is of the beautiful things. Then she proceeded to refute me by those kinds of speeches by which I refuted him, proving that he was neither beautiful nor good according to my argument." (201e2–7)

Diotima was Socrates' teacher. This is an extremely rare case, that Socrates appears in the role of a pupil. There is only one other case, and that is the dialogue *Parmenides,* where Socrates appears in the role of a pupil of Parmenides. In the beginning of this course I discussed the fact that there are only three narrated dialogues which are not narrated by Socrates: *Parmenides, Phaedo,* and the *Symposium.* The *Parmenides* and the *Phaedo* have one thing in common: they tell us something about the young Socrates. In the *Parmenides* this is obvious, and in the *Phaedo* Socrates himself tells of his early youthful attempts at philosophy. Now we see that the *Symposium,* too, belongs to this group, because here we also have an account of the young Socrates, the Socrates who had not yet undergone the change to the Socrates we know from the Platonic dialogues. This is not merely a historical question, which, as such, would be of no interest to us; it has great substantive importance, as we may see. The young Socrates held more or less the same view held now by Agathon. Eros is a great god, and eros is love for the beautiful things. His view is not identical with that of Agathon; he did not say that he is the most beautiful and best god, nor did he say in particular that eros is the youngest god. In other words, the young Socrates had not depreciated the other gods in favor of eros as Agathon did. Nor had Socrates said, as Agathon did, that the other gods act from eros of the beautiful. Diotima refutes Socrates on the basis of his assertion that he was neither beautiful nor good. She does exactly what Socrates did with Agathon, all on the premise granted by the other. In other words, Socrates has no originality whatsoever. One point I would like to mention: Originally, Socrates was a natural philosopher—we have had a specimen of the pre-Socratics in Empedocles—until he read a book by Anaxagoras, who said the cause of everything is nous. Hence, he expected Anaxagoras to show that everything was reasonably and beautifully ordered. But Anaxagoras did not make use of his intellectual principle, and therefore Socrates threw it away. In the *Parmenides* Socrates is presented to us as a man who says there are no ideas of the ugly. This is still in accordance with the first step: mind rules everything, therefore everything is well-ordered, beautifully ordered. And the view which he held of eros fits beautifully: eros is only love of the beautiful. From this point of view the discovery which transformed the young Socrates to the later Socrates is the discovery of the ugly, of the recalcitrant.

> "And I said, 'How do you mean, Diotima? Is Eros then ugly and bad?' And she said, 'Don't blaspheme! Or do you believe that whatever is not beautiful is necessarily ugly?' 'Yes, of course.' 'And if it is not wise, it is ignorant? Or have you not become aware that there is something between wisdom and ignorance?' 'What is that?' 'Don't you know,' she said, 'that to opine correctly without being able to give an account is neither to have precise knowledge—for how would precise knowledge be a matter without an account [irrational]?—nor is it ignorance—for how could ignorance be the hitting upon that which is?—but surely correct opinion is of this sort, between understanding *[phronesis]* and ignorance.'" (201e8–202a9)

The blasphemy of Socrates here consists in his absurdity. The first lesson which Socrates gets from Diotima is that there is something between the good and the bad. The example she uses is not the beautiful and the ugly but wisdom and ignorance; that which lies in the middle is correct opinion. Correct opinion shares with knowledge the fact that it hits the mark—the truth. It shares with ignorance the quality that it is ignorant of why it is so. This true opinion, which is only true opinion, is a very complicated problem. One can put it perhaps as follows: According to Plato, man has a natural capacity, an untrained capacity, for hitting the truth. Without that he could not be man. This natural capacity for hitting the truth concerns the fact as distinguished from the why. One requires techne, conscious consideration, to discover the causes. But there is one great difficulty regarding this wonderful thing, true opinion: can true opinion know that it is true opinion? How do we check without knowing that an opinion is a true opinion? There is only one criterion: universal agreement. If all men say it then it is true, though we don't know why it is true. Or, differently stated: that which one cannot consistently question. In other words, what is here called true opinion has something to do with what in the *Republic*, books 6 and 7, is called confidence and trust. You can say that there is in us a natural faith, but in order to avoid the religious connotation, it is safer to say a natural confidence, a natural trust. That there are such things as dogs, horses, justice—all those things we "know." We know that they are, but we do not know why, we do not know what they mean. But such a stratum exists. How does Diotima go on?

> "'Well, then, don't compel what is not beautiful to be ugly, any more than what is not good to be bad. So too in the case of Eros, since you yourself

> agree that he is not good any more than he is beautiful, don't any the more believe that he must be ugly and bad, but something,' she said, 'between the two.'" (202b1–5)

She adds now that eros is not good. From the fact that he is not beautiful it does not follow that he is not good. She assumes that Socrates will take it for granted that the beautiful is identical with the good, so natural is it to identify these two things, but it is also a question. There is no universal agreement. In some cases all men make a distinction between the beautiful and the good. Therefore, it is not true opinion to say that they are identical.

> "'And yet,' I said, 'it's agreed upon by all that he is a great god.' 'Do you mean by all,' she said, 'those who don't know or also those who know?' 'No, all inclusively.' And she said with a laugh, 'And just how,' she said, 'Socrates, could it be agreed that he was a great god by those who deny that he is even a god?'" (202b6–c2)

Socrates rebels against the conclusion that eros, since he is neither good nor beautiful, cannot be a god. For there is universal agreement as to his being a god. At this point Diotima laughs, a very rare occurrence in this dialogue. It has happened only in one case hitherto—Aristophanes laughed. She lacks the solemnity which one would expect from a prophetess. And now she says something absolutely overwhelming: He is not even a god—not even not a great god, but not a god at all. Diotima said that, not Socrates.

> "'Who are they?' I said. 'You are one,' she said, 'and I am one.' And I said, 'How,' I said, 'do you mean this?' And she said, 'Easily. Tell me, don't you assert that all gods are happy and beautiful? Or would you dare to deny that any one of the gods is not beautiful and happy?' 'No, by Zeus, not I,' I said." (202c3–9)

Do you see what she does? Do you see what pressure she puts on Socrates? "Would you dare to deny . . . ?" That is the first oath occurring in the dialogue itself. There was one in the beginning by Apollodorus.

> "'And don't you mean that those who possess the good things and the beautiful things are happy?' 'Certainly.' 'But you have agreed that Eros, on account of his lack of good and beautiful things, desires those very things of which he is in need.' 'I have agreed.' 'How then would he who has no share in the beautiful and good things be a god?' 'In no way, it seems.' 'Do you see then,' she said, 'You too hold Eros not to be a god?' 'Well, what then,' I said, 'would Eros be? Mortal?' 'Not in the least.' 'Well, what then?' 'Just as before,' she said, 'between mortal and immortal.' 'What's that, Di-

otima?' 'A great *daimon,* Socrates. For the *daimonion* is in its entirety between god and mortal.'" (202c10–e1)

Eros is not a god because he is neither good nor beautiful. Then she says he
is neither a mortal nor an immortal. As before, if there are things which are
neither beautiful nor ugly, then there is something which is in between.
There can also be something between mortal and immortal. Is this possible, we have to ask. We can easily see that something is neither beautiful
nor ugly, but is it true in all cases that there must be something in between?
What about numbers? Neither odd nor even. Can you say of a number it is
between odd and even? It wouldn't work. It seems that the case of mortal
and immortal is like the case of odd and even rather than of beautiful and
ugly. In other words, Socrates makes now the logical error opposite that
which he made in the beginning. In the beginning he denied a mean where
a mean was possible. Here he accepts a mean where a mean is impossible.
Eros is not a god but a demon, he belongs to the demonic world. This is
very interesting with a view to the broad theme of this dialogue. The *Symposium* is the only Platonic dialogue which deals with a god. Phaedrus had
said he is the oldest god, Aristophanes had said he is the most philanthrop-
ical, Agathon had said he is the youngest and the highest god. Diotima says
that he is not a god at all. If we assume that Socrates accepted the lesson of
Diotima, as I think is clear at the end, we must say that Socrates did not believe in any of these gods, i.e., in the gods of the city, and therefore he was
accused and condemned. When he was accused, the accuser said, "Socrates
does not respect the gods of the city, but introduces new *daimonia."* And
then, in the argument with the accuser Meletus, Socrates says, "What do
you mean to say, that I do not believe in the gods of the city, but that I believe in other gods?" And they said, "No, you are a simple atheist." Socrates
answered, "You say I believe in *daimonia,* but what are *daimonia* if not either gods or children of gods?" Hence, if he believed in demonic things as
the accuser admitted, he surely believed in the gods and even in the gods of
the city. This passage is quite interesting, in the *Apology* 26c, where a certain notion of *daimon* is developed.

Still, there is a great difficulty: Diotima had said eros is between the
mortal and the immortal. The whole demonic realm is between god and
the mortal. And then Socrates says, "With what power?" This is a very rich
and pregnant statement. To begin with it is wholly unintelligible how there
could be a being which is neither mortal nor immortal. If such a being
should exist it must have a power. In Plato's *Sophist* (247D–E) we find this

declaration: This and this only truly is which has the power to act on something else, or to be acted upon. On what does eros act and by what is eros acted upon? This question is answered by Diotima in the sequel.

> "'With what power?' I said. 'Interpreting and conveying the things from human beings to gods, and the things from gods to human beings, the requests and sacrifices of the latter, and of the former the injunctions and exchanges for the sacrifices, and being in the middle of both it fills it up, so as for the whole itself to have been bound together by itself.'" (202e3–7)

Everything demonic is between the mortal and the immortal. In a way, that is true, not because it itself is mortal or immortal but because it is the mediator between the immortal—gods—and the mortal—men. Therefore it is the bond of the whole. The implication is that the whole consists only of gods, men, and demons, which can, of course, not be the final truth. Both, gods and men, need a bond. The demonic realm makes them complete. Neither gods nor men are self-sufficient; the self-sufficiency is created by the demons. Since the demonic affects gods and men, it is. Because whatever acts, is. But how do we know that there is any truth to this assertion that there are such demonic things? She will say it in the sequel.

> "'All divination moves through this, as well as the art of the priests who deal with sacrifices, initiations, incantations, all of divination, and magic.'" (202e7–203a1)

Here is the empirical proof: there are arts of divining and the arts of the priests. These are two different facets of some importance.

> "'God does not mingle with human being, but through this there is the entire association and conversation that gods have with human beings, both asleep and awake.'" (203a1–4)

God does not mingle with men, and that includes also sexual relations. There are no sexual relations between gods and men—quite an assertion. That means there are no heroes, generated by an immortal father and a mortal mother or vice versa. In this connection I ask you to look up the *Apology of Socrates* (27d) where this question is discussed.

> "'And he who is wise in things of this sort is a demonic man *[daimonios]*, but he who is wise in anything else, whether it be about arts or some handicrafts, is vulgar *[banausos]*.'" (203a4–6)

She speaks here only of intercourse, or dialogue, of gods toward men. The intercourse leading from gods to men as distinguished from the one leading from men to gods. This intercourse requires a demonic man, a man possessing the mantic faculty as distinguished from the art of the priest. You see also that she speaks of a demonic man—male. Is there no place for demonic women? Strange. She, who should know, seems to speak only of demonic men.

> "'These *daimones* are many and of all sorts, and Eros too is one of them.' 'And who is his father,' I said, 'and who the mother?'" (203a6–8)

Eros is a demon, not a god. The distinction between demon and god as two distinct classes of beings seems to be of Platonic origin. As a demon, Eros is a mediator between men and gods. There are said to be of course many mediators, Eros being one of them, yet it is not wrong to say that *the* mediator is Eros. And Krüger, to whose book I have previously referred, makes the remark that this is really the difference between Christianity and Plato; the mediator is not Christ, it is Eros.

As a demon, Eros is not blessed or happy. Eros is, but he was not always. How do we know? That is not said. He is a living being, gods and demons being living beings. Now, since he was not always, and is a living being, he must have parents. This is Socrates' conclusion, Diotima did not say that. Hitherto, Phaedrus's contention that eros has no parents was never contested. Now it is denied: Eros does have parents. One thing is clear on the basis of Diotima's premise: Eros cannot have one divine parent and one human parent, since gods and men do not mingle. Could Eros not have sprung from one parent only? Pausanias spoke of the noble Aphrodite, who has only one parent, a male parent. Socrates tacitly denies this. In this respect he is rationalistic. If he is a living being who has come into being he must have two parents. Diotima says it would be too long to narrate, nevertheless I will tell you. She does not narrate but only tell. The brief account in the sequel is the only part of the whole *Symposium,* with the possible exception of Aristophanes' speech, which one could call a myth. There is an infinite literature on the Platonic myth. They all suffer, as far as I know, and I don't know all of them, from the fact that the scholar himself decides what is a myth, a most unscholarly procedure. One has to find out from Plato what a myth is. In other words, I would regard only that as a myth of which Plato or his characters say it is a myth. However this may be, in a loose way we can say that the genesis of a demon is in Plato a mythical statement. Precisely because this is so glaringly mythical, we see, when reading Diotima's speech as a whole, how amazingly unmythical it is. It is really a Socratic dialogue, but with the strange inversion that Socrates is on the receiving end.

> "'It is rather long to narrate,' she said, 'but I shall tell you. When Aphrodite was born, both all the other gods and Resource, the son of Metis, were holding a feast. When they had dined, Poverty came to beg— it was a festival after all—and she hung around the door.'" (203b1–5)

The translation is perhaps not quite clear that Resource, or power simply, is, of course, a god. That is clearly stated in the Greek. One other thing: There is only one Aphrodite. We had been told that there were two by Pausanias and Eryximachus. Since there is only one Aphrodite, there is only one Eros. That is strict logic. There is, however, Aphrodite without Eros, for on the birthday of Aphrodite Eros was generated. Aphrodite precedes Eros. This is also a correction of Pausanias. In other words, the demotion of Eros leads to a promotion of the other gods.

> "'Resource then got drunk on nectar—there was not yet wine—'" (203b5–6)

Why does she say there was no wine yet? Although it was in the very olden times, Eros is not so young as he might seem to be on the basis of Agathon's speech.

> "'. . . and heavy with it he went into the garden of Zeus and slept.'" (203b6–7)

Whether Eros is a descendent from Zeus is, to say the least, not clear. Poros, his father, was the son of Metis, the first wife of Zeus, but of course we don't know whether Zeus was the father. Eros has some relation to Zeus since he was generated in Zeus's garden. His relation to Zeus is obscure. This is not unimportant; we shall see later what it means.

> "'Poverty then, plotting to get a child from Resource because of her own resorcelessness, lay down beside him and conceived Eros.'" (203b7–c1)

Sexual intercourse antedates Eros.

> "'It's for this reason that Eros has become the attendant and servant of Aphrodite, being born on her birthday and, at the same time, being by nature a lover concerned with the beautiful, is a lover of Aphrodite because she is beautiful. Eros then, because he is the son of Resource and Poverty, has got settled in the same sort of fortune as theirs.'" (203c1–4)

Since Eros was generated on Aphrodite's birthday, Eros is her companion—that's simple. And, since Aphrodite, too, is beautiful, he is, by nature, in love with the beautiful. The accident—generated on Aphrodite's birthday—or the merely conventional, explains the nature of Eros. His love for the beautiful is here traced to his connection with Aphrodite, not to his descent from Resource. Now we come to the genealogy of Eros in a more precise sense.

> "'First, he is always poor, and far from being tender and beautiful, such as the many believe, he is rough and squalid and shoeless and homeless, always lying on the ground and without bedding, sleeping at doorways and on roads under the open sky, with the nature of his mother, always keeping house with neediness.'" (203c6–d3)

So, Agathon is mistaken. His error is a vulgar error. Eros is not delicate and tender, he is a tough fellow. Among the qualities ascribed to him here, one is outstanding: he is homeless, hence, perhaps, seeking a house; or is he satisfied without a house? We must first find out what he inherited from his father.

> "'And in turn, in conformity with his father, he is a plotter against the beautiful and the good, being manly, impetuous, and intense, an uncanny hunter, always weaving some devices, as desirous of understanding [*phronesis*] as capable of supplying it, philosophizing throughout his whole life, an uncanny magician, sorcerer, and sophist.'" (203d4–8)

He is desirous of knowledge, of practical wisdom. I would suggest that there is a connection between this and the fact that he is homeless. He is a traveler, an Odysseus who does not long for Ithaca. We see here that Eros's virtues from his mother's side can be called toughness, stamina. From his father he has inherited courage and wisdom, or at least love of wisdom—philosophy. We see two virtues he did not get from either side: moderation and justice. This is empirically meaningful. Some of you may remember Bizet's *Carmen*. Yet Eros is always poor as his mother, he is never rich like his father, and he is scheming for the beautiful. The same expression was applied to his mother. At 203b7 Poverty is scheming to have a child from Resource. Does he have any resemblance to his father?

> "'And he has a nature to be neither as an immortal nor as a mortal, but sometimes in the same day he flourishes and lives, whenever he is resourceful, and sometimes he dies, and again he lives again on account of the nature of his father, but the resources are always gradually flowing out, and hence Eros is never either resourceless or wealthy, and is in between wisdom and ignorance.'" (203d8–e5)

He is partly like an immortal and partly like a mortal. But is his mother mortal? His mother, too, is immortal. But, perhaps, he resembles his father because his mother is ignorant. This would be the only possible term of comparison. Let us see.

> "'For this is the way it is. Not one of the gods philosophizes, any more than he desires to become wise—for he is—and whoever else is wise, he does not philosophize either. And the ignorant in turn do not philosophize or desire to become wise. For this is the very thing in which ignorance is hard: not to be beautiful and good and thoughtful but to seem to oneself to be sufficient. So he who believes he is not in need does not desire that which he believes he does not need.'" (204a1–7)

So the gods are wise, therefore they do not philosophize, they do not seek wisdom. The most radical opponent of Plato, Nietzsche, taught exactly the opposite—the gods philosophize. He regarded this as one of his great innovations, which is, one could say, a mythical expression. There cannot be self-sufficient beings. But there may be others also who are wise. The ignorant are satisfied with their condition. Was Poverty, Eros's mother, satisfied with her condition? Did she behave like the ignorant? If she had been self-sufficient in the way the ignorant are self-sufficient, Poros would have taken the initiative in generating Eros. But he is a god and, hence, according to the hypothesis, self-sufficient. Poverty must have been dissatisfied with her state and not ignorant if Eros was to be conceived at all. Eros, I conclude, resembles only his mother and not at all his father. You remember, there was no relation of Eros to Zeus, only to Zeus's garden, nor was there any natural relation to Aphrodite, but only the accidental one that he was born on her birthday. For the understanding of Eros one need not have recourse to his father, to the gods in general, but recourse to the mother and, perhaps, something else which we may provisionally call the ideas, suffices.

Let me state the difficulty as follows: If the gods are, they are self-sufficient, and Eros could not have been generated by any one of them; if the gods are not self-sufficient, then they are not gods, and Eros could also not have been generated by one of them. Under no circumstances can Eros be a child of a god, or of a mortal. What is the conclusion? He must be always, and this is, indeed, the premise of the following argument. In the presentation of Poverty, Eros's mother we have an ambiguity: on the one hand she appears as simple, self-satisfied Poverty, self-satisfied ignorance, and on the other hand she appears as the one who wants to get out of that state of poverty, out of that state of ignorance. Exactly the same ambiguity is found in Aristophanes' presentation of poverty in his play *Ploutos*. I think Aristophanes' play is the model for this passage here. This would be one of the greater compliments which Plato pays to Aristophanes in this particular work. In that play, verses 550–554, the view that poverty is self-satisfied beggary is the view of the vulgar. But the view that poverty is love of work, to get out of the misery, is the view of that half-divine Poverty herself. Plato here imitates for his own reasons an ambiguity occurring in Aristophanes. The issue is settled. We know the parents of Eros by now and he turns to another subject: Who are these philosophers?

> "'Who then, Diotima,' I said, 'are those who philosophize, if they are neither the wise nor the ignorant?' 'This,' she said, 'is by now clear even to a child: those who are between them both, of whom Eros would be one. For wisdom is of the most beautiful things, and Eros is eros about the beautiful, and hence it is necessary that Eros be a philosopher, and being a philosopher to be between wise and ignorant. His birth is the cause of this, for he is of a wise and resourceful father, and a not wise and resourceless mother.'" (204a7–b7)

He says his mother is not wise, he does not say she is ignorant. The philosopher, too, is not wise by definition.

> "'Now the nature of the *daimonion,* my dear Socrates, is this.'" (204b7–8)

Diotima does not answer the question of Socrates regarding the philosophers. She turns back to the nature of eros. Why? Socrates was satisfied with her answer regarding the nature of eros. Why doesn't she answer Socrates' simple question? She knows what philosophy is. Later on she will give a long lecture on that. Well, she does not yet know whether Socrates is fit to receive that lesson. This she can give only later.

There is another question which I must mention here. The opposites which are ultimately important are those of wisdom and ignorance. What is in between? Philosophy. Is right opinion identical with philosophy? Have there not been philosophers who had atrociously paradoxical, untrue opinions? And cannot a man have right opinion and be satisfied with having only right opinion and not care at all for transforming that opinion into knowledge? Two entirely different things are here tacitly treated as identical. Perhaps Plato means that on the highest level they would be identical. A man who has right opinion on everything can exist only by virtue of some philosophizing and, on the other hand, the philosopher who is truly a philosopher is the one who starts from right opinions and does not throw out the right opinions.

> "'But whom you believed to be Eros, it's not a surprising experience that you underwent. You believed, as it seems to me in making an inference from what you say, that that which is loved is Eros, not that which loves. It's for this reason that Eros appeared to you to be altogether beautiful. For in fact the lovable is that which is really beautiful, delicate, perfect, and blessed; but that which is just loving is with the different kind of look [*idea*] that I described.'" (204c1–6)

According to Diotima, the basic error of Socrates was that he believed eros to be the beloved but not the loving. The truth is that eros is not the beloved but the loving. This subject is not wholly alien to us. Phaedrus said that the lover is inferior to the beloved—more divine than the beloved, but inferior to him. The beloved Achilles was more honored than Patroclus. Diotima says the lover is less divine that the beloved and inferior to him. What is the beloved according to her? The beautiful. The beloved is the truly beautiful, but the lover offers another sight, has another shape. You see also the words here "that which is loving" and "that which is loved" are neuters, not eros or the gods. The word which Plato uses here in the end [*idea*]) is the word from which *idea* is derived. At 204b7 he had spoken of the nature of eros. The nature of eros and the idea of eros are the same. To indicate the paradox one could make this remark: In a way eros is, for Plato, nature in the sense in which we commonly mean the word—things come into being and perish. Eros, we can say, is the heart of coming into being and perishing. Eros, we can say, is the nature of nature, the essence of nature. This is at least part of the Platonic argument.

A few words about IIIA. If one were to insert here, in the argument between Socrates and Diotima, Agathon's thesis, one would arrive at the conclusion that not only Eros, but all gods who are prompted by love of beauty, are not gods. But you see how difficult this is: it is divided between two different people. Can you impute to Diotima or Socrates what Agathon said? This implication is not brought up in the conversation between Socrates and Diotima. The conclusion she draws is that Eros is not a god but a demon, a mediator between gods and men, between mortals and immortals. To explain this she gives the genealogy of Eros. Eros descended from wealth and poverty. This means, however, from a god—the father—and a demon—the mother. Yet, as we have seen, Eros can be perfectly understood from his mother's side. Eros can be perfectly understood without recourse not only to his father but to any of the gods. All characteristics of Eros are found in his mother. In granting that desire, love, arises from lack, from poverty itself, do you not need another principle pointing toward fullness, indicating the direction which desire, lack, takes? And is not that toward which desire moves higher than the desire and therefore divine? One can say this: There must be something divine, something immortal, something unchanging. This condition is satisfied by the Platonic ideas, whatever they may mean. The beloved is higher than the loving, than eros, and the beloved may very well be the ideas. We shall find some evidence for this.

We must keep in mind another difficulty. Poverty and Wealth are compared to wisdom and ignorance. Eros is especially in between wisdom and ignorance. This state between wisdom and ignorance is described by Diotima in two entirely different terms: On the one hand it is called right opinion. Right opinion is in a way wisdom because it is true opinion. On the other hand, it is ignorance because it does not know why it is right. The stage between ignorance and wisdom is also called philosophy. At first glance philosophy and right opinion seem to be two entirely different things.

10 SOCRATES (2)

"And I said, 'That's all to the good, stranger, for you are speaking beautifully; but if Eros is of this kind, what use does he have for human beings?'" (204c7–8)

Here begins the next part (in my schema IIIB). The first part dealt with the nature of eros, and it said that eros is not a god but a demon. Here Socrates says "stranger," the only time Socrates uses this expression. In order to understand these little things one must consider them, because they tell us something about ourselves. The simplest explanation for his calling her stranger is that he is particularly aware of the fact here. She has evaded his question and he is bewildered by that.

The utility of eros, we can say, is the subject of the rest. But there is a very important subdivision in this section. The distinction is at 207a5, when he says she taught me all these things when she made speeches about erotic things and once upon a time she asked, etc. There is no comparable incision anywhere else. Let us begin at 204c7.

"'It is this, Socrates, that I shall try to teach you next. Eros is of this sort and has come to be in this way, but he is of the beautiful things, as you say. If someone should ask us, "In what respect is Eros of the beautiful things, Socrates and Diotima?" It's more plain in the following way: He who loves the beautiful things loves. What does he love?' And I said, 'For them to become his.'" (204d1–7)

Socrates is satisfied with the account of Eros' nature. He brings up the question of Eros' utility for human beings. Only in this section does Socrates take the initiative. This will be repeated in the central subdivision of IIIC. This question, however, of Eros's utility for human beings has been answered. Eros is a mediator in sacrifices, prayers, and all these things. Why, then, does the question arise? The superficial reason is this: The answer was not given with a view to Eros in particular, but with regard to all demons—it was a general answer. Now we shall learn what this mediation between gods and men means in terms of Eros. That will be clear in the sequel. Diotima is willing to answer this question of Socrates, as distinguished from the question regarding the philosophers, in 204a, which, as we have seen last time, she evades because she does not yet know whether

Socrates is mature enough to understand it. Given this nature of Eros, it does not necessarily follow that Eros is love of the beautiful things. For, if his mother Poverty were simple ignorance, which sometimes appears, Eros might have become desire for wholeness, i.e., desire for the extinction of intelligence, as Aristophanes implied. This, then, is a new condition. It does not simply follow from Eros's origin as appeared at first.

Diotima is willing to argue on the basis of Socrates' assertion that Eros is love of beautiful things. She argues—in the Aristotelian sense of the word, dialectically—accepting the other's premises. You also see something here which happens very frequently in Platonic dialogues, a dialogue within a dialogue. Diotima says, "If someone should ask us." The dialogues within the dialogue are contrived by the speaker. What is the meaning? The two people conversing, in this case Socrates and Diotima, are treated as a unity. The unity which is brought about is sometimes a spurious unity and is polite, disarming, ironical. We are attacked or questioned by someone outside. One more point: To speak of the love of the lover is clearer than to speak of love with a capital L. Love with a capital L does not love. Wherever we find love we find a loving being, something which is not merely love but something else, for example, a woman of thirty-five, a man of seventy, whatever it may be. But Love, absolutized, does not love.

Does this sound strange? Common sense has no objection to it, but something else might. Have you never heard of the Platonic doctrine of ideas? According to Aristotle, the true dog is the dog running around here: multicolored, five years old, male, with a wound on his right eye. For Plato this is not the true dog. The true dog does not run around. The true dog is dogness, that which is common to all dogs, in which all dogs participate. Why Plato thought of this apparently fantastic doctrine is a very difficult question. Here we see a Platonic character make this commonsensical remark: love, that which is in all love and in all lovers. How can this be explained without opening up a very large question? According to an interpretation which I read in certain writers, Plato teaches that there are ideas of everything which is designated by a term which is not a proper name. There is no idea of Socrates. But whenever you find a noun or an adjective, there is surely an idea conforming to that. My favorite example is the third undersecretary of the Garment Workers Union. Even if there exists only one of those, there could exist an indefinite number, and therefore there is an idea of it. Somehow this sounds like an absolutely absurd doctrine. What is the use of such a duplication? The principle can be stated as follows: If there are ideas in any sense, there must be something which are not ideas, and above all there is something connecting the two realms. It follows from the very distinction between ideas and nonideas, that there are no ideas of the connecting link. Now, we have seen that eros connects the unchangeable, the immortal, with the mortal; therefore there cannot be, in the simplest terms, an idea of love, love being essentially in between ideas and nonideas.

> "'But the answer,' she said, 'still longs for the following question: What will he have whoever gets the beautiful things?' I said I was hardly able any longer to give a ready answer to this question. 'Well,' she said, 'if one should change the question and ask using the good instead of the beautiful, Come, Socrates, he who loves the good things loves, what does he love?' 'To become his,' I said. 'And what will he have whoever gets the good things?' 'I can answer this more readily,' I said. 'He will be happy.'" (204d8–e7)

The subject is changed from the beautiful to the good and then the answer becomes easy. This implies one crucial thing: that the good is not identical with the beautiful.

> "'The reason is,' she said, 'that by the possession of good things the happy are happy, and there is no longer any need to ask further "And what does he who wants to be happy want?," but the answer seems to be complete.' 'You're speaking the truth,' I said." (205a1–4)

Seems to be, she says. Happiness seems to be an answer which does not need any further question. It seems to be the end of man. We have here an example of what right opinion is. It is right opinion; it is not knowledge, for "it seems." It is not knowledge because it leaves unclear what happiness consists in. Men divine that they seek happiness, and they have a general understanding of what it is and we can crudely say, Happiness is a state of contentedness, you want nothing further, and at the same time an enviable state. Because a moron, for example, might be perfectly content but we would no longer say he is happy. This all men divine.

> "'Now this wanting and this eros, do you believe it is common to all human beings and everyone wants the good things to be theirs always, or how do you say?' 'In this way,' I said. 'It is common to all.' 'Why, then, Socrates,' she said, 'do we deny that all love, if, that is, all love the same things and always, but we say some love and some do not?' 'I myself also wonder,' I said." (205a5–b3)

We have, then, at least a beginning for a possible interpretation. All men always desire to be happy. This is eros. Eros is not desire for the beautiful, as we shall see later. Eros is desire for happiness. But this brings us into a difficulty because we do not call every human being a lover. Every human being is a lover of happiness, but only a certain kind of man we call lover. Someone might find happiness in a good state of health and nothing else. This difficulty will be solved in the course of the discussion. Socrates says, "I myself also wonder." Diotima says, "Don't wonder." In other words, Socrates you are mistaken if you think I, Diotima, wonder. I don't, I know. Begin to understand, begin to know.

> "'But don't wonder,' she said. 'Are you surprised that we remove from eros a certain species *[eidos]* of it, and, in imposing on it the name of the whole, we name it eros, but for all the other different parts we employ different names?'" (205b4–6)

Strictly speaking, all desire for happiness in any form should be called love; but with a single arbitrariness we call a certain kind of seeking happiness love. Well, which kind, may I ask? Sexual love.

> "'Such as what?' I said. 'Such as the following. You know that making *[poiesis]* is quite extensive, for, you know, the cause for anything whatsoever, in going from what is not to what is, is in its entirety a making, and hence just as the productions subject to all the arts are makings, so all the craftsmen of them are makers—poets *[poietai].*' 'What you say is true,' I said. 'But all the same,' she said, 'you know they are not called poets but they have different names, and from all of making one species has been separated off, that which is concerned with music and meters, and gets addressed by the name of the whole. This alone is called poetry *[poiesis],* and those who have this part of making poets.'" (205a7–c9)

It is not uninteresting that the example for illustrating eros is poetry. Plato never chooses an example at random. The example always means more than just an example. He indicates here the kinship between eros and poetry. We know that, in a way, this is the problem of the whole dialogue. Eros is the subject, but eros is to be praised and adorned, which is a poetic activity. Furthermore, the dialogue is a contest between a philosopher and the poets. If eros is love for the beautiful, poetry will perhaps be the highest form of eros. Let us see what the fate of poetry will be in Socrates' speech. Poetry, poesis, making, producing, are used here to illustrate eros. You remember in Agathon's speech one form of illustrating the wisdom of eros was the making, the producing of living beings. Here we get an indication that eros is somehow not making or producing. We also notice that there are forms of eros from which usage abstracts, and we know that Socrates will abstract

201

from certain aspects of eros, from the seamy side of eros. Perhaps this is prepared by common sense, which also calls certain forms of the quest for happiness eros.

> "'So too in the case of eros. The entire desire for the good things and for being happy is, in general, "the greatest and deceitful eros for everyone." But those who turn in many different directions toward it, either in terms of money making or love of exercise or philosophy, they are not said to love and are not called lovers; but those who go along a certain single species of it and are in earnest about it get the name of the whole: "eros," "to love," and "lovers."' 'You run the risk of speaking the truth,' I said." (205d1–9)

Men who seek their happiness in wealth, or in strength and health, or in wisdom are not called lovers; but they are lovers because they seek their own happiness. The central example here is strength or health. Here we have already a clear notion of one point: the men who find their happiness in wealth. They, too, are lovers, but this is a base love. We know, then, that there are base forms of love, and therefore the distinction between noble and base love made by Pausanias and Eryximachus is not wholly groundless.

Now the answer of Socrates: "You run the risk of speaking the truth." This is the literal translation. But look at the preceding answer; Socrates said, "What you say is true." Why this strange change? It would require a long and detailed statistical study of the *Symposium* and perhaps also of the other reported dialogues before one can answer that. One thing only is clear: The *Symposium* is a report given by Aristodemus to Apollodorus and by Apollodorus to his comrade. This report contains Socrates' report of his conversation with Diotima. Look how complicated it is: Socrates reports to Aristodemus, among others, at the symposium; Aristodemus reports to Apollodorus, and Apollodorus reports to the comrade. With the beginning of Socrates' report of his conversation with Diotima, all indication that this report is itself reported, namely by Aristodemus or Apollodorus, is dropped. This does not solve the difficulty I mentioned but it is a condition to be observed. When you read it you get the impression that it is reported by Socrates and not further reported, but it is. One could give another example to illustrate this difficulty. For example, in 202c5 "And I said, 'How,' I said, 'do you mean this?'" The redundancy would need an explanation which I am unable to give. This is just one of many questions which we leave open.

Listener: It struck me that the three examples of love Socrates gives here correspond to the examples he gives in his first speech in the *Phaedrus.* This group seems to constitute a comprehensive list.

Mr. Strauss: This is doubtless true. You mean one could solve the difficulty regarding love of health by the fact that it is given in an ascending order. Nevertheless, I believe that Plato, as all writers of this kind do, would apparently explain it by this simple reason. But the question is also whether Plato does not mean a bit more. Later on we will see that this is very meaningful. Love will prove to be immortal possession of the good. Therefore the question of immortality of your body arises. This is one possibility which one must consider. You cannot have by nature immortality of your body. This explains the eros that you can have can only be of the body of someone generated by you.

> "'And still a certain logos is spoken of,' she said, 'that says that those, whoever seek their own half, love . . .'" (205d10–e1)

You see the interesting thing: this allegedly antedated Aristophanes' speech by decades. But we know better.

> "'. . . but my logos denies that love is either of a half or of a whole, unless no doubt, my comrade, it is in fact good, since human beings are willing to have their feet and hands cut off, if it seems to them that their own are no good. For each of them severally does not cherish their own, unless someone calls the good one's own and of oneself and the bad whatever is alien, since there is nothing else that human beings love than the good. Or do they seem so to you?'" (205e1–206a1)

All eros is love of the good, and all desire for the good, however understood, is eros. This is the exact view. Eros is, therefore, not in particular love of one's half or the whole, because there is no reason to assume that the other half or the whole as such should be good. Diotima flatly contradicts Aristophanes. There is a joke here. She said at first that the name eros is ascribed to a part of eros, let us say to a half of eros. Now she turns from the error which limits love to half of love to the error which limits love to love of half. It seems to be a mere joke, but it is more than that. Love consists of two parts—of two halves: one half of love is love of the good, the other half is love of the half. Namely, as Aristophanes understood it, love of one's own. Diotima denies the existence of the latter. But it is more precise to say she abstracts. Explicitly she denies that it exists. Yet on what grounds? Men don't care for their own, she says. Look at the people who have their legs amputated, their teeth extracted, etc.; they throw away their own if they are bad. To dig a little deeper, why do they do it? Because they love to live, because they love their own life, their own psyche, which means not only soul but also life. I refer you to *Laws* 873c, if you think this is not a thought which could have occurred in Plato. Men love themselves and they love the good things for themselves. They want to appropriate them, to make them their own. In the passage we have read, Diotima says, "unless no doubt, my comrade, it is in fact good." I don't know whether there is another instance in classical Greek literature where a woman calls a man comrade. I regard it as possible that Socrates here, as it were, drops the mask and speaks to Aristophanes.

> "'No, by Zeus, not to me,' I said. 'Is it really the case, then,' she said, 'that one is to say so unqualifiedly that human beings love the good?' 'Yes,' I said." (206a3–5)

In the sequel we shall see that it is not so simple. The young Socrates was simple in believing that men love the good. Now we get an addition.

> "'What about this?' she said. 'Mustn't one add also that they love the good to be theirs?' 'One must add it.'" (206a6–8)

You see "theirs"—I want the good for myself. I want to make it my own. You see the thing is more subtle. Socrates moves away from this self.

> "'And not only that it be theirs but also be always theirs?' 'One must add this too.'" (206a9–10)

There are two additions made, three points: All men love the good, all men love the good for themselves, they love to have it always. The center one has to do with one's appropriating it, making it one's own. Then she summarizes.

> "'So eros, in summary,' she said, 'is of the good being one's own forever?' 'You speak most truly,' I said." (206a11–13)

Now we know: eros is love for the sempiternal possession of the good. That is the strict and exact definition of eros. More precise: the sempiternal possession by oneself of the good. These are the three items and we must see what will happen to them in the future.

> "'Since eros is always this,' she said, 'in what manner and in what action would the zeal and intensity of those who pursue it be called eros? What in fact is this deed? Can you say?'" (206b1–4)

In other words, Diotima says, you still haven't answered my question. All eros is desire for sempiternal possession of the good, however a man may understand the good; but, in fact, we do not call all men who desire the sempiternal possession of money or of health lovers. Our old question has not yet been answered. Now, what does she say?

> "'Well, in that case, Diotima,' I said, 'I would not be admiring you for wisdom and be frequently coming to you in order to learn these very things.' 'Well, I shall tell you,' she said. 'This [deed] is birth in the beautiful both in terms of the body and in terms of the soul.' 'As to what you mean,' I said, 'there is need of divination, and I don't understand.' 'Well,' she said, 'I shall speak more plainly. All human beings, Socrates, are pregnant both in terms of the body and in terms of the soul, and whenever they get to be of a certain age, our nature desires to give birth.'" (206b5–c4)

All human beings are in a sense women, they all are pregnant. There is then a nonhuman begetter. This is said by a woman. She will correct herself later, but this is the way in which she begins. The subject of the pregnancy of all men will come up later, perhaps you know from another Platonic dialogue, about Socrates being a midwife, which implies that men, too, in a way can be pregnant. This whole subject is here alluded to. Now we get the answer.

> "It is incapable of giving birth in the ugly, but in the beautiful. For the intercourse [being together] of a man and a woman is birth. This matter is divine and is the deathless in the animal that is mortal, the pregnancy and the generation. And that which is in the disharmonious cannot come to be; the ugly is in disharmony with everything divine, and the beautiful is harmonious. Beauty [Kallone] is Fate [Moira] and Eilythuia for generation. It is on account of this that whenever the pregnant thing draws near the beautiful, it becomes cheerful and in its cheerfulness it dissolves [becomes relaxed] and gives birth and generates; but whenever it draws near the ugly, scowling and in pain it coils up and turns away and rolls up and does not generate, but in holding on to the embryo it bears it hard. It is from this source that for the one who is pregnant and already swelling the excitement about the beautiful becomes overwhelming, on account of its releasing the one who has it from great labor pains.'" (206c4–e1)

The question was this: Love is desire for sempiternal possession by oneself of the good, however that good may be understood. Yet, men, in fact, mean by love—eros—sexual love, especially of men and women. How can we understand this? Giving birth is possible only in the beautiful, for eros is every desire for sempiternal possession of the good. But only sexual desire is called eros. Why? Men and women are attracted to one another by beauty, especially beautiful bloom. Men think that eros is love of the beautiful. But the attraction between the two sexes leads to sexual union. In other words, love comes in only in an intermediate stage. It seems to culminate in sexual union. Yet sexual union itself is not the end. The end is giving birth. The latter—giving birth—and only it, is the divine thing, the immortal within the mortal. We need no extraneous, divine begetter. The union of mortal and mortal does not need an extraneous mediator, a demon. The immortal is discordant with the ugly. The beautiful is a reflection of the immortal in the mortal or, one can also say, the beautiful is only a means, a decoy, a condition for sempiternal possession of the good. The sempiternal possession of the good is giving birth to an offspring.

> "'For eros, Socrates,' she said, 'is not of the beautiful, as you believe.'"
> (206e1–2)

Now the break with Agathon occurs, if we forget for one moment that Diotima is said to be the speaker. In this section Socrates rejects the two notions regarding eros: Eros is love of one's own—Aristophanes' assertion; eros is love of the beautiful—Agathon's assertion. Eros is not love for the beautiful; the beautiful is only a transitional stage, a ruse of nature you could say.

> "'Well, what then?' 'Of the generation and birth in the beautiful.' 'Alright,' I said." (206e4–6)

"Alright" is here, in this connection, a somewhat grudging admission. Socrates is somehow disappointed.

> "'Indeed it is,' she said. 'Why then is it of generation? Because generation is always-becoming and deathless, for a mortal. On the basis of what has been agreed on, it is a necessity to desire immortality along with good, provided eros is to be of the good being one's own forever. So it is a necessity on the basis of this logos that eros is also of immortality.'" (206e7–207a4)

That is the end of this section which I call IIIB. It is the central section of the Socrates-Diotima conversation, and we see why it deserves to be put in the center. We have the two alternative interpretations regarding love—love as love of one's own and love as love of the beautiful—both rejected. The question which was raised is now answered. To repeat: Love is love for the sempiternal possession of the good. But the only form of love which we ordinarily know which meets this condition is sexual, heterosexual love. Everything is fine. Eros is desire for one's own sempiternal possession of the good, that was the premise.

But, there is a little difficulty here, which you can see from the passage we just read. What is sexual desire? Sexual desire is desire for immortality—sempiternity—together with the good. Do you see something? Is desire also for immortality? The desire for wealth cannot reasonably include immortality. Let me present it to you so you can see: sempiternal—I say my own—good. What about sexual limits? What have we here, according to the analysis up to now? Immortality together with the good—what's missing and is crucial? The entire later movement is needed in order to bring in my own. Why these strange goings-on we cannot answer before we have assembled the data, and, as the social scientists say, the data are not yet assembled.

The desire for one's own is dropped. Eros is directed toward immortality plus the good. This explains the usage regarding eros. If you apply it, for example, to health or wealth, the desire for health or wealth is incompatible with the desire for the immortality of these goods, because these goods are by their nature incapable of immortality. Only immortality of the species is naturally possible. Eros is desire for procreation for this reason. Many questions remain. Where does beauty come in? You see, Socrates made this great concession to Agathon. He says, "You are right, in a way; eros is love of the beautiful, but you take a transitional stage for the end." Is even this not a false concession of Socrates? Let us be commonsensical. I have heard of cases where procreation took place while both parents were ugly. What would you say to this objection? One could say love makes them more beautiful. I have even seen a case of a man who was not even particularly intelligent but had a great love for things of the mind, and that made him, without any great pretense on his part, to appear more intelligent than he was. Permit me to add some commonsensical qualification: they are more beautiful when in love, at least up to a point, at least in the eyes of one another. Therefore beauty must come in another way.

Listener: According to the text it is desire for procreation which creates beauty. Didn't you reverse this?

Mr. Strauss: Don't you have to start from the end to understand the transition, the condition?

Listener: In this case the end seems to create the precondition itself.

Mr. Strauss: It explains it. For example, if you see a movement made by a carpenter, this movement is created, to use your strong expression, by the end, the end being the making of the chair, and you have to start from the end. The dissatisfaction which you rightly feel, though not on the grounds stated, I will try to take care of by the following consideration: According to this analysis, eros implies the transcending of death, the negating of death. This means accepting one's own death. This is the beautiful—*kalon*. You must never forget that the word *kalon* means also noble or fair, both in the bodily and in the nonbodily sense. Everything ennobling is connected with one's transcending one's poor self. The most visible and the most impressive form of self-sacrifice is accepting death, willingness to die. The lovers as lovers, in this strict sense of sexual union, without knowing it, accept death. In the Song of Songs it is said "love is strong like death." This is essential to love, otherwise it is not love. I would like to explain this as follows: eros implies negating death and thus it presupposes death. You cannot understand eros without taking into consideration death. Just as in Aristophanes, where eros was revolt against the nomos, eros presupposes nomos. In Aristophanes, the desire for one's own is impeded by the convention and yet made possible by the convention. I presuppose now my interpretation. If the scission is establishment of the nomos and eros arises only after that, then the desire for one's own is both impeded by the convention . . .

[Tape change.]

In Socrates, eros is directed toward an open future, a future which is possible in nature, namely the preservation of the human species. That makes sense. What Aristophanes said does not make sense. He knew that it did not make sense, he was a comic poet, but he made a big mistake in spite of all his cleverness, as indicated here. Socrates' or Diotima's solution is really the sensible solution. It has only one defect: this immortality does not fulfill the desire of the individual for sempiternal possession of the good by the individual in question. Let us assume you are fortunate enough to have children of your own which continue your life: you cannot possibly know the situation two or three generations later. It is a mere gamble whether your blood will perpetuate itself sempiternally. In conclusion, I note that in this whole discussion there is not a trace of a place for pederasty. Love is heterosexual love directed toward procreation. This is, in a way, very comforting for our moral nature. But I have to add immediately that there is also no exclusion of incest. And this should not be surprising. For, as we have seen in the statement about eros's genealogy, eros has nothing to do with moderation and justice. The rules against incest belong either under the heading of justice or under the heading of moderation. I refer you to Aristotle's

Politics 1263b9–11, if you have any doubt about the connection with moderation. But the connection with justice is obvious because of the family, and the polis stands and falls by the prohibition against incest.

Now let me summarize the central part of the dialogue with Diotima. First, it explicitly refutes the contentions of Aristophanes and Agathon. Love is neither love of one's own nor love of the beautiful. Eros is one's desire for sempiternal possession of the good, but she drops one's possession. That means she drops the reference to oneself, to one's own. Eros is desire for sempiternity of the species, and therefore the individual's immortality, the individual's good, is forgotten. Another more striking feature about this section, in contrast to the preceding section, is the complete silence about the gods. For example, in the section on poetry—poesis—reference is made only to human making, no reference to the gods as makers. The divine, the neuter, is mentioned, not the gods. I believe there is a connection between these two features. With the rejection of these two notions of love and the silence about the gods I can try to explain it, though we have to wait for a confirmation of a point from what follows. The gods are essentially related to eros. We are speaking now of the Olympian gods, not of the cosmic gods of which Plato speaks elsewhere. The gods have been created by eros and it is only another version to say the gods have been created by the poets, or the poets were guided by eros in creating the gods. How? It is easiest to understand in the case of eros as love of the beautiful, why love of the beautiful should create the Olympian gods—eternal beauty, deathless youth, something man can never achieve and which he loves. Sempiternal strength and beauty of one's body. But what about love of one's own? The love of one's own leads to the polis. It leads first to the family, and the family cannot exist without the polis. The political society is, of course, always a closed society. By a closed society I mean one which does not include the human race. The universal society would be, strictly speaking, the community of all human beings. The polis is never that. The polis is always some men's own, even if there are 170 million. The human race is by nature sempiternal, at least as said here; the polis is not by nature sempiternal, it cannot be sempiternal but it wishes to be, and it is, therefore, in need of gods. These gods, as the guardians of the polis, are primarily the guardians of right. They are the avenging gods. The union of the beautiful gods and the avenging gods, which appears directly in the mythical presentation, has its common root in eros, but in two different manifestations—the love of one's own, on the one hand, and the love of the beautiful, on the other. With the provisional denial of love of one's own and love of the beautiful, the basis for these gods is destroyed and the question is what will be the next step. Because love of the beautiful and love of one's own will have to be restored. They exist and they are the most important manifestations of love. But the question is what will be the fate of the gods in this restoration.

Listener: Why are they guardians of the beautiful rather than the good?

Mr. Strauss: What is the good now here as distinguished from the beautiful? What quality of the gods do you have in mind when you speak now of the good?

Listener: Perfection.

Mr. Strauss: Which perfection?

Listener: Their immortality, happiness, beauty.

Mr. Strauss: I think their most outstanding feature, at first glance, apart from their beauty, would be their concern with right. For example, Zeus is the king. What does that mean? As he is presented by Homer, he is a very superior king who is concerned with right. That Homer questions this is of course true; but don't forget that it is a gross injustice, Helen and Paris, which underlies the Trojan War. If you would say the wisdom of the gods, then the question is whether this is truly achieved by the Olympian gods. If you take the notion of gods as the most perfect beings, the question arises, Can there be a plurality of such beings? Therefore the many monotheistic remarks occurring in Plato. But, if we disregard this great difficulty for one moment, what is characteristic of the gods? The mere fact that there is one goddess, Athena, singled out with a view to wisdom, Zeus more for his royal wiliness, shows that this is not characteristic of the gods. But what stands out in each case is their immortal beauty, and even that is qualified in the case of Hephaestus with his limping, and shows that there are other elements there too. These two heterogeneous elements—the sheer beauty, which in itself has no relation to guardianship of right, and the other one, the concern with avenging, with concern for right, which can lead to an aspect of the gods which is at least not emphatically beautiful—I believe that is what he means.

Listener: Eros understood as the sempiternal possession of the good does not exhaust eros because it still leaves the problem of the individual. Does generation come under the heading of the good?

Mr. Strauss: This is perfectly correct. That is what the good means here. We are told to find the answer to our question in the phenomenon of human procreation. We have the element of immortality in the fact of sempiternal procreation. Where do we find the fact of the good? It must be implied in there. Mere being. That might be, but I must tell you that this question will be taken up by Diotima in the next part of her speech. And in this part, where the same phenomenon is discussed—procreation—the good is dropped. Procreation supplies sempiternity. The good is out, because mere being in the narrow sense of the word is hardly good. Let us wait for that.

Listener: Procreation does not only mean the continuance of a being or of the blood, but you could say the good comes in by carrying on a set of social values, a value system which a person considers the good.

Mr. Strauss: May I take issue with the term 'value' you used, this is not translatable into Plato, and is a misleading term. You mean the good and noble and just things. No one every answered the question What is a value? Is an apple a value, if I desire it? There is really no clarity what a value means, whether it is an apple if desired or the principle why I desire it—say, because it is healthy, or pleasant. I think it is really a bad word. We can, of course, speak of the value of an umbrella, which is an entirely legitimate use of the term. But to come back to your question and forget what some might call the semantic side of the question, I would say this: The consideration on which you insist is absolutely reasonable and is, therefore, also considered in the next part, in the central section of the last part of Diotima's speech. I will indicate in what way: Plato always insists that in order to understand any human phenomenon you must look at the highest and most complete manifestation of it. Contrary to the tendency of social science today which looks mostly at the poorest manifestations of it—it looks at the narrowest, which can most easily be reproduced for questionnaire situations and things like that. To take up your question, Plato would say, let us look at that. He calls this, in a language which is somewhat metaphoric but at least as intelligible as the value terminology, the begetting, the generation in the souls of men. In other words, mere procreation will not produce the values of society, as you can easily see; when such a baby is transferred into an entirely different society, it will not be affected by the values of the society in which it was generated. The question is, then, the begetting of notions which are noble and just in the souls of men. Very well, Plato says, if you want to study that, let us look at it on the highest level. On the highest level it does not take place by the parents as parents. Parents as parents may not be the best, though they might be. On the highest level it is done by the highest form of educators. By educators you must not think of Columbia Teachers College. What Plato has in mind is the greatest poets. In other words, he has in mind, to speak of the Anglo-Saxon countries, the highest form of begetter—Shakespeare. There may be perfect concord among parents, though this is rare, but the mere need for concord shows the difficulty. In the case of this primary educator, a poet of the first order, the problem of concord does not arise. So the problem is not forgotten by any means. You can say what we have in the center part is the most dreary section of the whole presentation. Love of one's own is rejected, love of the beautiful is rejected, what remains? Mere concern with procreation. We should not minimize that, but it is surely an insufficient account of eros, even of heterosexual eros.

[In answer to a question:] I think one has to consider that, but I said, nevertheless, beauty does come in insofar as every overcoming of the concern with one's self-preservation is *kalon*.

Listener: Then the beauty is something which arises out of desire?

Mr. Strauss: That is the same from Plato's point of view. From any teleological point of view what you call the cause is a means. I believe that is your difficulty.

Listener: It seems to me in practice there is an essential difference between that which must exist before the activity can begin and that which arises out of the activity.

Mr. Strauss: For example, there must be trees before there can be wood. But the trees as trees are not wood, if I may express myself paradoxically. The tree as tree is not material for chairs. What Plato denies is that love of beauty has this absolute self-subsistence and self-sufficiency which tree has. Love of the beautiful is essentially ordered toward procreation. That it appears to be self-sufficient when two people are in love with one another, and they happen to be beautiful so that they are attracted by each other's beauty, they may very well believe, especially when they are very young, that this is it. If two human beings of different sex are attracted by one another's beauty, erotically they desire one another; this is essentially different from, say, the desire to possess a beautiful painting.

Listener: Isn't it still true according to Plato in this section, even where the possibility of procreation existed, it might be denied them for lack of beauty?

Mr. Strauss: Wouldn't this be an empirical falsehood of the first order? The text here is also a bit delicate. What Plato describes are certain phenomena which are described in textbooks of physiology. I think one can, without great difficulty, recognize that. Surely there is such a thing as repulsion. There are cases where a woman is repulsive to a man and he cannot generate, and there are other cases where attractiveness, beauty, actualizes the desire for generation—although it may in consciousness only be desire for sexual union, but since sexual union is by nature directed toward generation it has that.

Listener: This passage which begins with the notion that all men are pregnant, then shifts to the notion of procreation but with the earlier use of poetry—the artist bringing forth a work of art. Is this a kind of begetting and producing?

Mr. Strauss: Socrates and Diotima have a certain malice against the poets, and that will come out. To say briefly what will happen in the sequel: In A there will be a restoration of love of one's own; in B again love of one's own, where the beautiful comes in as an indispensable means. This is where he talks about the poets and he talks again about the mental parallel to bodily begetting, where the purpose of the whole thing is not beauty but immortality, though it does go through beauty. Homer produces beautiful children, the *Iliad* and the *Odyssey,* in order to become immortal. The production of beautiful things is not the end, which is a nasty accusation you can say, but here we are. In the third part, the final part, where he speaks of what people would call philosophy, the love of the beautiful triumphs. Socrates' whole speech is characterized by the following fact: It begins with a refutation of the assertion that love is love of the beautiful and it ends with an unbelievable reassertion that love is love of the beautiful. This massive contradiction is of course not done because Plato had a loose mind, but because he wanted to do something. He deliberately abstracted from the two forms of love—love of one's own and love of the beautiful—to see what comes out of it, a perfectly common scientific procedure, and then he restores them. This has also the following meaning, that eros, which is the subject, is subjected to a purification, to a catharsis. But what we call in the moral sense purification is, intellectually, an analysis, dividing it into essential parts and seeing the difference.

Listener: In this section there seems to be sometimes a false disjunction between love of the beautiful or love of the good versus love of one's own. Perhaps there is a third, what Aristotle calls friendship. I think this has to be taken into account.

Mr. Strauss: Surely. But the question is only that what Aristotle understands by friendship is not what one primarily means by eros. Aristotle also mentions the remarkable fact that when people are truly friends they like to be together. Don't underestimate that. This means not merely the writing of letters, but they themselves, i.e., their bodies, together. This has nothing to do with any indecencies, but it is not unimportant that the so-called personal presence is required for the highest fulfillment of friendship. But truly, it is not the same as eros as used here in this emphatic sense. Can one speak as easily as one can speak of passionate eros of passionate friendship? I believe that friendship is cooler than eros.

Listener: Suppose you put it in the realm of eros and speak of, say, what pertains between husband and wife, that somehow there seems to be a falsification of this reality by reducing it to an eros for the preservation of the race.

Mr. Strauss: That this is true is perfectly clear. This was the question which has been raised before, not only the procreation but also the education of the offspring.

Listener: It seems to me that there is an essential part of this relationship which can be legitimately abstracted from.

Mr. Strauss: That is a very great question and, as all these questions, it has been treated by the very great minds. In marriage two people of different sex lead a noble life together which they could not possibly do in any other way, and yet there is no reference to offspring. Kant, who was very far removed form Plato and Aristotle and who was very much concerned with universally valid formulations, tried to solve this question by his notorious definition of marriage—because he was thinking of this fact of childless marriage—and therefore he said, and I can only say I am not responsible for this definition: marriage is a lifelong union for the purpose of mutual use of the genitals. This happens when you try to have a universally valid formula for a complicated phenomenon which does not allow it. Plato and Aristotle were wiser. They said we can give a formula for the best, for the perfect, and we thus imply the various forms of deficiencies. Therefore I would say that a childless marriage between the noblest human beings is yet defective. This is perfectly compatible with the fact that a given marriage, productive of offspring, say twenty-five children, is humanly impossible compared with such a childless marriage. Yet the essential relation of the living together, in the highest sense, is the intention of nature, the procreation and education of children. This seems to me the only sensible view unless we say, Who cares for nature? Don't forget that the difference between men and women is also a bodily difference.

[In answer to a question:] This noble man and this noble woman, where there is no relation of the body but only friendship—why should they marry? Why should they live together? This friendship between a man and a woman may be very high, but it is not marriage. Human things are complicated and according to the Platonic and Aristotelian view the only universality we can legitimately find in human things is on the level of perfection, not on the behavioral level. On the behavioral level there is infinite variety, and if you really think something universally valid, which is true of all men, you will find on reflection that it is true only of all men who are not insane. Insane men are also human. The universally valid we cannot find behaviorally, by which I do not mean we should not watch human behavior very carefully, but we should do it in the proper perspective and with a view to the normal and perfection.

Listener: I still find it difficult to understand why the gods in relation to the city are products of the desire for beauty.

Mr. Strauss: Not in relation to the city. The gods as beautiful have no relation to the city, they are the product of the human love of beauty. This has no essential relations to the polis.

Listener: Why could one not argue that desire for bodily sempiternity creates the beauty?

Mr. Strauss: The point is this: one must always consider the essential difference between the unqualifiedly natural human society and qualified natural association—the polis. Let us see how this question will come out when we have made some headway. Let us only read the beginning where we left off.

> "'So all these things she used to teach me, whenever she talked about erotic things, and once she asked me . . .'" (207a5–6)

"Once she asked me." This is not a simple continuation of the conversation, which a superficial glance at what follows might lead one to believe, but a new beginning. The subject is no longer the nature of eros, or the works of eros, but, as appears from the immediate sequel, the cause of this eros and desire. This eros, not eros with a capital *E,* the demon. Eros is used here synonymously with desire, there is no longer any personification. What is the cause of that? This, one can say, is the beginning, though only sketched, of a philosophic inquiry. To use the older Greek term, of a physiological inquiry, which means making reasoned speeches about nature, not scientific as people would say today.

11 SOCRATES (3)

Today we must, if we can, finish our discussion of Socrates' discussion with Diotima, but it is necessary that we remind ourselves of some very broad features of the *Symposium* up to this point. The *Symposium* contains six speeches on eros, three uninspired and three inspired. There is a parallelism between these speeches: Phaedrus, Pausanias, Eryximachus, on the one hand; Aristophanes, Agathon, Socrates, on the other. Gain, moral virtue, techne: Phaedrus's gain and ugliness belong together; Agathon's beauty and moral virtue; and Eryximachus's techne and the good, Socrates' principle, belong together. But there is another idea which runs through the second, third, and fourth speeches: the defense of pederasty. We arrive, then, at this very interesting suggestion, that prior to Socrates are two speakers, Phaedrus and Agathon, who are, to say the least, indifferent to pederasty and do not defend it. They are, of course, judiciously chosen: they are the young ones; they are only the objects of pederasty and not the active pederasts.

A word about Socrates' speech in particular. This speech consists of seven parts: First, the introduction on how to speak, namely, the truth about the most noble thing about the subject. Second, Socrates' dialogue with Agathon; eros as love of the beautiful is not itself beautiful nor is he good. The third part is the dialogue of the young Socrates with Diotima. The first part of that speech is about the nature of eros; eros is not a god but a demon. The second part, which we discussed last time—the only part here which is due to Socrates' initiative—why is eros useful to human beings. In other words, what are the deeds, the actions, of eros. Diotima said eros is love for one's sempiternal possession of the good, for one's sempiternal happiness. But not every form of one's desire for sempiternal possession of the good is called eros. For example, if one finds one's happiness in the accumulation of gold, he is not called a lover. Eros, therefore, is desire for immortality together with the good, and that immortality is achieved by procreation. So the usage when we speak of lovers with a view to sexual love is justified. The broader meaning is the desire for sempiternal possession of any good. This is too broad and the reconciliation is that eros is desire for immortality together with the good, not merely for the good. Such desire for immortality is not implied in the love of money, for example. This immortality is achieved by procreation, where the mortal nature participates in the deathless by the constant re-creation of human beings.

Two special points follow from that: eros is neither love of one's own—this is said against Aristophanes—nor is it love of the beautiful, and this is said against Agathon. If two young people of different sex are attracted to one another by their beauty they do not know that what attracts them truly is the need for procreation, not the need for beauty. The second striking feature of this part is the silence on gods and on immortality proper, the immortality of the individual. The last point: eros is here compared to poetry. That eros has a very broad meaning, intelligently understood, but is, in fact, limited to sexual love, finds its parallel in the fact that poetry—poesis—means primarily all production, but is limited to poetic production. In this respect there is a similarity between eros and poetry.

The connection between these items is the following: By denying that eros is eros of one's own and that eros is love of the beautiful, one is led to the rejection of the gods, for the gods are created by poets, either the great poets, Homer and Hesiod, as Herodotus said, or anonymous poets antedating Homer and Hesiod. The gods are created through poets by love of the beautiful, on the one hand—therefore they are eternally young and eternally beautiful—and by eros of one's own, on the other. Of one's own, the descendant of one's own ancestor, the deification of the ancestor, and, on a higher level, the gods of the polis who are concerned with right, the avenging gods. Now we come to the last part of Diotima's speech, and this is the end of Socrates' speech.

"'What, Socrates, do you believe is the cause of this eros and desire?'" (207a6–7)

Diotima here begins the investigation of the cause of this eros or desire. Eros is here no longer treated as a demon, for if he were treated as a demon the question of his cause would no longer arise: the question of the cause of Eros with a capital E has been answered. The inquiry which begins here is philosophic and in no way mythological; it is physiologic, i.e., concerned with the nature of this particular phenomenon. Furthermore, she asks for the cause of this eros, namely, eros as desire for procreation. This eros alone will be discussed here.

"'Or aren't you aware how uncannily all beasts are disposed whenever they desire, both the terrestrial and the winged, that all are sick and erotically disposed, first in regard to mixing together, and second in regard to the raising of what is born, and they are ready to fight on their behalf, the weakest against the strongest and to die for them, while they themselves are racked by hunger, so as to bring them up, and there is nothing else which they don't do; for in the case of human beings,' she said, 'one might believe that they do these things on the basis of calculation; but what is the cause in the case of beasts that they are so erotically disposed? Can you say?'" (207a7–c1)

In her investigation of eros, Diotima, as physiologist, as a natural scientist, considers the brutes. The question raised by Socrates at the beginning of the preceding section was What is eros's utility for human beings? By this question Socrates conceived of eros somehow as controlled by man. What is its use? How must we guard against it? The consideration of the brutes is made in order to make clear that eros, in the case of man, is not based on calculation. The thought is not absurd. We find quite a few references in Aristophanes and in Xenophon to this effect, that parents generate children in order to have someone take care of them when they are old—social security. For all we know this may play a role with many parents, but Diotima is of the opinion that it is insufficient as an explanation, because the brutes are incapable of such social security calculation and therefore there must be something deeper—an instinct, not a deliberation. Since it is an instinct, men cannot control eros. Man is driven and can never overcome it.

The second point to observe is that we see here two elements of this eros common to all animals. The first is the direction toward sexual union; the second is the direction toward care for offspring, a point not made before. These two, sexual union and care for offspring, are the things with which animals are preoccupied, as distinguished from begetting and giving birth, for this, in principle at least, takes place without them. Once sexual union takes place the begetting takes place and giving birth follows in natural order without man interfering, except accidentally. These two elements, then, are described as a kind of sickness, there is nothing beautiful about it. Or, to look forward to another Platonic dialogue, the *Phaedrus,* they are a kind of madness, madness being the opposite of calculation. This means a complete forgetting of oneself. The calculating man never forgets himself. The madman, mad for good or ill, forgets himself. This self-forgetting can merely be low, but it can also be higher than any calculation. In eros, then, there is a complete forgetting of oneself, a complete forgetting of one's own. In this there is an element of beauty in eros, even in this limited form.

Let us never forget that the central figure in this dialogue, if we disregard Socrates, is Eryximachus, the physician. The medical point of view is that of the valetudinarian, which is the clearest opposition to the erotic point of view. You can also take the miser as the opposite to the erotic man, but I think it is more powerful to take the valetudinarian, because he too has to do with the body. The erotic man is concerned with the body but in an opposite direction. This remark about the loving dying for the loved was made by Phaedrus in 179b, but there it was said only about human beings and only about the lovers in their relation to the beloved, not of the offspring. The fact that the parents are willing to die for their offspring is a new consideration. This is also extended beyond man. All animals are willing to die for their offspring.

> "And I was saying once more that I did not know; and she said, 'Do you really think you will ever be skilled in erotic things, if you do not understand these things?' 'But it is for this reason, you see, Diotima, that I have come to you, just as I said just now, in the realization that I am in need of teachers.'" (207c2–6)

Socrates gets another rebuke from his severe teacher. One cannot become an outstanding erotic if one does not know these things. That is to say, they are the cause of the erotic things. This may seem to refer to 206b, which we read last time, and that would mean that the conversation takes place on the same day. But it is also possible that Socrates omitted something in his report of his conversation with Diotima and that he had made a similar remark in the omitted part. The most you can say is that it is ambiguous whether Socrates' conversation with Diotima consisted of two parts or of three. But if it is ambiguous, the plan of this section is ambiguous. What does this mean? We have to decide it, because Plato is not a loose writer. If Plato is ambiguous, the ambiguity is intended. The reader has to solve the ambiguity and must find which division is best. Is this a new part, as I contended, or not? Socrates does not repeat here the expression of his admiration for Diotima, which he did in the parallel passage in 206b. He now says that he needs teachers, plural, i.e., teachers other than Diotima. Naturally, he is not satisfied with Diotima's account of eros. There are other forms of eros, namely, other forms than heterosexual love, specifically human forms or higher forms. Socrates is young, he still despises the lowly things which everyone knows and everyone sees. Proof: *Parmenides* 130e, where Socrates is presented as because of his youth still despising the lowly.

> "'Well, then,' she said, 'if you trust that eros is by nature of that which we have often agreed to, don't go on wondering. In this case, there is the same logos as in that, that mortal nature as far as possible seeks to be always and immortal.'" (207c8–d2)

The cause of eros is the subject. The mortal nature craves immortality. Previously she had said, in section IIIB, that he craves immortality together with the good. Now she says eros is desire only for immortality; the good is tacitly dropped.

> "'It is only possible in this way, by becoming, because it is always leaving behind another young in place of the old. Since in whatever time each one of the animals is said to be alive and be the same—for example, he is spoken of as the same from childhood up to his becoming old—he, however, though he never has the same things in himself, nevertheless is called the same, but he is always becoming young, losing something, hair, flesh, bones, blood, and the body altogether.'" (207d2–e1)

Immortality is possible only by the substitution of one individual of the species for another. In a way, this is the preservation of the same individual. For what we call preservation of the same individual, is also a constant substitution of the new for the old. The change from a man to his offspring is not essentially different from the change in the same man from childhood to old age. This, I would say, is some exaggeration in order to make us swallow the bitter pill of our mortality. She speaks of a continuous loss of parts of the body; she does not place equal emphasis on their constant recovery. This is important. In Krüger's interpretation, this is taken to mean the following: Man is a being in time, a temporal being. To be in time means to decay. Time is the ground for decay because time is passing away. This applies even to science as will be stated shortly. This is apparently the doctrine of Aristotle in *Physics*, book 4. Aristotle makes some powerful remarks about this. But if one reads on, one sees that for Aristotle this is only a primary aspect of time. To the extent to which we can speak of time as a cause, Aristotle says time is also the cause of coming into being. Therefore the famous statement: truth is the fruit of time. That which underlies the modern idea of progress is, of course, also an effect of time. The "pessimistic" notion of time was a popular notion, not the view of Aristotle and Plato. The life of the individual is already a constant dying. The death of the individual is not so important. Therefore the concern with one's own immortality is not important. That is the meaning of this passage.

> "'And not only in his body, but also in his soul, his ways, characters, opinions, desires, pleasures, pains, fears—each of these never is present in him as the same, but some are coming to be, and some are perishing.'" (207e1–5)

What is true of the body, that it doesn't last, is true also of what in modern language would be called consciousness—the Greeks say the soul. But, interestingly enough, now she speaks not only of the loss taking place in time, but of the recovery as well. If living is dying, which, in a sense, is true, it is also reviving. There is a fundamental difference between the dying of a cell in me, or of hair by being cut off, and my death simply, because I cease to be.

> "'And still far stranger than this is that the sciences too, not only do some of them come to be and others perish for us, but also each one of the sciences undergoes the same thing. For what is called "to practice" is so on the grounds that the science is going out, for the going out of a science is forgetting and practice is the reinsertion again of a new memory in place of that which is going away, and it preserves the science, so as for it to be thought to be the same. In this manner everything mortal is preserved, not by absolutely being always the same, as the divine is, but by the fact that that which is going away and getting old leaves behind another young such as it itself was. By this device, Socrates,' she said, 'mortal partakes of immortality, both body and everything else, but the immortal does it in another way. So don't wonder that everything by nature honors its own offspring, for this kind of zeal and eros attends on everything for the sake of immortality.'" (207e5–208b6)

The key theme seems to be, eros is love of immortality. The good as good is no longer the theme. Let us consider a few details: We change constantly, she says, and that means, of course, we are. We remain alive. We could not change if we were not. We constantly change so much that every part of us changes; for instance, every single piece of knowledge we have changes. Let us assume you have complete possession of a mathematical theory—even that changes. In what sense? It is the same piece of knowledge which is recovered. In spite of the change there is permanence, whereas in the case of blood and bones it is not the same that is recovered. If a cell disintegrates a new cell is formed. But the Pythagorean theorem comes back as identically the same theorem. There is, then, also permanence of the same; but in the case of every individual living being there is a finite permanence. The transition from a living being to its offspring is essentially different from the transition of one stage in the life of one living being to the next stage. In other words, the immortality of the species is radically different from the immortality of the individual; but the immortality of the individual is not available to the brute, and tacitly to all living beings. Mortal beings partake of immortality regarding body and everything else only by generation or procreation. Hence, and now we come to the paradoxical conclusion, every mortal being honors its own offspring. That means that love of immortality, as discussed in this subsection, is love of one's own. The care for the offspring is care for one's own offspring, as can be shown by the many cases of stepmothers and stepfathers and by the famous stories told by biologists of how easily rats can be deceived about the identity of their offspring, whereas the human mother cannot be so easily deceived by such substitutions. In the *Republic* 330c, it is mentioned in the conversation with Cephalus that fathers love their children, as the poets love their poems, differently from the way they love someone else's poems. Love of one's own, which is in many ways silly, is nevertheless a phenomenon of human nature.

I summarize what we have seen in this section: It is a physiological study of the ground or reason or cause of the love for sexual union plus love of offspring. This study leads to the recognition of the fact that eros is eros of one's own but not of the beautiful. In this section there is no mention of either the beautiful or the good. Nor is there any mention of the gods of individual immortality. This part of the Diotima section—I will now introduce subdivision IIIC1—corresponds somehow to Agathon's speech. There is an important parallel: When Agathon praises eros, eros is wisdom, eros is the highest virtue; he mentions in the central part that wisdom is played by eros in procreation. You have an allusion to that here. She speaks of "this device" (208b2). This has something to do with wisdom in the wider sense. But in contradistinction to Agathon, Diotima does not say that this is the cleverness or wisdom of eros. On the contrary, eros is the cleverness of nature. This much about the first subdivision. To repeat: At this point love of the beautiful and love of one's own have been dropped. There is only love of sempiternal possession of the good. But this love of immortality proves to be love of one's own. When people generate children they are not concerned with preserving the human species; that is the intention of nature, but they are concerned only with perpetuating themselves. Love is love for one's own children. Love of one's own, then, has been restored. What happens to the other forms of love will come out in the next two sections.

Listener: In what sense can it not be said that men are willing to die because of their love of happiness?

Mr. Strauss: Because they regard their own, their children, as higher than their own in the more literal sense, their own body, which is destined to die sooner. This question will be answered as we go along.

"And I, when I heard the logos wondered and said, 'Very well.' I said, 'Wisest Diotima, is this the way these things truly are?' And she, just as the perfect sophists, said . . ." (208b7–c1)

Socrates again takes the initiative, the only other time he took it was at IIIB (204c7), the central part of the whole speech with Diotima; and now again in IIIC, the central part of the subdivision. Socrates had been told at 207C not to wonder, but after he heard Diotima's argument, he began to wonder, i.e., he is incredulous. Yet at the end he says, I have been persuaded by Diotima. If that is the case, it can only be by IIIC2 and 3. While Socrates was still incredulous, he called Diotima "wisest." When he delivers the speech to the symposium, he calls her the perfect sophist. In the *Symposium*, sophist is a term of praise; eros himself, for example, is called a sophist and at the same time a philosopher. As a philosopher he doesn't possess wisdom, he only seeks it; when he is called a sophist, he is not a perfect sophist, a complete possessor of wisdom.

"'Know well, Socrates, since if you are willing to glance at the love of honor in the case of human beings, you would wonder at its irrationality if you don't understand what I have said, when you reflect on how uncannily they are disposed by the eros of becoming renowned and "to lay down deathless fame for ever." On its behalf they are prepared to run all risks to a still greater degree than on behalf of their children, and to spend money and toil at any kind of toil whatsoever and to die for it.'" (208c1–d2)

Ambition is the theme in IIIC2, as procreation was in IIIC1, but ambition in the full sense, immortal fame. Can other than human beings have ambition? Who else can have love of honor, passion for honor? The gods. In particular, the gods as presented by Agathon; in 197a–b he speaks of the god's ambition. Here the argument is limited to human ambition, and human ambition shows the same irrationality, to an even higher degree than the desire for procreation and offspring does. What does irrationality mean here? Rationality, here, means calculation in the service of self-preservation. If you calculate correctly with a view of self-preservation, then you are a rational man. If you lack such calculation, you are an irrational man. Now, the parents dying for their children and the heroic man dying for immortal fame do not calculate with a view to their self-preservation, and, in this sense, they are irrational. This refers, of course, also to the fact that it is not something which can be controlled by calculation. It is the same instinctive power as eros in the narrower sense. Ambition too is concerned with immortality, immortality of fame. Up to now, eros is eros not for one's own, or for the beautiful, but for immortality. In the first case we have seen that love for immortality through procreation, is, in fact, an extended love for one's own. Let us see what love of eternal fame proves to be on closer inspection.

> "'Since do you believe,' she said, 'that Alcestis would have died for Admetus, or Achilles died after Patroclus, or your own Codrus die before on behalf of the kingship of his children, if they were not believing there would be an immortal memory of themselves about virtue, which we now have of them?'" (208d2–6)

Ambition is concerned with immortal fame for virtue—these are the really important cases of immortal fame. That means that ambition is not concerned with virtue as such. Virtue comes in only as an indispensable means for getting immortal fame. Can you see here an implication? If ambition, love of immortality in the form of immortal fame, is concerned with the immortality of fame and not with virtue, what kind of eros is it then? Eros of one's own. In the children your bodily image is perpetuated; here a shadow, your shadow, is perpetuated. The first two examples, as you may recall, were used by Phaedrus, 179b–180b, as examples of eros for other human beings, lovers and beloved, which prove that such sacrificial deaths were honored also by the gods. Diotima uses these two examples as examples of eros for fame and speaks only of their fame among men. Silence about the gods here. Phaedrus's central example was that of the singer Orpheus, who cut a poor figure, who was not prepared to die for his beloved, nor, it seems, for immortal fame. Diotima replaces Orpheus with an Athenian example, the old Athenian king Codrus. In Codrus's case, as distinguished from that of Alcestis and Achilles, love of offspring was combined with love of fame, and that throws light on the love of fame. Love of offspring and love of fame are akin to one another. Both forms of love are forms of love of one's own.

> "'That is far from being the case,' she said, 'but I suspect everyone toils at everything for the sake of deathless virtue and a famous reputation of this kind, and to the extent that they are better, to that extent they do it more; for they love the immortal.'" (208d6–e1)

In what sense is immortal virtue immortal? By memory. The three human beings mentioned have died. They died for those they loved, though actually for his fame, for his immortality. Love for immortal fame, it is said here, inspires all human action. Is this not a preposterous assertion? Think of the infinite actions committed, say, by Shakespeare, who was concerned with immortal fame, which surely had no reference to it. What does he mean? We must go a bit deeper. Love of one's own, self-love, inspires indeed all human actions, at least to the extent that it enters into all human actions, and that makes sense. This kind of eros is higher than the eros directed toward procreation and offspring, insofar as it includes concern with virtue. As is shown by the many spoiled brats, love of offspring does not necessarily go together with love of virtue, but love for immortal fame is inseparable from concern with virtue. On the other hand, however, love of immortal fame is more selfish: the man does not forget himself for the sake of other human beings. This is connected with the fact that love of immortal fame, in contradistinction to love of offspring and procreation, is specifically human. Man is not as much a member of his species as other animals are; he can be much more selfish than a brute. Man is also capable of the neglect of offspring in a way in which the brutes normally are not.

> "'Now those who are pregnant in their bodies,' she said, 'turn rather to women and are erotic in this way, supplying for themselves for all of future time, as they believe, through the generation of children, immortality, memory, and happiness.'" (208e1–5)

The first kind of eros is bodily, hence directed toward women—heterosexual love. It is based on a delusion, namely, no immortality of the individual can be achieved that way. The second kind of eros seems to belong to the soul, hence directed toward males, and seems to supply immortality of the individual. In what sense and to what extent that is true will be made clear in the sequel.

> "'But those who are [pregnant] in their soul—there are indeed,' she said, 'those who are pregnant in their souls still more than in their bodies—are pregnant with those things which it is fitting for a soul to conceive and give birth to. So what is suitable? Prudence *[phronesis]* and the rest of virtue—it is these things of which all the poets are generators, and all craftsmen who are said to be inventive.'" (208e5–209a5)

The second kind of eros strives for immortality, not through procreation but through giving birth to prudence and the other virtues. To this class belong all the poets and the inventor craftsmen. Why does he say all poets and not all craftsmen? An ordinary shoemaker cannot hope to acquire immortal fame by being a shoemaker. But the inventor of the art of shoemaking, the inventor of the cotton gin, can acquire immortal fame. You may also remember Agathon's remark about the gods who were inventor crafts-men—Hephaestus, etc.—prompted by love of the beautiful. Now we know one thing: giving birth to prudence.

> "'But by far the greatest and most beautiful kind of prudence is the order-ing and arrangement of cities and households, the name for which is mod-eration and justice.'" (209a5–8)

The second kind of eros strives in the highest case for giving birth to polit-ical or economic prudence. According to Plato there is no essential differ-ent between city and household, a thesis with which Aristotle takes issue at the beginning of the *Politics*. Political or economic prudence is the highest, and is identified here with moderation and justice. There is a passage in the *Phaedo*, 82a–b, where it is said: "The vulgar and political virtue which men call moderation and justice and which arises from habituation without phi-losophy and intellect." That is not the same as what he means here. There is no reference to habituation here, for example. We must take this as a much higher thing.

We must see not only what Plato mentions but also what he does not mention. Three virtues are mentioned here, but there are four. Diotima is silent about courage. As appears from the sequel, the begetters of this high-est practical wisdom do not die for the sake of their offspring. The states-men must die, but their begetters sit home. Here the case of Orpheus comes in, a poet who did not want to die and therefore became infamous in a sense, though he was still famous as a poet.

> "'And whenever in turn someone from youth onward is pregnant with these in his soul, being a bachelor and of a suitable age he by then desires to give birth and generate. In going about this he seeks, I suspect, the beautiful in which he would generate, for he will never generate in the ugly. So he cherishes the beautiful bodies rather then the ugly because he is pregnant, and if he meets up with a beautiful, noble, and naturally gifted soul, he very much cherishes the two together, and at once he is well sup-plied with speeches about virtue toward the human being, both about what sort the good man ought to be and what he must practice, and he tries to educate.'" (209a8–c2)

It appears that not everyone is pregnant with such political or economic prudence, hence, not everyone has the prospect of gaining immortality by generating such prudence. Those who are pregnant with it behave similarly to those who are pregnant in the body; they prefer beautiful bodies, but in this case only males, and beautiful souls too. But as in the first kind of eros, the eros directed toward procreation, does this make the second kind of eros ambition or love of the beautiful? Both are lovers of immortality, each of his own immortality, of his own.

You have here been given a brief description of what seems to be the highest form of educator. Anywhere in Plato one must always think of Socrates, even when he is not the speaker, as here. Is this not Socrates who begets the highest form of practical wisdom by generating in the proper souls of young men, preferably beautiful in body but surely beautiful in soul? He refers to himself as a midwife. But what does this mean? According to the explicit description, *Theaetetus* 149b, he is not productive. It's not Socrates. We shall see later. In this passage, he says, "He is well supplied with speeches about virtue toward the human being, both about what sort the good man ought to be and what he must practice." There is a fine distinction here, the virtue of a man is not identical with how a man must be and what he must pursue. Later on we shall see the solution to this problem.

Listener: He is resourceful in discoursing about virtue, that is to say, in something specifically human. Your earlier analysis of the myth, the parentage of Eros, may have been right in that context, but it seems to me as if Diotima is now allowing the father of eros to have his say.

Mr. Strauss: I would draw just the opposite conclusion, because in the lover there is both wealth and poverty. Is not the root of both poverty? Poverty knows itself to be poverty. If you take poverty as mere destitution, that is something else. But if Poverty implies the will to overcome poverty, then she does not need an outside incentive for seeking, she only needs, indeed, something outside. The question is What is the poverty of this rich man? The eros consists not in his wealth but in his poverty. Qua rich he is not an erotic man. Why does he need the poor young man? Immortality. In Socrates' concluding remark, 212b, he says that one could not easily take hold of a better helper for human nature than eros. That means that there might be an equally good helper or even a better helper, though he is not easy to come by, the natural gift. Eros is not a complete analysis of man; another very important point is what the Greeks call a good nature. Phaedrus made it perfectly clear that the men who are virtuous out of eros are only simulating the best natures. This rich man, as rich man, is the most gifted man. We will identify him very soon. Now the question is what is the motive of the poet in his poetic production. Is this eros? What kind of eros?

> "'For I suspect in touching the beautiful and associating with it, he gives birth to and generates the things with which he was long pregnant, both when he is present and when he is absent, in remembering, and he raises

up what is generated in common with him, and hence people of this kind conceive a far greater community and more solid friendship toward one another than that which is in the case of children, because they have a partnership in more beautiful and more immortal children.'" (209c2–7)

This man generates together with the beautiful men more beautiful and more immortal children than the parents of bodily children. Even in the case of the second kind of eros the children are not simply immortal, only the fame—though from Plato's point of view even the fame is not immortal. Today we would say the H-bomb, the classics said cataclysms. There will be earthquakes etc. which destroy civilizations, and therefore also the recollection of everything great. Some day not a single copy of Plato will exist, which shows that if we put our trust in culture or civilization we are not very wise. This is perfectly compatible with our great need to cherish the copies we have of Plato.

> "'And everyone would choose to have born to him children of this kind rather than human children, once he looks back in emulation at Homer and Hesiod and all the other good poets: think of what offspring they leave behind! Offspring of this kind supply on their own to them immortal fame and memory. And if you want,' she said, 'think of the children Lycurgus left behind in Sparta, saviors of Sparta and virtually of Greece. Solon too is honored among you on account of his generation of the laws, and other men in many other places, both among Greeks and among barbarians: in the generation of every kind of virtue, they showed forth many beautiful deeds. There have been before now many sanctuaries dedicated to them on account of children of this kind, but there has not yet been one on account of human children.'" (209c7–e4)

In the case of the poets, their fame is immortal—with the qualifications I mentioned—because their works are immortal. Why is this higher? Why is the offspring of a poet his to a higher degree than a son who looks exactly like the father? The work of the poet is much more his than is the child of the poet, because the life of the poem is entirely the poet's life, whereas the child has a life of its own. Then he says, "if you want." This indicates that it is a concession to a less exacting or a more popular demand. In other words, think of the legislators whom everyone admires.

He doesn't mention any laws in the case of Lycurgus. The fact stated in the last sentence is, I think, absolutely true. People are not praised by the community merely for having generated children. Lycurgus is not praised for his laws but for the men he educated, the saviors of Greece, as he says.

The mention of Solon, the Athenian legislator, is a concession of the foreign woman to the Athenian Socrates. In this school, which had a certain party line, it was understood that Lycurgus was much higher than Solon. The treatment given these two legislators in Aristotle's *Politics*, book 2, is exactly the same as the one given here. Solon is mentioned together with the barbarians, and they generated "every kind of virtue." The deification of the legislator is the last point mentioned, and that is important. The poets are much higher than the legislators here, and yet not the poets but the legislators are deified. Ultimately the ambitious gods were, in fact, deified humans.

Let me summarize this section: It occupies the same place in the Diotima-Socrates dialogue as Socrates' speech as a whole occupies in the *Symposium* as a whole, number six. This is perhaps the key to this section. Love of honor, ambition, the highest form of love of one's own, namely, love of one's own immortality, is concerned with the beautiful or noble to a much higher degree than with procreation and offspring. This second form is essentially concerned with the production of virtue and, in the highest case, with the production of the most beautiful prudence, namely political prudence, the prudence of the statesman. This immortality is the preserve, above all else, of the good poets, who are immortal in their works. This implies that poetry at its best generates political prudence, educates great statesmen and legislators. But is this not Socrates' peculiarity, as indicated not only in the *Republic* but even in such sober statements as Aristotle's *Metaphysics*, book 1, when he says that Socrates turned completely away from all 'metaphysical' things and limited himself entirely to the human things, i.e., to the things of concern to the statesman? Or is Socrates a competitor of the poets? The poets are concerned with virtue, and that means something beautiful for the sake of immortality, for the sake of their own. The poets are, then, not prompted by love of the beautiful or noble; they are not prompted by eros for morality as morality. Could this be the difference between Socrates and the poets, that Socrates is prompted by eros for the noble or the beautiful and is in love with moral virtue? We cannot yet answer this question. At any rate, this much is clear: the poets' eros is not the highest. The poets are pregnant, not Socrates. What does that mean? The poets are makers, producers, inventors. Socrates does not make, he is not a maker. And why is he not a maker? Because he is a philosopher. The philosopher is concerned with discovering the truth, not with inventing it. In this section there is again silence about the gods and about immortality proper. But in contradistinction to the preceding section, pederasty, as love of the souls of the young, is readmitted. This section is of special interest.

Long after Plato the attempt was made to understand the whole man, and therefore also the whole political life, in exactly the terms in which this second section understood man; namely, on the premise that the highest in man is his love of immortal fame. That was Machiavelli. To describe the relation between Machiavelli and Plato, one can simply say that if they should both stop here, they could agree. But something follows here which is omitted by Machiavelli. Now let us turn to the last section. As you will see right at the beginning, Socrates no longer has the initiative. It is started by Diotima in her own name.

> "'Now in these erotic things, Socrates, perhaps you too could be initiated; but into the perfect and highest grade of initiation *[epoptika]*, for the sake of which these things are, if someone pursues correctly, I don't know whether you would be able. Now I shall tell you,' she said, 'and I shall not fail in my eagerness; but try to follow along, if you are able.'" (209e5–210a4)

Diotima's speech as a whole is a revelation of mysteries. I have not drawn your attention all the time to the expressions which were taken from the language of the mysteries. This revelation of mysteries is now revealed by Socrates to a larger public. You remember what I said in the beginning about the scandal in Athens in 416. These here are foreign mysteries from a foreign woman; she was not the priestess of Eleusis, of the highest Athenian mysteries, whose mysteries were revealed. Now we come to the highest and culminating mystery, which is the end or purpose of the preceding forms of eros, and this occurs naturally only in the last part of Diotima's speech. There is a fine distinction which does not come out in the English translation. She says first she does not know "whether you would be able [to be initiated]." A little later she says "try to follow along, if you are able." Capable to be initiated means capable to follow, capable to grasp, capable to understand. The initiation is one of the mind. Diotima is in possession of these final mysteries. She is the complete owner of wisdom.

> "'He who goes correctly to this matter must begin when young to go to the beautiful bodies, and first, if the leader correctly leads the way, he must love one body and there generate beautiful speeches. Then he must realize that the beauty over any body whatsoever is akin to that over another body, and if he must pursue the beautiful as a class *[eidos]*—it is overwhelmingly foolish not to believe that the beauty over all bodies is one and the same—and with this realization must become the lover of all beautiful bodies, and relax in contempt that intensity for one in the belief that it is small.'" (210a4–b6)

230

We are now speaking of the highest stage. The first station on the way to salvation, one could say, is that in one's youth, if properly guided by the guider to the mysteries, the mystagogos, one must love first one beautiful body and generate therein beautiful speeches. One must make the distinction between beauty and this body. This body, this beautiful body, must be the beauty one loves. The beautiful body is not necessarily, to say the least, of the other sex. Yet, it would seem that the generation of the beautiful speeches is the end of the love of the beautiful body. But in the sequel it appears that this is not so. In this first stage the end is the beautiful body itself. We must learn next to love the beauty of all bodies as being one and the same beauty, and learn to despise as petty the extreme passion for one beautiful body. We are not to despise as petty the love for one beautiful body, only the extreme we must learn to despise. Surely the love of one beautiful body without generation of beautiful speeches would be simply base. That is implied. To love one beautiful body in brutish silence or in subbrutish foul language is not eros.

> "'And after this he must believe the beauty in souls is more honorable than that in the body, so that even if someone is decent in his soul and has but little bloom, it is enough for him to love and care for and seek and give birth to whatever sort of speeches will make the young better . . .'" (210b6–c3)

The next step is to turn to the beauty of the soul. Yet, it remains love of a young male who has at least a minimum of bodily beauty.

> "'. . . in order that he in turn may be compelled to observe the beautiful in practices and the laws and to see that this is in its entirety akin to itself, in order that he may believe that the beautiful of the body is something small.'" (210c3–6)

The final stage in the love of the soul, or at least in the first form of the love of the soul, is seeing the beautiful in pursuits and laws. This is, in a way, a compulsory thing. The pursuits and the laws are the first beautiful things mentioned as objects of contemplation. He was silent on seeing when he spoke of the love of bodies; of course the love of bodies is inseparable from beholding the bodies, but he did not mention it. What is happening in this section, and I will try explain it, is that in the first part there is constant reference to loving; then there is a shift from loving to beholding, and loving is no longer mentioned. This is the problem we will have to solve.

> "'And after the practices, one is to lead to the sciences, in order that he may see in turn the beauty of sciences, and in looking toward the beautiful that

> is by now vast, no longer cherishing the beauty in one—as if he were a ser-
> vant—of a little boy or some human being or one practice, and in being a
> slave be base and petty, but having turned toward the vast open sea of the
> beautiful and observing it, give birth to many beautiful and magnificent
> speeches and thoughts in bountiful philosophy . . . '" (210c6–d6)

This seems no longer to belong to the love of the soul, as the contemplation of laws or pursuits did. The next step is love of the sciences. No reason
is given here or before why the latter form of the beautiful is superior, i.e.,
more truly beautiful than the preceding one. But it is indicated. The pursuits are less beautiful than the sciences because the pursuits are necessary.
They are necessary, for example, for boxing or wrestling, for the strength of
the body, whereas the sciences are beautiful in themselves. Up to this point
the beautiful was viewed as this or that beautiful thing. Whenever everything of the kind is contemplated, for example, the beauty of all bodies,
there was already implied science. Let us compare three passages which are
relevant. In 210a Diotima said the lover of one beautiful body generates
beautiful speeches. In 210c she said the lover of one beautiful soul gives
birth to such speeches as make the young better. Here she says the lover
of the beautiful sciences gives birth to many beautiful and magnificent
speeches and thoughts.

If you take these three passages together, you see that the love of the
beautiful sciences is not in every respect superior to the love of one beautiful soul. Only the love of one beautiful soul can generate speeches which
make the young better. On the other hand, the speeches produced by the
love of one beautiful soul are not necessarily beautiful, which makes sense.
Is this not the case of Socrates? The lover of one beautiful soul who gives
birth to such speeches that make the young better. Is this not the difference
between Socrates and the poets? Is this not the reason why Socrates did not
write poetry? Here the transition from the love of one beautiful body to
the love of all beautiful bodies does not lead beyond generating beautiful
speeches. Love of the beautiful sciences is here presented as love of beauty,
not as love of truth. What does that mean? What are the beautiful sciences
anyway? The mathematical sciences. A pure music of which Eryximachus
spoke in 187c. Why are they beautiful? Because their objects are beautiful.
Because of their clarity and order. Note that the beautiful sciences are described as objects of beholding, contemplation, not of eros. If eros is directed toward the beautiful, that does not mean that all beautiful things are
objects of eros, there may be beautiful things which are not objects of passionate desire. In the first two stages, one body and all bodies, we had love

but no beholding. In the second two stages, pursuits and sciences, we had beholding but not love. There will be a fifth and final stage. Our expectation would seem to be, and that would be very fortunate for us, if on the highest level love and beholding would come together. Then we would have the unity of man on the highest plane, where his loving life, his affectionate life, his passionate life and his intellectual life would merge. Whether this is the case or not can be settled in one way: by reading what follows. To my great regret I must say that this problem is not so easily solved. There is again almost complete silence about love in the last part.

We are now at the third section of the third part. This is again subdivided. The third part deals with the highest form of eros, love of the beautiful and there are five stages: the first stage, love of one body; second, love of all bodies; third, love of beautiful pursuits and laws; fourth, love of the beautiful sciences; and we now turn to the fifth.

> "'. . . until with strength and increase gathered there he catches sight of one science of this kind, which is of the following kind of beautiful. Try to pay attention [apply your mind] to me,' she said, 'as best you can. Whoever up to this point has been guided to the erotic things, observing the beautiful things in order and correctly, in going then to the end of the erotic things he will suddenly catch a glimpse of something amazingly beautiful in its nature—and this is it, Socrates, for the sake of which there were also all the previous toils—'" (210d6–e6)

Toward the end of the erotic initiation he who has followed the way step by step and correctly sees some single sight of a beautiful thing of a certain description. What is beautiful is that with which the sight deals. He will suddenly see something strange. There is a kind of break of continuity here. There is a radical difference between this beautiful thing to be described in the sequel and all beautiful things either mentioned or not. On the basis of the remark in 210e1–2, one could perhaps say, try to apply your mind as much as you can and try to follow the parallel in 210a4. This section is subdivided into three parts: eros of the body, eros of the soul, and eros of the mind. What, then, is this one beautiful thing which appears at the end of the way?

> "'. . . [something beautiful] that in the first place always is and neither comes into being nor perishes, neither increases nor diminishes, and in the second place, is not in one respect beautiful and in another ugly, nor sometimes is and sometimes is not, nor in respect to one thing is beautiful and in respect to another ugly, nor here beautiful and there ugly, as being beautiful to some and ugly to some.'" (210e6–211a5)

Now this is a description of the beautiful, that beautiful thing which comes at the end. This beautiful thing is in every respect, and that implies, of course, that it is always, because that which is not always is also not. That beautiful thing is in every respect and is beautiful in every respect. These two considerations are inseparable, because for Plato, to be means to be something. There is nothing which merely is and is not something. There is no such thing as pure being. The whole Platonic notion of being is implied in this.

This may come as a surprise to us in modern times. When we speak of existence, do we necessarily mean that existence must be something, meaning something which is not implied in existence? This may not be so clear, but for Plato it is a matter of course. All other beautiful things, including all laws, pursuits, sciences, souls, etc., are not simply beautiful, they are also ugly in certain respects. How do we know that this beautiful is, which will prove to be the beautiful itself? If the meaning of eros is understood, we see that eros implies that there is such a thing, which is the beautiful itself. But is this perhaps a delusion? Could eros in its deepest meaning, namely, as tending toward the beautiful itself, not be a delusion? Think of Aristophanes' myth, where we have a description of the deepest meaning of eros. This deepest meaning of eros proves to be a delusion: that union is impossible. Or is the desire of the soul not necessarily the crown and criterion of true thoughts, as a modern interpreter says? Meaning, if eros is the deepest desire of our soul directed toward something, this something must be.

Eros as desire for the simply beautiful, the unqualifiedly beautiful, vouches for the being of the eternally beautiful. But before we know that the eternally beautiful and the unqualifiedly beautiful is, we do not know whether eros is simply natural or simply good. First we have to discover the true nature of eros before we can say that that which it divines is. I also draw your attention to the fact that in these sections of the speech eros is not mentioned. Now, what is this beautiful itself? It is the example in the *Symposium* of what is generally known as the idea in the Platonic sense. But it is not called an idea here, and that is not negligible. Ideas seem to be self-subsisting and simply unchangeable, the only beings which are truly. The usual view of this notion is that Plato hypothesizes universals or concepts. Plato says the universals or concepts are, and are more truly than any other thing. The question is whether this is based on a proper understanding of Plato. I can only remind you of a few things here: The word *eidos* means primarily the shape of a thing, the shape which can be seen only with the mind's eye, the character of a thing. Later on this was called the essence. Yet, if one says essence, one must consider this fact: essence as used later, became understood as the possible, in contradistinction to the actual or existing, whereas Plato surely means something which is more truly than sensible things. But, at the same time, *eidos* means a class of things. *Genos* is used synonymously in Plato for *eidos* and, prior to the logical distinction, it means the origin, the family, the race of a being. In other words, from this point of view, the *eidos* dog means all dogs, not something beyond it, all sensible dogs. The reasoning is this: every particular dog is dog and something else. Therefore not purely dog but, for example, a male, old and not young, black and not white; he is incomplete. Therefore, because of the incompleteness of every individual being, the *eidos* means also the completeness and, therefore, the goal of aspiration.

These are the three meanings of *eidos* in Plato: the shape, the class, and the goal of aspiration. What is the rationale of this doctrine? It is surely not set forth in the *Symposium*. There is only a partial indication of it anywhere in Plato. A particularly interesting case is that of the *Republic,* where the ideas are introduced at a certain point with a very insufficient preparation. When modern students read it they know through Aristotle or through modern literature the Platonic doctrine of ideas and, therefore, they naively assume that the listeners to Socrates also know the Platonic doctrine of ideas. But sometimes they are very young boys who have never heard of it. In some cases it appears that the people had heard of it, for example, in the *Phaedo.* But in the *Republic,* Glaucon probably had never heard of it before. So, it must have had an evidence which it no longer has for us. I only want to say a word about that: when you think of a statue, like that of Victory—and every young Greek was familiar with that—he understood in a way what an idea is. Here you have Victory. But this is not the victory of Marathon or Salamis, or whatever it might be. Nor is it the same statue in this temple as in another temple, yet they all mean the same. Victory is a self-subsisting thing which becomes visible, for example, in a statue but is not identical with it. This is, psychologically, the simple access to ideas. Therefore, we can say, the ideas take the place of the gods, and this is, ultimately, also true. The critical question which arises, and is not necessarily critical of Plato, is Are the ideas as ordinarily presented by Plato not also products of the eros for beauty, just as the gods are such products?

Everything beautiful is beautiful and something else. The beauty of the *Iliad* is not the beauty of the *Odyssey.* But both poems are beautiful. What is that identical thing which is responsible for any particular thing being beautiful? That is what is traditionally called the concept of beauty, but it is not quite what Plato means. What is the beautiful which we meet in everything beautiful? I will give you a few answers. For example, in Thomas Aquinas you get the beautiful is the apprehension of that which pleases. This, ultimately, goes back to the Platonic view. In Kant's notion it is that which creates disinterested joy or pleasure. The opposite of that is the view expressed by Stendhal as the promise of happiness; ultimately this is the Hobbesian view of beauty. The apprehension is not the crucial point. At any rate, we must try to find out what this is which underlies everything beautiful. Plato says that this universal alone is truly beautiful, that only the concept of beauty is truly beautiful. That's the paradox. Hence that this "concept" of beauty is the object of eros. For example, let the beautiful be the promise of happiness. Do we not love the promise of happiness as such in every love of a beautiful thing? Is the promise of happiness not that beautiful thing which we always love, whereas if we love this particular puppy we do not love another puppy. Is this not the way of understanding what Plato means by the fact that the universally beautiful, the beautiful itself, is the only thing which is truly beautiful? To repeat: Plato or his characters do not say here that we love the beautiful itself.

> "'Nor in turn will the beautiful appear to him as an illusion [*phantasthese-tai*], such as a face or hands or anything else in which body partakes, nor any logos nor any science, nor anywhere in something other, such as in an animal or on earth or in heaven, or in something else, but alone by itself, with itself, being always of a single species, and all other beautiful things partaking in it in the sort of way that everything else comes to be and perishes, while that does not become anything more or less or undergo anything.'" (211a5–b5)

This beautiful itself is not bodily. It is not, as we may tentatively say, an object of *phantasia;* it will not be imagined, nor is it an object of reasoning proper, nor does it subsist somewhere in something else—it is not in a god, for example. All beautiful things, all things which are by participating in the beautiful itself, come into being and perish. Apparently heaven too, and the souls. Only the idea, as we would say, only the beautiful itself, is immortal. This implies that the vision of the beautiful itself is only possible in this light. But everything said in this section is grammatically dependent on the word *phantasthesetai,* which means the beautiful itself will be imagined. If this is so, then the beautiful itself would appear as something imagined. And, if this is so, we would reach the conclusion, supported by some other considerations, that we have here a poetic presentation of philosophy and its object and not a philosophic one.

"'Whenever someone on the basis of these things, on account of his being a pederast correctly, goes on up and begins to catch sight of that beautiful, he would be touching pretty nearly the end. For this is to go correctly toward the erotic things, or to be led by someone else, beginning from those beautiful things to go on up for the sake of that beautiful, employing them as if they were steps, from one to two and from two to all the beautiful bodies, and from the beautiful bodies to the beautiful practices, and from the practices to the beautiful teachings, and from the teachings to end up at that teaching, which is a teaching of nothing else than that beautiful, and recognize finally what is beautiful itself.'" (211b5–d1)

Here we have a summary. It is thanks to the correct love of boys that the ascent takes place. That is the crucial point. This correct love of boys includes love of the beautiful body. Contemplation of the idea of the beautiful is from this point of view only the last and highest stage of the means for the correct love of boys. This should not be surprising, but in the *Republic* we have a strict parallel to that. In the *Republic*, philosophy is introduced only as means for the good polis. Here philosophy is introduced only as a means for the correct love of boys. But then, just as in the *Republic*, what first comes to sight as a means, proves to be the end. Philosophy not only as a means for good politics but as the end; similarly here regarding pederasty. You see also initiation is not indispensable. Whether one goes, or whether one is led by someone else, does not make a difference.

Here we have a repetition of the stages: one beautiful body, two beautiful bodies, all beautiful bodies, beautiful pursuits, beautiful teachings, and the teaching regarding the beautiful itself; six stages, i.e., as many as there are speeches on eros in the dialogue. What does he omit? General rule: there is never a repetition in Plato which is an identical repetition; there is always a change, though sometimes seemingly trivial. What is the change? The change is in the second step, and that means much greater emphasis on the body, accompanied by something else. When he makes the transition in the first statement from bodies to the other things, he speaks of the souls. There is no mention of the souls here, and that has grave implications regarding the meaning of the work itself. In the presentation itself, as distinguished from the summary, we have one body, all bodies, souls, pursuits and laws, sciences, and the one science. One other subtle thing: here he goes from one to two and then to all beautiful bodies, and from that to beautiful pursuits, to the beautiful pieces of learning, to that piece of learning, etc.; but whereas he repeats beautiful in the case of the bodies, he does not repeat it in the case of the pursuits and the sciences. Again, the emphasis is on the beautiful body.

> "'It is here in life, if anywhere, my dear Socrates,' the Mantinean stranger said, 'where it is worth living for a human being, observing the beautiful itself.'" (211d1–3)

The beautiful itself is the good. This is in glaring contrast to the teaching of the *Republic,* according to which the good is high and above the beautiful. That is the teaching not only of the *Republic* but of the *Symposium* too. What did we learn before about the relation of good and beautiful? To take the simple case of the love of the two sexes, which was presented as love of the beautiful—and then Diotima teaches not the beautiful but the good. So the teaching of the *Symposium* too is that the good is the highest. But in this final presentation the beautiful is substituted for the good, and this is another indication of what I call the poetic presentation of philosophy.

> "'If you ever see it, it will not seem to you to be on the level of gold and dress and the beautiful boys and youths, in looking at whom now you are thunderstruck and are ready, both you and many others, in seeing the beloveds and always being with them, neither to eat nor to drink, if it were somehow possible, but only to observe and be with.'" (211d3–8)

Here is the transition. First, in an earlier stage, it is the desire always to see the boys and to be together with them, if this were possible. Then, on the highest state, it is the desire to behold the beautiful itself and to be together with it, and nothing is said as to whether or not it is possible. The whole question of immortality is involved in that.

> "'What then,' she said, 'do we believe, if it should happen to someone to see the beautiful itself in its purity, cleansed and clean, unmixed, and not filled with human flesh and colors and much other mortal nonsense, but to be able to catch sight of the divinely beautiful itself as a single species? Do you believe,' she said, 'that life becomes mean when a human being looks in that direction, observing that and being with it by the means he should?'" (211d8–212a2)

That beholding leads to the substitution of the merely beholding and being together with the beautiful itself for merely beholding and being together with beautiful boys. Beholding the good is identical with being together with the good, and this is happiness. In the first description of the beautiful itself, always being was mentioned in the beginning at 211a1; in the second description 211b1–2, "being always" was at the end. Now "always being" is dropped. But in the central presentation, where he had spoken of always being, he had said that the beautiful itself will be imagined as always being. Let us keep this in mind.

> "'Or don't you realize,' she said, 'that here alone it will be possible for him, on seeing the beautiful by that by which it is visible, to give birth not to phantom images of virtue, because he is touching on that which is not a phantom, but to true virtue, because he is touching on the truth; and once he gives birth to true virtue and raises it, it is open to him to become dear to the gods, and if it is open to any other human being, for him too to become immortal?'" (212a2–7)

The question remains conditional. Here she describes the consequence of the vision of beauty itself, and this beauty stands for the good itself. The consequence of that vision, and only of that vision, is giving birth. Not to beautiful speeches, or to images of virtue, but to true virtue. The generation of true virtue is not intended. In the preceding part, where the poets and legislators were spoken of, they do not give birth to true virtue, obviously because they do not have that vision. He is not concerned with generating true virtue, he is only concerned with beholding beautiful things and beauty itself. Nor is he concerned with immortality, although he, more than anyone else, is most likely to become immortal. In what sense? The parallel in 209c–e shows: immortal in fame. Now the conclusion:

> "Here you have, Phaedrus and everyone else, what Diotima said and I have been persuaded of; and since I have been persuaded I try to persuade everyone else as well that one would not easily get anyone better than Eros for helping human nature gain this possession. Accordingly, I assert that every man should honor Eros, and I myself honor the erotic things and practice them to an exceptional degree, and I urge everyone else to do so, and now and always I celebrate the power and manliness of Eros to the extent that I can. So regard this logos, Phaedrus, as an encomium to Eros if you want, but if not, whatever and however you enjoy naming it, name it that." (212b1–c3)

"This possession"—possession is frequently used as a synonym for good. What is that possession? The vision of beauty followed by the generating of true virtue and immortality of fame. The acquisition of this possession does not simply require eros. Human nature cannot easily find a better helper— there may be a better helper; there may, at least, be an equally good helper. As the helper which can most easily be found, he addresses every man, but it may not be the best helper. This is the question which came up in the discussion of Phaedrus in the very beginning. Eros is productive of virtue, but the virtue produced by eros proved in Phaedrus's speech to be a lower kind of virtue, the highest that is accessible without the virtue of the best natures. Something of this kind is implied here. Eros is primarily eros for human beings. Therefore pederasty comes in. This is the first form of eros for the beautiful. Is this necessary for the highest good? Let us take the case of the entirely unerotic man, the lover of gain, who is guided by calculation alone, as presented in the *Republic*. Sheer calculation will make him a member of society, because he knows that he is not self-sufficient. As a member of society he becomes concerned with justice, and, if he is a thinking man, this leads him to seek right itself, justice itself. This justice itself is, according to the explicit statement in the *Republic,* as high in dignity as the beautiful itself. Each of these two, whatever that may mean, point to the good. Therefore, eros is not, in this sense, indispensable. At the end Socrates makes clear that his speech is not necessarily a praise of eros. It is a very qualified praise.

A few remarks about Diotima's speech: eros is not a god; eros is neither beautiful nor good. More precisely: eros is not directed toward the beautiful, nor is he directed toward one's own. That is the crucial meaning of the central part of Diotima's speech. In the third part of the speech love of one's own and love of the beautiful are restored, in contradiction to the central part. What does this mean? I suggest this explanation: By the denial of eros of the beautiful, as well as eros of one's own, the Olympian gods lose their basis. The Olympian gods are products of eros, but of a certain kind of eros: of the love of the beautiful—they are simply beautiful beings; but in a more indirect way, as avenging gods they are products of the love of one's own. One's own, culminating in the polis, one's right, and, therefore, in the need for avenging gods. Therefore, the gods do not reappear anymore, whereas love of one's own and love of the beautiful reappear. What is taking place is a purification of eros, and we can, perhaps, say that the task of the *Symposium* as a whole is the purification, the catharsis, of eros. We might even go further and say that the three, at first glance, most beautiful dialogues of Plato—the *Symposium,* the *Republic,* and the *Phaedo*—are devoted most obviously to purifications. To purify us from the fear of death—the *Phaedo;* to purify from the inherent danger of eros—the *Symposium;* to purify from the danger inherent in what we would now call political idealism and the delusions bred by it—the *Republic.*

In the last part of Diotima's speech, we find three forms of eros: love of immortality in generation, love of immortality through fame, and love of the beautiful. Love of immortality in generation proves to be love of one's own. The parents want to live on in their children; they are not merely concerned with producing human beings in general. This stage is strictly heterosexual. In the second stage, love of immortality through fame, there is also love of one's own immortality, but through the beautiful things as means. Here pederasty of the soul emerges. In the last stage, love of the beautiful, which includes pederasty of the body, culminates in the vision of the beautiful itself. When speaking of the higher levels, she speaks only of beholding the beautiful, not of eros for the beautiful. Why? Love of the beautiful is essentially directed toward bodies, this must be intelligently understood. We love essentially the soul, but we never love merely the soul. Eros can never be divorced from body. We cannot love a human being without loving his head. The first words of Antigone is a good illustration of that. Antigone says to her sister: "Oh, common head of Ismene." Antigone in loving Ismene loves her head. There is no eros except for living human beings, and this corresponds to usage. When we speak of an erotic man we mean that. Therefore the pederasty of the bodies is admitted. Yet the whole, and especially the vision of the beautiful itself, belongs, as is explicitly said, to the erotic things. So, in a way, there is an eros beyond the eros of bodies or connection with bodies. But this is no longer eros of the beautiful, and this is important. The eros of the beautiful leads to transcending the beautiful. In the highest stage the object of eros is no longer the beautiful but the good—beholding the good and being together with the good is true happiness. Erotics transcends love of one's own and love of the beautiful and is as such eros of the good as such, as is, indeed, also said.

Let us try to understand it as far as is possible on the basis of what is given here. It surely makes sense to distinguish empirically the following three forms of eros: First, love of one's own, love of one's kin, and, in the broadest form, love of the fatherland. Secondly, love of the beautiful, of glory, of moral virtue, but also what is known now as aestheticism. The third, love of the good, the crudest and most massive form; if a man is a lover of gymnastics with a view to getting a strong and healthy body, that is not love of the beautiful, nor love of one's own, but love of the good—valetudinarian, the lover of gain. From this point of view, and this is not unimportant, love of the good, as distinguished from love of one's own and love of the beautiful, is the lowest and most inconspicuous form of eros. And that is a typically Platonic notion, that what is so inconspicuous at first glance reflects, in a way more directly, the highest. Yet we have learned that all eros is eros of the good and, therefore, also the love of one's own and love of the beautiful must be love of the good. Diotima indicates how this is possible. Eros of the good is love for my well-being, my own perfection, virtue, the noble, and may even include fame. On the highest level all three elements are present. If a man loves what is most his own, namely his soul, he loves the truth, the good, and is attracted by boys and youths who are his kindred because they have the same potentiality.

We may distinguish, I have said, one's own, the beautiful, and the good; but this is not the tripartition made by Diotima. Her tripartition is procreation, glory, and, let us say, philosophy, or, perhaps, the beautiful instead of philosophy. What is the relation? Why does she replace the beautiful with glory and the good with the beautiful? As for the first question: why does she not speak of the beautiful in the second stage but of glory? This is identical with the demotion of poetry which she effects. The poets, she says, do not love the beautiful but their own. They are concerned with the beautiful only as a means for their own. But what is that beautiful? It is moral virtue and, in the highest case, political prudence, ultimately the polis. But they do not love these things for their own sake; they love them for their immortality. There is no eros for the polis and, hence, not for moral virtue and political prudence. For moral virtue and political prudence depend essentially on the polis, and the polis is not natural. It is constituted by an arbitrary selection from the natural whole, the human species, toward which eros is directed—procreation. There is no natural inclination comparable to procreation which is directed toward the polis as polis. There is no natural inclination toward moral virtue and the polis, that is, indeed, the crucial implication.

To understand that let us look at another tripartition which occurs much later but is related to it. That is Thomas Aquinas's distinction of man's threefold natural inclination, *Summa*, II, 1, question 94, article 2. Self-preservation is the first, then preservation of the species and raising of children, then knowledge of god plus social life, which is the equivalent of the polis. You see that here, too, there is no natural inclination toward moral virtue as moral virtue. Diotima is silent about self-preservation. Why? Because it can be said to be suberotic. We cannot call a man concerned with preserving himself an erotic man. She replaces, moreover, life in society with immortal fame, for the polis is not natural.

Let us also compare these distinctions with the three parts of the soul in the *Republic:* desire, spirit, and reason. Spiritedness is replaced with love of glory, eros for immortal fame. Why? Spiritedness, which includes indignation, is related to justice or right, and the *Symposium* abstracts from right because the right or the just is not, as such, an object of natural inclination. Furthermore, spiritedness means, more generally, repelling the hostile, the alien. From this point of view spiritedness is essentially related to love of one's own. But love of one's own is lower than love of the beautiful. The *Symposium* transcends the love of one's own. Eros is homeless. The *Republic*, as a political work, does not transcend the sphere of one's own. Perhaps more precisely: the *Republic* also suppresses in its way one's own and that is, indeed, the subtlety of the *Republic*. Proof: the so-called communism of the *Republic*. One can say in the *Republic*, too, one's own is abandoned in favor of the beautiful. When he speaks of the education of the guardians, in the center is education in music, and the function of this education is to make them love the beautiful. Nevertheless, the *Republic* does not transcend one's own in the way the *Symposium* does, because one can say one's own is transferred to the polis, which is also a limited part of the human race. In the *Republic* you no longer love your natural brothers and sisters but every fellow citizen of your age as an artificial brother and sister, and every older man and woman as your artificial parents. One's own, then, is radically modified in the *Republic*, it is not transcended. Because the *Republic* remains within the limitations of the love of one's own, the emphasis on spiritedness, repelling the foreign or the alien, is crucial. The *Symposium*, by transcending the sphere of one's own, is silent on spiritedness. We may learn from this the general point that spiritedness is essentially the companion of the lower forms of eros, and that is the crudity, if you will, of the psychology of the *Republic*. On the higher stages of eros there is no *thumos*, no spiritedness, as a companion. The simple proof of that is that philosophy can justly be called a form of eros, but there is no ingredient of spiritedness in philosophy as philosophy. Indignation has no place in philosophy proper. In its utterances or in its teaching, this is another matter.

Listener: Isn't there an immediate transcendence of one's own in the *Republic*?

Mr. Strauss: But it still remains one's own city. As ordinary human beings we love our polis. But there can be a split. For example, a nice man in Poland loves, in a way, the United States more than Poland. You can never completely separate the matter—the Polish soil, the Polish people—and the form, the government. Therefore, the famous problem of loyalty. But, on the highest level, you have undivided loyalty because you live in the best polis; it is precisely on the highest level also love of one's own polis as distinguished from the others. Never forget the complete silence in the *Republic* about the relations of the best polis to any other best city. Each city is perfectly self-sufficient and therefore has no motivation to go out toward other cities.

Listener: The only thing I didn't understand was when you said the *Republic* did not transcend the realm of one's own. It seems to me that the philosopher doesn't know what his own city is, so he has transcended this realm.

Mr. Strauss: You have to take the complete picture. There is a very big foundation, the polis, which has permitted him to study philosophy. But then he must pay his debt and go back to the cave. After all, the *Republic* presents the whole philosophic life, which includes not merely this sojourn on the island of the blessed. The *Republic* presents philosophy as transcending the polis and descent to the polis. The two aspects are inseparable. In the *Symposium* this is absent. What Socrates says in the end about generating true virtue has nothing to do with the polis. That is the relation of philosophers to young philosophers. The political relation is not mentioned here. What I said on the subject is difficult and arid, but it is necessary to see this complicated relation of the two dialogues in terms of the two forms of love here considered, love of one's own and love of the beautiful. The love of the beautiful triumphs completely over the love of one's own in the *Symposium*. It does not triumph over the love of one's own and is not meant to triumph in the *Republic*. You see also how difficult it is to find Plato's true teaching, because it is divided into many dialogues and must be put together. This question is perhaps the most theoretical I can find hitherto: how are the three stages—procreation, glory, and beauty itself—related to the three parts of the soul in the *Republic*. That would be a good exam question after a few years of study.

[Tape change.]

All that which we call interesting in human beings is in the sphere of *thumos*.

I repeat the question: Diotima replaces the beautiful with glory, with love of immortal fame, and this belongs to the context of the demotion of poetry, that is to say to the broad context of the *Symposium* as a whole. In the *Symposium* eros is discussed within the context of a contest between poetry and philosophy. This contest is decided and won by Socrates' speech in favor of philosophy. In Socrates' dialogue with Agathon and in the first part of his conversation with Diotima the tragic poet Agathon is refuted. In the second part of his conversation with Diotima, the central part, both the tragic poet and the comic poet are refuted; eros is not love of the beautiful, as the tragic poet said, nor is it love of one's own, as the comic poet had said, but eros is love of the good. This is, indeed, the philosophic point of view. In the first section of the third part the philosophic point of view is set forth unpolemically, namely in the form of a quest for the cause of eros, without any reference to the poets. But in the second section, and only there, poetry is presented from a philosophic point of view, the philosophic point of view being that love of the good is higher than any other form of love. Agathon had said that eros is love of the beautiful, and furthermore, not poetry but poetic fame is due entirely to love of the beautiful. I refer to 169d and 197a–b. Diotima says that poetry is inspired by nothing but love of the beautiful, but this love of the beautiful is truly not love of the beautiful but love of their own. The poets do not love the beautiful as such, they love their immortality, they love their own. The beautiful, moral virtue and political prudence, is only a means for the poets. When she speaks of love of the beautiful, in the last section, she is completely silent about both poets and political prudence, which was the highest object of the poets. The poets are in no way concerned with the truly beautiful, with the production of true virtue; they produce no more than a shadow of true virtue. This political prudence which we so admire, and rightly up to a point, is only a shadow of true virtue and this is the utmost the poets can achieve.

This criticism of poetry is infinitely more polite than the criticism of poetry given in the *Republic,* but ultimately it is identical with that criticism. The poets, these wonderful men, produce a virtue which is not genuine virtue. As could be shown, this criticism of poetry is not sufficient and not adequate from Plato's own point of view. Yet it must mean something. I limit myself to the question, What does the criticism, implied by the fact that poetry is mentioned only in the discussion of the second highest form of eros, mean in the context of the *Symposium?* Diotima says: poetry is related to love of one's own and leads to the production of immortal works of art. Homer lives on, speaks to us today, in a way infinitely more powerful than any of Homer's descendants we might discover today on the Greek islands. Philosophy, on the other hand, is love of the beautiful, not of one's own, not concerned with immortality, no writings. Since the philosopher is free from eros of one's own and animated only by love of the beautiful, he becomes immortal, perhaps, as Socrates and Plato did, without being concerned with immortality, namely, by generating genuine virtue. His happiness consists entirely in beholding beauty itself and leading others whom he individually selects to such beholding. No writer can select. Of course, I mention in passing, Socrates also generated bodily offspring, as we know, but, if we take the implication seriously, he was prompted not by any love of his own in doing so but, as Aristophanes says, by obedience to the nomos. Socrates did not write because of the purity of his eros. His eros was only directed toward the beautiful, not toward immortality. Socrates did not write because of his purity. How then did Plato and Xenophon write? How could Plato fall short so flagrantly of the highest standard of purity? You cannot have recourse to the flesh here, by which Plato would discredit himself eternally. So, in honor of Plato, we are compelled to say Socrates did not write because he could not write. But what does writing mean here? To write dialogues, to write drama of a certain kind. Drama is neither tragedy or comedy, because it is both. Socrates could not write; he was the midwife, i.e., barren, because he could not invent. And the poet is an inventor. Clearly that is not true. Proof: his many invention in the *Republic,* for example, the three waves.

Still, why could Socrates not write? There are two Platonic dialogues which deal with writing, that is to say with the writing of speeches as distinguished from the writing of laws in particular—the *Phaedrus* and the *Gorgias.* The *Phaedrus,* the sequel to the *Symposium,* sets forth the problem of writing, the objections to writing, the problem which writing must solve. The *Gorgias* sets forth the limitation of Socrates' rhetoric, of Socrates' art of speaking, and therefore also of his art of writing speeches and, therefore, of his art of writing. Now, what does the *Gorgias* tell us? Socrates was able to persuade Polus. The *Gorgias* has three parts: in the first part Socrates discusses rhetoric with Gorgias; in the second part with a pupil of Gorgias, Polus, also a teacher of rhetoric; and in the third part with Callicles. But the bulk is for the sake of exhibiting to Gorgias Socrates' own rhetoric. In the part with Polus Socrates is successful—he can persuade him. In the Callicles part Socrates fails. Socrates puts his cards on the table: he says my rhetoric reaches so far. Why? Socrates can persuade Polus because he can persuade him by dialectic, by proofs. He cannot persuade Callicles truly because Callicles could not be persuaded truly without recourse to threats, without recourse to punitive speeches, to speeches which in the last resort appeal to avenging gods. This is the reason why he failed to persuade Callicles. The myth at the end of the *Gorgias* is a specimen of Socrates' ineptness in such matters. With this myth you cannot persuade anyone to repent. Socrates lacked indignation, *thumos,* the quality so clearly displayed in Platonic dialogues. Here I must again pay homage to that great man who didn't know a line of Greek, a Turk, al-Farabi, who asserted that Plato's great achievement beyond Socrates was that he was able to combine the way of Socrates, by which you can teach, dialectically, nice people, with the way of Thrasymachus, by which you can persuade nondocile people who must be frightened and terrified. Socrates did not write because he could not write, more precisely, because he could not write on the highest level, and writing on the highest level includes the ability to write tragedy, the tragedy behind which are the avenging gods. The perfect speechmaker would write a tragedy, and as such he would also be a comedian. The inverse is not true. Socrates could have written comedies, and better ones than Aristophanes, though probably not such tough ones. But that was not enough because it would not become a philosopher to write comedies.

Yet Plato and Xenophon learned from Socrates how to make punitive speeches and how to act punitively. In the case of Xenophon we know it from his own mouth. When he came to Cyrus, he met a pupil of a sophist, Proxenos, a fine man, wonderful in handling gentlemen, but inept in handling nongentlemen. The pupil of Socrates, Xenophon, was excellent also in whipping people, in punitive action. Xenophon's whole affair in Asia Minor, where he almost founded a city and was even asked to become a monarch, and Plato's action in Syracuse show that they were politically active men, to some extent. The fact that Socrates was not politically active and the fact that he did not write are ultimately identical—the weakness of his *thumos,* of his spiritedness. And to that extent, Aristophanes' criticism of Socrates, that he was an unpolitical man, has a great element of truth. Socrates traced his withdrawal from politics, for which he was blamed, to his *daimonion,* to the demonic thing in him. In late antiquity it was said by commentators, the divine Plato and the demonic Aristotle, and that is, I think, a convincing though pagan statement of the order of rank of the two men. But it is more helpful for the understanding of Plato if we say that Socrates was demonic and Plato knew him. Plato had a gift which Socrates lacked. Whether there is a connection between Socrates' nonwriting and other limitations of Socrates would be an extremely interesting question. You know there are some dialogues where Socrates doesn't speak—in the *Timaeus, Critias, Sophist,* and *Statesman.* Does Plato indicate by that what Socrates could not have done? That's a moot question. But of one thing we can be certain: Socrates did not write and Plato did write, and that, I believe, can ultimately only be understood in the way in which I sketched it.

As for the fact that in one dialogue Socrates is completely absent, namely, in the *Laws,* one must also consider the connection between poetry and legislation as indicated by Diotima, as well as Socrates' being nonpolitical. So this absence in the *Laws* fits beautifully into what I said.

The philosophic presentation of poetry is the central section of the last part of Diotima's speech. What about the presentation of philosophy in the last section? We observe the complete silence about the ideas; only one such thing is mentioned, the beautiful itself, but not as idea. The idea of the beautiful is introduced and has, in effect, the function of the idea of the good, which, according to Plato, has an absolutely unique position. This is done without any preparation as well as certain other difficulties which I indicated. I suggest that the last part has the function of giving a poetic presentation of philosophy. What philosophy is does not in any reasonable way appear from these two pages. It gives an image to the imagination of the incredible superiority of philosophy to any other beautiful thing. In the light of what I said, this poetic presentation of philosophy is surely not tragic, ultimately it would perhaps appear to be highly comical. Unless we would say that this poetic presentation is given by Diotima, not Socrates, and Diotima perhaps did not suffer from Socrates' limitation. Socrates wins the contest with the poets by being able to give a philosophic presentation of poetry and a poetic presentation of philosophy. No poet has ever succeeded in doing that.

This poetic presentation of philosophy leads us to see that eros is, strictly speaking, only eros for human beings. Eros, then, is not the best helper for human nature. In other words, the dialogue ends with a depreciation of eros. This is, I think, the beginning of the *Phaedrus*. There, young Phaedrus, in his opinions entirely unerotic, preferring nonlovers to lovers, is corrected by Socrates who gives there an unqualified praise of eros. But precisely the *Phaedrus* is the only Platonic dialogue which ends with a prayer, not to eros but, above all, to the god Pan, who has much to do with fertility and, to that extent, with eros. But fertility in the wide sense: the god of natural wealth. Even here we are not permitted to forget the crucial importance of the love of gain, which is a humble representative of the love for true gain, true wealth, the wealth of the soul, wisdom. So much for this section.

Listener: Are you suggesting that Socrates lacked spiritedness whereas Plato and Xenophon did not?

Mr. Strauss: I am compelled to say that. Differently stated and perhaps more intelligibly, Socrates was more unqualifiedly the philosopher. I am also not satisfied with this as an answer, because I am sure there is something hidden there, but I have not been able to crack that nut. You might say Plato and Xenophon, too, were not angry but played angry when necessary. Apparently Socrates could not even do that. There is only one scene where Socrates is almost angry, in Xenophon's *Memorabilia,* in the first book, chapter 3, I believe. The object of his quasi anger is Xenophon. But I admit, what I said is not perfectly clear and satisfactory.

Listener: If eros is only eros for human beings, what would be the status, or what would you call the affinity, of the sensitive person to the good?

Mr. Strauss: If we take eros in this strict and proper meaning, what Aristophanes says could very well be true, that it contains more than the lovers know. But if this implication is brought out, it would no longer be eros proper. For example, there is implied, as you may know from the literature, in every deep erotic relation a desire for immortality of that relation, which cannot in this form be fulfilled. There is no such desire implied in the desire for food or drink. Would this implication of eros not lead us beyond eros? There are various other ways: for example, people are concerned whether their love is genuine or not. Therefore the question of human sincerity comes up. There are infinite ways which lead from the love of human beings in the strict sense beyond it. More generally stated: man cannot find his completion, his fulfillment, in the erotic life strictly understood. You can, of course, call it eros, but the question is whether this is not a metaphoric use of the term. But it is perhaps the best term we have.

Listener: If in the highest state man becomes purified of eros, is this his highest perfection?

Mr. Strauss: Apparently this is the case. If you see something beautiful without having looked for it, doesn't it strike you and attract you without any desire to possess it in any way? Whereas there is a lower kind of love which has necessarily a reflection to the self, health or wealth. But there is a love of the beautiful which is really self-forgetting and which is, in a way, of higher nobility than that love which is not self-forgetting. The remarkable fact is this: on the highest level self-forgetting is not possible. Love of the truth is higher than love of beauty, and love of the truth, if it is anything, is something you want to possess. This can be absent in love of the beautiful. That is what Plato means. There is that strange kinship between the highest and the lowest.

Listener: Does love of the good also presume that kinship with the lowest?

Mr. Strauss: In one way: the concern with self, with the health of the soul, is present on the highest level. Certain kinds of love of the beautiful do not have that implication.

Listener: Are you saying, then, that love of the beautiful is higher in a certain sense?

Mr. Strauss: That is probably not the only case in which a certain thing is higher than another thing while that which is the highest is from this point of view allied with the lowest. On the lowest level, the possession which we want is a possession, which as such cannot be shared. The beautiful is universally accessible. The good in the highest sense is common in principle to all, but the highest shares with the lowest the relation to appropriation which the central one does not have. The element of beholding is common to truth and beauty, the element of vital need is common to the highest and the lowest.

Listener: I don't quite understand why writing constitutes the superiority of Plato.

Mr. Strauss: There is a certain lacuna of my argument, I admit. But in the presentation of the *Symposium* it would appear that the production of immortal works belongs only to the second highest; only the poets, not the philosophers, produce as such immortal works. But since everything superfluous is a defect, is then Socrates not the consistent philosopher, by not writing at all? In this way the question comes up. Let us start from the most massive facts: Socrates did not write and has a strong argument against writing in the *Phaedrus*. Plato wrote, and these two things cannot be on the same level. One or the other must be the highest, and since Plato wrote it must be assumed that he regarded it as higher. Writing on the highest level is higher than nonwriting on the highest level, and we must find the reason for that.

Listener: Could this public spiritedness which you said was necessary for writing be understood somehow as a protection for philosophy?

Mr. Strauss: Still, you cannot abstract from the essential accidents, if I may say so, the essential externals of philosophy.

There is something else to which you draw my attention: the first part deals with rhetoric and, if my interpretation is correct, the last part deals implicitly with rhetoric insofar as, in contrast to that, it raises the question of the nonwriting of the philosopher.

Listener: If there are real desires, such as desire for immortality, for example, can we even on the highest level just leave them aside or do they have to be satisfied on that highest level?

Mr. Strauss: Sure. But the question is this: A natural desire must be fulfilled. But the question is what is a natural desire? In other words, if we have a natural phenomenon, is it in every respect natural? A desire may have been deformed in various ways, and you cannot expect that this should be satisfied. First you have to establish the fact that it is a natural desire. On the basis of the *Symposium* one would have to say that the immortality which here appears as possible is the beholding of the immortal, whereas the beholder, as this human being, is not immortal. Every Platonic dialogue is a half-truth, deliberately; it abstracts from something. One can say, and that is perhaps the best one can say, the *Symposium* abstracts from what one could call in the language of the Greeks, the cosmic gods. You can also put it as follows: the soul. And I believe that the silence in the enumeration, the six points he makes, is very characteristic. The Platonic demonstration of immortality and of gods is based on consideration of the soul. The *Symposium*, in a way, abstracts from the soul, which sounds very strange. There is a simple reason: the *Symposium* is concerned—and that is the connection with that scandal in 416—with the current beliefs in the Olympian gods, in immortality connected with the mysteries of Eleusis. In this respect the answer is simply negative. Whether the theoretical and physiological considerations proper would lead to the gods as superhuman thinking beings, and to immortality of the individual, can be settled only on the basis of the *Phaedo* and, to some extent, of the *Phaedrus* and the *Republic*.

12 ALCIBIADES

Last time we completed the study of Socrates' speech. All people present, invited or uninvited, with the exception of Aristodemus, have spoken. We are at the end. But the dialogue does not end with that—an eruption takes place, Alcibiades comes in. Why does the dialogue on eros end with Alcibiades' speech on Socrates? There is, of course, a dramatic motivation given, which we shall read. But let us first regard the issue without regard to specific evidence. One could argue as follows. The primary theme of the *Symposium* is not eros, but Socrates' hubris. This leads to the fact that the dialogue is placed in the year 416, at the time when the profanation of the mysteries took place, where Alcibiades was involved more than anyone else. So Alcibiades had to come in for this reason. Since the poet accused Socrates, or the philosophers in general, of hubris, it was necessary to link up the presentation of Socrates' hubris with the rebuttal of the poets. This required a contest with the poets, and the most elegant form in which this could be done by Plato was to take as his model Aristophanes' *Frogs,* where Alcibiades is, in a way, the key personage, for with a view to Alcibiades the contest between the tragic poets is decided in favor of Aeschylus. So Alcibiades had to come in from this consideration too. Yet we must, of course, understand Alcibiades' speech also as the fitting conclusion to a dialogue on eros; otherwise this would be a bit far-fetched. Socrates alone says of himself that he is only an expert in erotic things; therefore it is natural to present at the end of the dialogue someone who should best know Socrates as an erotician, if I may coin a word.

But perhaps more simply: eros, strictly understood, is love of human beings, a desire to be together with a human being or human beings whom one loves, and this means the being together of the bodies, not in any narrow sense. What we now call personal presence is, of course, presence of the body. Talk can only occur when both are present. Now if this is eros, eros is essentially limited to one's lifetime. But eros tends beyond one's lifetime and, therefore, it becomes desire for immortality for the sake of eros, of being together always, of bodily immortality. This would require incarnation of the soul so that it can survive the death of the body. The only natural form of this incarnation is writing. For a book is a bodily thing which can be present with human beings after the author's death. From this point of view the fact that Socrates did not write would seem to indicate that he scorned this kind of immortality. It indicates, we can also say, the problematic character of Socrates' eros, of his desire to be together either in his body proper or in this kind of body—the book—with those he loved. Was Socrates a lover? This question is imposed on us by the very fact that he did not write. The man who, at first glance, would seem to have known Socrates best as a lover was Alcibiades, and Alcibiades will give an answer to our question, which is not sufficient but part of our evidence. Socrates was not a lover. If you remember the argument I stated before, it means therefore he did not write. But we must go deeper into the argument. I believe the time has now come, before we turn to the text, for a consideration which I have postponed many times.

The *Symposium* contains six speeches on eros, six different views or theories of eros. But in a work such as this there must be some connection between the theory and the theoretician, between the speech and the speaker. The theories must somehow reflect typical human attitudes, as we would say today. Now, what are these attitudes? If the *Symposium* is not complete in its consideration of the possible human attitudes, it is, of course, incomplete as a presentation of eros. We must, therefore, get a survey of the possible attributes of eros on the basis supplied by the *Symposium*. This can be done by a simple mathematical operation. There are three considerations which are obviously relevant: (1) the speaker may be a lover or beloved; (2) he may be old or young, because it is not necessary that the lover be old and the beloved young; (3) as indicated by the attitude toward wild drinking in the beginning, is he cautious or not? The incautious are subdivided into two forms: the incautious who is soft and the incautious who is manly. We have, then, three different points of view, two consisting of two alternatives and one of three—twelve alternatives altogether.

Now let us look at the combinations and see whether we can identify them. Young, cautious, lover; young, cautious, beloved; old, cautious, lover; old, cautious, beloved; young, soft, lover; young, soft, beloved; old, soft, lover; old, soft, beloved; young, manly, lover; young, manly, beloved; old, manly, lover; old, manly, beloved. I don't claim that what I am going to say now is the last word on the subject. I will make now one premise which will not sound absurd, I believe, namely that old, manly, lover and old, manly, beloved are one and the same in our dialogue—Socrates. Old does not mean seventy, but old relative to his beloved. That he is loved is shown clearly by Aristodemus; that he is a lover is, at least, his claim; that he is neither soft nor cautious is evident. The total number of characters would be eleven on the basis of the following consideration: I assume, on the basis of some encouragement given to me by my friend Mr. von Blanckenhagen, that the number of people present at such an affair was the same as the number of Muses—nine, i.e., one host and eight invited guests. Two people came in uninvited—Aristodemus with Socrates and now Alcibiades. We assume then that the total number present is eleven and, hence, all the types would have spoken, or rather would have been identified. Eight are known to us, the six speakers plus Alcibiades and Aristodemus. There must be three speakers not known to us, three combinations that remain nameless.

Now let me try to identify them if possible. Let's begin with Phaedrus: he is surely young, cautious, and beloved. Then we turn to Pausanias, who is old, soft, and lover; then Eryximachus—old, cautious, and lover; then Agathon—young, soft, and beloved. I have already spoken of Socrates. I now anticipate Alcibiades, who is a simple problem, I believe: young, manly, and lover. I would now like to take the simple case of Aristodemus: young, cautious, lover. That he is young and a lover is clear, and I take his caution to be shown in his unwillingness to drink much. For Aristophanes I have this suggestion: old, soft, beloved. That he is, relatively speaking, old is clear; softness is characteristic of all poets (*Laws* 817D; *Republic* 607C). Beloved by whom? In Phaedrus's case, for example, we know by whom—Eryximachus; Agathon, by Pausanias. Aristophanes, I suggest, and this is a mere suggestion, by Plato. There is an old story, that when Plato died he had Aristophanes' comedies under his pillow.

If this is true, and all these points need careful consideration, three types are not represented by name. You remember that after Phaedrus's speech several men spoke who are not recorded. I think we can figure them out. I do not say that this is necessarily true, but this is surely the way one has to go about it in order to identify the general character of the speeches which are not recorded. The missing combinations are the old, cautious, and beloved—we have to figure out why his speech is not recorded. Then we have the young, soft, and lover. There is a young, soft, and lover there, though not at the symposium, in the book: Apollodorus, who is explicitly called soft—but even without that we could diagnose him as soft, because what is meant by soft is probably what we would call today emotional, easily given to crying, easily given to laughter. Some equivalent of Apollodorus must have been present among the speakers. Finally, young, manly, and beloved is, I believe, also not represented, and in this case I think one could understand why the speech of the young, manly, beloved is not given.

It would be unbearable. If someone is young and in addition manly and in addition beloved, that would be hubris incarnate. I only submit these things for your consideration because this reflection is absolutely necessary, but whether my statement is sufficient or not is unimportant.

Listener: Could young, manly, beloved apply to eros?

Mr. Strauss: That is not necessarily so. Compare the description to the one given by Agathon. There the emphasis was on his softness, which reveals Agathon's softness, whereas eros described by Socrates is characterized by manliness, reflecting Socrates' manliness. Now let us turn to the text:

> When Socrates had said these things, some praised, but Aristophanes tried to say something, because Socrates in speaking had mentioned him in regard to his logos . . . (212c4–6)

The one dissatisfied with Socrates' speech is Aristophanes. Incidentally, the applause which Socrates gets is by far inferior to the applause which Agathon got. Why is Aristophanes dissatisfied? His thesis, that love is love of one's own, is the target to a higher degree than Agathon's thesis that love is love of the beautiful.

> . . . and suddenly there was a knocking at the courtyard door which caused a lot of noise, as if of revelers, and one heard the voice of the flute girl. Then Agathon said, "Boys, go look. And if it's one of our acquaintances, invite him; if not, say that we are not drinking but are about to rest." Not much later they heard the voice of Alcibiades in the courtyard, very drunk and shouting loudly, asking where Agathon was and ordering them to lead him to Agathon. (212c6–d5)

Aristophanes is interrupted by Alcibiades. There is a parallel to that in the *Protagoras,* 347b, where Alcibiades interrupts Hippias, the sophist. Aristophanes has something in common with Hippias. Hippias was that sophist who claimed most to be a physiologist, a student of nature. Aristophanes, too, is such a physicist. The political man par excellence takes the side of Socrates against the physicist Hippias and against the physicist Aristophanes. Why? The cosmic gods, as understood by these physicists, are incompatible with the polis. The whole opposition of nature and convention is a consequence of this understanding of the whole. There is this difference: In the *Protagoras,* Alcibiades acts intentionally, here he acts unintentionally, because in the *Protagoras* everyone was sober, here he enters drunk.

> Then they lead him into them, the flute girl and some other attendants in support, and he stood at the door crowned with a dense crown of ivy and

violets, along with a great many fillets on his head, and he said, "Men, hello! Will you welcome an extremely drunk man as a fellow drinker, or are we to go away once we have crowned Agathon? It's why we came. I, you see," he said, "could not come yesterday, but now I have come with fillets on my head, in order that from my head I may crown just like this the head of the wisest and most beautiful, if I may say so. Will you really laugh at me because I am drunk? But even if you do laugh, all the same I know that I am telling the truth. But tell me, from where I am standing, am I to enter on these conditions or not? Will you drink with me or not?" (212d5–213a2)

Since Alcibiades has not yet seen Socrates he calls Agathon the wisest. He is sure that he tells the truth, as you see, in spite or because of his being drunk. *In vino veritas*—there is something to that. But, on the other hand, we can also say drunkenness doesn't necessarily guarantee the truth. How true will it then be, what he is going to say about Socrates later on in his speech? You see in the earlier part of this passage the decision is made by Alcibiades and his attendants, not by Agathon's servants. Alcibiades crashes the party.

All then cried out loudly and urged him to enter and lie down, and Agathon invited him. And he came, being led by human beings. (213a3–5)

"Led by human beings." *Anthropoi*, as distinguished from real men, hombres. In this particular connection, I believe, it means something very emphatic. Who is led by human beings emphatically? One who is not a human being, a kind of god. I suggest that Alcibiades is here presented as, let me say, the raw material out of which the poets make gods.

And taking off the fillets as if to crown, he was holding them in front of his eyes and did not catch sight of Socrates, but sat down beside Agathon, between Socrates and him, for when Socrates saw him he made room for him. Then sitting down beside Agathon he greeted him and was crowning him. Then Agathon said, "Take off Alcibiades' shoes, boys, so that he may lie down as the third." "Yes, of course," Alcibiades said, "but who is our third fellow drinker?" And as he turned around he saw Socrates, and on seeing him he jumped up and said, "Heracles!" (213a5–b8)

You will see that Alcibiades swears more than anyone else.

"What was this? Here's Socrates! Once more you were lying down here waiting in ambush, just as you're accustomed to pop up suddenly wherever I was thinking you would least be. And now why have you come? And why in turn did you recline just here? It wasn't by the side of Aristophanes or anyone else who is ridiculous and wants to be, but you contrived to lie down by the side of the most beautiful of those within." (213b9–c5)

Socrates' presence comes as an entire surprise to Alcibiades. But the point made at the end is particularly remarkable. Where would Alcibiades expect to find Socrates? By the comic poet. Socrates prefers the most beautiful youth only to the comic poet. This is five years after Aristophanes wrote the *Clouds,* his famous "attack" on Socrates. There was no enmity between them, and we must keep this in mind, for it is of the greatest importance for what follows.

> And Socrates said, "Agathon, see to it that you protect me, since the eros of this human being has proved to be not a trivial matter for me. From the time when I fell in love with him, it is no longer possible for me either to glance at or converse with even a single beauty, or else he is jealous of me and in his resentment does amazing things and reviles me and hardly keeps his hands off. See to it that he does not do something now, but reconcile us, or if he tries to use force, defend me, since I am very much afraid of his madness and love of a lover." (213c6–d6)

Who is the lover, Socrates or Alcibiades? Socrates says that he fell in love with Alcibiades, but Alcibiades is jealous of Socrates. Is the problem sufficiently solved by the fact that Alcibiades is the lover in response? You may know from the literature A falls in love with B, a young man with a young girl, and it may happen that B also falls in love with A, so there is nothing absurd about that. But we must see if this is the situation.

> "Well, there is no possibility of reconciliation between you and me," Alcibiades said, "but I shall take my vengeance on you for this at another time. But now, Agathon," he said, "lend me some of the fillets, in order that I may crown this wonderful head of his too, and lest he find fault with me because I crowned you, while he who wins over all human beings in speeches, not only as you did the day before yesterday, but always, and despite that I had the nerve not to crown him." And he immediately took some of the fillets and crowned Socrates and lay down. (213d7–e6)

Thus Alcibiades fulfills the prophecy. In the beginning Agathon had said to Socrates, "Dionysus shall be the judge between you and me." Now Dionysus, represented by Alcibiades, is the judge and crowns Socrates. While Agathon too is crowned, Socrates is given the highest praise: he wins always, not only once in a while. Therefore one can say, with reference to an earlier remark I made, the god, whose raw material is Alcibiades, would seem to be Dionysus. But that does not yet settle the issue. There may be other gods, greater gods, who could be made of Alcibiades by a great poet.

> When he had lain down, he said, "Alright, men. You seem to me to be sober. You mustn't be allowed to be, but you have to drink, for we have made this agreement. So I choose as the ruler of the drinking, until you drink enough, myself." (213e7–10)

You see the agreement is kept. There is a strange mixture of tyrannical and constitutional procedure. It is only for the purpose of executing what has been agreed upon. He is a typical tyrant, who would always say, "I fulfill what all of you want," but surely he elects himself.

> "Well, Agathon, let someone bring me some big cup, if there is any. But there is no need. Come, boy," he said, when he saw it had a capacity of more than eight pints, "bring me that cooler." He then had it filled up and drank out of it himself first, then he urged them to pour it out for Socrates and at the same time said, "Against Socrates, men, this sophism of mine is nothing, for however much one bids him drink, so much he drinks up and will never get any more drunk."
>
> Socrates drank as soon as the boy had filled it; but Eryximachus said, "How do we do this, Alcibiades? Is it in this way, without either saying or singing anything in our cups, but shall we drink simply like the thirsty?" (213e10–214b2)

Eryximachus protests. He is in a way the guardian of everyone, the physician. He does not forbid drinking, he only forbids mere drinking.

> Then Alcibiades said, "Eryximachus, the best of the best and most moderate [sober] father, hello!" (214b3–4)

He does not say most sober son, his father was most sober. This may mean that Eryximachus did have a little and is not altogether sober.

> "Greetings to you too," Eryximachus said. "But what are we to do?" "Whatever you command. One must obey you, 'For a physician is equivalent in worth to many others.' So order whatever you want." (214b6–8)

Alcibiades gives in to Eryximachus without any ado. Why? He quotes a verse from the *Iliad,* book 11, 514, where a physician is mentioned. This physician was the son of Asclepius who is, of course, inferior to Asclepius, just as Eryximachus is inferior to his father, as we have seen. Machaon was wounded by Paris, Helen's husband, and the verse occurs in connection with the value of physicians in war after a physician has been wounded. The fact that the physician is not available is much worse than if any hero were not available because he can save many. Physicians are eminently useful in war, and war is, of course, as we shall see later, the most important business. If this is so, it follows strictly that one must listen to physicians in every affair. If one must listen to them in the most important things, one must surely listen to them in less important things.

One more word about the situation in the eleventh book of the Iliad: It is a bad situation. Hector is loose and slays many Greeks. The Greeks are in greater danger than ever before. Nestor, eloquence incarnate, gives an eloquent description of the danger which Achilles' aloofness from the suffering of the Greeks has brought about. Achilles is still sulking in his tent, and the Greeks are in sore need of Achilles. This situation exists again in 407. The Athenians, and in a way all Greeks, are in sore need. Alcibiades is aloof, somehow aligned with the Persian king, and he is the only man who can save Greece. By the way, this fits beautifully with Thucydides' description of Alcibiades in this situation. Alcibiades divines the situation—he longs for it—where he, a new and greater Achilles, will be the one all Greece wants as their savior. So this verse of Homer is very revealing. One must always look up quotations in their context if the context is preserved. To repeat: Is it clear why Alcibiades obeys Eryximachus? That is surely a question. Why should such a grand seigneur obey a physician, however famous, if the physician was not, in a way, the most important man in war?

> "Listen then," Eryximachus said. "We had decided before you came in that each of us in turn, starting on the left, ought to speak as beautiful a speech about Eros as he could and praise him. Now all the rest of us have spoken; but you, since you have not spoken and have drunk, it is just for you to speak and, once you have spoken, give any order you want to Socrates, and then he to the one on his right and so on for all the rest." (214b9–c5)

Alcibiades must speak on eros, of course, like everyone else, and then give a commission to Socrates, and then Socrates to his neighbor on the right. Here we have this difficulty: Is Socrates not the last one on the right? And here I am subject to correction by anyone who knows better than I how the seating arrangement was. But, as I understand it, Eryximachus must have been mistaken, and if this is so, it would be additional proof that he is not altogether sober.

> "Well, Eryximachus," Alcibiades said. "Though you speak well, still I'm afraid it won't be quite equal to set a drunk man against the speeches of

the sober. And, you blessed innocent, does Socrates persuade you of anything of the things which he just now said? Or do you know that it is wholly the opposite of what he was saying? For he, if I praise anyone else than him, while he is present, either a god or a human being, he will not keep his hands off me." "Be quiet!" Socrates said. (214c6–d5)

Alcibiades says Socrates will not tolerate it if I praise in his presence any god or man. Therefore he cannot praise eros. For, contrary to what Socrates says, he is not a lover, not a worshiper of eros.

"No, by Poseidon!" Alcibiades said, "Say nothing against it, since I would praise no one else when you are present."

"Well, do it in this way," Eryximachus said, "if you want. Praise Socrates."

"How do you mean?" Alcibiades said. "Is it thought that I should, Eryximachus? Am I to attack the man and in your presence take my revenge on him?"

"You, there," Socrates said. "What do you have in mind? To praise me to make things funnier? Or what will you do?"

"I shall tell the truth. But see whether you allow it."

"Well, in that case," he said, "I allow and urge you to tell the truth."

"I couldn't begin too soon," Alcibiades said. "However, do as follows. If I say something untrue, check me in the middle, if you want, and say that I am lying on that point; for as far as my will goes I shall lie about nothing. If, however, in recollecting, I jump from one thing to another, don't wonder; for it is not at all easy for someone in the condition you see me in to enumerate fluently and in order your strangeness." (214d6–215a3)

Alcibiades will praise Socrates. This is settled. Socrates couldn't bear anything else being praised in his presence, at least when Alcibiades is the praiser. At the same time Alcibiades will take his revenge. Still, he will tell only the truth about Socrates. Socrates certainly cannot forbid that. Socrates does not refer to modesty for not wanting to be praised; he says that he cannot prevent anyone from telling the truth no matter what the subject might be.

Listener: Socrates spoke of his *daimonion* as preventing him from doing what is not proper, and this is essentially what Alcibiades is asking Socrates to do for him.

Mr. Strauss: That is not a bad point. Very good as a matter of fact, because Alcibiades later on speaks of Socrates as a demonic being.

Listener: Where the English says, "in the condition you see me in," does that specifically refer to Alcibiades' drunkenness or could it be a reference to Alcibiades' whole character?

Mr. Strauss: I believe it refers to his drunkenness.

Listener: Could it be construed as meaning that he is not the sort of fellow who can sit down and give an orderly presentation of the sort of person Socrates is because he does not really understand him?

Mr. Strauss: This would be a subtlety which Plato could have meant to convey without Alcibiades being aware of it. Surely. That is very good, if you understand it this way. That is exactly what will happen. Alcibiades is a man who does not know what he is talking about, and yet in a strange way through a screen sees everything.

[In answer to a question:] Eryximachus is corrupted by Alcibiades' tyrannical conduct to become a tyrant himself. Now let us begin with Alcibiades' speech.

> "I shall try to praise Socrates, men, in this way—through images. Now he, perhaps, will believe it is for making things funnier, but the image will be for the sake of the truth, not for the sake of the ridiculous." (215a4–6)

Alcibiades will praise Socrates by use of similes and thus give a truthful description. That is important. It is a new light on poetry which we have not yet received. Up to now it seems that poetry does not tell the truth: poetry magnifies, poetry adorns and therefore distorts the truth. But poetry can be truthful through similes, and this means also that poetry does not limit itself to generating political prudence. For example, the description of Socrates has no relation to that. At any rate, Alcibiades will give a poetic presentation of Socrates, and this follows naturally the poetic presentation of philosophy in the last part of Diotima's speech. Both presentations of philosophy and of Socrates are inspired. Diotima is a prophetess and Alcibiades is inspired by wine. The wine is that which makes possible the perfect frankness of his speech. This particular inspiration by wine is absent from the poetic presentation of philosophy by Socrates or Diotima.

It would seem, then, that we are likely to get a franker presentation here of Socrates than we have received of philosophy. Only one question remains: Is Alcibiades competent? That we don't know yet. He speaks through similitudes and the similitudes are, of course, not literally true. The similitudes refer to the whole Socrates, not any individual action. All details are literally true, that is Alcibiades' claim. One could say what Alcibiades wants to give is poetic history, where the whole is in similes and all details are true. The greatest example known to me at least of such poetic history is Thucydides.

So he will do to Socrates what Thucydides did to the Peloponnesian War. All details are true, and yet the overall picture is fiction. It is surely more than a prose statement. One wonders whether the opposite could not be said of Plato, that practically all details in the Platonic dialogues are invented yet the whole is literally true. Alcibiades' speech is poetic also in another way: it is an entirely nontheoretical speech. It is an account of his passions, his suffering, a term which recurs time and again, and the speech is an action prompted by his passion.

[In answer to a question:] That Agathon, Socrates, and Alcibiades should form a triad makes very much sense. At the very beginning, when Apollodorus talked to that nameless comrade, only these three names were mentioned. There is in other words a triad. We know already that Aristophanes is at the end of a triad beginning with Pausanias and including Eryximachus. Finally, there would be then, two triads preceded by an isolated speech of Phaedrus. That Phaedrus's speech is isolated is very clear.

After the introduction, we turn to the speech proper, which, as you will see, consists of three parts: The first part begins here and goes up to 216c and deals with the effect of Socrates' speeches.

> "I say he is most like those Silenuses which sit in the shops of herm sculptors, the ones craftsmen make with pipes or flutes, which on being opened up in two show they have images of gods within. And I say in turn, he resembles the satyr Marsyas." (215a6–b4)

This is the exterior of Socrates, an ugly exterior, but within are contained images of the gods. What is visible at first glance is ugly; what is audible at first glance is beautiful—flute, etc. Those who are attracted by the sound and not repelled by the sight are eventually led to a beautiful vision. We remember the end of Diotima's speech, the vision of the beautiful itself. "Sit[ting] in the shops of herm sculptors" refers to something we can recognize. In the *Apology*, Socrates is described as sitting in the marketplace with all kinds of craftsmen. Also his father was a sculptor, though not in this precise sense.

> "Now that you are like them in looks *[eidos]*, Socrates, surely not even you yourself would dispute; but how you are like them in all other respects, hear after this. You are hubristic. Aren't you? If you don't agree, I shall supply witnesses. Well, are you not a flautist? Yes, far more wonderful than he. Since he was wont to enchant human beings through instruments by the power from his mouth, and still now whoever plays his songs on the flute—for those which Olympus played, I say they are Marsyas's, since he

taught him—these songs of his, whether a good flutist or a poor flute girl plays them, they alone make one possessed and reveal those who are in need of gods and initiatory rites, because they are divine." (215b4–c6)

Socrates is first like the artificial Silenus and then like the true Marsyas. Since he is not an artifact the first simile is insufficient. In three respects he is like the satyr Marsyas: in shape, in hubris, and in marvelous flute playing. Hubris is central and is not proven here. Alcibiades enlarges here only on the flute playing. That brings about possession and the revelation of those who are in need of the gods and of sanctification. The vision of the images of the gods in the first comparison is now replaced by possession through higher powers. Socrates' effect is deep, it affects the whole man. As for Marsyas's hubris, we know this story: he challenged Apollo to a contest in regard to wisdom, in which Marsyas was defeated and flayed by Apollo. Was Socrates too defeated by Apollo? We cannot yet answer that, because Socrates is a far more marvelous flute player than Marsyas and perhaps he was not defeated. Let us see.

One more point before we go on, concerning modesty. The clearest statement on this subject you can find is in Aristotle's *Ethics,* in the chapter on magnanimity. The virtue of magnanimity consists in this, that a man being worth much knows his worth and lays claim to the honors becoming his worth. Then he discusses the alternative to this—which is, in a way, the highest moral virtue from Aristotle's point of view—and that is the modest man, as we would say. The modest man is the man who is not worth much and therefore does not claim any particular honors for himself. This is not particularly admirable. Socrates is not modest. If he says he is ignorant, for example, that would simply be a statement of fact. But if he alone knows the abyss of his ignorance, whereas we do not know it, he has, of course, reason for pride. The notion of modesty does not fit in.

The more striking example is that of humility, a term never used by Plato or Aristotle or Xenophon in a positive sense. It is used only once by Plato and once by Xenophon as far as I remember in a laudatory sense, and in both cases it occurs when they speak of Sparta, the most archaic part of the Greek mainland, where old habits survive. So the words modesty and humility are really not applicable in Socrates' case. Therefore, Socrates would listen without blushing in the least to the strongest praise if true. Someone has tried, and with success as far as I remember, to show that the whole *Apology* is really quasi modeled on Aristotle's description of the magnanimous man. Socrates, knowing himself to be a man of outstanding virtue, claims for himself the highest honors. The mere fact that Socrates says nothing to contradict Alcibiades would, on the face of it, mean that Alcibiades has not said an untruth. We must also not forget that, whatever hubris may mean, this dialogue serves the purpose of presenting Socrates' hubris, and therefore it would be artistically impossible to destroy that. Within the limits of his understanding he makes clear what Socrates' hubris is.

> "But you differ from him by only this much, that without instruments, with bare speeches, you have the same effect." (215c6–d1)

That is the only different between Socrates and Marsyas. That is to say there is no difference between Socrates and Marsyas regarding the defeat by Apollo. How could Socrates have been defeated by Apollo, on the basis of what we know? Where did Apollo enter into Socrates' life? The Delphic oracle. The oracle said Socrates was the wisest man, and then Socrates goes around in Athens and examines every Athenian. Perhaps this was Socrates' defeat, that he had to walk around and examine every Athenian. You could, of course, say Alcibiades was drunk and every word would, therefore, not have to be taken seriously, but Plato wasn't drunk.

> "We, at any rate, whenever we hear anyone else speaking other speeches, even of a very good public speaker, virtually no one has any concern; but whenever someone hears you speak or someone else speaks your speeches, even if the speaker is very poor, regardless of whether a man, a woman, or a youth hears them, we are thunderstruck and possessed." (215d1–d6)

Socrates is the only speaker whose speeches take possession of the hearer. He does not say now that his speeches, like Marsyas's speeches, make manifest those who are in need of the gods. Every hearer of Socrates' speeches is entranced, even if the speaker is a very low fellow, even women and young men. Socrates is a master of swaying the demos.

> "I, at any rate, men, if I were not going to be thought utterly drunk, would have sworn to you exactly the sort of things I myself have experienced by his speeches and how I still experience them even now. For whenever I hear them, to a far greater extent than Corybants, my heart leaps and tears pour out of my eyes by the effect of his speeches; and I see many many others experiencing the same things. In hearing Pericles and other good public speakers, though I was thinking they spoke well, I was experiencing nothing like this, nor was my soul in turmoil and experiencing vexation at my slavish disposition, but this Marsyas put me in this state

quite often, so as to think that life was not worth living for me, being in the state I am. And you won't say, Socrates, that these things too are not true." (215d6–216a2)

You see the repetition: after all, Alcibiades should know best how Socrates' speeches affected him. How would you describe that effect of Socrates' rhetoric, which has no parallel in present or past according to Alcibiades? Perhaps we should read on.

"And still even now I am conscious within myself that should I be willing to lend my ears, I would not resist but I would experience the same things. He compels me to agree that, in being need of much myself, I still neglect myself and handle the affairs of the Athenians. So forcibly stopping my ears as if from the Sirens I flee and am gone, in order that I do not sit here idly beside him and grow old. I have experienced in relation to him alone of human beings what one would not suspect was in me, to experience shame before anyone whatsoever. I feel ashamed only before him. I know within myself that I cannot contradict him and say that I should not do what he urges, but whenever I go away [I am conscious] that I have been defeated by the honor from the many. So I scurry away [like a runaway slave] and avoid him, and whenever I see him, I am ashamed about what has been agreed upon. And often I would see him with pleasure no longer among human beings, but if this should happen, I know well that I would to a much greater extent be grieved, and hence I don't know what I am to do with this human being." (216a3–c3)

This is the end of the first part of Alcibiades' speech. How would you describe the effect of Socrates' speeches as described here by Alcibiades? I think there is one modern word, which has no equivalent in Greek, which could be used to describe this: religion. Alcibiades feels like a sinner—to use a biblical expression—like one who knows that he sins but cannot help going on sinning. That is perfectly true, provided we make one distinction which is now very popular, I understand, between shame cultures and guilt cultures. Indeed, Alcibiades speaks only of shame, not of guilt. I do not want to identify myself with this theory, because guilt plays, of course, a great role among the Greeks as well, but certainly not in the case of Alcibiades. Socrates, we may say, successfully preaches repentance. In his effect he appears almost like, what in an entirely different context would be, religious speakers. Socrates is a successful preacher of repentance, a religious effect.

Alcibiades, however, is defeated; he cannot live up to what he learns from Socrates. The thing that prevents him from complying with Socrates is vulgar ambition. Socrates, we know, is free from ambition, vulgar or high. The ancient poets are free from vulgar ambition, but not from the highest ambition. Alcibiades is below the poets. Socrates' voice is not compared to the voice of the conscience, naturally, but to the voice of the Sirens, which may sound very strange. How can the voice of the conscience be compared to the voice of the Sirens? You know the Sirens in the *Odyssey*—when listening to them you get into mortal danger, and only the wise Odysseus could safely hear them because he was tied to the mast of the ship. But if you look up Xenophon's *Memorabilia,* book 2, chapter 6, you will see there too the Sirens' voice is said to call to virtue, which is the same that you have here. This is the first part of this speech. There is a central reference to Socrates' hubris but no explanation or proof. The theme is the religious effect of Socrates' speeches.

Some of these effects which Alcibiades describes are mentioned in different contexts by Plato: that we are entranced, deeply moved, that we cry. What sort of thing has this effect? Tragedy. In this first part of the speech, Alcibiades compares the effect of Socrates with that of tragedy. Here begins the second and central part of the speech, which goes to 221c. This second part takes up the suggestion mentioned in the beginning but suppressed in the first part, that there is a difference between Socrates' exterior and interior. If you know merely the speeches, no difficulty arises, but once you consider the difference between exterior and interior, the problem of Socrates' hubris comes up. The explicit theme of the second and central part can be described as moderation, insensibly shifting into endurance. But the primary thing is moderation. The connection between moderation and endurance can be shown very simply: moderation means primarily, in the usage at that time, the proper attitude toward food, drink, and sex. That is the sense in which the word is used in Aristotle's *Ethics*. Take thirst; the transition to endurance of thirst is very simple.

The key consideration, however, for the understanding of the sexual instinct, is a different kind of moderation than that for food or drink. It is the opposite of hubris. A moderate man is the opposite of a man of hubris. There is another alternative to moderation, and that is madness. That is the antagonism which is the core of the *Phaedrus,* but not here. Here we are concerned with the opposition of Socrates' moderation and hubris. Externally, Socrates appears to be a man of hubris, but his interior is moderation. These two qualities are strangely connected, according to Alcibiades; they are two aspects of the same thing. Why? What Alcibiades has primarily in mind as Socrates' hubris is his attitude toward himself: Socrates is not in love with him, he rejects him, he scorns him, he scorns his amorous advances. But why does he do that? Because he is moderate. So, Socrates' hubris toward Alcibiades is identical with his moderation. That is by no means the full story, but it is the external connection of the two themes.

> "And by his flute songs both many others and I have experienced things of this sort by this satyr; but hear me speak of other things, how like he is to those to whom I likened him and how marvelous is the power he has. Know well that no one of you is acquainted with him, but I shall make it plain, inasmuch as I started. You see that Socrates is erotically disposed to the beauties, thunderstruck in awe and always around them, and that in turn he is ignorant of everything and knows nothing. How isn't this figure of his Silenic? Yes it is, exactly. He has cast it about himself on the outside, just as the sculpted Silenus; but inside, on his being opened, can you believe how great is the moderation he is filled with, oh my fellow drinkers?" (216c6–d7)

No one except Alcibiades knows Socrates, that is the claim. Socrates becomes visible as the lover of the beautiful and as an ignoramus. His outside is ugly, but inside he is full of moderation. That is a very strange statement. Why is the lover of the beautiful ugly? We have seen it in Pausanias. In Athens there was a very strange thing: on the one hand they were encouraged by the nomos and on the other hand they were discouraged. But Alcibiades does not say Socrates in his interior is full of moderation and knowledge, he says only full of moderation. The moderation takes the place of wisdom. Alcibiades is not concerned with wisdom; he tells in the following story his strange quest for Socrates' secret wisdom, and absolutely nothing is discovered by Alcibiades. He discovers only Socrates' moderation.

> "Know that neither if someone is beautiful is it of any concern to him, but he despises it to an extent that not one would even suspect, nor if someone is rich or if he has any other honor of those blessed by the multitude; but he regards all these possessions as worthless and ourselves to be nothing— I am speaking to you—but he continues to be ironical and playful all his life toward human beings." (216d7–e5)

Socrates is moderate because he is utterly unerotic, which, of course, one can also say is not very meritorious. He is contemptuous of all men, just as Apollodorus in the beginning. His whole life is ironical. As Nietzsche put it when he speaks of married philosophers: Socrates, the great exception, the married philosopher, is married only ironically. He implies, since he limits himself entirely to the moderation aspect, that Socrates' ignorance too is mere pretense. How could Socrates' interior be beautiful if he were also ignorant in his interior? Alcibiades surely does not say that.

One could say, of course, that Alcibiades has refuted the charge of Socrates' ignorance by his praise of Socrates' speeches. How could a man make such speeches without possessing knowledge? I used almost inadvertently the expression "the charge of ignorance." But that is the point. Alcibiades, seventeen years in advance, meets the charge against Socrates. What was the charge for which he was condemned? He does not believe in the gods of the city and he corrupts the young, also a bipartite charge, just as here. Here it is his love for the beautiful ones and his ignorance. Is there a possible connection between these two charges? The first impression you get when you hear of a man corrupting the young is, of course, pederasty. Plato does not allude to that, but Xenophon does. I contend that ignorance and the charge of impiety also correspond. If he only says, "I do not know whether Zeus is," that has practically the same effect. He cannot simply worship the gods of the city. Here we come somewhat closer to the problem of Socrates' hubris. His hubris has very much to do with the issue of the gods, as indicated in the beginning, starting from the consideration that the *Symposium* is the only dialogue devoted to one of the recognized gods.

Alcibiades has some awareness of treasures hidden in Socrates which would not appear in his speeches. He has seen that the outside, love of beautiful young males and assertion of ignorance, is mere dissimulation. The inside is divine, namely, pure moderation. But what about the inner side of Socrates' ignorance? Alcibiades wanted to know Socrates' knowledge, which he was sure was concealed behind his pretended ignorance. What does he do in order to discover that hidden knowledge? That is told at great length in the sequel. He thinks that if he achieves bodily intimacy, Socrates will no longer be able to withhold from him anything he knows. What he discovers in this very ambiguous story, verging on the unbearable, is that Socrates was a man of perfect moderation. Socrates' knowledge, what he was about, he never discovered. Alcibiades had undergone the effect of Socrates' ugliness and his pretended eroticism. He had also undergone the effect of his moving speeches. Then he discerns that there is something else and he tries to discover it. He never discovers it. On the contrary, it ends with a great humiliation for Alcibiades. How does he get out of it? He tells the story with great frankness, though he is not fully aware of the connection. How does he get out of that state of humiliation brought about, on the one hand, by Socrates' speeches and, on the other hand, by that strange night he spent with Socrates? There is only one way in which a man like Alcibiades can get rid of this overpowering feeling of inferiority, as the psychologists would say. He goes to war. War is the great savior. In war he finds that he can be superior to Socrates. He is on a horse comforting the infantryman Socrates. This gives him back his self-esteem. But the crucial point is the story of moderation and hubris. The final solution is found only in the last part of the speech, in which Socrates' speeches become again the theme. In the central part the speeches are not the theme; the theme is Socrates' conduct with regard to eros, the flagrant contradiction between Socrates' claim to be in love with Alcibiades and his complete freedom from such love.

Today we must finish, by fair means or foul, our discussion of the *Symposium*. To recapitulate briefly the main points: In the first part Socrates is compared to the Silenuses; he has an ugly exterior and a beautiful interior. He is compared to Marsyas, the satyr, regarding his shape, his hubris, and his flute playing. Only the theme of his flute playing is developed. The flute playing of Socrates is his speaking: his speeches have an effect like tragedies; we may also say a religious effect. In this most important section of the first part of Alcibiades' speech, no distinction is made between the exterior and interior of Socrates' speeches. In the second part, Socrates is compared in the beginning again to the satyr but also to the Silenuses, who have an ugly exterior and a beautiful interior. The ugly exterior: Socrates' claim to be a lover of the beautiful ones and his claim to be ignorant. The beautiful interior of Socrates is his moderation. Nothing is said about the beautiful interior including wisdom. Moderation is used here in opposition to his alleged eroticism, and there is no opposite to his ignorance. The sequel describes Alcibiades on the quest for Socrates' hidden interior. But again, the inside he seeks is not the inside of Socrates' speeches. Alcibiades seeks the inside of Socrates' conduct, of his deeds. His external deeds are those of an erotic man. What is their inside?

> "With this intention, though I had previously not been accustomed to be with him without an attendant, I then sent the attendant away and was with him all alone—I have to tell you the whole truth, but pay attention, and if I lie, Socrates, refute me. So I was alone with him alone, men, and I believed he would converse with me at once in just the way a lover converses with a beloved in isolation, and I was joyful; but really none of these things occurred, but just as he was accustomed he would continue to converse with me, and having spent the day would go away." (217a6–b7)

So that was the first attempt. At first Alcibiades was always in company when he met Socrates. Now he wants to find the secret. He is alone with him, but nothing happens. Yet one thing is clear. Alcibiades expects or divines that Socrates' secret knowledge is of an erotic kind.

> "After that I invited him to join me in exercising, and I joined him in exercising, as I intended that here I would get somewhere. So he exercised with me and wrestled with me often when no one else was present. What need is there to speak any more about it? It did not do me any good. And when I was getting nowhere in this way, I decided I should attack the man at full strength and not let up, inasmuch as I had now started on the attempt, but I now had to know what the business is." (217b7–c6)

The business of Socrates. That is the formula used in the *Apology*, the business of Socrates. What is it? No one knows. Alcibiades has the same embarrassment, but he has the particular notion that this business has to do with eros, and therefore he proceeds in an erotic fashion.

> "So I invited him to join me at dinner, simply as a lover plots against a beloved. Not even in this case did he quickly accept, but nevertheless in time he was persuaded. When he had come the first time, he wanted to go away once he had dined; and then out of shame I let him go. But on the second occasion I plotted, and when we had dined I kept on conversing far into the night, and when he wanted to go away, I pretended that it was too late and compelled him to stay. He was resting on the couch next to mine, the one he had dined on, and no one else was sleeping in the room except us." (217c7–e1)

So that is the last stage, and an account of it will follow. Alcibiades is driven to reverse roles and play the lover. Socrates claimed to be the lover of Alcibiades, but that did not work. Alcibiades has to woo Socrates. There are six stages. Alcibiades in the company of attendants; Alcibiades alone; training, i.e., stripping, together; the invitation to dinner refused; dinner without consequence; and six—I have to use the hard word—to sleep together. That will come now.

> "Now up to this point in the logos it would be fair to tell it to anyone at all; but what followed you would not have heard from me unless, in the first place, as the saying goes, wine without boys and with boys is after all true, and, in the second place, it appears to me unjust, now that I have come to the praise, to hide from view the overweening deed of Socrates. And thirdly, the experience of one bitten by a viper holds me too. They surely say that anyone who experiences it is unwilling to say what sort it

was except to those who have been bitten, on the grounds that they alone will know and sympathize if he brought himself to stop at nothing in speaking and doing by the effect of the pain. Now I was bitten by a more painful bite and in the most painful place in which one could be bitten— the heart or soul or whatever one must call it—struck and bitten by the speeches in philosophy, which hold on more savagely than a viper does whenever they seize someone young with a not ungifted soul, and they make him do and say anything whatsoever. And seeing Phaedruses, Aga- thons, Eryximachuses, Pausaniases, Aristodemuses, and Aristophane- ses; and Socrates—what need is there to speak of him?—and everyone else. All of you have partaken of philosophic madness and bacchic frenzy. Therefore all of you will hear, for you will forgive the things then done no less than the things now said. But the servants, and whoever else is profane and a boor, place very large gates on your ears." (217e1–218b7)

Six stages—does this ring a bell? Six speeches and six levels of the erotic quest according to Diotima. In other words, just as the highest stage in Diotima's quest for beauty is a vision of beauty itself, Alcibiades will see now in his way the beautiful itself in Socrates. But that will be a kind of car- icature of what Diotima or Socrates sees. It is a secret story which Alcibi- ades is going to tell, which can be told only to those who have been bitten by the speeches occurring in philosophy, or those who have participated in philosophic madness and frenzy. This madness or frenzy is, of course, the opposite of moderation. A secret story about Alcibiades' nocturnal attempt to get hold, ultimately, of Socrates' secret knowledge. Let us see what he finds. Incidentally, this makes it perfectly clear that Alcibiades does not even claim to be closer to philosophy than any of the others present, even those whom he leaves nameless.

"When, men, the lamp had been extinguished and the boys were outside, I thought I should not embroider anything before him, but freely say what I was thinking; and as I nudged him I said, 'Socrates, are you asleep?' 'Certainly not,' he said. 'Do you know then what I have resolved on?' 'What in particular?' he said. 'You seem,' I said, 'to have proven to be the only deserving lover of mine, and you appear to me to hesitate to make mention of it to me. This is my situation: I believe it is very foolish not to gratify you in this, and in whatever else of my wealth or my friends that you are in need of. There is nothing more estimable than for me to be- come as good as possible, and I believe there is no one who is a more com- petent helper in this than you. So I would be far more ashamed before the wise [phronimoi] in not gratifying a man of your sort than in gratifying be ashamed before the many and senseless.'" (218b8–d5)

Alcibiades makes it clear and proves it that he is altogether frank. Whether Socrates is altogether frank remains to be seen. Alcibiades makes Socrates what we can only call an improper advance, and his problem is the same as that of Pausanias, who was also worried about decency. But in contradistinction to Pausanias, Alcibiades does not suggest a change in the law. Alcibiades has a tyrannical nature, he disregards the law in favor of the opinion of the sensible. The sensible will accept his conduct and that is sufficient; the law is of no interest.

> "And he, when he heard me, very ironically, and very characteristically of him, said in his usual way, 'My dear Alcibiades, it's probable that you really are not a bad sort, if it is in fact true what you say about me and there is some power in me through which you would become better. You must, you know, be seeing some indescribable beauty in me and very far superior to the beauty of form in you. So if in catching sight of it you are trying to have a share in it and exchange beauty for beauty, it's not by a little amount that you intend to gain an advantage over me, but you are trying to acquire the truth of beautiful things in place of this opinion [seeming; *doxa*], and you have in mind to exchange in reality gold for bronze. But, you blessed innocent, consider better, lest I be, without your being aware of it, nothing. The sight of thought, you know, begins to look sharply when the sight of the eyes tries to fall off from its peak, and you are still far from that.'" (218d6–219a4)

How does Socrates get out of this delicate situation? He says, as it were, you, Alcibiades, see in me an indescribable beauty, but precisely if you are right you are trying to cheat me. You will get my true beauty and I would get your spurious beauty, and that is not fair. It is like the exchange of Glaucus and Diomedes, exchanging gold for bronze weapons in the *Iliad*. The alternative is that you are mistaken as to my beauty. In that case I would cheat you. Socrates declines Alcibiades' offer on grounds of justice, perhaps ultimately on the side of law, seeing the connection between justice and law.

Alcibiades is, of course, unaware of the ground of this rejection, and that is characteristic of him because he has all kinds of qualities but surely no sense of justice. We must also not overlook the element of selfishness in Socrates. Socrates, too, does not wish to be cheated.

> "And I, when I heard this, said, 'Nothing on my side has been stated in any other way than how I think it; so on this condition you yourself deliberate and decide whatever you believe is best for you and me.' 'Well,' he said, 'that is a good point. In the ensuing time we shall on deliberation do

whatever appears to the two of us the best about these things and every-thing else.' Now I, once I had spoken and heard him say this, and with the discharge of all my weapons as it were, I believed he had been wounded, and getting up, I did not allow him to say anything anymore, but I wrapped my own himation around him—it was winter—and lying down under that threadbare cloak of his, I threw my arms around this truly de-monic and wonderful being and lay down beside him the whole night. And not even on these points, Socrates, will you say I am lying. And when I had done this, he proved to be so far superior to my youthful bloom and scorned and laughed at and insulted it—and I was thinking I was some-thing, in this regard at least. Oh, judges! You are judges of the high and mighty disdain of Socrates—know well, by the gods, by the goddesses, I slept and got up with Socrates, and nothing more untoward occurred than if I were sleeping with my father or older brother." (219a5–d2)

Another oath of Alcibiades, a very unusual oath. He is a big swearer, as we have seen. He calls those present the jury, the judges. This is a judgment of Socrates, and we must see the divination of Alcibiades. Alcibiades knows, divines, that Socrates will have to stand before a jury.

But Alcibiades' speech is both an accusation of Socrates and a defense of Socrates. Socrates is guilty of hubris. He disdained arrogantly Alcibiades. But he is not guilty of corrupting the young. Why is he not guilty of cor-rupting the young? Because he is a man of moderation. But the ground of his acquittal, moderation, is at the same time the ground of his hubris. His hubris toward Alcibiades is a necessary consequence of Socrates' modera-tion. Now let us translate it into the terms of the charge made later on: be-cause Socrates is moderate, because his eros has been purified, he does not believe in the gods of the city. Therefore, because of his moderation he is guilty of hubris. No one was ever as close as that to Socrates in body, if we disregard Xanthippe. Yet Alcibiades learned absolutely nothing about the secret of Socrates' business, he learned only of his moderation. You can also say Socrates has no hidden business, he has no hidden knowledge. These beautiful statues within Socrates, of which Alcibiades spoke, are equally ac-cessible to all through Socrates' speeches. Which of these interpretations is correct can only appear from the sequel. This bedroom scene, the most dar-ing scene ever occurring in Plato, recalls another bedroom scene, but this time in Socrates' bedroom, in the beginning of the *Protagoras*—which be-gins, incidentally, with a brief dialogue, the main theme of which is Soc-rates' being in love with Alcibiades. There it is early morning; here it is at the end of the dialogue, in Alcibiades' bedroom, during the whole night.

The implication is clear: the *Protagoras* is infinitely less intimate than the *Symposium*. The *Symposium* alone reveals Socrates' hubris.

But there remains an entirely unsolved problem. Socrates despises all men, as Alcibiades says, even Alcibiades. Yet he somehow cares for all men, and especially for the young. How is this possible? For Alcibiades this is one aspect of the riddle of Socrates, of Socrates' strangeness. Socrates is not a lover, nor is he filled with love of glory or prestige. What prompts Socrates to care for men? A very simple, perhaps too simple, solution, though worthy of consideration: Out of justice, though it is clear that Alcibiades would not understand that motivation. This may be the reason why Alcibiades has no access to Socrates' business. I do not go into the dramatic situation now, although that would, of course, require attention. But you must always watch where they are. It is the most embarrassing situation in which Alcibiades finds himself. You may have to translate it into heterosexual relations to recognize it in modern literature.

> "Then what thought do you believe I had after this? While I believed I had been dishonored, I still admired his nature, moderation, and manliness, having come across a human being of this kind, such as I believed I would never have encountered in respect to prudence *[phronesis]* and endurance [resistance]. Hence, just as I did not know how I could get angry at him and be deprived of the being-together with this man, so I was utterly at a loss as to how I was to draw him over." (219d3–e1)

He admired his nature as well as his moderation and manliness, and later on he says, I didn't ever believe I would encounter someone as outstanding in prudence and in endurance. He apparently identifies moderation with prudence and manliness with endurance.

One virtue, however, is glaringly absent: justice. He did not discover any justice in Socrates; one reason, which is sufficient reason, is that it was not in him, in Alcibiades. Justice, we could perhaps say, is replaced by endurance. While Alcibiades has no sense for the just, he has a strong sense of the noble or beautiful. But of what kind of the beautiful? Of that kind of beautiful which appeared at the peak of Diotima's speech on the poets— prudence, political wisdom. Alcibiades had identified prudence with moderation and in the sequel he is going to speak of Socrates' endurance. I conclude, the moderation of which Alcibiades spoke is identical with endurance. The difference is trivial. Moderation has to do with the right attitude toward pleasures, and endurance with the right attitude toward pain. This virtue swallows up everything, including Socrates' manliness. Socrates is a composite of superhuman endurance and, as we must not forget from the first part of the speech, of superhuman rhetoric. This superhuman, absurd, demonic character explains for Alcibiades Socrates' care for other men. But it is somehow connected with the two phenomena he sees, namely, Socrates' superhuman endurance and his superhuman rhetoric. In 219d4–5, "his nature, moderation, and manliness"—I believe this means that Socrates' virtue is his nature. His nature is not something separate from his virtue. Alcibiades indicates it by saying that Socrates is a demonic man. He is by nature virtuous.

> "For I well knew that he was far more immune in all respects to money than Ajax was to iron, and that alone by which I thought I would catch him he had escaped me. I was going around at a loss, enslaved by that human being as no one had been by anyone else." (219e1–5)

Alcibiades is completely enslaved by Socrates, as no man ever was by any other man. The extreme humiliation he, a most beautiful human being, had suffered, to say nothing of the humiliations he had suffered before that night by virtue of Socrates' speeches, which made him aware of his defects—that was so many, many years ago. And now Alcibiades is a great man, on the verge of his greatest political action, the Sicilian expedition. He is no longer enslaved, he is almost the ruler of Athens. How did he get out of that enslavement? That story is told in the sequel. The general answer is by military action.

> "All these things had happened to me earlier. After this we were on campaign together against Potidaea, and we were messmates there. Now first of all, he surpassed not only me in toils but everyone else as well; whenever we were compelled—cut off somewhere, the sort of thing to be expected on campaign—to go without food, everyone else was as nothing compared to his endurance. And in turn, in festivities he alone was able to enjoy both everything else and drinking, and though unwilling, whenever he was compelled, he used to beat everyone; and what is the most amazing thing of all, no human being ever saw Socrates drunk. Now of this point there will soon be proof, I think." (219e5–220a6)

Alcibiades shows first Socrates' endurance regarding hunger and drinking. You see the lack of parallelism; he doesn't say hunger and thirst but hunger and drinking. Socrates did not boast that he could eat more than anyone else. So the great theme of Socrates' endurance opened here and continued in the sequel.

"And again in regard to his feats of endurance during winter—the winters are terrible there—everything else he did was amazing. Once when there was a most terrible frost—you can't imagine—and everyone either did not go out, or if they did go out wrapped themselves in amazing quantities of clothes and put on shoes and wrapped their feet in felt and sheepskins, he used to go out in those times with the sort of himation he used to wear even before, and without shoes he walked through the ice more easily than everyone else who was shod, and the soldiers used to give him sidelong glances as if he was despising them." (220a6–c1)

Here he describes Socrates in winter. Even in winter he goes unshod. Going unshod was also used for a description of eros, you will remember, and one can show throughout the description that unwittingly it is somehow a description of eros. But that is not the main point. One point, however, I would make: if Socrates is eros, then his concern for human beings, especially for young human beings, would be explained. Unless we remember the statement that Eros with a capital *E* does not love, only human beings love.

"Now this was the way it was; but it is worthwhile to hear 'the sort of thing the enduring man did and endured there' once on campaign." (220c1–3)

This verse is from Homer's *Odyssey,* book 4, 242; it is said by Helen of Odysseus. Alcibiades compares Socrates to Odysseus, whereas Alcibiades is rather comparable to Achilles, as we have seen on a previous occasion. The interesting point is that Socrates, too, is a man who suffers much. He did much and suffered much. Socrates is a much-suffering man, just as Odysseus was.

"He conceived a thought there and stood from dawn considering it, and when he couldn't make any progress, he refused to let up but kept on standing considering. It was now already noon, and the soldiers became aware of it, and in amazement one said to another, 'Socrates has been standing there since dawn reflecting.' Finally, some of the Ionians, when it was evening, once they had dined—it was then summer—brought out their bedding and slept in the cold while keeping watch on him, to see whether he would stand also through the night. He stood till dawn and the sun came up; and then he went away after he had prayed to the sun." (220c3–d5)

The object of admiration here is not Socrates' contemplation but his endurance. Here his endurance is shown in summer, as distinguished from his endurance in winter in the preceding story. Contemplation in summer as distinguished from winter. What could that possibly mean? That theme is known to those of you who have read Cicero's *Republic* and *Laws*. Cicero's *Republic* is a dialogue in winter, where they seek the sun, and the *Laws* is a dialogue in summer, where they seek the shade. Socrates seeks the sun in summer, when it is hardest to bear; he seeks the light of the sun at its strongest. In accordance with that he prays to the sun at the end. Let us not forget that the sun is a cosmic god. But why did some of the Ionians and not the Athenians watch Socrates' contemplation? I read a commentator who said the Athenians knew all about it, but I think we can dismiss this suggestion. I think the main point is that Alcibiades did not watch it. He watched Socrates in battle, as we shall see in the immediate sequel.

> "And if you want, in battles—for it is quite just to give him this—when there was a battle after which the generals gave me the prize of valor, no other human being saved me except him: he refused to leave me when I had been wounded, and he saved me along with my weapons. And I, Socrates, even then urged the generals to give you the prize of valor, and in this at least you won't find fault with me or say that I am lying; but when the generals looked at my rank and wanted to give me the prize of valor, you yourself proved to be more eager than the generals for me to take it rather than yourself." (220d5–e7)

Socrates admitted that he should get the prize. Don't forget that. It is true that it had something to do with the fact that Alcibiades came from one of the noblest families and Socrates did not, but still it is something to come from one of the noblest families. Thus, Alcibiades began to get out of his state of inferiority to Socrates.

> "Still further, men, it was worthwhile to observe Socrates when the army was retreating in flight from Delium, for I happened to be there on a horse, and he was a hoplite. He and Laches were withdrawing together when the soldiers had already scattered. I happened by, and as soon as I saw them I urged the pair to be confident, and I said I would not desert them. Here, indeed, I observed Socrates in a finer way than I had in Poti-daea—for I was less in fear because I was on horseback—first, how far he surpassed Laches by his keeping cool *[emphron]*, and then, it seemed to me—Aristophanes, that line of yours—even there he was walking as he does here, 'swaggering and casting his eyes sideways,' calmly giving side-long glances at the friendly and the enemy, making it clear to everyone even from a great distance that if anyone attacks this man here he will de-fend himself very vigorously. Accordingly, he went away in safety, he and

his comrade; for it's pretty nearly the case that they don't attack people of such a disposition in war but pursue those who are fleeing headlong." (220e7–221c1)

You see now the final scene: Alcibiades sitting on a horse is literally superior to Socrates. He is the one who encourages Socrates and Laches. "I said I would not desert them." That is the exact parallel to what happened in the earlier battle, where Socrates did not desert him. Socrates had not deserted him, and that was not a favorable position for a proud man; in the second case he is superior. He doesn't say that Socrates had his wits about him simply, only more so than Laches. Some fear was inevitable, because he didn't sit on a horse. Socrates' conduct at Delium proved his reasonableness, his reasonable calculation: it is foolish to run away; you run less risk if you retreat cautiously and with your eyes open. In this whole account he does not mention a single time Socrates' manliness. Alcibiades confirms Aristophanes' description of Socrates in the *Clouds*. But it is the least interesting verse in the play. What about the other descriptions of Socrates? For example the awful verse where Socrates says Zeus does not exist. Alcibiades, one can say, tacitly confirms Aristophanes' description of Socrates altogether by not taking exception to any particular point. This is the end of the second and central part of Alcibiades' speech. Now we come to the third and last part, which is much shorter and which deals with the subject of Socrates and his speeches.

> "Now one could praise and admire Socrates for many other things, but of all his other practices one could perhaps say they were like those of someone else. But that in which he is like no other human being, neither of the ancients nor of those now, this deserves every wonder. One might liken Brasidas and others to the sort that Achilles was, and as for the sort Pericles was, one would liken him to Nestor and Antenor—and there are others too—and one would make likeness on the same terms of everyone else; but the sort of human being that he has been in his strangeness, both him and his speeches, no one, should he seek it, would find even a close resemblance, neither to those now nor to the ancients, unless after all if one should liken him to those I am speaking of—to no human being but to Silenuses and satyrs, him and his speeches." (221c2–d6)

"Him and his speeches," that is the theme. However extraordinary Socrates' endurance may be, there may have been someone now or in the past who was his equal, in this respect or perhaps in any other respect. But in one respect Socrates is simply unique: in his strangeness, his absurdity, and this applies both to him and to his speeches. In this respect he resembles no human being but only the Silenuses and satyrs. And then he gives some examples of contemporary equivalents to heroes: Brasidas is comparable to Achilles, Brasidas the Spartan gentlemen general; and Pericles is comparable as an orator to Nestor and Antenor. That Odysseus is not mentioned I note in passing. You see here that Alcibiades inverts the times. He treats Achilles as a contemporary and Pericles as a mythical hero. In both cases it amounts to the same thing. Just as he sees himself as an Achilles, or perhaps a super Achilles, he divines something of Odysseus in Socrates.

> "I omitted this too in the first part, that his speeches are most similar to the opened-up Silenuses. For should one be willing to hear the speeches of Socrates, they would appear very ridiculous at first: they put around themselves those kinds of words and phrases, on the outside—it's the kind of hide of a hubristic satyr. He speaks of asses and pack-asses and blacksmiths and shoemakers and leather workers, and he appears to be always speaking of the same things through the same things, so that every inexperienced and foolish human being would laugh at his speeches; but should one see them opened up and get inside them, he will find that they alone of speeches had mind within and, secondly, that they were most divine and had the greatest number of statues of virtue in themselves and pertaining over the greatest range, or rather over the entire range that it is fitting for him who is going to beautiful and good to survey." (221d7–222a6)

He turns now to Socrates' speeches in particular. Socrates' speeches are like the Silenuses. These speeches have an ugly exterior and a beautiful interior. In the first part of Alcibiades' speech he had compared Socrates chiefly to Marsyas and noted the contrast between Socrates' external shape—his famous ugliness—and his quasi-internal flute playing, i.e., his speeches. But now he will speak of the external of Socrates' speeches and the internal of his speeches. Socrates' speeches, if heard, are ridiculous, let us say comical. But if one looks inside they prove to contain most wonderful images of virtue. He no longer says most wonderful images of the gods, as he had said in the beginning. Socrates' speeches are like comedies. You remember in the beginning, when he came in, Alcibiades was surprised that Socrates did not sit with Aristophanes, where he belonged. These Socratic speeches show only the inconspicuous things, which gentlemen wouldn't talk about. That of course is true. Socrates' philosophy has the character of ascent, which means necessarily from the low to the highest, but they ascend. What do they ascend from? What would we expect them to ascend from, on the basis of what we have learned from Diotima? From beautiful bodies. But Socrates speaks of such inconspicuous bodies as tanners, etc. The mature Socrates is not the young Socrates trained by Diotima, let us not forget that. Socrates had learned to realize the importance of the nonbeautiful, the dreary, the insignificant. The outside of Socrates is hubris, according to this repeated statement; the inside of Socrates is an imitation of virtue, images of virtue, not virtue itself.

In the first part of his speech, Alcibiades had not spoken of the hubris in Socrates' speeches but only of the religious or tragic effect of these speeches on everyone. In the second part of his speech Alcibiades did speak of Socrates' hubris, but as a hidden hubris. The exterior of his speeches was eroticism and ignorance, by which I mean the claim that he is a lover and the claim that he is ignorant. The inside was hubris, somehow identical with moderation. I remind you again that according to the meaning of the Greek terms, moderation and hubris are opposites. In classical times, as I said before, moderation meant moderation in sensual pleasures—food, drink, sex. But in a deeper sense, moderation means much more, and then its opposite is either hubris, insolence, rebellion, or madness or insanity. To repeat: the inside of the speeches prove to be hubris and its opposite— moderation. Now Alcibiades says that the external of Socrates' speeches is comical, hubris, and that the moral effect of Socrates is limited to a very few. I cannot now, at this advanced stage of the course, put together all the threads; you have to do some figuring out yourself. You see also a little point in 221e5–6: Socrates does not in fact always say the same things about the same subjects, this is only the appearance. This is only another way of saying that Socrates is ironical, because irony consists in not saying the same thing to everyone. The word *pack-asses* is very strange. Does he ever talk of pack-asses? I can only say the Platonic lexicon does not give any other passage, and Xenophon's Socrates doesn't use it either. The word occurs once in Xenophon's *Education of Cyrus,* book 7, chapter 5, and that is an interesting point. Xenophon uses this expression when he describes the deeds of the Persian king Cyrus in connection with the siege of Babylon, in a military context, and Cyrus is presented as the political, military man. Precisely the military, political man must speak of these matters which are so ridiculous and comical, according to Alcibiades. That is the greatest irony. Think of modern war: must the general not be concerned with engineers and transportation? So what Alcibiades conveys very unknowingly is that Socrates is so comical, so ungentlemanly, so ridiculous, because he speaks of political and military matters. He ridicules himself without knowing it.

"Here you have, men, the things in which I praise Socrates; and again I mixed them up with what I blame him for when I spoke of the things in which he insulted me. He has done this not only to me, however, but also to Charmides the son of Glaucon, Euthydemus the son of Diocles, and very many others, in deceiving whom, as if he were a lover, he becomes rather himself the beloved instead of a lover. It's precisely on these points, Agathon, that I am talking to you: Don't be deceived by him but take precautions against him. Learn from our sufferings, and don't, as the proverb goes, just like a fool learn by suffering." (222a7–b7)

Alcibiades says Socrates deceives people. He says it twice. What is it which prompts Socrates to deceive people? The fact he is sure of; he has experienced it. He deceives people, i.e., he thinks differently than he speaks. He speaks as if he were in love with Alcibiades, for example, though he is not in love with him. But what prompts him to deceive people? We found one answer which escaped Alcibiades completely, namely, he does it out of justice. Here we get an Alcibiadean answer to the question: he wants them to love him. Is this not a strange answer? In other words, Alcibiades says Socrates often does things because he desires to be loved. It is not desire for the beautiful, it is desire for being loved. He leads others to his hidden treasures, to those images or statues of virtue hidden within him, in order to lead them to himself. Does this ring a bell? Who does this? The poets. The poets produce these beautiful things only for the sake of their own immortality. Socrates is in a way a poet as described by Diotima. But, we have to add immediately, to the extent to which Socrates is a poet, he is of course a comic poet, because the externals are as he has emphasized, comical.

When Alcibiades had said this, there was laughter at his frankness, because he seemed to be still erotically inclined toward Socrates. (222c1–3)

Isn't this delicacy admirable? They don't laugh about the daring scene he described, but about the naive way in which he displayed his still existing love for Socrates.

Then Socrates said, "You seem to me to be sober, Alcibiades. Otherwise you would never have so cleverly thrown a cloak around the reason why you have said all this and made it disappear from view, and just as if you were speaking parenthetically you placed it at the end, as if you had not said everything for this reason, to set me and Agathon apart, in the belief that I should love you and no one else, and Agathon be loved by you and by no one else. But you did not get away with it; that satyric and silenic drama of yours became perfectly obvious. But, my dear Agathon, let it not

281

do him any good, but make sure that no one will set me and you apart."
(222c3–d6)

Socrates had been asked by Alcibiades in the beginning to correct him if he
said anything untrue. Socrates never corrects Alcibiades at any point. He
even goes so far as to say at the end, You are sober; no drunkenness prevented you from saying something wrong.

[Tape change.]

Alcibiades is, I think, in a great error because the love affair which is
coming is the one between Socrates and Phaedrus, of which Alcibiades is
completely unaware. In the order of the speeches we have these arrange-
ments: Agathon, Socrates, Alcibiades. These are three speeches which are
related to another triad: Pausanias, Eryximachus, and Aristophanes. In the
first Socrates is in the center, in the second Eryximachus, which is important for other reasons too. The first triad, as you will remember, had pederasty as its common theme, and this culminated in Aristophanes' speech
on the understanding of eros as love of one's own, which was identical with
rebellion against the law. But if Alcibiades is the completer of the triad here,
as Aristophanes was the completer in the first triad, we must say again that
the whole thing culminates in the understanding of love as love of one's
own. For this is exactly what Alcibiades said at the end of his speech:
Socrates loves himself, he tries to bring the others not to love the beautiful
in Socrates, but Socrates. In other words, what Alcibiades unknowingly
suggests is an agreement between Socrates and Aristophanes, between the
two high points of the dialogue. But there is still one great difference, because the love of one's own as Aristophanes understood it is something
outside the individual, the other half, however this may have to be understood; but in Socrates' case it is not outside of him. Let us keep this in mind.

May I remind you of another point I made in the beginning of this
course: There are six speeches; there is a seventh speech, that of Phaedrus in
the beginning, which is set off from all the other speeches by the interven-
ing omitted speeches. But Phaedrus's point of view, as I have tried to show,
is that of gain or profit—also love of one's own. That is the great theme remaining almost underground in the *Symposium*, but yet very powerful, and
brought to the fore in other Platonic dialogues.

We must comment on Socrates' remark when he calls Alcibiades' speech
a satyric drama. What was it? A conclusion of a tragedy. What would follow
from that? That the *Symposium* prior to Alcibiades' speech is a tragedy, and
that is very strange. How is this possible if Socrates is not capable of tragic

speech, as I claim? I will try to answer this question in four different ways, though they are probably not sufficient. First, by this remark Socrates seems to confirm Alcibiades' initial description of Socrates' speeches, when he described their tragic effect. One could then say that Socrates describes the *Symposium* with a view to its possible effect on Alcibiades. Socrates' effect on Alcibiades was like that of a tragedy. Alcibiades, this political man par excellence, can understand the effect of Socrates on himself only in terms of the effect of tragedy. But the following answer I believe goes somewhat deeper: the *Symposium* does not contain a single speech by Socrates. That is a pedantic remark but a necessary one. There are only the speeches of the five others, and Socrates' speech, as you know, is the speech of Diotima. The *Symposium* as a whole is an enchanting work, and a certain kind of enchantment is the function of tragedy. The *Symposium* as a whole is a praise of eros as a god or at least as a demon and, therefore, it belongs together with tragedy. The third consideration: the Socrates who speaks in the *Symposium*, if we assume him to be the same as Diotima, is the young Socrates, the Socrates who had not yet understood the place of the ugly or the base in the economy of the world. This Socrates who had not yet understood the necessity of the ugly or base had a tragic effect. The last suggestion I would make is this: Is not the tragedy which is beyond the competence of Socrates strictly speaking the punitive speech—the speech referring to the punitive gods? But punishment presupposes law, nomos, and therefore we can say tragedy in a more radical, in a more primary sense, is the production of nomos or, more worthily, of true nomos. I read to you a passage from the *Laws*. The tragic poets come and wish to be admitted to the city. The legislator says:

> This should be the answer: Most excellent of strangers, We ourselves, to the best of our ability, are the authors of a tragedy, at once superlatively fair and superlatively good. At least all our polity is framed as a representation of the fairest and best life which is in reality as we assert the truest tragedy. Thus, we are composers of the same things as yourselves, rivals of yours as artists and actors of the fairest drama, which, as our hope is, true law and it alone is by nature competent to complete. (817b)

The *Symposium*, I would say, is "tragic" because it supplies the true nomos regarding eros, which as a nomos, however true, is a problem. That it supplies the true nomos, I believe, can be shown from the end of Socrates' speech, 212b5, where Socrates says, Every man should honor Eros." The *Symposium* supplies the true nomos regarding eros and, therefore, is in the deepest sense of the word tragic, where nomos means a beautiful, salutary, but spurious unit. Socrates is a legislator regarding eros, but only by virtue of Diotima, not by his own power. The fact that he is not a legislator is, of course, also indicated by the fact that he is absent from Plato's *Laws*. But even if Socrates were able to give laws, he could not present properly the sanctions for violations of the law. Now let us go on.

> Then Agathon said, "Well, Socrates, you are probably speaking the truth. I infer it also from the fact that he lay down in the middle, between me and you, in order that he may keep us apart, but it won't do him any good, for I shall come to you and lie down beside you." "Yes, of course," Socrates said. "Come over here and lie down below me." (222d7–e5)

So the order desired by Alcibiades is this: Socrates, Alcibiades, Agathon. The actual order was Agathon, Alcibiades, Socrates. Agathon and Socrates suggest that the order should be Alcibiades, Socrates, Agathon. Let us see what Alcibiades replies.

> "Zeus!" Alcibiades said, "Think of what I once more suffer at his hands! He believes he must be superior to me everywhere. Well, if nothing else— you are a marvel!—allow Agathon to lie down between us." (222e6–9)

So what he wants is Alcibiades, Agathon, Socrates. There is again another conflict. How do we get out of that?

> "But it's impossible," Socrates said. "For you praised me, and I must praise in turn the one on my right. So if Agathon lies below you, he surely won't praise me again before, rather, he has been praised by me. Let it go, Oh demonic one, and don't begrudge the youth to be praised by me, for I very much desire to praise him." (222e10–223a2)

Do you get the point? Why is Alcibiades' suggestion impossible? Because Agathon would have to praise Socrates, and Socrates is very eager to praise Agathon. Socrates aggravates the situation.

> "Oh, joy! joy!" Agathon said, "Alcibiades, it's impossible that I should remain here, but as certain as anything I shall get up and move, in order that I may be praised by Socrates." (223a3–5)

Socrates wins completely, as usual, except at his trial.

> "That's it!" Alcibiades said. "It's just the usual. When Socrates is present it's impossible for anyone else to have a share in the beauties, and now how resourcefully he found a persuasive speech as well, so as for him [Agathon] to lie down beside himself." Now Agathon was getting up to

lie down beside Socrates, when suddenly a great number of revelers came to the door, and, finding it open when someone was going out, they came in straight to them and lay down, and everything was full of noisy confusion, and they were compelled to drink a great deal of wine without any order. Now Aristodemus said that Eryximachus, Phaedrus, and some others went away and left, but as for himself sleep overtook him and he slept very deeply, because the night was far advanced, and he woke up toward the day and the cocks were already singing, and on waking up he saw that all the rest were asleep or had gone away, but only Agathon, Aristophanes, and Socrates were still awake and were drinking from a large cup, starting on the left. Then Socrates was conversing with them, and Aristodemus said he did not remember all the rest of the speeches—for he had not been present from the beginning and he was still dozing. However, the chief point, he said, was that Socrates was compelling them to agree that it belonged to the same man to know how to write comedy and tragedy, and that he who was a tragic poet by art was also a comic poet. And they were being compelled in this and were not very intently following and were dozing off, and Aristophanes fell asleep first, and when it was already day Agathon did. Then Socrates put them to bed, got up, and went away, and he [Aristodemus], just as was usual for him, followed along, and when Socrates had come to the Lyceum, he washed himself off, and just as he spent the rest of the day at other times, so too he spent that day and toward evening rested at home. (223b1–d12)

Alcibiades, of course, is not awake. Let us not forget that. Only the three wisest are awake.

The word before the last in the Greek text is "at home," Socrates went home only to rest, he is never at home, just as eros, who is homeless. Socrates has no eros for the things belonging to the home. The most important remark in this closing statement is what Socrates says about comedy and tragedy. Let us consider this for a moment: Socrates forces them to agree that it is within the same man to make comedy and tragedy and that he who is by art, meaning not merely by natural gift, a maker of tragedy is also a maker of comedy. The statement is repeated and there is never an identical repetition. The first statement seems to be to the effect that on the highest level, on the level of conscious production, based of course on natural gift, the same man is capable of both. But the second statement modifies this: it speaks only of him who is by art a maker of tragedy as also a maker of comedy, not the other way around. This is confirmed by the sequel. The comic poet Aristophanes falls asleep before the tragic poet Agathon. He who by art produces tragedy, who by art can enchant men through the production of the beautiful gods, by this very fact is disenchanted and therefore also can disenchant. But the man who can disenchant, the comic poet, is not yet, for this reason, able to enchant, to produce the gods in their awful beauty. Therefore I think Socrates could have written comedies, he could not have written tragedies; and therefore he did not write. This implies the assertion, the proof of which is quite a job, that properly understood the works of Plato, and to some extent also of Xenophon, are in the more subtle sense of the word tragedies. Tragedies which carry within themselves the comedy.

In this course and in this effort we have reached the end, which means only that we are in a good position, after a pause, to begin again on a higher level of understanding, and that may go on for many readings. Because, ultimately, as I said in the beginning, one cannot believe that one has understood fully any Platonic dialogue if one has not understood all the dialogues. We have become aware here of a number of difficulties which we could not explain or which we could explain only in a complicated and unconvincing manner. But apart from this obvious observation one can say this a priori: there will be other dialogues—the *Phaedrus, Euthydemus, Laws*, etc.—crucial points of which one would have to consider for understanding any other dialogue and therefore the *Symposium* in particular. In this way, Plato's dialogues are truly in imitation of what we call reality. The enigma of reality is limited by the Platonic dialogue. People used to speak of art as imitation, and that is a very profound word. It means the imitation of the riddle of reality, and this riddle Plato imitates by writing many dialogues, each giving some articulation of a part. But even the greatest possible articulation of any part cannot give more than partial truth, and that means, of course, partial truth about that part discussed in that dialogue, and therefore one must go on.

Listener: What is it in Socrates that Alcibiades admires and loves?

Mr. Strauss: It is surely connected with the fact of Socrates' amazing intelligence, that is clear. But that alone doesn't do it, partly because Alcibiades is not able and tough enough to follow Socrates in his pursuit. Therefore it must be something else. Socrates is a demonic man, to use the Platonic word. What does this mean? Did you ever hear the expression "a magnetic personality"? That is as revealing as any answer you could give on that level. Socrates must have had an indescribable fascination which led to either intense attraction or equally intense repulsion. Generally speaking, the more noble natures were attracted by Socrates and the lower ones were repelled. That Alcibiades is unable to give a clear account of Socrates is obvious. But then one has to ask whether anyone was able to give a clear account. If you think, for example, of the remark at the end of the *Phaedo,* where a much nicer and simpler man tells the story and he says Socrates was the wisest, justest, and most moderate of human beings, that, too, does not tell of the fascination of Socrates. One would have to answer this question by going through all of Plato and seeing the demonic thing in Socrates. The usual interpretation says it is something like the conscience, but that cannot be true, because the conscience is something which is supposed to be effective in all men, and the *daimonion* is the peculiarity of Socrates. Secondly, the *daimonion* is only another aspect of the erotic character of Socrates, meaning the strange attractiveness Socrates had for some human beings and, on the other hand, that Socrates was also strangely attracted by human beings. He had an amazing sensitivity to the souls of men. I don't know if one can say much more about that. One should analyze it more fully, but it remains a kind of riddle. One could, perhaps, say that Alcibiades senses this in Socrates with unusual power, but he is also unusually unable to discern what it is. Callicles, too, is important in this respect; he is a lower Alcibiades. One also has to consider Thucydides' description of Alcibiades.

Listener: You mentioned Socrates' *daimon,* and as I remember the charges brought against him it was not that he didn't honor the gods of the city but that he brought in *daimonia.* In that connection I noted that when Alcibiades is about to reveal the secret of Socrates he says he would reveal it only to the initiated.

Mr. Strauss: There is something to that. In what you mentioned I also thought of the general point which I made in the beginning, that the *Symposium* is a description of the revelation or profanation of the mysteries in 416—the real description. I think the crucial one is that which is given partly by Aristophanes and especially by Diotima. I could not say now any more about what the *daimonion* is. It is surely an excess beyond the philosophic nature as such. There are philosophic natures—Parmenides—who did not have a *daimonion.* There is a passage about that in the *Republic.* As far as Socrates knows there has never been anyone who has this strange quality, this strange link between the pure *theoria,* pure contemplation and the desire for it, and human beings. One could say that the *daimonion* is the link between the strictly philosophic, the contemplative, and human beings—which also makes the philosopher himself, Socrates, as distinguished from his doctrines, his questions, an object of concern. We have a vulgar term for that: the educating element in Socrates, which does not essentially belong to philosophy, as is shown by the greatest examples of philosophy, and yet Socrates had it. But we must not lose sight of the fact, which Plato conveys, that the man who is demonic, in the Greek sense of the word, is not divine; and Plato, I am almost certain, regarded himself as in this sense divine. This is a very difficult question and our studies this quarter are not sufficient to establish that.

Listener: Are you suggesting that the young Socrates is also divine?

Mr. Strauss: I do not know. That Aristophanes intended that I could not say. But the statement of Aristotle that nature is demonic and the nous divine is also of some help. What Plato means is also that Socrates' nature, his physis, was singularly philosophic, must less dependent on training, habituation, than that of other philosophers—his instinctive awareness of the questions. There are some humorous illustrations at the beginning of the *Crito:* Socrates is in prison, he dreams, and Crito comes in to effect a jailbreak so that Socrates can get out to Thessaly, far away, lawless but safe for a fugitive from justice. Then Socrates tells him his dream. A woman of superhuman stature had appeared to him and quoted a verse from the *Iliad:* on the third day from now you will be in Phthia, which is not very far from Thessaly. In other words, Socrates had in a fantastic way divined the plan hitherto wholly unknown to him. This divinatory quality Socrates must have possessed in a way in which philosophers do not possess it. This divinatory quality is, of course, not essential to theoretical perfection. But that Socrates had something in addition to that theoretical quality which made him as a human being both attractive and repulsive is part of that mysterious point.

[In answer to a question:] Poet is too general a term and among the many objections you can raise to my presentation is that we have not gone deeply enough into that problem. When we speak of tragedy we cannot help but begin understanding these terms as they are used now. When we speak of gods what do we know of the gods? Factual knowledge doesn't help us to know what is a god for a thinking Greek, or for that matter also for a nonthinking Greek. It is quite true that what we mean today by a poet or perhaps by an artist is some demonic quality. But is that the poetic quality in the way Plato understood it? I think one must pay great attention to the information derived from the *Gorgias* about the limitations of Socrates' rhetoric and how they are connected with the fact that Socrates cannot produce very fine speeches.

If there are no further questions I terminate this session and this course.

INDEX

Achilles: as contemporary, 279; Diotima's interpretation of, 224; Phaedrus's praise of, 52–53

Adultery: Aristophanes on, 135

Agathon: argument of with Socrates, 180–82; beloved of Pausanias, 61; character of, 32; 254; difference from Aristophanes, 147; on Homer, 157, 159; and "I" *(ego)*, 155; inside of, 155; and Phaedrus, 157–58, 162–63; and Socrates, 153–54; softness of, 76; speech of, 156, summarized, 168–69; thesis of in relation to Diotima's, 196, 206; verses of on Eros, 166; victory of, 15

Alcestis: Diotima's interpretation of, 224; praise of, 50–51

Alcibiades: accusation and defense of Socrates, 268, 273; as Achilles, 259; in Athens, 15; character of, 254, 260–61; humiliation of, 268, 275; as raw material for a god, 256–57; "religious" experience of, 265; self-ridicule of, 279–80; six stages of in seduction of Socrates, 270–71; on Socrates' speeches, 279–80; superiority of to Socrates, 269

Al-Farabi: achievement of, 246–47

Ancestors: deified, 217

Ancestral: and the good, 48, 158

Antigone: first words of, 241; praise of Eros in, 46

Aphrodite: in Diotima, 191; in Pausanias, 62–63

Apollo: in Aristophanes' speech, 129–30; defeat of Socrates by, 264

Apollodorus: character of, 14, 20, 22; as soft, 23, 254

Apology of Socrates: as account of Socrates' magnanimity, 263; on business of Socrates, 270; on gods and *daimonia,* 189; on heroes, 190

Aquinas: on beauty, 236; on justice, 86; on natural inclination, 242

Aristodemus: image of Eros, 29; importance of, 13; noblest lover in *Symposium,* 66; silence of, 152; in Xenophon, 21

Aristophanes: absence of in *Protagoras,* 25–26; accuser of Socrates, 40–41; agreement of with Socrates, 282; Alcibiades' interruption of, 255; character of, 254; comedies of, 149–50; difference from Agathon, 147; and Eryximachus, 148–49; and Euripides, 152; on gods, 142; on hierarchy in Eros, 119; on incest, 144–45, 180; laughter of, 121; next greatest not highest, 151; nonpettiness of, 119; and order of speaking, 95; on philosophy, 150; alone praises piety, 127, 132, 142; *Ploutos* of, 194–95; proponent of religious revolution, 122; and Socrates, 140, 257; speech of summarized, 147–48; tragedy and comedy of Eros in, 172. *See also* Eryximachus; Plato

Aristotle, 226; on Empedocles, 107; *Ethics* of, 85; on human nature, 151; on magnanimity, 263; on mind and nature, 288; on moderation and endurance, 266; on polis, 6; *Politics* of, 133; *Rhetoric* of, 77, 160; on Socrates, 229; on time, 220

Art *(technē):* abandonment of by Aristophanes, 119, 132; as controller of chance, 110; and Eros, 97, 100, 111–12; and law, 104; noble or base, 98; and pan-eroticism, 113–14; theory and practice of, 99, 102

Astronomy: and divination, 106–7

Ate: and Eros, 159

Athens: in Plato, 22; pederasty in, 67, 77–82

Attraction: and repulsion, 112

Barbarism: two forms of, 68

Battle morality: in Athens, 79

Beauty: of actions, 65; of body and soul, 231; of Eros, 160; and good, 238; always imperfect, 155; reflection of immortal in mortal, 206; self-forgetting in love of, 249; and virtue, 161